SOUTH AMERICA

INVESTMENT RESOURCES AND CAPITAL FOR SOUTH AMERICAN COUNTRIES HANDBOOK

STRATEGIC INFORMATION, OPPORTUNITIES, CONTACTS

International Business Publications, USA
Washington DC, USA

SOUTH AMERICA

INVESTMENT RESOURCES AND CAPITAL FOR SOUTH AMERICAN COUNTRIES HANDBOOK

STRATEGIC INFORMATION, OPPORTUNITIES, CONTACTS

UPDATED ANNUALLY

We express our sincere appreciation to all government agencies and international organizations which provided information and other materials for this handbook

Cover Design: International Business Publications, USA

2016 Edition Updated Reprint International Business Publications, USA
ISBN 978-0-7397-2763-8

For customer service and information, please contact:

in the USA: **International Business Publications, USA**
P.O.Box 15343, Washington, DC 20003
Phone: 202 546-2103, Fax: 202 546-3275.
E-mail: rusric@erols.com

Printed in the USA

SOUTH AMERICA

INVESTMENT RESOURCES AND CAPITAL FOR SOUTH AMERICAN COUNTRIES HANDBOOK

STRATEGIC INFORMATION, OPPORTUNITIES, CONTACTS

TABLE OF CONTENTS

SOUTH AMERICAN COUNTRIES - STRATEGIC INFORMATION AND DEVELOPMENTS

BASIC INFORMATION

South America is a continent situated in the Western Hemisphere, mostly in the Southern Hemisphere, with a relatively small portion in the Northern Hemisphere. It is also considered a subcontinent of the Americas, which is the term used in Spanish-speaking nations and most of South America.

It is bordered on the west by the Pacific Ocean and on the north and east by the Atlantic Ocean; North America and the Caribbean Sea lie to the northwest. It includes twelve sovereign states – Argentina, Bolivia, Brazil, Chile, Colombia, Ecuador, Guyana, Paraguay, Peru, Suriname, Uruguay, and Venezuela – and two non-sovereign areas – French Guiana, an overseas department of France, and the Falkland Islands, a British Overseas Territory (though disputed by Argentina). In addition to this, the ABC islands of the Netherlands and Trinidad and Tobago may also be considered part of South America.

South America has an area of 17,840,000 square kilometers (6,890,000 sq mi). Its population has been estimated at more than 400,000,000. South America ranks fourth in area (after Asia, Africa, and North America) and fifth in population (after Asia, Africa, Europe, and North America). Brazil is by far the most populous South American country, with more than half of the continent's population, followed by Colombia, Argentina, Venezuela and Peru.

Most of the population lives near the continent's western or eastern coasts while the interior and the far south are sparsely populated. The geography of western South America is dominated by the Andes mountains; in contrast, the eastern part contains both highland regions and large lowlands where rivers such as the Amazon, Orinoco, and Paraná flow. Most of the continent lies in the tropics.

The continent's cultural and ethnic outlook has its origin with the interaction of indigenous peoples with European conquerors and immigrants and, more locally, with African slaves. Given a long history of colonialism, the overwhelming majority of South Americans speak Portuguese or Spanish, and societies and states commonly reflect Western traditions.

South America occupies the southern portion of the Americas. The continent is generally delimited on the northwest by the Darién watershed along the Colombia–Panama border, although some may consider the border instead to be the Panama Canal. Geopolitically and geographically all of Panama – including the segment east of the Panama Canal in the isthmus – is typically included in North America alone and among the countries of Central America. Almost all of mainland South America sits on the South American Plate.

South America is home to the world's highest uninterrupted waterfall, Angel Falls in Venezuela; the highest single drop waterfall Kaieteur Falls in Guyana; the largest river (by volume), the Amazon River; the longest mountain range, the Andes (whose highest mountain is Aconcagua at 6,962 m [22,841 ft]); the driest non-polar place on earth, the Atacama Desert; the largest rainforest, the Amazon Rainforest; the highest capital city, La Paz, Bolivia; the highest commercially navigable lake in the world, Lake Titicaca; and, excluding research stations in Antarctica, the world's southernmost permanently inhabited community, Puerto Toro, Chile.

South America's major mineral resources are gold, silver, copper, iron ore, tin, and petroleum. These resources found in South America have brought high income to its countries especially in times of war or of rapid economic growth by industrialized countries elsewhere. However, the concentration in producing one major export commodity often has hindered the development of diversified economies. The fluctuation in the price of commodities in the international markets has led historically to major highs and lows in the economies of South American states, often causing extreme political instability. This is leading to efforts to diversify production to drive away from staying as economies dedicated to one major export.

South America is one of the most biodiverse continents on earth. South America is home to many interesting and unique species of animals including the llama, anaconda, piranha, jaguar, vicuña, and tapir. The Amazon rainforests possess high biodiversity, containing a major proportion of the Earth's species.

Brazil is the largest country in South America, encompassing around half of the continent's land area and population. The remaining countries and territories are divided among three regions: The Andean States, the Guianas and the Southern Cone.

OUTLYING ISLANDS

Traditionally, South America also includes some of the nearby islands. Aruba, Bonaire, Curaçao, Trinidad, Tobago, and the federal dependencies of Venezuela sit on the northerly South American continental shelf and are often considered part of the continent. Geo-politically, the island states and overseas territories of the Caribbean are generally grouped as a part or subregion of North America, since they are more distant on the Caribbean Plate, even though San Andres and Providencia are politically part of Colombia and Aves Island is controlled by Venezuela.

Other islands that are included with South America are the Galápagos Islands that belong to Ecuador and Easter Island (in Oceania but belonging to Chile), Robinson Crusoe Island, Chiloé (both Chilean) and Tierra del Fuego (split between Chile and Argentina). In the Atlantic, Brazil owns Fernando de Noronha, Trindade and Martim Vaz, and the Saint Peter and Saint Paul Archipelago, while the Falkland Islands are governed by the United Kingdom, whose sovereignty over the islands is disputed by Argentina. South Georgia and the South Sandwich Islands may be associated with either South America or Antarctica

SOVEREIGN STATES

A sovereign state is a political association with effective sovereignty over a population for whom it makes decisions in the national interest. According to the Montevideo convention, a state must have a permanent population, a defined territory, a government, and the capacity to enter into relations with other states. The following states are all membersof the United Nations and members of the Union of South American Nations.

Names	**Domestic short and formal names**	Capital	Population	Area
Argentina **Argentine Republic**	**Spanish:Argentina — República Argentina**	Buenos Aires Spanish:Ciudad de Buenos Aires	41,769,726	2,780,400 km^2(1,073,518 sq mi)
Bolivia **Plurinational State of Bolivia**	**Spanish:Bolivia — Estado Plurinacional de Bolivia**	Sucre Spanish:Sucre	10,118,683	1,098,581 km^2(424,164 sq mi)

Names	Domestic short and formal names	Capital	Population	Area
Brazil **Federative Republic of Brazil**	**Portuguese:Brasil — República Federativa do Brasil**	Brasília Portuguese:Brasília	203,429,773	8,514,877 km^2(3,287,612 sq mi)
Chile **Republic of Chile**	**Spanish:Chile — República de Chile**	Santiago Spanish:Santiago	16,888,760	756,102 km^2(291,933 sq mi)
Colombia **Republic of Colombia**	**Spanish:Colombia — República de Colombia**	Bogotá / Santa Fe de Bogotá Spanish:Bogotá	46,366,364	1,138,910 km^2(439,736 sq mi)
Ecuador **Republic of Ecuador**	**Spanish:Ecuador — República del Ecuador**	Quito Spanish:Quito	15,007,343	283,561 km^2(109,484 sq mi)
Guyana **Co-operative Republic of Guyana**	**English: Guyana — Co-operative Republic of Guyana**	Georgetown Spanish:Georgetown	744,768	214,969 km^2(83,000 sq mi)
Paraguay **Republic of Paraguay**	**Spanish:Paraguay — República del Paraguay** **Guarani:Paraguai — Tetã Paraguai**	Asunción Spanish:Asunción	6,459,058	406,752 km^2(157,048 sq mi)
Peru **Republic of Peru**	**Aymara:Perú** **Quechua:Perú** **Spanish:Perú — República del Perú**	Lima Spanish:Lima	29,248,943	1,285,216 km^2(496,225 sq mi)
Suriname **Republic of Suriname**	**Dutch:Suriname — Republiek Suriname**	Paramaribo Dutch:Paramaribo	491,989	163,820 km^2(63,251 sq mi)
Uruguay **Eastern Republic of Uruguay**	**Spanish:Uruguay — República Oriental del Uruguay**	Montevideo Spanish:Montevideo	3,308,535	176,215 km^2(68,037 sq mi)
Venezuela	**Spanish:Venezuela — República**	Caracas	27,635,743	912,050 km^2(352,144 sq mi)

Names	**Domestic short and formal names**	Capital	Population	Area
Bolivarian Republic of Venezuela	**Bolivariana de Venezuela**	Spanish:Caracas		

DEPENDENT TERRITORIES

English name	Legal status	Domestic name	Capital	Population	Area
Falkland Islands	British overseas territory	English: Falkland Islands	Stanley English: Stanley	3,140	12,173 km^2(4,700 sq mi)

OTHER AREAS

English name	Legal status	Domestic name	Capital	Population[1]	Area
French Guiana	French overseas region	French:Guyane	Cayenne French:Cayenne	250,109	83,534 km^2(32,253 sq mi)

DEVELOPMENT AND INVESTMENT CONDITIONS OF SOUTH AMERICA - STRATEGIC DEVELOPMENTS

Population	358,941,000
GDP	nominal: US$3.205 trillion PPP: $3.990 trillion
GDP growth	Per capita: 5.5%
GDP per capita	nominal: US$8,929 PPP: US$11,115
Millionaires (US$)	400,000 (0.07%)
Unemployment	9%
Top 10% income	44.37%

The **economy of South America** comprises around 382 million people living in twelve nations and three territories. It contributes 6 percent of the world's population.

From the 1930s to 1980s, countries of South America used what is called the Import Substitution. Import Substitution is an economic policy which replaces foreign businesses as well as imports with domestic production. This was a policy made to produce more development and help grow domestic businesses, which are not competitive with other international industries. However, this policy created a debt crisis in the South America.

It was only from 1990s when countries in South America switched over to the system of Free-Market economy. This eventually pulled countries in South America out of the debt crisis. Now, major economic activities include agriculture, forestry, and mining.

The main agricultural products include: Coffee, soybeans, wheat, rice, corn, sugarcane, cocoa, citrus, beef, bananas and shrimp are also important agricultural products for many countries.

Chile contributes about a third of the world copper production. Brazil is the world's leading producer of niobium and tantalum, and Peru is the largest silver producer and the second-ranked producer of bismuth and copper

ARGENTINA - INVESTMENT AND BUSINESS CLIMATE - STRATEGIC INFORMATION AND CONTACTS FOR STARTING BUSINESS

Argentina is one of Latin America's largest and wealthiest countries, possessing abundant human and natural resources, highly-diversified industries, and a 43 million person market. Argentina is estimated to have the world's second largest shale gas resources and fourth largest shale oil resources in the world. Investors face a difficult operating environment (e.g. currency and price controls, import restrictions, and double-digit inflation), but are more optimistic with regard to the medium- to long-term in Argentina.

Argentina is still dealing with issues related to its 2001 default on nearly USD 100 billion in debt, the largest sovereign debt default in history. In late 2013 and early 2014, the government of Argentina (GOA) made some progress in normalizing its relations with the international financial community. The GOA settled several outstanding international arbitral awards, engaged with the International Monetary Fund (IMF) to improve economic reporting data, and compensated the Spanish firm Repsol for the partial expropriation of YPF in 2012. Argentina also signed bilateral agreements to repay nearly USD 10 billion in arrears with the Paris Club group of creditors.

Argentina's refusal to comply with a U.S. court ruling ordering the GOA to pay a group of U.S. creditors who sued the country for the full value of their defaulted Argentine bond holdings continues to restrict Argentina's ability to service some of its sovereign debt both at home and abroad. Argentina's limited access to international financial markets will continue to discourage investment until the issue is settled.

Longstanding concerns regarding the lack of transparency in government policymaking also diminish the attractiveness of prospective investments in Argentina. Decisions that affect both foreign and domestic companies are frequently made without industry input and are rarely open to a consultation period. GOA actions to curb the remittance of profits abroad limit foreign companies' ability to repatriate earnings, causing some companies to reconsider locating new business ventures in Argentina. Currency controls delay companies' access to dollars to pay suppliers while recently amended laws allow the GOA to set profit margins and the prices of goods in the private sector in certain circumstances. Businesses and investors also report concerns about Argentina's currency exchange rate policies, which affect the competitiveness of Argentine goods internationally and delay investment decisions.

The World Trade Organization (WTO) in January 2015 ruled that the GOA's all-encompassing import licensing system violated international trade norms. The GOA affirmed that it will comply with the WTO decision, but did not specify a timeframe for adjustment. In the meantime, the system remains in place and reportedly causes shortages and complicates the operations of businesses that are reliant on the importation of goods for production and distribution. Factories and distributors occasionally sit idle while the GOA delays granting approval to move inputs through customs, a process that can be restrictive and unpredictable.

In 2014, in accordance with official figures, Argentina's economic growth slowed to 0.5 percent and unemployment remained steady at 6.9 percent. Private sources reported that the economy contracted about 2 percent and inflation reached 38 percent in 2014. Central Bank international reserve levels ended 2014 around USD 30 billion, a slight improvement from the previous year despite the GOA running current and financial account deficits in 2014. Some private economists contend that liquid reserves are actually lower. Argentina's trade surplus, the country's main source of foreign currency, fell nearly 17 percent in 2014 compared with the previous year.

After several years of publishing non-credible statistics, Argentina's official statistics agency (INDEC) released substantially revised inflation and GDP growth data in 2014 and 2015 that are closer to private estimates. The IMF had formally censured Argentina in February 2013 because of the manipulation of inflation and GDP data, a breach of obligation to the Fund under the Articles of Agreement. The IMF has recognized that Argentina has made progress on its statistics but the new methodology is still subject to final review, the results of which will be released later in 2015. However, some concern remains about the difference between official economic data and private source estimates. The government has not released to the public its new methodologies.

Argentina will hold presidential elections in October 2015, which will bring a change in administration, as the current president is constitutionally precluded from standing for a third term.

1. OPENNESS TO, AND RESTRICTIONS UPON, FOREIGN INVESTMENT

ATTITUDE TOWARD FOREIGN DIRECT INVESTMENT

The GOA has signaled its desire to see continued foreign direct investment (FDI) flows to enhance the nation's productive capacity and GDP growth potential, and it took actions in the past year to improve the investment climate in Argentina. To regain investor confidence, the GOA settled several outstanding international arbitral awards, engaged with the IMF to improve economic reporting data, and compensated the Spanish-firm Repsol for the partial expropriation of YPF in 2012. Argentina also reached agreements with the Paris Club group of creditors to repay USD 9.7 billion in arrears over the next five years, including USD 642 million owed to the United States. Argentina has already made two payments in the first year. The GOA revamped its hydrocarbon regulations in 2014 with the aim of attracting new investments to develop Argentina's world class oil and gas resources.

OTHER INVESTMENT POLICY REVIEWS

Argentina was last subject to an investment policy review by the Organization of Economic Cooperation and Development (OECD) in 1997 and by the World Trade Organization (WTO) in 2013 (https://www.wto.org/english/tratop_e/tpr_e/tp377_e.htm). United Nations Conference on Trade and Development (UNCTAD) has not done an investment policy review of Argentina.

LAWS/REGULATIONS OF FOREIGN DIRECT INVESTMENT

According to a Presidential decree governing foreign investment in Argentina, foreign companies may invest in Argentina without registration or prior government approval, and on the same terms as investors domiciled in Argentina. Investors are free to enter into mergers, acquisitions, green-field investments, or joint ventures. Foreign firms may also participate in publicly-financed research and development programs on a national treatment basis. Central Bank restrictions (both formal and de facto) on the purchase of foreign currency limit the ability of a company or investor to remit profits, dividends, or investments out of the country.

The Argentine Ministry of Economy (http://www.mecon.gov.ar), the Investor's Information Service for Argentina (http://www.infoarg.org), the Undersecretariat of Investment Development and Trade Promotion (http://www.inversiones.gov.ar), the Embassy of the Argentine Republic in the United States of America (http://www.embassyofargentina.us/en/invest-in-argentina.html), and the Central Bank of Argentina (www.bcra.gov.ar) have additional detailed information on investment policies in Argentina.

INDUSTRIAL PROMOTION

The GOA has established a number of investment promotion programs. These programs allow for Value-Added Tax (VAT) refunds and accelerated depreciation of capital goods for investors and offer tariff incentives for local production of capital goods. They also include sectorial programs, free trade zones, and a Special Customs Area in Tierra del Fuego Province, among other benefits. A complete description of the scope and scale of Argentina's investment promotion programs and regimes can be found at http://www.industria.gob.ar, http://www.inversiones.gob.ar and http://www.mecon.gob.ar/.

Information about programs that specifically apply to small and medium businesses may be found at http://www.industria.gob.ar/secretaria-pyme.

LIMITS ON FOREIGN CONTROL

The GOA limits land foreign ownership of rural land through Law 26.737 (Regime for Protection of National Domain over Ownership, Possession or Tenure of Rural Land) established in 2011. Foreign ownership of rural land is restricted to a maximum of 15 percent of all national productive land. Individuals or companies from the same nation may not hold over 30 percent of that amount; and individually each foreign individual or company faces an ownership cap of 1,000 hectares (2,470 acres) in the most productive farming areas, or the equivalent in terms of productivity levels in other areas. As approved, the law is not retroactive. Section 11 of the Law establishes that "for the purposes of this Law and according to the Bilateral Investment Treaties (BITs) underwritten by the Republic of Argentina that are in force at the time this Law becomes valid, the acquisition of rural land shall not be considered an investment as it is a non-renewable natural resource provided by the host country."

Regarding taxes, foreign and Argentine firms generally face the same tax liabilities. In general, taxes are assessed on consumption, imports and exports, assets, financial transactions, and property and payroll (social security and related benefits).

COMPETITION LAW

The National Commission for Protection of Competition and the Secretary of Commerce, both within the Ministry of Economy, have enforcement authority of the Antitrust Law (Law 25.156). The law is aimed at ensuring the general economic interest and promotes a culture of competition in all sectors of the national economy.

INVESTMENT TRENDS

Investor confidence remains low in the short-term and is more optimistic with regards to the medium- and long-term. Argentina's investment climate is dampened by concerns with Argentina's currency controls, deteriorating macroeconomic conditions, and unresolved sovereign debt dispute with litigating U.S. hedge funds. Many established companies in Argentina reported that they are planning to expand investment in Argentina in the immediate or near future, with more economic stability and policy certainty. Sectors of heightened interest are energy, mining, agribusiness, telecommunications, technology, financial and infrastructure development. In early 2015, the City of Buenos Aires and national oil company YPF raised about USD 500 million each through bond issuances, demonstrating significant investor demand for Argentine bonds. The bonds were bought mostly by European and U.S. fund managers and hedge funds.

Table 1

Measure	Year	Index or Rank	Website Address
TI Corruption Perceptions index	2014	107 of 175	transparency.org/cpi2014/results
World Bank's Doing Business Report "Ease of Doing Business"	2015	124 of 189	doingbusiness.org/rankings
Global Innovation Index	2014	70 of 143	globalinnovationindex.org/content.aspx?page=data-analysis
World Bank GNI per capita	2013	No Info	data.worldbank.org/indicator/NY.GNP.PCAP.CD

2. CONVERSION AND TRANSFER POLICIES

FOREIGN EXCHANGE

Argentina has a managed float exchange rate policy. Conversion of the peso into foreign currency is limited.

Remittance Policies

The GOA began imposing significant restrictions on remittances of capital overseas in 2011, which were formally implemented by law in December 2012 with Resolution 3417. In 2012, the Central Bank issued Regulation A-5318 officially banning the purchase of dollars by residents (either Argentine or foreign) as a form of financial savings (although it does not prevent residents from maintaining existing dollar saving accounts and time deposits). This measure formally ended the previous norm that had allowed individuals to buy up to USD 2 million per month without having to specify the destination of the funds (e.g., debt payment, investments, savings, international travel expenses, etc.) Residents can only buy foreign currency for international tourism purposes as allowed by Resolution 3333 and these purchases are subject to caps and controls by the GOA and a 35 percent withholding tax that can be deducted from an individual's income and wealth tax obligation. Requestors must provide information as to the source of their money and proof that it was acquired legally. In addition to other personal data such as birth date, profession, and tax ID numbers, they must provide details about their planned trips, including where, when, and why they are traveling. Since the issuance of this norm, the government has reportedly provided additional verbal instruction to banks and foreign exchange houses that further limit the purchase of foreign exchange.

Beginning in January 2014, the GOA allowed residents to purchase a limited quantity of foreign exchange for savings depending on the person's declared income. The buyer can choose to either withdraw the foreign currency within the first year and pay a 20 percent tax or leave the funds in a local bank for at least a year and pay no tax.

Since 2011, government restrictions on foreign currency purchases have led to the expansion of an informal retail foreign exchange market. The informal dollar rate reached a high of nearly 16 Argentine Pesos to the U.S. Dollar (ARS/USD) in September 2014, exceeding the official exchange rate (approximately ARS 8.5 pesos to the USD) by more than 80 percent. The GOA launched aggressive investigations and enforcement operations in the unofficial dollar markets in late 2014, leading to a reduction in the gap between the official and unofficial rates. As of this publication, the gap has dropped below 40 percent.

Companies have reported difficulties in exchanging pesos for dollars in order to pay for imports. These measures reportedly are in place to address balance of payments concerns. Such restrictions have resulted in occasional goods shortages and difficulties for companies doing business in Argentina. Companies must complete multiple steps to import a good into the country. Certificates-of-origin for some goods must be notarized by the Argentine embassy or consulate in the country in which they were produced. This procedure is the same for products that have multiple parts from multiple countries. The company must then obtain import license approval, which is known by its Spanish-language acronym DJAI. Following DJAI approval, companies must then petition the Central Bank for access to foreign exchange. As of April 2015, about USD 5 billion of requests were pending at the Central Bank.

In order to import goods, companies are also often asked to submit detailed financial and operational information such as their investment plans for the following year. During 2014, the private sector has reported a strengthening of various non-tariff barriers to the importation of goods into the country. Companies reported that the inability to budget for inventory limits their ability to plan for investment.

The GOA subjects speculative capital inflows to three major requirements: (a) investments may not be transferred out of the country for 365 days after their entry; (b) proceeds from foreign exchange transactions involving these investments must be paid into an account in the local financial system; and (c) a 30 percent unremunerated reserve requirement, meaning 30 percent of such transactions must be deposited in a local financial entity for 365 days in an account that is denominated in dollars and receives no interest payment . There are some notable exceptions to the deposit requirement. A deposit is not required for capital inflows to finance energy infrastructure. Nor is a deposit required on inflows for the purchase of real property by foreigners as long as the foreign exchange liquidation occurs on the day of settlement (and transfer of the title). A deposit is also not required for inflows from foreigners to be used for (a) tax payment and (b) social security contributions within 10 days of the settlement of the foreign currency. In October 2011, the Central Bank imposed new market controls on non-residents. They are now required to immediately "register capital inflows into the local foreign exchange market when they purchase a local company, contribute capital, or purchase real estate."

Foreign entities are banned from participating in Central Bank initial bond offerings, but foreign firms may trade Central Bank debt instruments on the secondary market. The Central Bank also requires that exporters deposit the proceeds in U.S dollars from exports into local banks (cuentas de corresponsalía de entidades financieras locales) within a specified number of days depending on the good exported (usually between 10-30 days).

Hard currency earnings on exports, both from goods and services, must be converted to pesos in the local foreign exchange market. In 2011, the GOA eliminated the exceptions previously granted to hydrocarbon and mining exports. These firms must now convert their revenues to pesos on the local foreign exchange market. Revenues from re-exports of some temporary imports and exports to Argentine foreign trade zones are still exempted from this requirement.

In October 2011, the Argentine insurance regulator issued Resolution 36.162 requiring all investments and cash equivalents held by locally registered insurance companies be located in Argentina. This has exposed insurance companies to greater country risk since they are unable to diversify their assets outside of Argentina. In 2012, the GOA further expanded the investment requirements for insurance companies requiring them to allocate part of their overall investments in "instruments related to local productive projects." The minimum percentage required ranges from 5 percent for labor risk insurers to 10 percent for property insurers and 12 percent for life insurers. A government committee composed of the secretaries of Finance, Economic Policy and Development, Internal Trade, Industry, and SMEs as well as the superintendent of Insurance determine the projects eligible to receive such investments.

The Argentine Central Bank issued Circular A5272/73 in January 2012 increasing bank liquidity requirements for operational risks and minimum capital requirements, which sharply limited dividend payments.

The Central Bank expanded in 2012 the list of activities involving the transfer of money abroad by local subsidiaries to headquarters that require prior approval (Circular A5295). These activities now include: IT services; business and professional services' royalties, patents, trademarks and copyrights; commercial guarantee payments on exports of goods and services; foreign film, audio and video rights; and services for technology transfer, and rental and leasing income, among other activities. The regulations apply to transactions greater than USD 150,000 in value; however, in practice every payment requires a so-called DJAS license approval, the services equivalent of the DJAI.

In February 2014, the Central Bank issued Circular A5536 capping the foreign exchange exposure of private banks. The norm limits a financial institutions' foreign currency exposure to 30 percent of their net worth and future exchange rate contracts to 10 percent. Private estimates suggest that 50 percent of the positions held by banks in Argentina are dollarized, representing nearly USD 9 billion in assets.

In October 2014, the Financial Action Task Force recognized Argentina's progress in improving its Anti-Money Laundering/Combating the Financing of Terrorism (AML/CFT) regime and removed the country from the FATF's monitoring process. The FATF determined the country had established the legal and regulatory framework to meet its commitments in its action plan regarding the strategic deficiencies that the FATF had identified in June 2011. Argentina continues to work with FATF to address the full range of AML/CFT issues identified in its mutual evaluation report and will make annual reports on its progress.

3. EXPROPRIATION AND COMPENSATION

Section 17 of the Argentine constitution affirms the right of private property and states that any expropriation must be authorized by law and be previously compensated. The United States-Argentina Bilateral Investment Treaty states that investments shall not be expropriated or nationalized except for public purpose upon prompt payment of the fair-market value in compensation. In October 2008, the government nationalized Argentina's private pension funds, which amounted to approximately one-third of total GDP, and transferred the funds to the government social security agency. In December 2008, the Argentine parliament also passed legislation nationalizing the Spanish-owned flag air carrier Aerolineas Argentinas.

President Cristina Fernandez de Kirchner expropriated 51 percent of oil and gas company YPF from Spanish-owned Repsol in 2012. The state takeover of the company was widely criticized by the European Union and others and increased investor caution. The government settled with Repsol approximately two years later in 2014, which the Argentine congress approved on April 23, 2014.

The GOA announced the nationalization of the train and railway system in March 2015, which was approved by Congress in April 2015.

4. DISPUTE SETTLEMENT

LEGAL SYSTEM, SPECIALIZED COURTS, JUDICIAL INDEPENDENCE, JUDGMENTS OF FOREIGN COURTS

Domestic investment dispute adjudication is available through local courts or administrative procedures. Many foreign investors prefer to rely on private or international arbitration when those options are available.

Argentina follows a Civil Law system. The Civil and Commercial Code provides regulations for civil and commercial liability, including ownership of property. Contracts include provisions for settlement of disputes, where parties agree to bring their controversies to definite courts in the event of disagreements. In 2014, GOA passed a new Civil and Commercial Code that will go into effect in August 2015.

Intellectual property claims fall under the federal civil and commercial courts. There have been complaints of executive branch's interference in judicial matters, mainly through the appointment or dismissal of prosecutors and judges. The current judicial process is lengthy and suffers from significant backlog, causing it to be considered ineffective and not reliable for many individuals.

BANKRUPTCY

Argentina's bankruptcy law was codified in 1995 in Law 24,522. The full text can be found at: http://www.infoleg.gov.ar/infolegInternet/anexos/25000-29999/25379/texact.htm. Under the law, debtors are generally able to begin insolvency proceedings when they are no longer able to pay their debts as they mature. Debtors may file for both liquidation and reorganization.

INVESTMENT DISPUTES

Prior to and following the 2001-02 Argentine economic crisis, a number of U.S. investors in privatized public utilities filed in the International Centre for the Settlement of Investment Disputes (ICSID Convention) claims against the GOA, arguing that government rulings decentralizing public utility tariffs to foreign inflation indices and a January 2002 known as pesofication of dollar-denominated contracts was a form of indirect expropriation of their investments. In addition, some U.S. investors filed ICSID claims based on unforeseen changes to the tax laws. Customs treatment and delays in re-negotiating public utility rate changes also provoked investment disputes. Following the 2001-2002 economic crisis, more than fifty ICSID claims, throughout several sectors were tied to Argentina's nationalization and pesofication initiatives.

In 2013, Argentina settled three of the ICSID awards involving U.S. investors by paying them a portion of the judgment. A number of ICSID cases filed by U.S. investors are pending resolution with Argentina.

Argentina continues to deal with its historic sovereign debt default from its 2001 financial crisis. The government swapped ninety-two percent of the USD 82 billion in defaulted sovereign debt in 2005 and 2010 for a mix of new bonds with a substantial loss in net present value. Some bondholders, known as the holdouts, did not participate in the swaps and continue to pressure Argentina via the U.S. courts to settle its outstanding debt for the actual amount owed plus interest. A U.S. court ruling in 2012 (and affirmed in 2014) determined that Argentina may not pay on its restructured debt unless it also makes equal treatment payments to the holdouts. Argentina has failed to settle with the holdouts, but attempted to pay on the restructured debt despite the U.S. court order. To try to enforce compliance, the U.S. court issued an injunction barring financial intermediaries from passing along any bond payments Argentina makes on its restructured debt unless the country also pays the holdouts, which has effectively blocked the payments. On March 12, 2015, the U.S. judge in the case issued a ruling that the injunction covering financial intermediaries extends to payments on a series of restructured bonds governed by Argentine law and denominated in U.S. dollars. At the time of this report, negotiations were ongoing between Argentina and the holdouts.

INTERNATIONAL ARBITRATION

The GOA officially accepts the principle of international arbitration. The United States-Argentina BIT provides for international arbitration of investment disputes that cannot be settled amicably.

ICSID Convention and New York Convention

The GOA is a member of the International Center for the Settlement of Investment Disputes (ICSID), the United Nations Commission on International Trade Law (UNCITRAL), and the World Bank's Multilateral Investment Guarantee Agency (MIGA). Argentina ratified the United Nations' Convention on the Recognition and Enforcement of Foreign Arbitral Awards in 1989. Companies that seek recourse through Argentine courts may not also pursue recourse through international arbitration.

DURATION OF DISPUTE RESOLUTION

Domestic and international dispute resolution could be lengthy, sometimes spanning years. Other alternative dispute resolution methods could be stipulated in contracts.

5. PERFORMANCE REQUIREMENTS AND INVESTMENT INCENTIVES

WTO/TRIMS

Argentina has been a World Trade Organization (WTO) member since 1995. Argentina's import licensing requirements often cause delays in, or prevent, the importation of goods necessary for production and consumption. The WTO in January 2015 ruled that the import licenses and other trade balancing schemes required by Argentina violate international trade rules, in a case filed by the United States, Japan, and the European Union. The GOA has publicly stated its intent to comply with the WTO ruling but has yet to make adjustment to its trade regime.

In addition to the import licenses, companies also need to apply for authorization to make payments abroad for services received. This mainly affects international companies' ability to pay foreign headquarters or branches for centralized services such as executive oversight, accounting and human resource management services. During the last year, companies reported increased scrutiny by the GOA over their transfer pricing and foreign payments transactions. In November 2014, the GOA established a Unit of Monitoring and Traceability of Foreign Trade Operations, through decree 2013/2014, with the stated aim of tracking all international trade operations to ensure transparency and accuracy and to prevent over- and under- invoicing by commercial entities.

Since September 2014, any foreign payments amounting to more than USD 150,000 require Central Bank authorization. Companies reported that this requirement further creates delays in their ability to import goods.

These practices are not written in regulation or law but are administrated by the Secretary of Commerce. In practice, any significant payment even of less than USD 150,000 can be delayed by the Central Bank depending on the amount of dollars it thinks it can spend on any given day.

INVESTMENT INCENTIVES

Government incentives apply to both foreign and domestic firms alike. The federal government, as well as provincial and municipal, offers several incentives to attract investment to specific economic sectors such as capital assets and infrastructure, innovation and technological development and energy. More details of these programs can be found here: http://www.inversiones.gov.ar/es/incentivos-la-inversion or http://www.prosperar.gov.ar/

Research and Development

Argentina does not restrict foreign firms from participating in government-funded or subsidized research and development programs.

PERFORMANCE REQUIREMENTS

There are no performance requirements.

DATA STORAGE

Argentina does not have forced localization of content in technology or requirements of data storage in country.

6. RIGHT TO PRIVATE OWNERSHIP AND ESTABLISHMENT

In general terms, foreign investors have the same rights as Argentines to establish and own businesses, or to acquire and dispose of interests in businesses.

The media law caps foreign capital ownership of media outlets at 30 percent; requires a minimum national content of between 60 to 70 percent; requires that all transmission signals be owned totally or partially by the national government; establishes a minimum screen quota for Argentine movies; imposes a 0.5 percent of annual revenue fee on foreign programmers for acquiring Argentine films; requires advertisement transmitted by broadcast channels or national channels be produced locally; dictates that all investment in advertising on a non-national signal be covered by exemptions and reductions to income tax; gives foreign media operations differing tax treatment from local companies; and limits the number of broadcasting licenses (based on geography and market segment) to be held by a single licensee.

Measures regarding the limitation of foreign ownership in media outlets are not retroactively applied to existing foreign investments currently covered by BIT provisions of non-discriminatory treatment. The U.S.-Argentina BIT contains such protection for U.S. firms.

7. PROTECTION OF PROPERTY RIGHTS

REAL PROPERTY

Secured interests in property, including mortgages, are recognized and common in Argentina. Such interests can be easily and effectively registered. They also can be readily bought and sold. Argentina manages a national registry of real state ownership (Registro de la Propiedad Inmueble) at http://www.dnrpi.jus.gov.ar/.

INTELLECTUAL PROPERTY RIGHTS

The government of Argentina adheres to most treaties and international agreements on intellectual property and belongs to the World Intellectual Property Organization and the World Trade Organization (WTO). The Argentine Congress ratified the Uruguay Round agreements, including the provisions on intellectual property in Law 24425 on January 5, 1995. Since 1996, however, Argentina has been on the Office of the U.S. Trade Representative's intellectual property rights Priority Watch List. Argentina was listed in USTR's Notorious Markets Report and Special 301 Report in 2014.

Regarding patents, protection remains a theme of particular importance in Argentina's intellectual property rights regime. Extension of adequate patent protection to pharmaceuticals and genetically modified seeds has been a source of bilateral disagreement. Representatives of U.S. companies with significant interest in patented product sales in Argentina say that the patent issuance process is slow and that the backlog of patent applications remains substantial. The National Intellectual Property Institute (INPI) has taken a number of steps recently to reduce the backlog, including the implementation of fast-track procedures and opportunities for companies to prioritize their patent applications before INPI. However, problems persist. The average wait time observed in 2014 was between seven to eight years for pharmaceutical and biotechnology patents and an average of 3 to 4 years for software and electronics.

In April 2002, the United States and Argentina reached an agreement with respect to most of the claims in a WTO dispute brought by the United States with respect to Argentina's implementation of its Trade Related Aspects of Intellectual Property Rights (TRIPS) obligations. New patent legislation implementing part of the April 2002 agreement was passed in December 2003. Several issues remain unresolved, however. The United States and Argentina have agreed to leave these issues within the WTO dispute settlement mechanism for action.

Some U.S. and European pharmaceutical firms have expressed concern that some provisions in the amended legislation limit their ability to protect patented products via the use of judicial injunctions to prevent patent violations. The unlicensed production by Argentine firms of pharmaceuticals whose patent rights are owned by foreign companies is a longstanding concern to foreign pharmaceutical companies. In May 2012, INPI published a joint Resolution (118/2012, 546/2012 and 107/2012) that sets new standards for chemical and pharmaceutical patent applications. The guidelines instruct patent examiners to reject new use, new form, and new formulation patents, and specify a number of other changes to drugs that will no longer be acceptable. Companies have stated that the measures were implemented without sufficient transparency and that they significantly diminish protection of their intellectual property, and that these regulations are inconsistent with Argentina's Trade Related Intellectual Property Rights (TRIPs) commitments. Also, INPI does not always offer a formal comment period when implementing new procedures. The pharmaceutical and biotechnical industries are the most affected by these regulations, especially, with regard to the prohibition of secondary inventions.

Pharmaceutical and biotech firms assert that during 2014, the GOA did not provide effective data protection for their products (data protection refers to the protection of confidential and proprietary information that companies demonstrate to the health regulators that approve the sale of a new drug). Firms are concerned that the lack of data protection could lead to unfair commercial use and hinder investments in the sector.

Many industry observers claim that the trademark law, passed in 1980, provides civil damages that are insufficient to be an effective deterrent. The judiciary is reluctant to impose deterrent penalties such as prison sentences in criminal cases, and it is rare that companies press criminal charges. The government of Argentina has passed laws designed to allow authorities to mount undercover operations; to flag electronically-suspect shipments; to facilitate the seizure and detention of suspect merchandise; and to rotate more frequently customs personnel. Also, the Customs administration in 2006 instituted a voluntary trademark registry and owner notification program. Some industry actors have noted that further protection for trademark owners should include the right to demand destruction of fraudulent goods to prevent reentry to the market. Currently, when a customs official encounters counterfeit goods, he must notify police authorities to seize the goods and proceed with appropriate legal procedure for each given case. The rights holders are responsible for paying for the storage and destruction of counterfeit goods. The government has decreased the time needed for trademark registration and increased the rate at which trademarks are registered. Argentina has no specific law on trade secrets although penalties for unauthorized revelation of trade secrets are applied to a limited degree under commercial law. Argentina has signed the WIPO Treaty on Integrated Circuits, but has no law dealing specifically with the protection of layout designs and semiconductors.

Although Argentina's copyright law dates to 1930, it does provide a sound legal framework to protect intellectual property such as books, films, music, and software. Copyright piracy of audio and video in CD and DVD formats continues to flourish. Industry reports that the level of enforcement against piracy of copyrighted goods is "very weak" both in law enforcement and the judicial branch. Vendors selling illegal copies can be seen through Buenos Aires subway stations and street corners. Industry reported street vending of pirated goods increased significantly in 2014, unchecked by local law enforcement.

Electronic delivery of copyright infringing materials is still widespread. While Argentine courts have been responsive to civil suits against pirated content, criminal prosecution is lacking. The website Cuevana continues to stream unauthorized copyrighted content and has expanded its distribution network to several more Cuevana websites. The site, although based outside of Argentina, is owned and operated by Argentines. Argentine courts thus far declined to proceed with criminal prosecution against the owner, who lives in Buenos Aires. In June 2014, the Argentine Copyright Association (known by its Spanish acronym SADAIC) succeeded in winning an injunction in Argentine court against the Sweden-based Pirate Bay website. The site has since resurrected via a different IP address. Industry claims Argentine IPR law is outdated and does not provide for IPR protection in newly developed forms of media and operating platforms. Enterprises reported that lack of technical and technological knowledge prevents prosecutors from pursuing cases and judges from making rulings, leaving cases in limbo. Industry continues to call on Argentina to pass its own version of the U.S. Digital Millennium Copyright Act.

Argentina has the largest black market in South America, called La Salada, that sells counterfeit and pirated products. La Salada itself has reportedly continued its expansion to now include multiple stories and more stores and several branches throughout Argentina. Smaller Las Saladitas have proliferated throughout Buenos Aires. The number of illegal street vendors selling counterfeits and pirated goods increased more than 100 percent during 2014 compared to 2013, according to the Argentine Chamber of Commerce.

For additional information about treaty obligations and points of contact at local IP offices, please see WIPO's country profiles at http://www.wipo.int/directory/en/.

Resources for Rights Holders
Embassy's Contact:
María Soledad Iglesias Liste
IglesiasS@state.gov
U.S. Embassy, Buenos Aires, Argentina

8. TRANSPARENCY OF THE REGULATORY SYSTEM

Argentine government authorities, including the Ministries of Economy, Production, and Planning and a number of quasi-independent regulatory entities, have mandates to foster competition and protect consumers. Some international investors have expressed concern about abrupt changes in sector-specific regulatory regimes that in their view increase uncertainty. Decisions that affect companies, both foreign and domestic, are frequently taken without industry input and rarely with a formal comment period. Government interventionist policies affect foreign and domestic companies alike.

Over the last year, the GOA passed a number of laws that increase the ability of the government to determine companies' profits and production quotas. The national Supply Law, approved September 2014, allows the Secretary of Commerce to determine profit margins and reference prices for every stage of the productivity chain and set supply quotas. The Law also establishes severe sanctions ranging from fines to temporary closure for businesses found by the government to be artificially or unjustifiably increasing prices or hoarding inventories.

The Argentine government approved the Argentine Digital Law in early 2015 that enables the government to regulate the interconnection tariffs of telecommunications and cable companies.

In general, national taxation rules do not discriminate against foreigners or foreign firms (e.g., asset taxes are applied to equity possessed by both domestic and foreign entities). Government tax authorities scrutinize tax declarations of foreign corporations operating in Argentina with the intent of curbing the use of offshore shell corporations to shelter profits and assets from taxation. This has led to tax disputes with foreign-owned firms that have structured their operations in a manner they believe to be consistent with Argentine law, while minimizing total corporate tax obligations to all of the countries in which they operate.

Argentina is a member of the U.N. Conference on Trade and Development's international network of transparent investment procedures. Lomas de Zamora, the second largest municipality of Buenos Aires offers detailed information on administrative procedures applicable to income generating operations, including the number of steps, name and contact details of the entities and persons in charge of procedures, required documents and conditions, costs, processing time, and legal bases justifying the procedures: http://lomasdezamora.eregulations.org/. Two other municipalities (Berazategui and Vicente Lopez) plan to offer the same information system online by the end of 2014.

9. EFFICIENT CAPITAL MARKETS AND PORTFOLIO INVESTMENT

The Argentine Securities and Exchange Commission (Comisión Nacional de Valores - CNV) is the federal agency that regulates securities markets offerings. Securities and accounting standards are transparent and consistent with international norms. Foreign investors have access to a variety of options on the local market to obtain credit.

The Argentine Congress approved in November 2012 a new law to amend regulations over the domestic stock market. The bill expands the local capital market, but it also provides for greater regulatory intervention in financial deals and corporate administration of listed companies.

U.S. banks, securities firms, and investment funds are well-represented in Argentina and are dynamic players in local capital markets. In 2003, the government began requiring foreign banks to disclose to the public the nature and extent to which their foreign parent banks guarantee their branches or subsidiaries in Argentina. In April 2015, the Argentine Securities Exchange Commission (CNV) suspended Citibank Argentina from operating in capital markets and ordered the removal of its CEO due to the bank's efforts to extricate itself from a dispute over the country's bond payments tied to litigation in U.S. courts between the GOA and a group of U.S. hedge funds.

The private pension fund system -- consolidated in 1995 -- provided a growing base for capital markets until the 2001-02 economic and financial crises. Following the government's 2005 debt restructuring, private pension funds once again became significant players in domestic capital markets. The government's nationalization of the private pension funds' assets in November 2008 shut down the funds' investment activities, however. As a result of the nationalization, Argentina's Social Security Agency (ANSES) now holds large equity stakes in domestic and foreign firms trading on the local stock exchange, and has also taken on the private pension funds' holdings of federal and provincial government debt. This nationalization considerably decreased the liquidity and depth of the securities market in Argentina.

Following new provisions introduced in the Central Bank charter reform approved in mid-2012, the Central Bank has required banks operating in Argentina holding at least 1 percent of total market deposits to lend at least 5 percent of their deposits -- for "productive investments" at an interest rate that are below market rates, and even below private estimates of inflation. This program has been extended and recently the loans have been oriented to focus on small and medium sizes enterprises. Since its implementation, banks have issued over ARS 100 billion in loans. The government also mandates interest rate caps and limits on bank fees, limiting banks' profit margins. Banks are required to offer credit to both corporate borrowers and small and medium-sized enterprises at below-market rates, which further constrains profitability.

MONEY AND BANKING SYSTEM, HOSTILE TAKEOVERS

Argentina has a relatively sound banking sector. The largest bank is the Banco de la Nación Argentina. In recent years, the GOA has imposed a range of policies that have negatively affected business conditions and banks' financial strength, including dividend payment and foreign exchange market restrictions, caps on lending rates and fees, and lending requirements to targeted sectors. However, non-performing private sector loans constitute less than 2 percent of banks' portfolios. The ten largest private banks have total assets of approximately ARS 564 billion (USD 64 billion). Total financial system assets are approximately ARS 1.230 trillion (USD 140 billion).

10. COMPETITION FROM STATE-OWNED ENTERPRISES

The Argentine government owns state owned enterprises (SOEs) in the following sectors: civil commercial aviation, water and sanitation, oil and gas, electricity generation, transport, paper production, banking, railway, shipyard, and aircraft ground handling services. A list of state-own enterprises and enterprises under concession can be found here: http://www.adminpublica.org.ar/EF_EmpresasPublicas.htm.

By Argentine law, a company is considered a public enterprise if the state owns 100 percent of the company's shares. The state has majority control over a company if the state owns 51 percent of the company's shares. The state has minority participation in a company if the state owns less than 51 percent of the company's shares. Argentine Law 25.156 regulates state-owned enterprises and enterprises with state participation.

Through the government's social security agency (ANSES), the GOA owns stakes ranging from 1 percent to 31 percent in 46 publically-listed companies. U.S. investors also own shares in some of these companies. As part of the ANSES takeover of Argentina's private pension system in 2008, the government agreed to commit itself to being a passive investor in the companies and limit the exercise of its voting rights to 5 percent, regardless of the percentage of a company the social security agency actually owned. In April 2011, the GOA removed the 5 percent cap and moved to increase ANSES' influence over these companies by nominating members for their boards of directors and exercising influence over issues such as dividend payments.

Most of Argentina's state-owned enterprises (SOEs) operate as providers of public services and do not face competition in the private sector. SOEs do purchase and supply goods and services from the private sector and foreign firms. Private enterprises may compete with SOEs under the same terms and conditions with respect to market share, products/services, and incentives. Private enterprises also have access to financing terms and conditions similar to SOE. SOEs are subject to the same tax burden and tax rebate policies as their private sector competitors. SOEs are not currently subject to firm budget constraints under the law. Argentina does not have regulations that differentiate treatment of SOEs and private enterprises. Argentina has observer status under the WTO Agreement on Government Procurement and, as such, SOEs are subject to the conditions of Argentina's observership.

OECD Guidelines on Corporate Governance of SOEs

Argentina generally adheres to the OECD Guidelines on Corporate Governance of SOEs. SOEs are in compliance with some policies and practices for transparency and accountability set out in the OECD Guidelines. The general rule in Argentina is that requirements that apply to all listed companies also apply to publicly-listed SOEs.

11. CORPORATE SOCIAL RESPONSIBILITY

There is an increasing awareness of corporate social responsibility (CSR) among both producers and consumers. CSR practices are welcomed by beneficiary communities throughout Argentina.

OECD Guidelines for Multinational Enterprises

Foreign and local enterprises both tend to follow generally accepted CSR principles. Argentina subscribed to the Declaration on the OECD Guidelines for Multinational Enterprises on April 1997.

12. POLITICAL VIOLENCE

Demonstrations are common in metropolitan Buenos Aires and occur in other major cities and rural areas. Protesters on occasion block streets, highways, and major intersections, causing traffic jams and delaying travel. While demonstrations are usually nonviolent, individuals sometimes seek confrontation with the police and vandalize private property. Groups occasionally protest in front of the U.S. Embassy or U.S.-affiliated businesses. Though political violence is always concerning, it is not widely considered a hindrance to the investment climate in Argentina.

13. CORRUPTION

According to the World Bank's worldwide governance indicators, corruption remains an area of concern in Argentina. In the latest Transparency International Corruption Perceptions Index (CPI) that ranks countries and territories by their perceived levels of corruption, Argentina ranked 107 out of 175 countries. Lack of transparency, autonomy, and clear rules in the selection of judges as well as inefficiencies and pervasive delays compromise the judicial system and create the potential for political influence. Few Argentine companies have implemented anti-foreign bribery measures beyond limited codes of ethics. According to Transparency International, weak enforcement of anti-corruption measures remains Argentina's greatest corruption weakness.

Argentina's legal system incorporates measures addressing public sector corruption and a number of government institutions tasked with using them to fight corruption including the Anti-Corruption Office (ACO), the National Auditor General, and the General Comptroller's Office. Public officials are subject to financial disclosure laws, and the Ministry of Justice's ACO is responsible for analyzing and investigating federal executive branch officials based on their financial disclosure forms. The ACO is also responsible for investigating corruption within the federal executive branch or in matters involving federal funds, except for funds transferred to the provinces. While the ACO does not have authority to independently prosecute cases, it can refer cases to other agencies or serve as the plaintiff and request a judge to initiate a case.

UN Anticorruption Convention, OECD Convention on Combatting Bribery

Argentina is a party to the OAS Inter-American Convention Against Corruption. It ratified the OECD Convention on Combating Bribery of Foreign Public Officials in International Business Transactions in 2001. Argentina also has signed and ratified the UN Convention against Corruption (UNCAC) and is an active participant in UNCAC's Conference of State Parties. Argentina also is an active participant in the Mechanism for Follow-up on the Implementation of the Inter-American Convention against Corruption (MESICIC).

Since Argentina became a Party to the OECD Convention in 2001, ten allegations of Argentine individuals or companies bribing foreign officials have surfaced. Three of the allegations are under investigation. An investigation into one allegation was not opened because of a lack of information. Investigations into two allegations ended without charges. A seventh allegation was determined not to involve foreign bribery but other offences after an investigation. At the time of OECD's last reporting in December 2014, it remains unconfirmed whether the remaining cases involve foreign bribery.

Argentina is a member of the OECD Working Group on Bribery, the organization that monitors compliance with the OECD Convention. Argentina underwent its Phase 3 Working Group evaluation in December 2014 at which time the group found that Argentina was "seriously non-compliant with key articles of the convention, including introducing corporate liability for foreign bribery." The Working Group also found persistent, systemic deficiencies in Argentina's criminal justice system and ability to detect and report foreign bribery. As a consequence, Argentina will be required to undergo a supplemental Phase 3 evaluation before the end of 2016.

Resources to Report Corruption

Oficina Anticorrupción, Ministerio de Justicia y Derechos Humanos
anticorrupcion@jus.gov.ar
Tucumán 394
Código Postal (C 1049 AAH)
Ciudad Autónoma de Buenos Aires,
República Argentina

Poder Ciudadano (Local Transparency International Affiliate)
Phone: +54 11 4331 4925 ext 225
Fax: +54 11 4331 4925
Email: comunicaciones@poderciudadano.org
Website: http://www.poderciudadano.org

14. BILATERAL INVESTMENT AGREEMENTS

In 1991, Argentina and the United States signed a Bilateral Investment Treaty (BIT). The agreement was ratified by both countries entering into force on October 20, 1994. The Argentina-United States BIT can be found on the following site:**http://2001-2009.state.gov/documents/organization/43475.pdf**.

The BIT provides protections against capital movement restrictions, expropriations, and performance requirements; it also establishes a means for the settlement of investment disputes. The BIT lists sectors in which Argentina maintains exceptions to national treatment for U.S. investors: real estate in border areas, air transportation, shipbuilding, nuclear energy, uranium mining, and fishing. U.S. investors must obtain permission from the Ministry of Defense's Superintendency for Frontiers to invest in non-mining activities in border areas.

Currently, Argentina has over 50 BITs and double taxation treaties (DTAs) in force. Among those countries there is Australia, United Kingdom, Denmark, Germany, Belgium, France, Italy, Sweden, Canada, Bolivia, Brazil, Finland, Norway, and the Netherlands. In addition, a number of treaties concerning the exemption of income tax from international transport are in force.

In October 2014, the Government of Argentina signed a resolution with 50 other countries, agreeing to the automatic exchange of banking information to improve fiscal transparency. The agreement, which was spearheaded by the Organization for Economic Co-operation and Development (OECD), will allow the Argentine Tax Authority AFIP access information on foreign bank accounts held by Argentines. The agreement is expected to begin implementation in 2017. Detailed information of the Argentina's international agreement related to taxes can be found at http://www.afip.gov.ar/institucional/acuerdos.asp

In 2015, Argentina and the United States signed a Memorandum of Understanding to renew the exchange of trade and fiscal information between the countries, increasing the transparency of commercial transactions.

During the last year, several commercial and investment agreements have been signed between the GOA and China. The specific terms and conditions of the agreements are not publicly available, causing consternation in the private sector over the lack of transparency.

BILATERAL TAXATION TREATIES

Argentina does not have a bilateral tax treaty with the United States.

15. OPIC AND OTHER INVESTMENT INSURANCE PROGRAMS

The GOA signed a comprehensive agreement with the Overseas Private Investment Corporation (OPIC) in 1989. The agreement allows OPIC to insure U.S. investments against risks resulting from expropriation, inconvertibility, war or other conflicts affecting public order. OPIC programs are currently used in Argentina. Argentina is also a member of the World Bank's Multilateral Investment Guarantee Agency (MIGA).

16. LABOR

Argentine workers are among the most highly educated in Latin America. Wages in dollar terms have historically been competitive. Argentina has relatively high social security charges and other labor taxes. As of the fourth quarter of 2014, the unemployment rate was 6.9 percent according to official government statistics. The Ministry of Labor, Employment, and Social Security estimated that 33.1 percent of the urban workforce worked in the informal sector as of the third quarter of 2014, although other private sector and civil society sources estimate that the number is higher (around 45 percent).

Organized labor plays an active role in labor-management relations and in the Argentine political system. Standoffs between management and union activists do occur. Many managers of foreign companies say that they have good relations with their unions. While negotiations between unions and industry are largely market-driven, they occasionally require mediation by the Ministry of Labor. Labor-related demonstrations in Argentina remained high in 2014, with over 1,600 protests that ranged in size, taking place between the months of January and October. Reasons for strikes include complaints from disgruntled workers, unemployed, and other social groups' demonstrations.

Argentine law affords unions the right to negotiate collective bargaining agreements and offers recourse to mediation and arbitration. The Ministry of Labor ratifies collective bargaining agreements, which covered roughly 75 percent of the formally employed work force. There are no special laws or exemptions from regular labor laws in the Foreign Trade Zones (FTZs).

Labor laws are usually protective of workers in Argentina. However, when employers can show a true decrease or lack of activity in their sectors that do not derive from their negligence or recklessness, employers can adjust employment by reducing the working days or assigning employees to shiftwork. This provision is implemented only in emergency situations, which cannot last longer than a month in a given year.

The Labor Ministry has different hotlines to report labor abuses and the Superintendencia de Riesgos del Trabajo monitors health and safety standards in all sort of operations. Nevertheless, unions also play a key role in monitoring labor conditions, reporting abuses and filing complaints with the proper authorities.

In 2014, Congress passed a law that reduced employers' required contributions for small businesses. This move came as part of the government's effort to fight "under-the-table" or unregistered workers. Also in 2014, Congress passed a law – the Supply Law – against 'business abuse" that entitles the executive branch to set earning margins and prices during the different stages of the economic process.

17. FOREIGN TRADE ZONES/FREE PORTS/TRADE FACILITATION

Argentina has two types of tax-exempt trading areas: Free Trade Zones (FTZ), which are found throughout the country; and the more comprehensive Special Customs Area (SCA), which covers all of Tierra del Fuego Province.

Argentine law defines an FTZ as a territory outside the "general customs area" (GCA, i.e., the rest of Argentina) where neither the inflows nor outflows of exported final merchandise are subject to tariffs, non-tariff barriers, or other taxes on goods. Goods produced within a FTZ generally cannot be shipped to the GCA unless they are capital goods not produced in the rest of the country. The labor, sanitary, ecological, safety, criminal, and financial regulations within FTZs are the same as those that prevail in the GCA. Foreign firms receive national treatment in FTZs.

Under the current law, the GOA may create one FTZ per province, with certain exceptions. More than one FTZ per province may be allowed in sparsely populated border regions (although this provision has not been fully utilized). Thus far, the GOA has permitted FTZs in many of the 23 Argentine provinces. The most active FTZ is in La Plata, the capital of Buenos Aires Province.

Merchandise shipped from the GCA to a FTZ may receive export incentive benefits, if applicable, only after the goods are exported from the FTZ to a third country destination. Merchandise shipped from the GCA to a FTZ and later exported to another country is not exempt from export taxes. Any value added in an FTZ or re-export from an FTZ is exempt from export taxes.

Products manufactured in an SCA may enter the GCA free from taxes or tariffs. In addition, the government may enact special regulations that exempt products shipped through an SCA (but not manufactured therein) from all forms of taxation except excise taxes. The SCA program provides benefits for established companies that meet specific production and employment objectives. The SCA program applies only to Tierra del Fuego Province and is scheduled to expire at the end of 2023. In late 2006, the Economy Ministry through Resolution 776 abolished the export tax exemption enjoyed by oil companies operating in Tierra del Fuego Province. The Argentine Congress passed a law in November 2009 establishing value-added tax rates up to 21 percent on cell phones, televisions, digital cameras and other electronic items not produced in the southern Tierra del Fuego foreign trade zone. According to the government, the bill aims to increase government revenue through higher tax collection, and encourage investment in Tierra del Fuego to promote local manufacturing and job growth. Argentina's import restrictions are often the primary reason that foreign firms choose to assemble electronic products in Argentina.

18. FOREIGN DIRECT INVESTMENT AND FOREIGN PORTFOLIO INVESTMENT STATISTICS

Table 2: Key Macroeconomic Data, U.S. FDI in Host Country/Economy

	Host Country Statistical source*		USG or international statistical source		USG or International Source of Data: BEA; IMF; Eurostat; UNCTAD, Other
Economic Data	Year	Amount	Year	Amount	
Host Country Gross Domestic Product (GDP) ($M USD)	2013	610,288	2013	609,900	www.worldbank.org/en/country
Foreign Direct Investment	Host Country Statistical source*		USG or international statistical source		USG or international Source of data: BEA; IMF; Eurostat; UNCTAD, Other
U.S. FDI in partner	2013	N/A	2013	15,171	BEA data available 3/19/14 at http://bea.gov/international/direct investment multinational

country ($M USD, stock positions)					companies_comprehensive_data.htm
Host country's FDI in the United States ($M USD, stock positions)	2013	N/A	2013	119	BEA data available 3/19/14 at http://bea.gov/international/direct_investment_multinational_companies_comprehensive_data.htm
Total inbound stock of FDI as % host GDP	2013	N/A	2013	1.68%	

*Argentine Statistics Agency, www.indec.gob.ar. Difference between figures is due to statistical corrections done by INDEC on a regular basis.

Table 3: Sources and Destination of FDI

The IMF does not have recent direct investment data on Argentina. Argentina was censured by the IMF in February 2013 for reporting unreliable economic data.

According to the United Nations Conference on Trade and Development (UNCTAD) World Investment Report 2012, the latest information for Argentina, the total stock of FDI in Argentina at the end of 2012 was estimated at USD 110.7 billion. The stock of U.S. FDI in Argentina in 2012 was estimated at USD 14.4 billion by the U.S. Bureau of Economic Analysis. In 2012, according to UNCTAD, total FDI inflows were estimated at USD 12.5 billion and outward FDI flows amounted to USD 1.1 billion.

Source: UNCTAD, http://unctadstat.unctad.org/TableViewer/tableView.aspx

Table 4: Sources of Portfolio Investment

PORTFOLIO INVESTMENT ASSETS								
TOP FIVE PARTNERS (MILLIONS, US DOLLARS)								
TOTAL			EQUITY SECURITIES			TOTAL DEBT SECURITIES		
All Countries	23,459	100%	All Countries	14,211	100%	All Countries	Amount	100%
United States	22,092	94%	United States	13,169	93%	United States	8,923	96%
Luxembourg	680	3%	Luxembourg	680	5%	Brazil	305	3%
Brazil	427	2%	Spain	149	1%	Germany	7	0.08%

Spain	149	1%	Brazil	121	1%	Mexico	6	0.04%
China P.R.	24	0.10%	China, P.R.	24	0.17%	Chile	4	0.03%

Source: IMF Coordinated Portfolio Investment Survey, 2014

IMPORTANT INVESTMENT AND BUSINESS CONTACTS

CONTACT FOR MORE INFORMATION

Economic Counselor
U.S. Embassy Buenos Aires
Avenida Colombia 4300
(C1425GMN)
Buenos Aires, Argentina
+54-11-5777-4747
ECONBA@state.gov

LAWYERS

BUENOS AIRES

ESTUDIO BRONS & SALAS ABOGADOS
Maipú 1210, Piso 5º
C1006ACT, Buenos Aires
Tel: (11) 4891-2715, (11) 4891-2717
Fax: (11) 4314-0399
E-mail: brons@brons.com.ar erepresas@brons.com.ar gmalmgreen@brons.comar
Web site: www.brons.com.ar

PRACTICE:
Marriage/Divorce, Insurance, Banking/financial, Commercial/Business Law, Foreign Investments, Marketing Agreements, Patents/Trademarks/Copyrights, Civil Law, Damages, Collections, Contracts, Transportation Law, Aeronautical/Maritime, Corporations, Foreign Claims, Government Relations, Estates, Taxes, Immigration
LANGUAGES SPOKEN: English, Spanish

CARABELLI, CECILIA
Tel: (+54-9-11) 5409-2826 (calling from abroad), 15-5409-2826 (calling from Argentina)
E-mail: cecicarabelli@hotmail.com
PRACTICE:
Marriage/Divorce, Insurance, Civil Law, Damages, Estates, Labor Relations, Immigration, Auto/Accidents
LANGUAGES SPOKEN: English, Spanish, French and Italian (limited)

ESTUDIO DOUGALL ABOGADOS
Córdoba 971, Piso 7°
1054, Buenos Aires
Tel: (11) 4322-7006
E-mail: mvd@dougallabogados.com.ar
Web site: www.dougallabogados.com.ar
PRACTICE:

Family Law, Child Custody, Parental Child Abduction, Marriage/Divorce, Commercial/Business Law, Foreign Investments, Civil Law, Damages, Collections, Corporations, Foreign Claims, Taxes, Immigration, Auto/Accidents.
LANGUAGES SPOKEN: English, Spanish

ESTUDIO DURRIEU ABOGADOS S.C.
Maipú 1300, Piso 6
C1006ACT, Buenos Aires, Argentina
Tel: (54-11) 4311-9500
Fax: (54-11) 4311-9800
E-mail: rdf@estudiodurrieu.com.ar
Web site: www.estudiodurrieu.com.ar
PRACTICE:
Family Law, Banking/ Financial Criminal Law, Corporations, Government Relations, Auto/Accidents
LANGUAGES SPOKEN: English, Spanish, French and Portuguese

CONSUELO GARCIA LAW OFFICES
Talcahuano 736, piso 10A
(1013) Buenos Aires
Tel: (11) 4373-0549, Cell phone: (9-11) 44754998 (calling from the U.S.); Cell phone: 15-4475-4998 (calling from Argentina)
Fax: (11) 4773-4582 E-mail: cg@consuelogarcia.com
Web site: www.consuelogarcia.com

PRACTICE:
Family Law, Adoptions, Child Custody, Parental Child Abduction, Marriage/Divorce, Civil Law, Damages, Contracts, Foreign Claims, Estates
LANGUAGES SPOKEN: English, Spanish
LIMERES, BARASSI, VES LOSADA & STANZIONE
Tucumán 766, piso 2°-196,
(1049) Buenos Aires
Tel: (11) 5263-3262
E-mail: LIMERES@LIMERES.com
Web Site: https://www.limeres.com
P
RACTICE:
Marriage/Divorce, Insurance, Banking/Financial, Commercial/Business Law, Foreign Investments, Patents/Trademarks/Copyrights, Civil Law, Damages, Commercial Law, Contracts, Transportation Law, Corporations, Foreign Claims, Estates, Taxes, Auto/Accidents
LANGUAGES SPOKEN: English, Spanish.

ESTUDIO MARTEAU ABOGADOS / ATTORNEYS-AT-LAW
Santa Fé 1339, piso 1°
(1059) Buenos Aires
Tel: (11) 4815-6888, (11) 4811-8498
Fax: (54-11) 4815-6888, (11) 4811-8498
E-mail: institucional@marteau.pro jfm@mareau.pro
Web site: www.marteau.pro
PRACTICE:
Banking/Financial, Foreign Investments, Criminal Law, Narcotics
LANGAUGES SPOKEN: English, French, Portuguese, German, Italian

ESTUDIO QUAINI
Maipú 267, piso 6
C1084ABD – Buenos Aires
Tel: (11) 5199-2446, (11) 4328-3939, Cell Phone: (9-11) 3295-8221 (calling from the U.S.) Cell phone: 15-3295-8221 (calling from Argentina)
Fax: (11) 4328-3939
E-mail: fquaini@lexaustralis.com
Web site: www.lexaustralis.com

PRACTICE:
Family Law, Adoptions, Child Custody, Parental Child Abduction, Child Protection, Marriage/Divorce, Civil Law, Damages, Collections, Foreign Claims, Auto/Accidents
LANGUAGES SPOKEN: English, French, Italian, Portuguese and Spanish

ESTUDIO SASSE & ASOCIADOS
Rodríguez Peña 546, piso 8°A
Buenos Aires
Tel: (11) 4374-9325/2397
Cell phone: (911) 4477-2364 (calling from the U.S.); 15-4477-2364 (calling from Argentina)
E-mail: estudiosasseyasoc@gmail.com

PRACTICE:
Banking/Financial, Commercial/Business Law, Foreign Investments, Marketing Agreements, Civil Law, Damages, Contracts, Transportation Law, Corporations, Foreign Claims, Estates, Taxes, Government Relations, Labor Relations, Immigration, Auto/Accidents
LANGUAGES SPOKEN: English, Spanish
ESTUDIO TAMINI & ASOCIADOS
Av. Córdoba 836, Piso 12, Oficina 1212
1054 – Buenos Aires
Tel: (11) 4328-0172
Fax: (54-11) 4328-0172
E-mail: adolfotamini@speedy.com.ar
PRACTICE:
Criminal Law, Narcotics
LANGUAGES SPOKEN: English, Spanish

WEINER, SOTO, CAPARÓS
Av. Pte. Roque Saenz Peña 637, piso 1
C1035AAB – Buenos Aires
Tel: (11) 5272-9960
Fax: (11) 4326-4789
E-mail: gsoto@wsclegal.com ; mcaparros@wsclegal.com ; lwiener@wsclegal.com
Web site: www.wsclegal.com

PRACTICE:
Insurance, Banking/Financial, Commercial/Business Law, Foreign Investments, Marketing Agreements, Patents/Trademarks/Copyrights, Damages, Contracts, Transportation Law, Corporations, Foreign Claims, Estate, Taxes, Government Relations, Labor Relations, Immigration
LANGUAGUES SPOKEN: English, Spanish.

FREE JUDICIAL ASSISTANCE

COLEGIO DE ABOGADOS DE LA CIUDAD DE BUENOS AIRES
Montevideo 640 (C1019ABN) Buenos Aires
Tel: 43 71 11 10
E-mail: consultorio@colabogados.org.ar
Web site: http://www.colabogados.org.ar/consultorio-juridico-gratuito/funcionamiento.php

MINSTERIO PÚBLICO DE LA DEFENSA
México 890/92
(1097) Buenos Aires
E-mail: defgral@jusbaires.gov.ar
Web site: http://defensoria.jusbaires.gov.ar/
CENTRO DE FORMACIÓN PROFESIONAL UNIVERSIDAD DE BUENOS AIRES
Talcahuano 550, piso 8º, Buenos Aires
Tel: 4371-2861
E-mail: patrociniouba@hotmail.com

DEFENSORÍA DEL PUEBLO DE LA CIUDAD DE BUENOS AIRES
Discrimination, the Elders, Retirement Pensions, Immigration, Consumer Protection Law
Venezuela 842, Buenos Aires
Tel: 4338-4900
Monday through Friday 9am – 6pm
E-mail: consultas@defensoria.gov.ar
Web site: www.defensoria.gov.ar

PROCURACIÓN DEL GOBIERNO DE LA CIUDAD DE BUENOS AIRES
General legal counsel and assistance in domestic violence cases
Dirección: Uruguay 440, Buenos Aires
Tel: 4323-9200, ext. 7400
Monday through Friday 9 am – 3 pm
Email: priv_procur@buenosaires.gov.ar
BARILOCHE
ESTUDIO GIRAUDY ABOGADOS
Libertad 299 1 "B", oficina B
8400 San Carlos de Bariloche, Rio Negro
Tel: (294) 442-1600, (294) 442-3709
Fax: (294) 442-3709, (294) 442-1600
E-mail: giraudyabogados@bariloche.com.ar

PRACTICE:
Insurance, Banking, Financial, Commercial/Business Law, Foreign Investments, Real Estate, Auto/Accidents
LANGUAGES SPOKEN: English (limited)

CÓRDOBA
ARIAS
Manuel E. Pizarro No. 2025, Barrio Cerro de las Rosas
X5009KSC – Córdoba
Tel/Fax: (351) 4814-141
E-mail: dr.mauriciorodriguez@gmail.com abogados@arias.com.ar
Web site: www.arias.com.ar

PRACTICE:
Family Law, Marriage/Divorce, Insurance, Commercial/Business Law, Foreign Investments, Marketing Agreements, Patents/Trademarks/Copyrights, Civil Law, Criminal Law, Damages, Narcotics, Collections, Contracts, Corporations, Foreign Claims, Estates, Taxes, Labor Relations, Auto/Accidents.
LANGUAGE SPOKEN: English, Spanish

MENDOZA

ESTUDIO BISERO PARATZ &GIMÉNEZ RIILI - ABOGADOS
Dr. J. E. Serú 270,
M5500FNF, Mendoza
Tel: (54-261) 424-7473
Fax: (54-261) 424-7497
E-mail: abisero@bpgr.com.ar
Web site: www.bpgr.com.ar
SPECIALITY:
Insurance, Banking/Financial, Commercial/Business Law, Foreign Investments, Marketing Agreements, Patents/Trademarks/Copyrights, Civil Law, Damages,
Collections, Commercial Law, Contracts, Transportation Law, Corporations, Estates, Taxes, Government Relations, Labor Relations, Immigration, Auto/Accidents.
LANGUAGES SPOKEN: English, Spanish, French, Italian, Portuguese
ESTUDIO QUAINI
Mitre 1685, Chacras de Coria,
M5500GEQ - Mendoza
Tel: (261) 476-0667, Cell phone: (9-261) 5438134 (calling from abroad), Cell phone: (261) 5438134 (calling form Argentina)
E-mail: fquaini@lexaustralis.com
Web site: www.lexaustralis.com
PRACTICE:
Family Law, Adoptions, Child Custody, Parental Child Abduction, Child Protection, Marriage/Divorce, Civil Law, Damages, Foreign Claims, Auto/Accidents
LANGUAGES SPOKEN: English, French, Italian, Portuguese and Spanish

ROSARIO

ESTUDIO STRAZIUSO & MORCHI
Av. Fancia 2278 – Planta Alta –
2000, Rosario, Santa Fé
Tel: (341) 4326590
Fax: (341) 4361625
E-mail: a.straziuso@gmail.com
PRACTICE:
Family Law, Adoptions, Child Custody, Parental Child Abduction, Child Protection, Marriage Divorce, Civil Law
LANGUAGES: English (good) and Italian

BOLIVIA INVESTMENT AND BUSINESS CLIMATE - STRATEGIC INFORMATION AND CONTACTS FOR STARTING BUSINESS IN BOLIVIA

CONTACT FOR MORE INFORMATION

Don Frerichs
Economic Officer
U.S. Embassy La Paz
+591-2-216-8210
CommerceLaPaz@state.gov

Bolivia is a landlocked country in west central South America. Investing in Bolivia is challenging for both domestic and international companies due to a lack of transparency, a cumbersome legal system, and a regulatory system in transition. Bolivia is currently awaiting the implementation of more than 100 laws and regulations needed to bring the country's legal framework into agreement with the nation's Constitution.

The 2009 Constitution stipulates that:

The government will prioritize Bolivian investment over foreign investment (Article 320)

Economic activity cannot damage the collective good (Article 47)

Citizens are entitled to the right to private property -- as long as it serves a social function and is not against the collective interest (Article 56)

Transferring national resources that are the "social property of the Bolivian people" in favor of companies, people, or foreign states can be considered an act of treason (Article 125)

Bolivian Constitutional law supersedes international law and treaties (Article 410) with the exception of human rights treaties.

The Bolivian government has signaled that its upcoming legislative agenda will include new hydrocarbons, electricity and arbitration regulations. Such regulations have been in the works for years, with little progress.

In 2014, the Bolivian government approved an investment law that lacks specificity in terms of incentives and leaves the topic of dispute resolution to be covered by a separate future law. Despite this, the business community hopes its passage indicates a change in the government's attitude towards investment. The 2014 law recognizes foreign investment (Article 4). It also recognizes legal security for national and foreign investment (Article 3), but without elaborating on how it intends to ensure legal security, given the 2009 Constitution's restrictions on international dispute resolution and domestic legal shortcomings. The 2014 Investment law states that the government will establish incentives for investment in key sectors within three months and that an arbitration law will be enacted within three months. However, the Bolivian government has not enacted either provision.

Potential investors in Bolivia should conduct very careful due diligence before investing. Using the Bolivian judicial system to settle disputes can be slow and decisions may be arbitrary. The Bolivian government does not recognize third country arbitration in any of its commercial agreements, so potential investors working directly with the government should consider how disputes would be resolved if they arise. Companies in Bolivia are subject to arbitrary requirements such as the 2013 announcement of the requirement to provide a second Christmas bonus (repeated in 2014), as well as annual, retroactive wage increases.

Despite the real challenges to investing in Bolivia, investors who have adequately assessed the risks can find many profitable opportunities. With real GDP growth of 5.4 percent in 2014, Bolivia experienced an 18 percent increase in nominal per capita GDP; still robust, but slightly lower growth is projected for 2015. This increased wealth led to a 6 percent increase in imports from the United States. Sectors such as heavy construction equipment, hydrocarbon and mining machinery, and telecommunications have all benefitted from Bolivia's growing economy.

1. OPENNESS TO, AND RESTRICTIONS UPON, FOREIGN INVESTMENT

ATTITUDE TOWARD FOREIGN DIRECT INVESTMENT

In general terms, Bolivia remains open to foreign direct investment (FDI). The 2014 investment law guarantees equal treatment for national and foreign firms, however it also stipulates that public investment has priority over private investment (both national and foreign) and that the Bolivian government will determine which sectors require private investment.

The Government of Bolivia has delivered to the United States a notice of termination for the BIT between the countries, a termination that will take effect on June 2012. As of June 2012, the treaty will cease to have effect except that it will continue to apply for another 10 years over covered investments existing at the time of termination.

OTHER INVESTMENT POLICY REVIEWS

Bolivia has been a World Trade Organization (WTO) member since 1995. Bolivia's last trade policy review was in 2005.

LAWS/REGULATIONS OF FOREIGN DIRECT INVESTMENT

Article 320 of the 2009 Constitution directly affects potential foreign investments because Bolivia no longer recognizes international arbitration forums. In case of controversy, the parties cannot settle the dispute in an international court. However, the legal standard of implementation is still uncertain because there is no implementing law to accompany the Constitutional framework.

Article 320 of the Bolivian Constitution states the following regarding foreign investments in Bolivia:

Bolivian investment takes priority over foreign investment.

Every foreign investment will be subject to Bolivian jurisdiction, laws, and authorities, and no one may invoke a situation for exception, nor appeal to diplomatic claims to obtain more favorable treatment.

Economic relations with foreign states or enterprises shall be conducted under conditions of independence, mutual respect and equity. More favorable conditions may not be granted to foreign states or enterprises other than those established for Bolivians.

The state makes all decisions on internal economic policy independently and will not accept demands or conditions imposed on this policy by states, banks or Bolivian or foreign financial institutions, multilateral entities or transnational enterprises.

Public policies will promote internal consumption of products made in Bolivia.

Article 262 of the Constitution states the following regarding foreign investments near the border:

"The fifty kilometers from the borderline constitute the zone of border security. No foreign person, individual, or company may acquire property in this space, directly or indirectly, nor possess any property right in the waters, soil or subsoil, except in the case of state necessity declared by express law approved by two thirds of the Plurinational Legislative Assembly. The property or the possession affected in case of non-compliance with this prohibition will pass to the benefit of the state, without any indemnity."

Part of the stated purpose of the Bolivian judicial system is to uphold the sanctity of contracts. In practice, however, the judicial system faces a huge backlog of cases, is short staffed, and has problems with corruption. Swift resolution of cases, either initiated by investors or against them, is unlikely. Also, the Marcelo Quiroga Anti-Corruption law of 2010 makes companies and their signatories criminally liable for breach of contract with the government, and the law can be applied retroactively. Authorities can use this threat of criminal prosecution to force settlement of disputes. Commercial disputes can often lead to criminal charges. Cases are processed slowly, and suspects can be held legally for 18 months without formal charge as a case is investigated and for 36 months before their case is resolved by a judge. Foreigners are more likely to be deemed a flight risk than Bolivian nationals and, as such, may not receive bail in lieu of pretrial incarceration. Foreigners considering investing in Bolivia would do well to review our Human Rights Report as background on the judicial system, labor rights and other important issues.

INDUSTRIAL PROMOTION

Although the Bolivian government frequently mentions that it would like to attract new foreign direct investment (FDI), it has done little to do so. There are no active campaigns to recruit foreign companies at this time.

LIMITS ON FOREIGN CONTROL

With the exception of the broadcasting sector, there is no requirement that Bolivian nationals own shares of companies, or that foreign equity be reduced over time. There are some areas where investors may judge that special treatment is being given to their Bolivian competitors, for example in key sectors where private companies compete with state owned enterprises. Additionally, foreign investment is not allowed in matters relating directly to national security, and only the government can own natural resources.

The Constitution specifies that all hydrocarbon resources are the property of the Bolivian people and that the state will assume control over their exploration, exploitation, industrialization, transport, and marketing (Articles 348 and 351). The state-owned and operated company, Yacimientos Petrolíferos Fiscales Bolivianos (YPFB), manages hydrocarbons transport and sales and is responsible for ensuring that the domestic market demand is satisfied at prices set by the hydrocarbons regulator before allowing any hydrocarbon exports. YPFB benefitted from government action in 2006 that required operators to turn over all of their production to it and to sign new contracts that gave YPFB control over the distribution of gasoline, diesel, and liquid petroleum gas (LPG) to gas stations. The law allows YPFB to enter into joint venture contracts for limited periods with national or foreign individuals or companies wishing to exploit or trade hydrocarbons or their derivatives. For companies working in the industry, contracts are negotiated on a service contract basis and there are no restrictions on ownership percentages of the companies providing the services.

The Constitution (Article 366) also specifies that every foreign enterprise that conducts activities in the hydrocarbons production chain representing Bolivia will submit to the sovereignty of the state, and to the laws and authority of the state. No foreign court case or foreign jurisdiction will be recognized, and foreign investors may not invoke any exceptional situation for international arbitration, nor appeal to diplomatic claims.

According to the Constitution, no concessions or contracts may transfer the ownership of natural resources or other strategic industries to private interests. Instead, temporary authorizations to use these resources may be requested at the pertinent ministry (mining, water and environment, public works, etc.). The Bolivian Government is still renegotiating more than 10,500 commercial agreements related to forestry, mining, telecommunications, electricity, and water services in order to comply with these regulations

The Telecommunications, Technology and Communications General Law (Law 164, Article 28) stipulates that the licenses for radio broadcasts will not be given to foreign persons or entities. Further, in the case of broadcasting associations, the share of foreign investors cannot exceed 25 percent of the total investment, except in those cases approved by the state or by international treaties.

PRIVATIZATION PROGRAM

There are currently no privatization programs in Bolivia.

SCREENING OF FDI

In accordance with the new investment law, investments will be monitored by the ministry related to the particular sector. For example, the Mining Ministry is in charge of overseeing all public and private mining investments. Each Ministry should assess industry compliance with the incentive objectives. The Central Bank of Bolivia is responsible for registering all foreign investments.

COMPETITION LAW

Bolivia does not have a competition law. However, Article 314 of the 2009 Constitution prohibits private monopolies. Based on this article, in 2009 the Bolivian government created an office to supervise and control private companies (http://www.autoridadempresas.gob.bo/). Among its most important goals are: regulating, promoting, and protecting free competition; trade relations between traders; implementing control mechanisms and social projects, and voluntary corporate responsibility; corporate restructuring, supervising, verifying and monitoring companies with economic activities in the country in the field of commercial registration and seeking compliance with legal and financial development of its activities; and qualifying institutional management efficiency, timeliness, transparency and social commitment to contribute to the achievement of corporate goals.

INVESTMENT TRENDS

At 16 percent, the investment rate as percentage of GDP in Bolivia is fairly low. The average in South America is 20 percent and reaches 22 percent on average in Colombia, Chile and Peru. There has also been a shift from private to public investment. In recent years, private investment was particularly low because of the deterioration of the business environment since the beginning of the nationalization process in 2006. From 2006 to 2014, private investment, including local and foreign investment, averaged 7.5 percent of GDP; in previous years it was above 11 percent. From 2006 to the present, public investment grew significantly, reaching an annual average of 10 percent of GDP. Prior to 2006 public investment averaged 6 percent of GDP.

Foreign Direct Investment (FDI) is highly concentrated in natural resources, especially hydrocarbons and mining, which account for nearly two-thirds of FDI. Since 2006 the net flow of FDI averaged 3 percent of GDP. Before 2006 it averaged around 8 percent of GDP.

In an effort to attract more investment, the government enacted an investment law in 2014, which says that each Ministry will provide incentives for sector-specific investment. To date, no Ministry has provided any such incentives. The law notes that dispute resolution will be codified in a separate law. The Bolivian government has said that it is currently working on this law and will enact it during 2015.

Table 1

Measure	Year	Index or Rank	Website Address
TI Corruption Perceptions index	2014	103 of 174	transparency.org/cpi2014/results
World Bank's Doing Business Report "Ease of Doing Business"	2015	157 of 189	doingbusiness.org/rankings
Global Innovation Index	2014	111 of 143	globalinnovationindex.org/content.aspx?page=data-analysis
World Bank GNI per capita	2013	USD 2,550.00	data.worldbank.org/indicator/NY.GNP.PCAP.CD

Millennium Challenge Corporation Country Scorecard

The Millennium Challenge Corporation (MCC) Scorecard for Bolivia is mixed. Bolivia received "red" grades (i.e. not good enough for the MCC to recommend working with Bolivia) on regulatory quality, gender in the economy, access to credit, and business start-up in the economic freedom category. In terms of investing in people indicators, girls' secondary education enrollment, child health, rule of law, and control of corruption, all received red scores. The full results can be found at: https://assets.mcc.gov/scorecards/score-fy15-english-bolivia.pdf. Information the methodology of indicator calculation can be found at: https://www.mcc.gov/pages/docs/doc/report-guide-to-the-indicators-and-the-selection-process-fy-2015.

2. CONVERSION AND TRANSFER POLICIES

FOREIGN EXCHANGE

Currency is freely convertible at Bolivian banks and exchange houses. The official exchange system is described as an incomplete crawling peg. Under this system, the exchange rate is fixed, but undergoes micro-readjustments which are not pre-announced to the public. There is a spread of ten basis points between the exchange rate for buying and selling U.S. dollars. The Peso Boliviano (Bs) has remained fixed at 6.96 Bs/USD 1 for selling and 6.86 Bs/USD 1 for buying since October 2011. The parallel rate closely tracks the official rate, suggesting the market finds the Central Bank's policy acceptable. In order to avoid distortions in the exchange rate market, the Central Bank requires all currency exchange to occur at the official rate ±1 basis point.

The banking law (#393, 2013) establishes regulations for foreign currency hedging and authorizes banks to maintain accounts in foreign currencies. A significant, but dropping, percentage of deposits are denominated in U.S. dollars (currently less than 20 percent of total deposits). Bolivian law currently allows repatriation of profits, with a 12.5 percent withholding tax. However, a provision of the 2009 Constitution

(Article 351.2) requires reinvestment within Bolivia of private profits from natural resources. Until specific implementing legislation is passed, it is unclear how this provision will be applied. In addition, all bank transfers in U.S. dollars within the financial system and leaving the country must pay a Financial Transaction Tax (ITF) of .03 percent. This tax applies to foreign transactions for U.S. dollars leaving Bolivia, not to money transferred internally.

Any banking transaction above USD 10,000 (in one operation or over three consecutive days) requires a form stating the source of funds. In addition, any hard currency cash transfer from or to Bolivia equal to or greater than USD 10,000 must be registered with the customs office. Amounts between USD 50,000 and USD 500,000 require authorization by the Central Bank and quantities above USD 500,000 require authorization by the Ministry of the Economy and Public Finance. The fine for underreporting any cash transaction is equal to 30 percent of the difference between the declared amount and the quantity of money found. The reporting standard is international, but many private companies in Bolivia find the application cumbersome due to the requirement of the Bolivian government for detailed transaction breakdowns rather than allowing for blanket transaction reporting.

Administrative Resolution 398/10 approved in June 2010 forces Bolivian banks to reduce their investments and/or assets outside the country to an amount that does not exceed 50 percent of the value of their net equity.

The Central Bank charges a fee for different kinds of international transactions related to banking and trade. The current list of fees and the details can be found at http://www.bcb.gob.bo/webdocs/2014/Normativa/Resoluciones/175%202014.PDF

The Tax Reform (Law 843) is the one directly affects the transfer of all money to foreign countries. All companies are charged 25 percent tax on profits under the Tax Reform Law, but when a company sends money abroad, the presumption of the Bolivian Tax Authority is that 50 percent of all money transmitted is profit. Under this presumption, the 25 percent tax is applied to half of all money transferred abroad, whether actual or only presumed profit. In practical terms it means there is a payment of 12.5 percent as a transfer tax.

Remittance Policies

The Bolivian government has a lax remittance policy. Each remittance transaction from Bolivia to other countries has a USD 2,500 limit per transaction, but there is no limit to the number of transactions that an individual can remit. The volume of remittances sent to and from Bolivia has increased considerably in the past five years, and the central bank and banking regulator are currently analyzing whether to impose more regulations sometime in the future. Foreign investors are theoretically able to remit through a legal parallel market utilizing convertible, negotiable instruments, but practically the availability of these financial instruments is limited in Bolivia. For example, the Bolivian government mainly issues bonds in Bolivianos and the majority of corporate bonds are also issued in Bolivianos.

The official exchange rate between Bolivianos and dollars is the same as the rate on the street. The government allows account holders to maintain bank accounts in Bolivianos or dollars and make transfers freely between them. Business travelers may bring up to USD 10,000 in cash into the country. For amounts greater than USD 10,000, government permission is needed.

Bolivia is a member of the Financial Action Task Force of Latin America (GAFILAT). GAFILAT works toward developing and implementing a comprehensive global strategy to combat money laundering and terrorist financing.

Since November 2011, Bolivia officially has a fixed rate of exchange and the government does not engage in currency manipulation.

3. EXPROPRIATION AND COMPENSATION

The Bolivian Constitution allows the government to expropriate property for the public use or when the property does not fulfill a social purpose (Article 57). In the case of land, this social purpose (FES) is understood as "sustainable land use to develop productive activities, according to its best use capacity, for the benefit of society, the collective interest and its owner." In all other cases where this article has been applied, the Bolivian government has no official definition of collective interest and makes decisions on a case-by-case basis. Noncompliance with the social function of land, tax evasion, or the holding of large acreage is cause for reversion, at which point the land passes to the Bolivian people (Article 401). In cases where an expropriation is deemed a necessity of the state or for the public good, such as when building road or laying electricity lines, payment of just indemnification is required. However, in cases where there is non-compliance, the Bolivian government is not required to pay for the land because the land title reverts to the state.

The Constitution also gives workers the right to reactivate and reorganize companies in the process of bankruptcy, insolvency, or liquidation, or those closed in an unjust manner, into employee-owned cooperatives (Article 54). The mining code of 1997 (last updated in 2007) and hydrocarbons law of 2005 both outline procedures for expropriating land to develop underlying concessions.

Between 2006 and 2014, the Bolivian government nationalized companies that were previously privatized in the 1990s. The government nationalized all of hydrocarbons, transport, and sales companies (private and foreign state owned firms remain in production and services), a majority of the electricity sector, the biggest telecommunications company, a tin smelting plant, and a cement plant. To take control of these companies, the government forced private entities to sell shares to the government, but often at below market prices. Some of the affected companies have cases pending with international arbitration bodies.

There are still some former state companies that are under private control, including the railroad, and some electricity transport and distribution companies. The first company not previously owned by the government was nationalized in December of 2012. The Bolivian Government has not discriminated by country; some of the countries affected were the United States, France, the UK, Spain, Argentina, and Chile, amongst others. In numerous cases the Bolivian government has nationalized private interests in order to appease social groups protesting within Bolivia. Although the 2014 investment law does not prohibit nationalization of companies, President Morales has signaled in the press that the new law will curb future nationalizations.

4. DISPUTE SETTLEMENT

LEGAL SYSTEM, SPECIALIZED COURTS, JUDICIAL INDEPENDENCE, JUDGMENTS OF FOREIGN COURTS

Property and contractual rights are enforced through domestic courts but the legal process is time consuming and may be subject to political influence and corruption. Bolivia's Commercial Code (Law 14379, 1977) continues to provide general guidance for commercial activities. The Constitution has precedence over international law and treaties (Article 410), and stipulates that the state will be directly involved in resolving conflicts between employers and employees (Article 50).

BANKRUPTCY

In the case of bankruptcy, the average time to complete the procedures to close a business in Bolivia is 20 months. The Bolivian Commercial Code includes (Article 1654) three different categories of bankruptcy:

No Fault Bankruptcy – when the owner of the company is not directly responsible for its inability to pay its obligations.

At- Fault Bankruptcy – when the owner is guilty or liable due to the lack of due diligence to avoid harm to the company.

Bankruptcy due to Fraud – when the owner intentionally tries to cause harm to the company.

If a company declares bankruptcy, the company must pay employee benefits before other obligations.

In general, the application of laws related to commercial disputes and bankruptcy are inconsistently applied and charges of corruption are common. Foreign creditors often have little redress beyond Bolivian courts, and judgments are generally more favorable to local claimants than international ones. Workers have broad-ranging rights to recover pay and benefits from foreign firms in bankruptcy, and criminal actions can be taken against individuals the Bolivian government deems responsible for failure to pay in these matters.

INVESTMENT DISPUTES

Between 2006 and 2014, a variety of foreign companies were affected by the government's nationalization policy. In 2014, the government passed a new investment law announcing there would be no more nationalization.

Since 2006, there have been five known investment dispute cases between the government and U.S. persons. Three of the cases were settled outside of the court. One of these three cases was submitted to international arbitration but it was never heard because the parties settled outside of court. Two U.S families who owned large farms had them expropriated by the government after allegations of unfair labor practices and misuse of land. The use of the farm did not comply with the economic and social function (FES) law which states that its use must be a social benefit for Bolivians.

INTERNATIONAL ARBITRATION

Investment contracts between the Government of Bolivia and investors granted the right to pursue international arbitration in all sectors. Bolivia and stated that international agreements, such as the Convention on the Settlement of Investment Disputes between States and Nationals of Other States and the New York Convention of 1958 on the Recognition and Enforcement of Foreign Arbitral Awards, must be honored. Current Bolivian law also mandates the recognition of foreign decisions and awards and establishes procedures for the Supreme Court's execution of decisions. However, these rights conflict with the 2009 Constitution, which states (Articles 320 and 366) that arbitration is not recognized in any case and cannot proceed under any diplomatic claim, and specifically limits foreign companies' access to international arbitration in the case of conflicts with the government. The 2009 Constitution also states that all bilateral investment treaties must be renegotiated to incorporate relevant provisions of the new Constitution. The Investment Law of 2014 states that arbitration provisions must be drafted within three months, as of this time they have not been completed.

ICSID Convention and New York Convention

In November 2007, Bolivia became the first country ever to withdraw from the International Center for the Settlement of Investment Disputes (ICSID). In August 2010, the Bolivian Minister of Legal Defense of the State said that the Bolivian government would not accept ICSID rulings in the cases brought against them by the Chilean company Quiborax and Italian company Euro Telcom. However, the Government of Bolivia agreed to pay USD 100 million to Euro Telecom for its nationalization; this agreement was ratified by a Supreme Decree 692 on November 3, 2010. Additionally, in 2014 a British company that owned the biggest electric generation plant in Bolivia (Guaracachi) won an arbitration case against Bolivia for USD 41 million. In 2014, an Indian company won a USD 22.5 million international arbitration award in a dispute over the development of an iron ore project. The Bolivian government has appealed that award.

In another case, a Canadian mining company with significant U.S. interests failed to complete an investment required by its contract with the state-owned mining company. The foreign company asserts it could not complete the project because the state mining company did not deliver the required property rights. The foreign company entered into national arbitration (their contract does not allow for international arbitration) and in January 2011, the parties announced a settlement of USD 750,000, which the company says will be used to pay taxes, employee benefits, and pending debts. The company also retained responsibility for future liabilities.

Duration of Dispute Resolution

Since companies choose to resolve disputes with the government before going to formal international arbitration, there is no data on the length of a complete dispute resolution in international courts. The one case that did attempt to go to international arbitration took seven years before reaching agreement and receiving government payment outside of the arbitration system. Other cases have been resolved outside of arbitration in one to two years.

5. PERFORMANCE REQUIREMENTS AND INVESTMENT INCENTIVES

WTO/TRIMS

Bolivia is a member of the World Trade Organization (WTO) and has not registered any objections to the Trade Related Investment Measures under WTO agreements. The latest WTO Trade Policy Review for Bolivia was conducted in 2005. At that time, the WTO noted that "the trade regime has improved but greater predictability is needed."

Investment Incentives

Article 14 of the 2014 investment law requires technology transfer from foreign companies operating in Bolivia to Bolivian workers and institutions. The law specifies that Bolivians should work in operational, administrative, and executive offices foreign companies. Also, companies investing in Bolivia should donate equipment and machinery to universities and technical schools in the same area as the investment, and conduct research activities that will find solutions that contribute to public welfare.

Article 21 of the investment law stipulates that the government can incentivize investment in certain sectors that contribute to the economic and social development of the country.

Research and Development

There are very few government financed research and development programs. Any company can participate in research if they receive the appropriate permission from the government. There is a de facto practice to reject U.S. companies and NGOs from research and development projects.

Performance Requirements

Bolivian labor law requires businesses to limit foreign employees to 15 percent of their total work force and requires that such foreign hires be part of the technical staff. These workers require a work visa that can be obtained in any Bolivian consulate, and in the case that they work for a Bolivian company, both the company and the workers should also contribute to the Bolivian Pension System (Pension Law Article 104.1)

Supreme Decree 27328 regulates national and local level government procurement, which give priority to national sourcing. If an item required is not produced in Bolivia, buying decisions are made based on price. Supreme Decree 28271 (Article 10), establishes the following preference margins for sourcing with Bolivian products:

Except for national tenders, 10 percent preference margin for Bolivian products regardless of the origin of materials.

For national public tenders, if the cost of Bolivian materials represents more than 50 percent of the total cost of the product, the producers receive a 10 percent preference margin over other sellers.

In national and international public tenders, if Bolivian inputs and labor represent more than the 50 percent of the total cost of the product, the seller receives a 25 percent preference margin over other sellers. If the Bolivian inputs and labor represent between 30 percent and 50 percent of the total cost of the product, the seller receives a 15 percent preference margin over other sellers.

Under the Bolivian Criminal Code (Article 226), it is a crime to raise or lower the price of a product based on false information, interests, or actions. For those caught doing so, punishment is six months to three years in prison. It is also a crime to hoard or conceal products in order to raise prices. The Bolivian government has aggressively applied these provisions in a number of cases, applying regulations that allow them to request accounting records and audit companies' financial actions looking for evidence of speculation.

DATA STORAGE

Bolivian legislation does not specify requirements for foreign information technology providers to turn over source code. Also the Bolivian government does not follow forced localization policies. Information technology providers are only required to provide access to surveillance with a court order.

Article 14 of the 2014 Investment Law requires companies investing in Bolivia to invest in research to improve industrial processes and the general well-being of the public.

6. RIGHT TO PRIVATE OWNERSHIP AND ESTABLISHMENT

The Constitution recognizes the right for both foreign and domestic private entities to establish and own business enterprises. Article 52, Paragraphs 1-2 state:

The right to free business association is recognized and guaranteed.

The state guarantees the acknowledgement of the legal personality of business associations, as well as of the democratic organizational business forms, in accordance with their own by-laws.

There are several markets that have restrictions on foreign investment. For example, the Telecommunications, Technology and Communications General Law (Law 164, Article 28) stipulates that the licenses for radio broadcasts will not be given to foreign persons or entities. Further, in the case of broadcasting associations, the share of foreign investors cannot exceed 25 percent of the total investment, except in those cases approved by the state or by international treaties.

The right of private entities to freely establish, acquire, and dispose of interest in business enterprises is recognized by the Bolivian Commercial Code (Article 6.3) that states that the purchase or sale of a mercantile company or commercial establishment of shares, quotas, or equity are considered part of the commercial process.

For more information on opening a business in Bolivia, see the World Bank Doing Business report at http://www.doingbusiness.org/data/exploreeconomies/bolivia/.

7. PROTECTION OF PROPERTY RIGHTS

REAL PROPERTY

The Bolivian Constitution stipulates the right to private property as long as it serves a social function and is not against the collective/public interest (Articles 56 and 57). The Constitution specifically allows expropriation in cases of public necessity, or where property is not serving an economic/social function. Revisions that were made to the Agrarian Law (#1715, 1996) in November 2006 reflect this concept. The law was modified (#3545) to stipulate that property deemed unproductive in bi-annual reviews by the National Institute of Agrarian Reform (Instituto Nacional de Reforma Agraria, or INRA) would revert to the state; the modification placed limits on landowners' legal recourse in such cases. This modification has limited banking interest in long term agricultural investments due to uncertainty over possible future confiscation of the landowners' property. In January 2013, Congress passed a law to provide an amnesty to landowners with plots being reverted to the state due to unauthorized forest clearings. The Bolivian private sector considered this a government move to improve the conditions for the agricultural sector. Farmers are still waiting for a promised law that would grant them a seven year hiatus from INRA reviews, but at a national agriculture summit in April 2015, the Bolivian government agreed to reduce the frequency of land inspections to every five years.

The Constitution also grants formal, collective land titles to indigenous communities, in order to restore their former territories (Article 394.3), stating that public land will be granted to indigenous farmers, migrant indigenous communities, afro-Bolivians, and small farmer communities that do not possess or have insufficient land (Article 395). Under law 3545, passed in 2006 and still valid, the government will not grant public lands to non-indigenous people or agriculture companies. The Mother Earth Integral Development Law to Live Well (Mother Earth Law, or Law #300) passed in October 2012 specifies that the State control access to natural resources, particularly when foreign use is involved. In action, the law limits access to land, forest, water and other natural resources by foreigners in Bolivia. The law, though signed, is likely to be reviewed before implementing regulations are enacted.

The Office of Property Registry oversees the acquisition and disposition of land, real estate, and mortgages. Mortgages are easy to obtain. It takes at most 60 days to obtain a standard loan. However, Bolivia lacks an adequate system of title verification and challenges to land titles are common. Competing claims to land titles and the absence of a reliable dispute resolution process create risk and uncertainty in real property acquisition. Nevertheless, illegal occupation of rural private property is decreasing since the government passed law 477 to combat land seizures. While some properties are still occupied or disputed, some illegal occupants have already been tried and jailed.

INTELLECTUAL PROPERTY RIGHTS

The Mother Earth Law recognizes the intellectual property rights (IPR) of indigenous peoples, the Afro-Bolivian community, and Bolivian migrant groups related to ancestral knowledge and biodiversity. The medicinal properties of plants and animals found in the Bolivian Amazon and other regions within Bolivia are included in these rights.

The Bolivian Intellectual Property Body SENAPI (Servicio Nacional de Propiedad Intelectual), has recently published a complete set of regulations related to IPR. This list is available on SENAPI's webpage at: http://www.senapi.gob.bo/MarcoLegal.asp?lang=ES.

Bolivia does not have a specific industrial property law, only a 1916 industrial privileges law is currently in force. However, Bolivia belongs to the World Intellectual Property Organization (WIPO) and is a signatory to the Nice Agreement and the Paris, Berne, and Geneva Conventions on intellectual property. As a member of the Andean Community (CAN), it has pledged to abide by the intellectual property decisions of the CAN. Last year SENAPI finished a draft law on industrial property, which they expect to present to Congress before June 2015.

Bolivia has no laws protecting trade secrets. However, Bolivia respects related international conventions, including with respect to protection of foreigners. CAN Decision 486 is legally binding in Bolivia and deals with industrial property (trade secrets). The most relevant sections of Decision 486 are:

I. Each Member Country shall accord the nationals of other members of the Andean Community, the World Trade Organization, and the Paris Convention for the Protection of Industrial Property, treatment no less favorable than it accords to its own nationals with regard to the protection of intellectual property, subject to the exceptions already provided in articles 3 and 5 of the Agreement on Trade-Related Aspects of Intellectual Property Rights (TRIPS) and in article 2 of the Paris Convention for the Protection of Industrial Property.

Member Countries may also accord such treatment to the nationals of a third country under the terms of their respective domestic legislation.

IV. The protection granted by this Decision shall accrue to all literary, artistic and scientific works that may be reproduced or disclosed by any known or future means.

SENAPI reviews patent registrations for form and substance and publishes notices of proposed registrations in the Official Gazette. If there are no objections within 30 working days, the organization grants patents for a period of 20 years. The registration of trademarks parallels that of patents. Once obtained, a trademark is valid for a 10-year renewable period. It can be cancelled if not used within three years of the date of grant.

Bolivia's copyright law (Law 1322) predates the international standards established under the WTO Agreement on Trade-Related Aspects of Intellectual Property (TRIPS). It also falls short of obligations under the World Intellectual Property Organization (WIPO) Copyright Treaty and the WIPO Performances and Phonograms Treaty.

Existing Bolivian copyright law protects literary, artistic and scientific works for the lifetime of the author plus 50 years. Bolivian copyright protection includes the exclusive right to copy or reproduce works; to revise, adapt, or prepare derivative works; to distribute copies of works; and to publicly share works. Although the law does not explicitly grant the exclusive right to translate works, the law does prevent unauthorized adaptation, transformation, modification, and editing. The law also provides protection for software and databases.

The copyright law protects the rights of Bolivian authors, foreign authors domiciled in Bolivia, and foreign authors published for the first time in Bolivia. Foreigners not domiciled in Bolivia are protected to the extent provided in international conventions and treaties to which Bolivia is a party.

The 1991 Film and Video Law (#1302, 1991) also contains elements of IPR protection but its implementation is lacking. The law established a National Movie Council (CONACINE) to oversee the domestic film industry and required that all locally produced films and videos shown or distributed in

Bolivia be registered with that organization. Between 2011 and 2012 CONACINE tried to reach agreements with street vendors' associations, in an effort to have them sell legal copies of movies; however this effort failed because street vendors continued to make illegal copies of the legal copy provided by the registered owners.

The 2009 Constitution provides for protection of all domestic genetic resources, and locally available microorganisms, as well as the knowledge associated with their use and exploitation. The Bolivian government plans to protect these resources through a registration system managed by the Genetic Resources Conservation National Center of the Agriculture and Forestry Innovation Center. Article 381 of the Constitution says Bolivia will establish procedures for the protection of all microorganisms and genetic resources even if they are not registered, but as of May, 2015 the government had not written the implementing regulations.

The 2012 Mother Earth Law states that the Bolivian government will take actions to avoid the commoditization of genetic resources, bio-piracy, and the participation of monopolies in the production of seeds. Nevertheless, it does not specify which actions the government will take. This law targets companies that bioengineer seeds and that would normally rely on IPR to protect their products.

Indigenous intellectual property rights are highly protected by the Bolivian legal system. Article 100 of the Constitution stipulates that the Bolivian government will protect the learning and knowledge of indigenous people through intellectual property registration. The Constitution acknowledges the right of indigenous nations and people to "the collective intellectual property of their intelligence, sciences, and knowledge, as well as the right to indigenous intellectual property's regained and appreciative value, use, promotion, and development" (Article 30). Article 304 further specifies that indigenous people can safeguard, through registration, collective intellectual property related to knowledge of genetic resources, traditional medicine, and germ plasma. There are not yet any regulations governing the implementation of these constitutional provisions.

The Constitution specifically limits IPR related to medicines in Article 41, which specifies that the right of access to medicines cannot be restricted by intellectual property or trade rights. The Bolivian intellectual property body SENAPI coordinates with the Medicines and Health Technologies Unit UNIMED (Unidad de Medicamentos y Tecnología en Salud) on the regulation of medicine patents.

In 2013, Bolivia passed a law requiring Bolivian institutions to use only open source software. Government agencies need to get special permission to acquire any branded software. However, government institutions are still using branded software, with the use of legal versions of these programs on the rise. Despite government efforts to avoid the dilemma of purchasing software copyrights, it is still possible to find that a government office owns fewer licenses than it has copies of branded software.

The Constitution (Article 41) states that the Bolivian state will guarantee access to prescription drugs and that property and commercial rights cannot restrict this right. Although this provision has not yet been written into law, it is likely to affect intellectual property rights. At present, registration of prescription drugs is regulated by Law (#1737), which establishes control over the production, importation, commercialization, quality control, selection, purchase, distribution, prescription, and sale of medicines through an obligatory sanitary registry, which is valid for five years. After five years, renewed registration of a drug can be requested from the Ministry of Health through DINAMED (the Dirección de Medicamentos y Tecnología en Salud). The registry can be canceled or suspended if the requirements and technical standards mentioned above are not fulfilled.

Resources for Rights Holders
For questions regarding Intellectual Property issues, contact:
Mauricio Ballesteros
ESTH and IPR Specialist

+591 (2)-216-8431
BallesterosM@state.gov

8. TRANSPARENCY OF THE REGULATORY SYSTEM

The lack of congruency between the 2009 Constitution and the laws being implemented creates legal discrepancies between constitutional guarantees and the dated policies currently enforced. All of this creates an uncertain investment climate. Adding to the uncertainty, the political agenda can determine what laws will be issued according to the needs of the moment.

The tax code has not changed, and will probably not change in the near future. The government is also discussing a tax increase on profits, focusing on financial institutions that generate very high profits.

Environmental regulations can slow projects due to the constitutional requirement of "prior consultation" for any projects that could affect local communities. This has affected projects related to the exploitation of natural recourses, both renewable and nonrenewable, as well as public works projects. Issuance of environmental licenses has been slow and subject to corruption.

In 2010, the new pension fund was enacted; it increased the contributions that companies have to pay from 1.71 percent of payroll to 4.71 percent.

Formal bureaucratic procedures are lengthy, difficult to manage and navigate, and considered by some to be debilitating. Many firms complain that a lack of administrative infrastructure, corruption, and political motives impede their ability to perform. The one exception is when registering a new company in Bolivia. Once a company submits all documents required to the Bolivian entity charged with registration of new enterprises (FUNDEMPRESA) the process takes between 2-4 working days.

There is no established public comment process allowing social, political, and economic interests to provide advice and comment on new laws and decrees. However, the government generally -- but not always -- discusses proposed law with the relevant sector.

Most accounting regulations follow international principles, but they do not always fully conform to international standards. Only the largest private companies and a few government institutions, such as the Central Bank and the Banking Supervision Authority, have transparent and consistent accounting systems.

Article 308 of the Constitution establishes that the state recognizes, respects, and protects private initiatives that contribute to economic and social development and the strengthening of the economic independence of the country. In addition, as mentioned in the section on Right to Private Ownership and Establishment, the Constitution guarantees free enterprise and the full exercise of business activities as regulated by law.

9. EFFICIENT CAPITAL MARKETS AND PORTFOLIO INVESTMENT

Established Bolivian firms may issue short or medium-term debt in local capital markets, which act primarily as secondary markets for fixed-return securities. Bolivian capital markets have sought to expand their handling of local corporate bond issues and equity instruments. Over the last few years, several Bolivian companies and some foreign firms have been able to raise funds through local capital markets. However, the stock exchange is small and is highly concentrated in bonds and debt instruments (more than 95 percent of transactions). The amount of total transactions per year generally hovers around one-third of the GDP.

Since 2008, the financial markets have experienced high liquidity, which has led to historically low interest rates. This situation is expected to continue for the near future, despite the strains in the international financial markets. The Bolivian financial system is not well integrated with the international system and the presence of foreign banks is very low, with only one external bank amongst the top ten banks of Bolivia.

In October 2012 Bolivia returned to global credit markets for the first time in nearly a century, selling USD 500 million worth of 10-year bonds at the New York stock exchange. The sovereign bonds were offered with an interest rate of 4.875 percent and demand for the bonds well surpassed the offer, reaching USD 1.5 billion. U.S. financial companies Bank of America, Merrill Lynch, and Goldman Sachs were the lead managers of the deal. In 2013 Bolivia sold another USD 500 million at 5.95 percent for ten years. HSBC, Bank of America, and Merrill Lynch were the lead managers of the deal. According to the Ministry of Economy, the resources gained from the sales will be used to finance infrastructure projects.

Money and Banking System, Hostile Takeovers

The Bolivian banking system is small, composed of 13 banks, 3 private financial funds, and 34 savings and credit cooperatives. Of the total number of personal deposits made in Bolivia through December 2014 (USD 18.0 billion), the banking sector accounted for 80 percent. Similarly, of the total loans and credits made to private individuals (USD 14.4 billion) through December 2014, 78 percent were made by the banking sector, while private financial funds and the savings and credit cooperatives accounted for the other 22 percent.

Bolivian banks have developed the capacity to adjudicate credit risk and evaluate expected rates of return in line with international norms. The banking sector is stable and healthy with delinquency rates at less than 2 percent.

In 2013 the financial services bill was signed into law. This new law enacted major changes to the banking sector, including deposit rate floors and lending rate ceilings, mandatory lending allocations to certain sectors of the economy and an upgrade of banks' solvency requirements in line with the international Basel standards. The law also requires banks to spend more on improving consumer protection, as well as providing increased access to financing in rural parts of the country.

Credit is now allocated on government-established rates for productive activities, but foreign investors may find it difficult to qualify for loans from local banks due to the requirement that domestic loans be issued exclusively against domestic collateral. Since commercial credit is generally extended on a short-term basis, most foreign investors prefer to obtain credit abroad. Most Bolivian borrowers are small and medium-sized enterprises (SMEs).

In September 2010, the Bolivian government bought the local private bank Banco Union as part of a plan to gain control of part of the financial market. Banco Union is medium-sized, with a share of 9 percent of total national credits and 11 percent of the total deposits; its principal activity is managing public sector accounts. Bolivian government ownership of Banco Union was illegal until December 2012, when the government enacted the State Bank Law, allowing for state participation in the banking sector.

In 2007, the government created a Productive Development Bank to boost the production of small, medium-sized and family-run businesses. The bank was created to provide loans to credit institutions which meet specific development conditions and goals, for example by giving out loans to farmers, small businesses, and other development focused investors. The loans are long term and have lower interest rates than private banks can offer in order to allow for growth of investments and poverty reduction.

There is no strong evidence of cross-shareholding and stable-shareholding arrangements used by private firms to restrict foreign investment, and the 2009 Constitution forbids monopolies and supports antitrust measures. In addition, there is no evidence of hostile takeovers (other than government nationalizations).

The Financial sector is regulated by ASFI (Supervising Authority of Financial Institutions), a decentralized institution that is under the Ministry of Economy. The Central Bank of Bolivia (CBB) oversees all financial institutions, provides liquidity when necessary, and acts as lender of last resort. The CBB is the only monetary authority and is in charge of managing the payment system, international reserves, and the exchange rate.

10. COMPETITION FROM STATE-OWNED ENTERPRISES

The Bolivian government is actively expanding the state's role in the economy. Actions include re-nationalization in key sectors, establishment of State-owned enterprises (SOEs), and passage of laws and regulations that stipulate state ownership of natural resources.

In recent years, the Bolivian government has re-nationalized, by obtaining a controlling stake, a number of private entities that were formerly public enterprises prior to the 1990s. These include Bolivia's largest tin mine, a smelting plant, the largest telecommunications company, the gas production and transport industry, hydroelectric and thermoelectric plants, and a cement company.

Rather than sweeping nationalizations, the Bolivian government has set up companies in sectors it considers vital to the national interest and social well-being, and has stated that it plans to do so in every sector it considers strategic or where there is either a monopoly or oligopoly. Areas possibly affected in the next year include the cement industry and the banking sector. Many of these public companies are less efficient than their private counterparts.

At present, the Bolivian government owns and operates more than fifty businesses including a sugar factory, an airline, a supermarket chain, a packaging plant, a cement plant, a construction company, paper and cardboard factories, and milk and Brazil nut processing factories. In 2005, income from state-owned business in Bolivia represented only a fraction of a percentage of Gross Domestic Product (GDP). As of 2014, public sector contribution to GDP (including SOEs, investments, and consumption of goods and services) has risen to nearly 41 percent of GDP.

A government-appointed Board of Directors runs each state-owned company. Each director represents a ministry, and some are informally obligated to consult with government officials for decision-making purposes. Supreme Resolution usually appoints the general manager. Private sector entities complain that public companies generate subsidized, unfair competition with the existing private sector. There is currently no law specifying preferential treatment for state-owned businesses, though industry experts anticipate a law on public enterprises that clarifies roles may be on the near horizon.

The largest SOEs are able to acquire credit from the Central Bank at very low interest rates and convenient terms. Some private companies complain that it is impossible for them to compete with this financial subsidy. Moreover, SOEs appear to benefit from easier access to licenses, supplies, materials and land; however, there is no law specifically providing SOEs with preferential treatment in this regard.

Budget constraints have not been a problem for SOEs. Government budget surpluses over the past six years, as well as financing from the Central Bank, have enabled public companies to have large budgets. According to the 2009 Constitution, all SOEs are required to publish an annual report and are subject to financial audits. Additionally, SOEs are required to present an annual testimony in front of civil society and social movements, a practice known as social control

OECD Guidelines on Corporate Governance of SOEs

Not applicable.

Sovereign Wealth Funds

In 2010 Bolivia began discussions around creating a sovereign wealth fund (SWF) unfortunately those discussions did not amount to any conclusive decisions being made. Bolivia still does not have a sovereign wealth fund.

All legally established companies are required to present auditing and financial statements to the tax office annually. This requirement is for private and public companies. Financial institutions must present financial statements quarterly.

11. CORPORATE SOCIAL RESPONSIBILITY

Both producers and consumers in Bolivia are generally aware of corporate social responsibility, but consumer decisions are ultimately based on price and quality. Because the Bolivian Constitution stipulates that economic activity cannot damage the collective good (Article 47), CSR activities are generally looked upon favorably by the government of Bolivia. However, during pre-electoral periods, government officials occasionally accuse companies of using CSR practices as political tools against the government and suggest that the government pioneer tighter CSR regulations.

Though Bolivia is not part of the OECD, it has participated in several Latin American Corporate Governance Roundtables since 2000. Neither the government of Bolivia nor its organizations use the OECD Guidelines for CSR. Instead, Bolivian companies and organizations are focused on trying to accomplish the UN's Millennium Development Goals, and they use the Global Reporting Initiative (GRI) methodology in order to show economic, social and environmental results. While the Bolivian government, private companies, and non-profits are focused on the UN's Millennium Development Goals, only a few private companies and NGOs focus on following the UN standard ISO 26000 guidelines and methodologies. Another methodology widely accepted in Bolivia is the one developed by the ETHOS Institute, which provides measurable indicators accepted by PLARSE (Programa Latinoamericano de Responsabilidad Social Corporativa, the Latin American Program for CSR).

Bolivia has laws that regulate aspects related to CSR practices, but the Bolivian authorities rarely enforce them. Article 8 of the Bolivian Constitution promotes a nation of "common well-being, responsibility, social justice, distribution and redistribution of the products and social assets, to live well," but even the government does not fulfill the regulations focused on accomplishing these objectives.

The 1942 General Labor Law is the basis for employment rights in Bolivia, but this law has been modified more than 2,000 times via 60 supreme decrees since 1942. As a result of these modifications, the General Labor Law has become a complex web of regulations that is difficult to enforce. An example of the lack of enforcement is the Comprehensive System for Protection of the Disabled (Law 25689) which stipulates that at least 4 percent of the total work force in public institutions, state owned enterprises, and private companies should be disabled. Neither the public nor private sectors are close to fulfilling this requirement, and most buildings lack even basic access modifications to allow for disabled workers.

In support of consumer protection rights, the Vice Ministry of Defense of User and Consumer Rights were created in 2009 (Supreme Decree 29894) under the supervision of the Ministry of Justice. This same year the Consumer Protection Law (Supreme Decree 0065) was enacted, which gave the newly created Vice Ministry the authority to request information, verify and follow up on consumer complaints. Though the Vice-ministry has yet to report on its activities, an example of its work can be seen in local airports and bus stations, where customers can make a complaint on service or other matters to a representative of the Vice-ministry and receive compensation from the transport company if deemed appropriate.

The Mother Earth Law (Law 071) approved in October of 2012 promotes CSR elements as part of its principles (Article 2), such as collective good, harmony, respect and defense of rights. The Ministry of Environment and Water is in charge of overseeing the implementation of this law, but the implementing regulations and creation of new institutions to enforce this law are still in process.

Even though Bolivia promotes the development of CSR practices in its laws, the government gives no advantage to businesses that implement these practices. Instead, businesses implement CSRs in order to gain the public support necessary to pass the prior consultation requirements or strengthen their support when mounting a legal defense against claims that they are not using land to fulfill a socially valuable purpose, as defined in the Community Land Reform laws (# 1775 and #3545).

In April 2009, the Bolivian government reorganized the supervisory agencies of the government (formerly Superintendencias) to include social groups, thus creating the Authorities of Supervision and Social Control (Supreme Decree 0071). This new authority now controls and supervises the following sectors: telecommunications and transportation, water and sanitation, forests and land, pensions, electricity, and enterprises. Each sector has an Authority of Supervision and Social Control assigned to its oversight, and each Authority has the right to audit the activities in the aforementioned sectors and the right to request the public disclosure of information, ranging from financial disclosures to investigation of management decisions.

There are some organizations working in CSR, ranging from those focusing on education and training, to clean technology promotion, to fair labor practices. Additionally, individual sectors have undertaken CSR initiatives, most notably in mining and forestry. For example, miners developed a working partnership focused on education, infrastructure, and environmental issues with local communities, and communities now exhibit a relatively higher level of awareness of CSR practices than in the past. Since 1996, the Bolivian forestry sector certified almost 2 million hectares of forest.

Additionally, a leading trade think tank, the Instituto Boliviano de Comercio Exterior (IBCE) developed a certification called the Triple Sello (triple seal) that will certify that a business that receives the stamp is free from child labor, discriminatory practices, and forced labor. The Triple Sello certification is currently coordinated with the IBNORCA (Bolivian Institute of Quality Normalization) and in 2014 the first Bolivian company, Guabira, was awarded the triple seal.

OECD GUIDELINES FOR MULTINATIONAL ENTERPRISES

The Bolivian government does not force companies to adhere to the OECD Guidelines for Multinational Enterprises.

12. POLITICAL VIOLENCE

Bolivia is prone to social unrest that includes violence. Given the country's reliance on a few key thoroughfares, conflict often disrupts transportation and distribution networks. The majority of civil disturbances are related to domestic issues, usually workers pressuring the government for concessions by marching or closing major transportation arteries. Over the past year, there has been no political violence that targeted foreigners.

While protests and blockades are frequent, they only periodically affect commerce. Less than a half-dozen conflicts in La Paz directly affected distribution of essential services or travel in and out of the city for periods greater than 24 hours during 2014. However, numerous others caused businesses to close for short periods or impeded business operations.

13. CORRUPTION

Bolivian law stipulates criminal penalties for corruption by officials, but the government does not implement the law effectively, and officials often engage in corrupt practices with impunity. In 2014, there were numerous reports of government corruption.

According to the World Bank's 2011 worldwide governance indicators, government corruption and lack of transparency remained serious problems. According to Transparency International's 2013 Global Corruption Barometer, 86 percent of citizens believed the police were corrupt or extremely corrupt, and 76 percent labeled the country's judiciary as corrupt or extremely corrupt.

Police corruption remains a significant problem. In March 2014, U.S. authorities convicted police officer Fabricio Ormachea Aliga in Miami on two counts of extortion. Ormachea, an investigator in the police anticorruption unit, allegedly promised to suspend a pending investigation involving a Bolivian living in Miami in exchange for approximately 205,000 bolivianos (USD 30,000). There is also widespread corruption in the country's judiciary.

The Ministry of Anticorruption and Transparency and the Prosecutor's Office are both responsible for combating corruption, but most corrupt officials operate with impunity. In September 2014, former Transparency Minister Nardy Suxo reported that the Ministry was investigating 388 complaints against public servants. The Ministry has obtained 97 convictions since 2006. Cases involving allegations of corruption against the president and vice president require congressional approval before prosecutors may initiate legal proceedings, and cases against pro-government public officials are rarely pursued. Local courts have found that granting immunity for corruption charges is unconstitutional; the government ignored their rulings.

UN Anticorruption Convention, OECD Convention on Combatting Bribery

Bribery is a criminal offense in Bolivia. Bolivia signed the UN Anticorruption Convention in December 2003 and ratified it in December 2005. Bolivia is not a signatory of the OECD Convention on Combating Bribery of Foreign Public Officials.

Bolivia is part of the Organization of American States' Inter-American Convention against Corruption and the Follow-Up Mechanism for its Implementation. There is an Ombudsman appointed by Congress and charged with protecting human rights and guarding against government abuse. In his 2014 annual report, the Ombudsman cited the judicial system, the attorney general's office, and the police as the most persistent violators of human rights due to widespread inefficiencies and corruption. Public opinion reflected the Ombudsman's statements. The 2014 Transparency International corruption perception index found that Bolivian citizens believe the most corrupt institutions in Bolivia are the judiciary, political parties, public officials, and the Bolivian Police.

Resources to Report Corruption

Contact at government agency or agencies are responsible for combating corruption:

Lenny Tatiana Valdivia Bautista
Transparency Minister
Ministry of Institutional Transparency and the Fight against Corruption
Calle Capitan Ravelo, esq. Montevideo, Edificio Capitan Ravelo Piso 3 – 9, La Paz Bolivia
591-2-2115773, 591-800-10-9988

No email address available, but the Ministry does have a webpage, Facebook page, and Twitter account

Reports of corruption can also be made to Transparency International, but the organization does not have a physical presence within Bolivia.

14. BILATERAL INVESTMENT AGREEMENTS

Government policy changes stemming in part from the adoption of the 2009 Constitution have raised concerns among foreign investors. Although the new Constitution has yet to be fully implemented, one of its most troubling provisions limits foreign companies' access to international arbitration in cases of conflicts with the government. It also states that all bilateral investment treaties (BIT) must be renegotiated to adjust to this and other new constitutional provisions.

Citing these provisions, the government of Bolivia terminated the BIT with the United States in June 2012. Existing investors in Bolivia at the time of termination continue to be protected by the U.S. BIT's provisions for 10 years. The BIT with Bolivia was the first to be terminated by a U.S. treaty partner. In a related action, in October 2007, Bolivia became the first country to withdraw as a member state from the International Centre for Settlement of Investment Disputes (ICSID convention).

BILATERAL TAXATION TREATIES

Bolivia does not have a bilateral taxation treaty with the United States.

15. OPIC AND OTHER INVESTMENT INSURANCE PROGRAMS

OPIC provides financing assistance to U.S. firms through direct loans and guarantees issued by U.S. financial institutions. There are currently no OPIC projects operational in Bolivia.

The International Bank for Reconstruction and Development's (IBRD) Multilateral Investment Guarantee Agency (MIGA) has offered a complete line of investment guarantees to foreign investors in Bolivia since October 1991. MIGA has one active project in Bolivia at this time. In December 2011, it issued a guarantee of USD 10.8 million to cover an investment made by a German holding company by its Bolivian subsidiary. The coverage is for a period of up to 10 years against the risk of expropriation of the mandatory reserves held by the subsidiary in the central bank of Bolivia. Past guarantees included assurances for the financing and investment of the Santa Cruz to Brazil gas pipeline, and financial guarantees for a Peruvian bank's mandatory reserves held by the Bolivian Central Bank against expropriation.

16. LABOR

Approximately two-thirds of Bolivia's population is considered "economically active." Overall, between 60 and 65 percent of workers participate in the informal economy, where no contractual employer-employee relationship exists. Relatively low education and literacy levels tend to limit labor productivity, a fact reflected in wage rates. Unskilled labor is readily available, but skilled workers are often harder to find.

The 2009 Constitution specifies that unjustified firing from jobs is forbidden and that the state will resolve conflicts between employers and employees (Articles 49.3 and 50). Bolivian labor law guarantees workers the right of association and the right to organize and bargain collectively. Most companies are unionized, and nearly all unions belong to the Confederation of Bolivian Workers (COB).

The law, including related regulations and statutory instruments, provides for the freedom of association, the right to strike, and the right to organize and bargain collectively. The law prohibits antiunion discrimination and requires reinstatement of workers fired for union activity. The law does not require government approval for strikes and allows peaceful strikers to occupy business or government offices. General and solidarity strikes are protected by the Constitution, as is the right of any working individual to join a union.

Workers may form a union in any private company of 20 or more employees, but the law requires that at least 50 percent of the workforce be in favor of forming a union. The law requires prior government authorization to establish a union and confirm its elected leadership, permits only one union per enterprise, and allows the government to dissolve unions by administrative fiat. The law also requires that members of union executive boards be Bolivian by birth. The labor code prohibits most public employees from forming unions, but some public-sector workers (including teachers, transportation workers, and health-care workers) were legally unionized and actively participated as members of the Bolivian Workers' Union without penalty.

The National Labor Court handles complaints of antiunion discrimination, but rulings generally take a year or more. In some cases, the court rules in favor of discharged workers and requires their reinstatement. Union leaders state that problems are often resolved or are no longer relevant by the time the court rules. For this reason, government remedies and penalties are often ineffective and insufficient to deter violations.

The government and under-resourced labor courts limit freedom of association. Moreover, the 20-worker threshold for forming a union proved an onerous restriction, as an estimated 72 percent of enterprises had fewer than 20 employees. Labor inspectors may attend union meetings and monitor union activities. Collective bargaining and voluntary direct negotiations between employers and workers without government participation was limited. Most collective bargaining agreements were restricted to addressing wages.

Violence during labor demonstrations continues to be a serious problem. In March 2014, two miners, Johnny Huisa Condori and Jaime Cachiaca, were shot and killed during a conflict between miners and police on the Oruro-Cochabamba highway; another 50 miners were injured. In the same incident, 43 police officers were taken hostage by miners; all were eventually released with minor injuries. Despite President Morales' 2012 executive order outlawing the use of dynamite during public protests, the practice continues.

In July 2014, Vice President Garcia Linera signed a new child and adolescent code that permits children as young as 10 to work legally. The law states that the minimum working age is 14; however, the Child and Adolescent Ombudsman's Office may permit children as young as 10 to work if the child chooses to do so voluntarily and he or she works independently or with the family. The child must also obtain permission from his or her parent(s). Children as young as 12 can work for outside employers provided the same permissions are obtained. The law states that work should not interfere with a child's right to education and should not be dangerous or unhealthy, which includes work in sugar cane and brazil nut harvest, mining, brick making, hospital cleaning, selling alcoholic beverages, and working after 10PM, among other conditions. A request to the ombudsman must be answered within 72 hours. The Ministry of Labor is responsible for authorizing work activity for adolescents over 14 years of age who work for a third-party employer. The new code establishes that the Ministry of Justice, rather than the Ministry of Labor, is responsible for enforcing child labor laws, including laws pertaining to the minimum age and maximum hours for child workers, school completion requirements, and health and safety conditions for children in the workplace.

17. FOREIGN TRADE ZONES/FREE PORTS/TRADE FACILITATION

There are nine free trade zones in Bolivia, more than half of which are in cities along the Bolivian borders. The free trade zones were created to facilitate commercial and industrial operations for national and international companies. Any transaction that takes place inside a free trade zone is exempt from tariffs and national taxes. Private companies with 40-year contracts administer the free trade zones, which are located in the cites of El Alto, Cochabamba, Santa Cruz, Oruro, Puerto Aguirre, Cobija, Guayaramerin, Yacuiba, and Desaguadero. The National Council on Free Trade Zones (CONZOF) oversees all industrial and commercial free trade zones and authorizes operations.

18. FOREIGN DIRECT INVESTMENT AND FOREIGN PORTFOLIO INVESTMENT STATISTICS

Table 2: Key Macroeconomic Data, U.S. FDI in Host Country/Economy

	HOST COUNTRY STATISTICAL SOURCE*		USG OR INTERNATIONAL STATISTICAL SOURCE		USG OR INTERNATIONAL SOURCE OF DATA: BEA; IMF; EUROSTAT; UNCTAD, OTHER
ECONOMIC DATA	YEAR	AMOUNT	YEAR	AMOUNT	
Host Country Gross Domestic Product (GDP) ($M USD)	2013	34,824	2013	30,6001	www.worldbank.org/en/country
Foreign Direct Investment	Host Country Statistical source*		USG or international statistical source		USG or international Source of data: BEA; IMF; Eurostat; UNCTAD, Other
U.S. FDI in partner country ($M USD, stock positions)	2013	897	2013	617	http://bea.gov/international/factsheet/factsheet.cfm?Area=201
Host country's FDI in the United States ($M USD, stock	2013	N/A	2013	N/A	http://bea.gov/international/factsheet/factsheet.cfm?Area=201

positions)					
Total inbound stock of FDI as % host GDP	2013	34%	2013	34%	

*Bureau of Statistics and Central Bank of Bolivia

Table 3: Sources and Destination of FDI

Direct Investment from/in Counterpart Economy Data					
From Top Five Sources/To Top Five Destinations (US Dollars, Millions)					
Inward Direct Investment			Outward Direct Investment		
Total Inward	10,558	100%	Total Outward	N/A	100%
Spain	3,386	32%			
Brazil	1,134	11%			
United Kingdom	1,045	10%			
Sweden	1,040	10%			
United States	897	8%			
"0" reflects amounts rounded to +/- USD 500,000.					

Source: Bolivian Central Bank and International Monetary Fund

Table 4: Sources of Portfolio Investment

Portfolio Investment Assets								
Top Five Partners (Millions, US Dollars)								
Total			Equity Securities			Total Debt Securities		
All Countries	533	100%	All Countries	23	100%	All Countries	510	100%
United States	452	85%	United States	23	100%	United States	429	84%
Peru	26	5%				Peru	26	5%
Brazil	12	2%				Brazil	12	2%

Colombia	11	2%				Colombia	11	2%
Chile	11	2%				Chile	11	2%

Source: Bolivian Central Bank and International Monetary Fund

LIST OF ATTORNEYS

La Paz Consular District

AGUIRRE B., Fernando
Ave. Jose Salmon Ballivian (Los Alamos) No. 322, La Florida, La Paz, Bolivia.
Phone: (591) 2-278-6528/2-278-6527, Fax: 211-4222. Email: abogados@bufeteaguirre-lawfirm.com
Provides legal advice in the following areas: Commercial and administrative law, banking, mining, petroleum, international contracts and civil law. Languages: SPANISH, ENGLISH, FRENCH and GERMAN

APT ESTUDIO JURIDICO
Calle Capitan Ravelo #2328, La Paz, Bolivia. P.O. Box 1261-1231. La Paz, Bolivia.
Phone: (591) 2-244-1809. Fax: 244-1088. Email: apt@legalapt.com
Specializes in the following areas: Commercial law, taxes, insurance, and transportation.
Languages: SPANISH, ENGLISH and GERMAN

BALDIVIA UNZAGA & ASOCIADOS
Edificio Torre Lydia No 8227, Piso 8, Of 801, Calle 21 Calacoto (frente Ketal), P.O. Box 5223, La Paz, Bolivia.
Phone/Fax: (591) 277-4561 / 277-4901. Email: rbaldivi@entelnet.bo
Provides legal advice on corporate, regulatory, administrative and financial matters, energy (oil, gas and electricity), project financing, and arbitrage.
Languages: SPANISH, ENGLISH, and PORTUGUESE.

B., BERMUDEZ & BERMUDEZ LAW OFFICES
Edificio Alfa Centauro #73, Calle "E", Entre Calles "D" y "F". Dpto 2-C, Achumani, Sector San Ramón, La Paz, Bolivia.
Phone: (591) 2-271-0459; Cell: 705-75357, Fax: 271-0458. Email: bermudez@unete.com
Provides professional services in the following areas: Civil law, banking, insurance, administrative law, corporate law, copy rights, industrial property, customs and international commerce, arbitrage and alternative solutions to disputes.
Languages: SPANISH, ENGLISH, and FRENCH

BLACKWOOD CONSULTING CORP
Alvaro Otero Gamabarte & Ivan Pecka Otero
Ave. Julio C.Patiño #551, Calacoto, La Paz, Bolivia. Phones: (591) 2-279-9288, 277-2438; Cell: 765-06060. Email: haotero@backwoodbw.com
Provides professional services in the following areas: Commercial, Immigration Services, Labor and Financial
Languages: SPANISH, ENGLISH, and FRENCH

CRIALES, URCULLO & ANTEZANA ABOGADOS
Av. Arce #2799, Edif. Fortaleza, Piso 12. La Paz, Bolivia. P.O. Box 12556, La Paz, Bolivia.

Phone: (591)2- 243-2343; Fax: 243-4940. Email: jcriales@bolivialaw.com ; www.bolivialaw.com
Provides professional services in corporate, civil and labor law, taxes, oil and energy, telecommunications, foreign investment, regulatory matters, acquisitions and mergers, stock market, privatizations and private participation procedures, transportation, mining, insurance, arbitration and alternative solutions to disputes.
Languages: SPANISH , ENGLISH, PORTUGUESE and FRENCH

FABBRI & ASOCIADOS
Calle Federico Suazo esq. Reyes Ortiz #73, Edificio Gundlach, Torre Oeste, Piso 16, Of. 1602, La Paz, Bolivia
P.O. Box 1420, La Paz, Bolivia. Phone: (591) 2-231-1782; 231-1783, Fax: 231-1782. E-mail: info@fabbri.com.bo
Provides professional services in corporate and administrative law, civil and criminal law, taxes, and others.
Languages: SPANISH and ENGLISH

GAMARRA & PEREZ ASOC.:
Calle Loayza #233, Edif. Mariscal de Ayacucho, 11avo Piso, Of. 1108, La Paz, Bolivia.
Phone: (591) 2-220-4473. Fax: 220-0817. Cell: 725-06544; 671-24574
Provides professional services in corporate law, mining, oil and gas, banking, taxes, administrative law, intellectual property, financial law, labor law, family and criminal law, constitutional law.
Languages: SPANISH and ENGLISH

MIRANDA & ASOCIADOS
Ave. Arce 2299, Edif. Multicentro, Torre B, Piso 11, Of. 1104, La Paz, Bolivia. P.O. Box 4122.
Phone: (591) 2-244-2222; Fax: (591) 2-244-2222.
Email: abogados@miranda-asociados.com
Provides specialized services in commercial, administrative, labor, taxation, environmental, agricultural, transportation, civil law, regulatory matters, conciliation, arbitration and intellectual property.
Languages: ENGLISH, FRENCH, PORTUGUESE, and SPANISH

MORENO BALDIVIESO ESTUDIO DE ABOGADOS
Calle Capitán Ravelo #2366, La Paz. P.O. Box 830, La Paz, Bolivia.
Phone: (591) 2-244-1600; Fax: 244-1550. Email: morenob@emba.com.bo ; www.emba.com.bo
Provide professional services in corporate law, mining, oil and gas, intellectual property, finance, labor, investment, and telecommunications.
Languages: SPANISH and ENGLISH

REYNOLDS & ASOCIADOS SOC. CIV.
Jorge Gregory Reynolds Rivera Socio & Gonzalo Rolando Davila Maceda
Pasaje Fabiani final Sanchez Lima, Sopocachi #2687 D
Phone: (591) 2-243-1345. Email: Gonzalo.davila@reynolds-legal.com ; www.reynolds-legal.com
Provide professional services in administration, environmental, international, oil and gas, electricity, water, telecommunications, transportation, constitutional, commercial and civil law.
Languages: SPANISH, ENGLISH and FRENCH

C.R. & F. ROJAS - ABOGADOS
Calle Federico Zuazo 1598, Edif. Park-Inn, Piso 11, La Paz, Bolivia. P.O. Box 662. La Paz, Bolivia.
Phone: (591) 2-231-3737; Fax: 237-6380. Email: rojas@rojas-lawfirm.com
Provides professional services in the following areas: civil law, aviation, banking and finances, mining, oil, corporate law, environment, mining, labor law, civil and criminal law, intellectual property and copy rights, telecommunications, biodiversity, energy, family law, arbitrage, privatization,

Languages: SPANISH, ENGLISH, FRENCH, and PORTUGUESE

SALAZAR, SALAZAR & ASOCIADOS
Calle Rosendo Gutierrez #550, 1er Piso, La Paz, Bolivia. P.O. Box 11228. La Paz, Bolivia. Phone: (591) 2-241-7836; 241-5309; 241-0459. Fax: 211-2407. Email: estudiojuridico@salazar-law.com.bo
Provides professional services in civil and investment law, corporate law, taxes, privatization, criminal law, contracts, joint ventures, constitutional law, capitalization schemes, extradition matters, commercial and financial law, government and environmental law and litigation in general.
LANGUAGES: SPANISH, ENGLISH AND FRENCH

VERASTEGUI PALAO, Paulino
Av. Sanchez Lima No. 2520, Edificio Anibal Piso 11, Departamento "D". La Paz, Bolivia.
Phone: (591) 2-279-9480; (591) 2-271-3882; Cell (591) 725-91577; Email: paulinoverastegui@hotmail.com
Provides professional services in international arbitration.
LANGUAGES: SPANISH

COCHABAMBA

CORTES DE SORIANO, Ana María
Calle Lanza # 0621, Edificio Concordia, 1er Piso, Cochabamba, Bolivia. Casilla Postal188, Cochabamba, Bolivia.
Phone: (591) 4-452-1623. Fax: 425-5291. Email: soriano.cortes@gmail.com; anamcortes@gmail.com
Specializes in family and civil law. Languages: SPANISH and ENGLISH

DE LA REZA SUAREZ, Luis
Calle España esq. Heroínas, Edificio La Promotora, 5to Piso, Oficina 501, Cochabamba, Bolivia. Casilla Postal 1340, Cochabamba, Bolivia.
Phone: (591) 4-425-3668 and 450-1617. Fax: (591)4-425-0848. Email: delareza@supernet.com.bo
Specializes in commercial and civil law. Languages: SPANISH and ENGLISH

SAHONERO MOLINA, Jankarla
Ave. San Martín #123, Edif. Raquel, Piso 2 Of. 2A, Entre Heroínas y Bolivar. Calle Bolívar #639, Edificio Profesional, Mezzanine, Cochabamba, Bolivia. Phone: (591) 4-450-9086; Fax: 4-422-7989. Cells: 703-64525, 717-20790.
Specializes in commercial, family, criminal and narcotics law. Languages: SPANISH

LEVY DE TEJADA, Cecilia
Av. Gaby de la Reza esq. Ave. Ramón Rivero, Edificio Los Tiempos, Torre II, Piso 14, Cochabamba, Bolivia.
Phone/Fax: (591) 4-453-2728/453-2729. Email: osvaldo_tejada@yahoo.es
Specializes in family, tax, civil, commercial law and arbitration and conciliation. Language: SPANISH
TEJADA FERRUFINO, Osvaldo Fernando
Av. Gaby de la Reza esq. Ave. Ramón Rivero, Edificio Los Tiempos, Torre II, Piso 14, Cochabamba, Bolivia.
Phone/Fax: (591) 4-453-2728/453-2729. Email: osvaldo_tejada@yahoo.es
Specializes in civil, commercial and tax law, arbitration and conciliation. Languages: SPANISH AND ENGLISH

VIDAURRE BALDIVIESO, Gretzel Giselle
Calle Colombia entre Av. San Martin y calle Lanza No 576, Edificio Basan, 4to. Piso Of. 7, Cochabamba, Bolivia.

Phone: (591) 4-450-2127, Cell: 779-90448; 707-73722. Email: gretzelvb@gmail.com
Specializes in civil, business (commercial), and family law. Language: SPANISH

SANTA CRUZ

CALLAU BALCAZAR, Walter
Avenida Irala #585, esq. Ejército Nacional, Edificio Irala, 4to Piso, Oficina 401, Santa Cruz, Bolivia.
Phone: (591) 3-332-5109; Fax: 332-234; Cell 768-52811. Email: wcallau@cotas.com.bo
Specializes in commercial (contracts) law. Languages: SPANISH AND ENGLISH.
COSTA DU RELS, Mauricio
Av. San Martin No. 115, Edificio Taqmarindo, Of.#3. Santa Cruz, Bolivia.
Phone: (591) 3-339-4555/339-4543; Cell: 770-45095; Email: mcostadurels@wkc.com.bo
Specializes in professional services in international commercial and investment arbitration, commercial, civil, corporate law and energy law. Language: SPANISH, ENGLISH, GERMAN, ITALIAN, COREAN and FRENCH.

HERRERA AÑEZ, William
Calle Murure #100 (cerca de Ave. Beni), Santa Cruz, Bolivia.
Phone: (591) 3-343-3561; Cell: 716-48303; Fax: 343-3560. Email:
wherrera@bibosi.santacruz.entelnet.bo
Specializes in adoptions, civil, criminal and administrative law. Language: SPANISH

INDACOCHEA, Ricardo
Firm: Indacochea & Asociados
Avenida Piraí esquina Baracea #2115, Santa Cruz, Bolivia. Casilla 6661, Santa Cruz, Bolivia
Phone: (591) 3-353-5356. Fax: 358-1200;
Email: indacochea@indacochea.com.bo
Specializes in corporate, financial law. Masters in Comparative Jurisprudence, New York University. Experience as Associate at Dewey Ballantine in New York. Languages: SPANISH , ENGLISH, PORTUGUESE and GERMAN.

LACIO LINO, German
Calle Padre Perez #40, Santa Cruz, Bolivia. Phone: (591) 3-353-0691; Cell: 712-64759.
Specializes in civil, family and labor law. Languages: SPANISH, FRENCH and ENGLISH

MENACHO, Yolanda B.
Barrio Sirari, Calle Flaboyanes #33, Santa Cruz, Bolivia
Phone: (591) 3-342-3523; Cell 726-20700.
Specializes in adoptions, family and civil law. Language: SPANISH

URENDA, Juan Carlos
Urenda Abogados
Calle Rafael Peña #222, Santa Cruz, Bolivia. Casilla 1286, Santa Cruz, Bolivia
Phone: (591) 3-336-7788. Fax: 334-4669
Email: jcu@urenda.bo
Specializes in commercial, bank, cooperative law and foreign investment. Languages: SPANISH AND ENGLISH.

BRAZIL - INVESTMENT AND BUSINESS CLIMATE - STRATEGIC INFORMATION AND CONTACTS FOR STARTING BUSINESS

CONTACT FOR MORE INFORMATION

TITLE: Economic Counselor
ADDRESS: U.S. Embassy, Brasilia SES – Av. das Nações, Quadra 801, Lote 03 Brasilia
TELEPHONE: +55-61-3312-7000

Brazil is open to and encourages foreign direct investment (FDI). According to the United Nations Conference on Trade and Development (UNCTAD), Brazil was the fifth largest destination for global FDI flows in 2014. New FDI into Brazil reached approximately USD 64 billion in 2013, and Brazil typically receives close to half of South America's total incoming FDI. The Government of Brazil (GOB) has made attracting private investment in infrastructure a top priority for 2015.

The United States is a major foreign investor in Brazil; according to the Brazilian Central Bank (BCB), the United States had the highest stock of FDI in Brazil as of 2013. While Brazil is generally considered a desirable market for investment given its large economy and growing middle class, complex tax, local content, and regulatory requirements exist. In most cases, these impediments apply without discrimination to both foreign and domestic firms. The GOB generally makes no distinction between foreign and national capital in cases of direct investment.

The Brazilian economy disappointed in 2014 with 0.1 percent GDP growth, and market participants surveyed by the Brazilian Central Bank expect a contraction in 2015. Since 2014, Brazil's anti-corruption oversight bodies have been investigating allegations of widespread corruption involving state-owned energy firm Petrobras and a number of private construction firms. A separate tax bribery investigation, announced in 2015, is also ongoing. Medium- and long-term prospects still remain favorable, however, supported by strong domestic demand, anticipated investments in infrastructure, development of offshore oil reserves, and prudent macroeconomic policies.

1. OPENNESS TO, AND RESTRICTIONS UPON, FOREIGN INVESTMENT

ATTITUDE TOWARD FOREIGN DIRECT INVESTMENT

Foreign Direct Investment (FDI) is prevalent across Brazil's economy. Brazil is open to and encourages FDI.

OTHER INVESTMENT POLICY REVIEWS

The latest Organization for Economic Cooperation and Development (OECD) Economic Survey for Brazil was released in 2013. The OECD Survey applauds Brazil's efforts to promote inclusive growth and to sustainably manage natural resources, but recommends continued fiscal consolidation, more aggressive monetary policy to bring inflation closer towards the center of the target band, and improvements to productivity and competitiveness. The OECD report can be found at: http://www.oecd.org/eco/surveys/Brazil_2013_Overview_ENG.pdf.

LAWS/REGULATIONS OF FOREIGN DIRECT INVESTMENT

The GOB currently restricts foreign investment in domestic airline companies to a maximum of 20 percent (Law 7565/1986, Article 181). A bill in the Chamber of Deputies (PL6716/2009) that would increase the ceiling to 49 percent has been pending since 2009. On March 19, 2011, representatives from the U.S.

and Brazilian governments signed an Air Transport Agreement that will lead to an Open Skies relationship between the United States and Brazil, eliminating numerical limits on passenger and cargo flights between the two countries. If it is approved by Brazil's Congress, the agreement will take effect in October 2015. The agreement currently sits with the Brazilian executive branch waiting to be reviewed and sent to Congress for ratification. On March 18, 2011, both parties also signed a Memorandum of Consultation (MOC) that incrementally increases flight limits in the interim.

To enter Brazil's insurance and reinsurance market, U.S. companies must establish a subsidiary, enter into a joint venture, or acquire or partner with a local company. Market entry for banks may occur on a case-by-case basis. Of the top 50 banks in Brazil, 20 are owned or controlled by foreign interests. The Brazilian reinsurance market opened to competition in 2007. In December 2010 and March 2011, however, the Brazilian National Council on Private Insurance (CNSP) rolled back market liberalization through the issuance of Resolutions 225 and 232, which disproportionately affect foreign insurers operating in the Brazilian market. Resolution 225 requires that 40 percent of all reinsurance risk be placed with Brazilian companies. Resolution 232 allows insurance companies to place only 20 percent of risk with affiliated reinsurance companies. In December 2011, the CNSP issued Resolution 241, which walked back some of the restrictions of Resolution 225 by allowing the 40 percent requirement to be waived if local reinsurance capacity does not exist.

In September 2011, President Rousseff signed into force a law covering the subscription television market that removed the previous 49 percent limit on foreign ownership of cable TV companies. Under Law 12485/2011, telecom companies will be allowed to offer television packages with their service. Content quotas require every channel to air at least three and a half hours per week of Brazilian programming during primetime. Additionally, one-third of all channels included in any TV package have to be Brazilian.

Foreign ownership of land within 150 km of national borders remains prohibited unless approved by Brazil's National Security Council, per Law 6634/1979. On August 23, 2013, the National Land Reform and Settlement Institute (INCRA) published a set of rules covering the purchase of Brazilian land by foreigners. Under the new rules, the area bought or leased by foreigners cannot account for more than 25 percent of the overall area in any municipal district. Additionally, no more than 10 percent of the land in any given municipal district may be owned or leased by foreign nationals from the same country. The rules also make it necessary to obtain congressional approval before large plots of land can be purchased by foreigners, foreign companies, or Brazilian companies with the majority of shareholders from foreign countries.

On February 25, 2014, the Attorney General of Brazil and the Minister of Agrarian Development co-signed a bill that stipulates the rural lands purchased by foreigners between June 7, 1994 and August 22, 2010 in which companies that have foreigners as partners will be considered Brazilian and be regulated to prevent judicial insecurity. In the state of São Paulo, due to a judicial impasse, foreigners have been able to buy unrestricted amounts of land since the end of 2013. Companies controlled by foreign entities have been taking advantage of the opportunity and have been seeking investment properties.

INDUSTRIAL PROMOTION

In August 2011, Brazil announced a new industrial policy, Plano Brasil Maior (the "Bigger Brazil" plan), to support domestic producers, encourage investment, and spur innovation. The plan, covering the period of 2011-2014, set targets for investment spending to reach 22.4 percent of GDP by 2014, up from a 2010 baseline of 18.4 percent. Private investment in R&D was to reach 0.90 percent of GDP by 2014, up from the 2010 figure of 0.59 percent. Brasil Maior also set targets for making the economy more energy-efficient, reducing the amount of petroleum used per unit of GDP by 9 percent, and nearly tripling broadband internet penetration from 13.8 million households in 2010 to 40 million households in 2014. The GOB is still assessing the results of the 2011-2014 period.

LIMITS ON FOREIGN CONTROL

FDI is prevalent across Brazil's economy, although certain sectors are subject to foreign ownership limitations as specified in the sections above. A 1995 constitutional amendment (EC 6/1995) terminated the distinction between foreign and local capital in general, but there are laws that restrict foreign ownership within some sectors, notably aviation, insurance, and media.

PRIVATIZATION PROGRAM

Brazil has begun an ambitious USD 133 billion Logistics Investment Program (PIL) to draw in private capital and managerial expertise to upgrade the nation's infrastructure, including projects in roads, ports, airports, energy, and urban mobility. All of the infrastructure concessions are open to foreign companies. In fact, in the airport concessions, foreign companies have not only been encouraged to bid, but the auction criteria have been defined in a way that has the effect of requiring the participation of foreign airport operators. The bidding process is non-discriminatory, transparent, and performed without political interference.

In addition to the PIL mentioned above, between January 2011 and December 2014, the government's Program to Accelerate Growth (PAC) disbursed USD 530 billion to fund transportation, energy, housing, and sanitation projects, representing 96.5 percent of total spending projected by the end of 2014. The next phase of PAC will launch in 2015.

SCREENING OF FDI

Foreigners investing in Brazil must register their investment with the BCB within 30 days of the inflow of resources to Brazil. Registration is done electronically. Investments involving royalties and technology transfer must be registered with Brazil's patent office, the National Institute of Industrial Property (INPI). Investors must also have a local representative in Brazil. Portfolio investors must have a Brazilian financial administrator and register with the Brazilian Securities Exchange Commission (CVM).

COMPETITION LAW

Regulatory review of mergers and acquisitions are carried out by the Administrative Council for Economic Defense (CADE). In October 2012, Brazil performed its first-ever pre-merger review of a pending merger, bringing Brazil in line with U.S. and European practices. This shift in merger review was a result of 2011 legislation (Law 12529), which was adopted to modernize Brazil's antitrust review and to combine the antitrust functions of the Ministry of Justice and the Ministry of Finance into those of the so-called "Super CADE." This government body is be responsible for enforcement of competition laws, consumer defense, and combating abuse of economic power.

INVESTMENT TRENDS

Brazil was the fifth largest destination for global FDI flows in 2014. New FDI into Brazil reached approximately USD 64 billion in 2013, and Brazil typically receives close to half of South America's total incoming FDI. The GOB has made attracting private investment in infrastructure a top priority for 2015.

Table 1

Measure	Year	Index or	Website Address

		Rank	
TI Corruption Perceptions index	2014	69 of 175	transparency.org/cpi2014/results
World Bank's Doing Business Report "Ease of Doing Business"	2015	120 of 189	doingbusiness.org/rankings
Global Innovation Index	2014	61 of 143	globalinnovationindex.org/content.aspx?page=data-analysis
World Bank GNI per capita	2013	USD 11,690	data.worldbank.org/indicator/NY.GNP.PCAP.CD

2. CONVERSION AND TRANSFER POLICIES

FOREIGN EXCHANGE

There are few restrictions on converting or transferring funds associated with a foreign investment in Brazil. Foreign investors may freely convert Brazilian currency in the unified foreign exchange market where buy-sell rates are determined by market forces. All foreign exchange transactions, including identifying data, must be reported to the BCB. Foreign exchange transactions on the current account have been fully liberalized.

All incoming foreign loans must be approved by the BCB. In most instances, the loans are automatically approved. Automatic approval is not issued when the costs of the loan are "not compatible with normal market conditions and practices." In such instances, the BCB may request additional information regarding the transaction. Foreign loans obtained abroad do not require advance approval by the BCB, provided the recipient is not a government entity. Loans to government entities, however, require prior approval from the Brazilian Senate as well as from the Finance Ministry's Treasury Secretariat, and must be registered with the BCB.

Interest and amortization payments specified in a loan contract can be made without additional approval from the BCB. Early payments can also be made without additional approvals, if the contract includes a provision for them. Otherwise, early payment requires notification to the BCB to ensure accurate records of Brazil's stock of debt.

On March 6, 2014, the Federal Revenue Service of Brazil consolidated the regulations on withholding tax (IRRF) applicable to earnings and capital gains realized by individuals and legal entities resident or domiciled outside Brazil. The regulation states that the cost of acquisition must be calculated "in reais." The drafting is not clear enough to determine, however, whether the acquisition cost in reais is obtained by converting the value of the direct foreign investment registered with the BCB using the quoted exchange rate on the date of acquisition (the historic rate), or the quoted rate for the date of the sale, or the rate for day two days prior to the sale. Additional requirements were also created for the application of a zero-rate IRRF, such as good tax standing (formalities not specified). Also, the "technical services" definition was broadened to include administrative support and consulting services rendered by individuals (employees or not) or resulting from automated structures having clear technological content. This change is significant for the purposes of determining the applicable IRRF rate, whether the Contribution of Intervention in the Economic Domain (CIDE) tax applies, and for the application of Treaties to Avoid Double Taxation.

Remittance Policies

Foreign investors, upon registering their investment with the BCB, are able to remit dividends, capital (including capital gains), and, if applicable, royalties. Remittances must also be registered with the BCB. Dividends cannot exceed corporate profits. The remittance transaction may be carried out at any bank by documenting the source of the transaction (evidence of profit or sale of assets) and showing that applicable taxes have been paid.

Capital gain remittances are subject to a 15 percent income withholding tax, with the exception of the capital gains and interest payments on tax-exempt domestically issued Brazilian bonds. Repatriation of the initial investment is also exempt from income tax. Lease payments are assessed a 15 percent withholding tax. Remittances related to technology transfers are not subject to the tax on credit, foreign exchange, and insurance, although they are subject to a 15 percent withholding tax and an extra 10 percent CIDE.

3. EXPROPRIATION AND COMPENSATION

There have been no known expropriation actions in Brazil against foreign interests in the recent past, nor have there been any signs that the current government is contemplating such actions. Some claims regarding land expropriations by state agencies have been judged by Brazilian courts in U.S. citizens' favor; however, compensation has not always been paid, as states have filed appeals to these decisions, and the Brazilian judicial system moves slowly. In June 2014, a amendment to Article 243 of the Constitution was approved, determining that assets can be expropriated if human slavery or planting of illegal psychotropic plants is confirmed on the grounds. Expropriation will be done through all lawful means, with the right to appeal, but once determined, the owner will not receive the money generated through the sale of the asset.

4. DISPUTE SETTLEMENT

LEGAL SYSTEM, SPECIALIZED COURTS, JUDICIAL INDEPENDENCE, JUDGMENTS OF FOREIGN COURTS

The Brazilian court system is overburdened, and contract disputes can be lengthy and complex. Brazil has both a federal and a state court system, and jurisprudence is based on civil law. Federal judges hear most disputes in which one of the parties is the State and rule on lawsuits between a foreign State or international organization and a municipality or a person residing in Brazil. Five regional federal courts hear appeals of federal judges' decisions.

BANKRUPTCY

Brazil has a commercial code that governs most aspects of commercial association, except for corporations formed for the provision of professional services, which are governed by the civil code. In 2005, bankruptcy legislation (Law 11101) went into effect creating a system modeled on Chapter 11 of the U.S. bankruptcy code, which allows a company in financial trouble to negotiate a restructuring with its creditors outside of the courts. In the event a company does fail despite restructuring efforts, the reforms improve creditors' ability to recover their debts.

INVESTMENT DISPUTES

Article 34 the 1996 Brazilian Arbitration Act (Law 9307) defines a foreign arbitration judgment as any judgment rendered outside the national territory. The law established that the Brazilian Federal Supreme

Court must ratify foreign arbitration awards. Law 9307 also stipulates that the foreign arbitration award is to be recognized or executed in Brazil in conformity with the international agreements ratified by the country and, in their absence, with domestic law. [Note: A 2001 Brazilian Federal Supreme Court ruling established that the 1996 Brazilian Arbitration Act, permitting international arbitration subject to Federal Supreme Court ratification of arbitration decisions, does not violate the Federal Constitution's provision that "the law shall not exclude any injury or threat to a right from the consideration of the Judicial Power."]

INTERNATIONAL ARBITRATION

Brazil has ratified the 1975 Inter-American Convention on International Commercial Arbitration (Panama Convention) and the 1979 Inter-American Convention on Extraterritorial Validity of Foreign Judgments and Arbitration Awards (Montevideo Convention).

ICSID Convention and New York Convention

Brazil has ratified the 1958 Convention on the Recognition and Enforcement of Foreign Arbitration Awards (New York Convention). Brazil, however, is not a member of the International Center for the Settlement of Investment Disputes (ICSID), also known as the Washington Convention.

DURATION OF DISPUTE RESOLUTION

The 2015 World Bank, Doing Business report found that on average it takes 44 procedures and 731 days to litigate a contract breach at an average cost of 16.5 percent of the claim.

5. PERFORMANCE REQUIREMENTS AND INVESTMENT INCENTIVES

WTO/TRIMS

Brazil is not a signatory to the World Trade Organization (WTO) Agreement on Government Procurement (GPA). U.S. companies seeking to participate in Brazil's public sector procurement effectively need to partner with a local firm or have operations in Brazil. Foreign companies are often successful in obtaining subcontracting opportunities with large Brazilian firms that win government contracts.

INVESTMENT INCENTIVES

The Brazilian government uses a variety of tax incentives and attractive financing through the National Bank for Economic and Social Development (BNDES) to actively encourage both domestic and foreign investment. BNDES is one of the largest development banks in the world, outpacing the lending of even the World Bank. BNDES lending in 2014 was concentrated in infrastructure and Micro, Small and Medium Enterprises, accounting respectively for 36.7 and 32 percent of total disbursements. Industry accounted for 26.7 percent of total disbursements, a setback of 14 percent compared to 2013. The telecommunications sector saw the largest proportional growth in lending, with total disbursement of R$5.3 billion, a 97 percent increase over the previous year.

As part of its package of fiscal tightening, in December 2014, the GOB announced its intention to scale back the expansionary activities of BNDES. The GOB will end direct Treasury support to the bank, which provided 20 percent of BNDES cash flow in 2014, and raised the Long Term Interest Rate that serves as the basis for BNDES loans from 5.0 to 5.5 percent.

The GOB extends tax benefits for investment in less developed parts of the country, such as the Northeast and the Amazon regions, with equal application to foreign and domestic investors. These incentives have been successful in attracting major foreign plants to areas like the Manaus Free Trade Zone, but most foreign investment remains concentrated in the more industrialized southern part of Brazil.

Individual states have sought to attract investment by offering ad hoc tax benefits and infrastructure support to specific companies, negotiated on a case by case basis. These benefits have spurred a so-called "fiscal war" between the states, with some states challenging the tax benefits as harmful fiscal competition. In June 2011, the Brazilian Supreme Court ruled that the benefits granted by 14 states on interstate commerce are unconstitutional, since they were implemented without unanimous consent from the National Council of Fiscal Policy (Confaz). In November 2012, the Ministry of Finance proposed to Congress an end to the "fiscal war" by setting the interstate tax rate on goods at 4 percent for all states, thus limiting states' ability to offer special tax incentives to attract investment away from other states. However, state finance secretaries have been unable reach consensus on the tax rate exemptions proposal.

In January 2015, the Minister of Finance proposed reversing an October 2012 decree (7819) in support of domestic auto manufacturers. The decree raised the Industrial Products Tax (IPI) by 30 percentage points of the price of the vehicle on all vehicle sales in the Brazilian market on or after January 1, 2013. This change affected all vehicles in Brazil. Auto manufacturers are able to apply for a tax credit based on their ability to meet certain criteria, including the number of manufacturing processes performed in Brazil, enhancing fuel efficiency, committing to invest in research and development in Brazil or to use Brazilian engineering services, and agreeing to participate in a fuel-efficiency labeling scheme.

In September 2014, the GOB issued Decree 8304 to reinstate the Special Regime for the Reinstatement of Taxes for Exporters, dubbed the Reintegra Program. Under the program, exporters of products covering 8,630 tariff codes receive a subsidy of 3 percent of the value of their exports. To qualify, the imported content of the exported goods cannot exceed 40 percent, except in the case of high-tech goods, such as pharmaceuticals, electronics, and aircraft and parts, which are permitted to have up to 65 percent of inputs imported. In addition, Reintegra exempts exporters from so-called indirect taxes on capital expenditures, including the PIS/Cofins social contribution taxes and the IOF tax on financial transactions. On February 27, 2015, Decree 8415 revoked Decree 8304 and determined new regulations for the program; however, the three percent subsidy on the value of the exports is still in effect.

In May 2010, the GOB launched a National Broadband Plan, which featured fiscal incentives, private sector participation, and regulatory reform to build out internet infrastructure under the leadership of state-owned firm Telebras. While the plan provided commercial opportunities for foreign investors, it also sought to boost Brazilian technology by granting domestic IT equipment tax exemptions, favorable BNDES financing, and preference in the procurement process.

Research and Development

Tax credits are available based on a producer's ability to meet certain criteria, including investing in research and development in Brazil.

PERFORMANCE REQUIREMENTS

In firms employing three or more persons, Brazilian nationals must constitute at least two-thirds of all employees and receive at least two-thirds of total payroll, according to Brazilian Labor Law Articles 352 to 354. Foreign specialists in fields where Brazilians are unavailable are not counted in calculating the one-third permitted for non-Brazilians.

Law 8666 (from 1993) covers most government procurement other than information technology/telecommunications and requires non-discriminatory treatment for all bidders regardless of nationality or origin of the product or service. GOB procurement rules apply to purchases by government entities and state-owned companies. Brazil has an open competition process for major government procurements. The GOB may not make a distinction between domestic and foreign-owned companies during the tendering process; however, when two equally qualified vendors are considered, the law's implementing regulations provide for a preference for Brazilian goods and services. Price is to be the overriding factor in selecting suppliers. However, the law's implementing regulations also allow for consideration of non-price factors, giving preferences to certain goods produced in Brazil and stipulating local content requirements in order to qualify for tax benefits. Additionally, nearly all bids require establishment of a local representative for any foreign company bidding.

Government procurement is just one of thirty-five industrial policy components under Brasil Maior intended to support Brazilian industry and protect domestic producers, particularly the labor-intensive sectors threatened by imports. The textile, clothing and footwear industries – among the few industries to have lost jobs during the current growth period – were the first to benefit from Brasil Maior when, in November 2011, the Ministry of Development, Industry and Commerce implemented an 8 percent preference margin for domestic producers in these industries when bidding on government contracts. In April 2012, Decrees 7709 and 7713 expanded the use of preference margins to pharmaceuticals and medicine (8 or 20 percent) and excavators and bulldozers (15 and 25 percent). The preference margins for these goods are valid until December 31, 2015.

Decree 7174 (2010), which regulates the procurement of information technology goods and services, requires federal agencies and parastatal entities to give preferential treatment to domestically produced computer products and goods or services with technology developed in Brazil based on a complicated price/technology matrix.

Data Storage

In general, the government does not explicitly practice “forced localization” in which foreign investors must use domestic content in goods and technology, but local content products have the advantage of tax breaks, BNDES financing, and price preferences of up to 25 percent in government purchases. To date, there is no general requirement for foreign IT providers to turn over source codes or otherwise provide access to surveillance, but Decree 8135 of 2013 calls for auditing of hardware and software used in government data communications.

In 2014, Brazil passed the comprehensive Marco Civil Internet Law without an explicit data localization requirement. The law states, however, that data collected, stored, retained, or treated in Brazil shall respect Brazilian law, implying that certain data stored overseas by foreign companies might be subject to the law. Penalties for non-compliance could include fines of up to 10 percent of gross Brazil revenues and/or suspension or prohibition of related operations in country.

6. RIGHT TO PRIVATE OWNERSHIP AND ESTABLISHMENT

Foreign and domestic private entities may establish, own, and dispose of business enterprises.

7. PROTECTION OF PROPERTY RIGHTS

Real Property

Brazil has a system in place for mortgage registration, but implementation is uneven and there is no standardized contract. Foreign individuals or foreign-owned companies can purchase real property in Brazil. These buyers frequently arrange alternative financing in their own countries, where rates may be more attractive. Law 9514 (from 1997) helped spur the mortgage industry by establishing a legal framework for a secondary market in mortgages and streamlining the foreclosure process, but the mortgage market in Brazil is still underdeveloped, and foreigners may have difficulty obtaining mortgage financing. Large U.S. real estate firms, nonetheless, are expanding their portfolios in Brazil.

INTELLECTUAL PROPERTY RIGHTS

The quality of Intellectual Property Right (IPR) protection and level of enforcement within Brazil is improving. The country has an array of domestic laws and regulations that address IP, and government entities and private industry pay attention to the issue. National and local authorities are active in carrying out enforcement actions, but a long land border and active ports complicate this effort. While Brazil itself is not a major producer of counterfeit and pirated products, societal attitudes toward their purchase remain permissive, and industry stakeholders are increasingly concerned about online IP violations.

Brazil is a member of the WTO, and has legislatively implemented its obligations under the Trade Related Aspects of Intellectual Property (TRIPS) agreement through through its 1996 Industrial Property Law and 1998 Copyrights Law. Brazil is a signatory of the Berne Convention for the Protection of Literary and Artistic Works, the Patent Cooperation Treaty, the Convention on Plant Variety Protection, and the Paris Convention on Protection of Intellectual Property, and plays an active role at the World Intellectual Property Organization (WIPO). Brazil is not a party to the WIPO Copyright Treaty or the WIPO Performances and Phonograms Treaty, collectively known as the WIPO Internet Treaties, nor the Anti-Counterfeiting Trade Agreement (ACTA). Brazil has been taking steps to join the Madrid Agreement Concerning the International Registration of Marks ("Madrid Protocol"), which would make the process of obtaining a trademark in Brazil faster.

In multilateral negotiations and the WTO TRIPS Council, Brazil, together with other countries, presses demands for unlimited technology transfer that could lead to coercion of private rights holders, weakening their property rights. These outcomes could undermine innovation, trade, and investment in IP-intensive products and services that are critical parts of the response to climate change, sustainable economic development, and other challenges. By advancing such positions, the Brazilian government is creating uncertainty with respect to its commitment to create a domestic environment that will encourage innovation and investment in innovative industries.

Brazil is developing a revised copyright law that will more directly address digital issues, as well as other bills to address such items as the ownership of genetic biodiversity resources. These laws might clarify the IP landscape, but foreign industry stakeholders are watching carefully to see how they might affect their IP interests.

Brazil does not publish a comprehensive database on counterfeit seizures, but a recent non-government estimate placed losses to illicit commerce (including contraband) at over USD 20 billion in 2014**http://arte.folha.uol.com.br/mercado/2015/03/12/crime-sem-castigo/** . Brazil has remained on the "Watch List" of the U.S. Trade Representative's Special 301 report since 2007, when it was upgraded from the "Priority Watch List" in recognition of improvements in its IPR regime. Continuing challenges include regulatory issues such as the longstanding role of the health regulator in reviewing pharmaceutical patent applications before the patent office considers them, long wait time in the patent application process, and high levels of digital and hard-goods piracy and counterfeiting. USTR's 2015 "Notorious Markets" report flagged Sao Paulo's Galeria Page market for its high levels of illicit goods and low levels of enforcement. The report also flagged baixeturbo.org, an overseas website with infringing content that targets Brazilian users.

Customs officers have ex-officio authority to seize suspected counterfeit goods. The authorities, however, are required to retain such goods throughout the investigative and legal process, rather than merely keeping a representational sample. This taxes physical storage and budget capabilities of the authorities, hampering overall enforcement. Rights holders are not responsible for paying for the storage and destruction of counterfeit goods. Counterfeit goods readily available in Brazil include apparel, fashion accessories, toys, and audiovisual entertainment products; these items are produced within Brazil, in neighboring countries such as Paraguay, and in Asia. Smuggled genuine goods, such as cigarettes and beverages, are also a serious concern.

Industry stakeholders continue to voice concern over INPI's backlog of pending patent applications. INPI has increased its hiring and training of new examiners, but it still takes about 10 years for a patent to be granted. The average time from application to grant of trademark is 46 months. Brazil has modern trade secret laws, including criminal penalties, and Brazilian courts are accessible and equitable to foreigners. In most respects, the Industrial Property Law meets the international standards specified in TRIPS regarding patent and trademark protection. The law does provide for compulsory licensing if a patent owner has failed to adequately commercialize the technology, but there are several exceptions to this that can be referenced by the patent holder so that compulsory licensing can be averted.

IP protections in general are improving in Brazil, exemplified by continued whole-of-government dialogue and efforts under the National Council on Combating Piracy. Authorities conduct and publicize raids in cities like Brasilia and Rio. The 2014 FIFA soccer World Cup helped draw attention to IP issues, and it is expected that the 2016 Olympics will further boost enforcement and IP protection efforts.

Resources for Rights Holders

Embassy point of contact: Albert Keyack, U.S. Patent and Trademark Office, Rio de Janeiro, **Albert.Keyack@trade.gov**

Local lawyers list: **http://brazil.usembassy.gov/lawyers.html**

8. TRANSPARENCY OF THE REGULATORY SYSTEM

In the 2015 World Bank "Doing Business" report, Brazil ranked 120th out of 189 countries in terms of overall ease of doing business, an improvement of three positions compared to the 2014 report. According to the study, it takes an average of 12 procedures and 102.5 days to start a new business in São Paulo, significantly longer than the OECD high-income economies' average of 9.2 days. In Rio de Janeiro, it takes an average of 11 procedures and 54 days to start a new business. The study noted that the annual administrative burden to a medium-size business of tax payments in Brazil is an average of 2,600 hours versus 176 hours in the OECD high-income economies. According to this same study, the total tax rate for a medium-sized business in Brazil is 69 percent of profits, compared to 41.3 percent in the OECD high-income economies. Business managers often complain of not understanding tax regulations, despite their investments in large tax and accounting departments.

Tax regulations, while burdensome and numerous, do not differentiate between foreign and domestic firms. However, there have been instances of complaints that the value-added tax collected by individual states (ICMS) favors local companies. Although the tax is designed to be refunded when goods are exported abroad, exporters in many states have had difficulty receiving their ICMS rebates. Taxes on commercial and financial transactions are particularly burdensome, and businesses complain that these taxes hinder the international competitiveness of Brazilian-made products. In addition, the U.S. government is evaluating Provisional Measure 668, which increases the PIS/Cofins tax rate on imported goods only and is scheduled to take effect May 1, 2015.

Of Brazil's ten federal regulatory agencies, the most prominent include ANVISA (the Brazilian equivalent of the U.S. Food and Drug Administration), which has regulatory authority over the production and marketing of food, drugs and medical devices; ANATEL, the country's telecommunication agency, which handles licensing and assigning of bandwidth; ANP, the National Petroleum Agency, which regulates oil and gas contracts and oversees the bidding process for oil blocks, including for pre-salt oil; ANAC, the agency that oversees the civil aviation industry; and ANEEL, the country's electric energy agency. In addition to these federal regulatory agencies, Brazil has at least 27 state-level agencies and 17 municipal-level agencies.

The Office of the Presidency's Program for the Strengthening of Institutional Capacity for Management in Regulation (PRO-REG), created in 2007 by Decree 6062, has tried to introduce a broad program for improving the regulatory framework in Brazil including via a 2014 Work Plan with the White House Office of Information and Regulatory Affairs to exchange best practices in developing regulations. Five exchanges under the work plan occurred in 2014.

Pursuant to the GOB's priority to improve transparency, the general public has online access to both approved and proposed federal legislation via websites for the Chamber of Deputies, Federal Senate, and the Office of the Presidency. Brazil is seeking to improve its public comment and stakeholder input process. Since 2004, the Brazilian government has instituted a Transparency Portal, a website in which data is available on funds transferred to and from the federal, state and city governments, as well as to and from foreign countries. It also includes information on civil servants' salaries. The Brazilian Transparency Portal has been a model for other developing countries, and the United States partnered with Brazil to replicate the portal in El Salvador.

Foreign investors have encountered obstacles engaging with regulatory agencies. Notable examples include companies in the electric power sector that have complained about the high level of regulatory risk, including the tariff review process. Additionally, some industries have reported challenges in obtaining licenses from IBAMA, the environmental regulator, citing unclear licensing requirements, though the process was reportedly streamlined in 2008. There have also been examples of federal agencies levying significant fines on U.S. companies.

9. EFFICIENT CAPITAL MARKETS AND PORTFOLIO INVESTMENT

Brazil's credit market has grown significantly over the past several years. Real interest rates, once among the highest in the world, fell dramatically in 2012, driven by continued decreases in the BCB's benchmark overnight Selic lending rate and a concerted effort by the GOB to reduce lending spreads charged by public and private banks. The BCB initiated a cycle of monetary policy tightening in April 2013, which continued into 2014 and 2015, and real interest rates have increased again.

While local private sector banks are beginning to offer longer credit terms, BNDES, the state-owned national development bank, has been the traditional Brazilian source of long-term credit, and also provides export credits. BNDES provides foreign- and domestically-owned companies operating in Brazil financing for the manufacturing and marketing of capital goods. As part of its package of fiscal tightening, in December 2014 the GOB announced its intention to scale back the expansionary activities of BNDES. The GOB will end direct Treasury support to the bank, and it has raised the Long Term Interest Rate that serves as the basis for BNDES loans from 5.0 to 5.5 percent. Further increases are expected.

All stock trading is performed on the Sao Paulo Stock Exchange (BOVESPA), while trading of public securities is conducted on the Rio de Janeiro market. In 2008, the Brazilian Mercantile & Futures Exchange (BM&F) merged with the BOVESPA to form what is now the fourth largest exchange in the Western Hemisphere, after the NYSE, NASDAQ, and Canadian TSX Group exchanges. BOVESPA has launched in 2000 a "New Market" in which the listed companies comply with stricter corporate governance requirements. A majority of initial public offerings (IPOs) are listed on the New Market. There are currently 133 companies listed under the "New Market" program. In 2014, two new IPOs and follow-ons raised over R$ 14 billion in capital.

At the end of 2014, there was an average of 367 companies traded on the BM&F/BOVESPA. Total daily trading average volume has risen from R$ 2.4 billion in 2006 to R$ 7.29 billion in 2014, and the number of trades has reached historical high and increased to 228,100,922.

The BM&F/BOVESPA currently has no competition, but that may change soon. In January 2013, Direct Edge, the fourth-largest stock exchange operator in the United States, applied for a license to launch its services in Brazil in 2013. Direct Edge's position in the Brazilian market may be strengthened after its proposed merger with BATS Global Markets in 2014. Direct Edge is expected to begin operations in Brazil in 2015.

Foreign investors, both institutions and individuals, can directly invest in equities, securities and derivatives. Foreign investors are required to trade derivatives and stocks of publicly held companies on established markets. At year-end 2014, foreign investors accounted for 51.2 percent of the total turnover on the BOVESPA. Domestic institutional investors were the second most active market participants, accounting for 28.9 percent of activity. Individual investors comprised 13.7 percent of activity, followed by financial institutions (5.1 percent), and public and private companies (1 percent). Law 10303 of 2001 limits preferred shares to 50 percent of new issuances.

Wholly owned subsidiaries of multinational accounting firms, including the major U.S. firms, are present in Brazil. As of 1996, auditors are personally liable for the accuracy of accounting statements prepared for banks.

MONEY AND BANKING SYSTEM, HOSTILE TAKEOVERS

The Brazilian financial sector is large and sophisticated. Banks lend at Brazilian market rates, which remain high. Reasons cited by industry observers include high taxation, repayment risk, concern over inconsistent judicial enforcement of contracts, high mandatory reserve requirements, and administrative overhead.

The financial sector is concentrated, with BCB data indicating that the 10 largest commercial banks (excluding brokerages) account for approximately 89.6 percent of the commercial banking sector. Three of the five largest banks (in assets) in the country -- Banco do Brasil, Caixa Economica Federal, and BNDES -- are partially or completely federally owned. Lending by the large banking institutions is focused on the largest companies, while small- and medium-sized banks primarily serve small- and medium-sized companies.

The BCB has strengthened bank audits, implemented more stringent internal control requirements, and tightened capital adequacy rules to better reflect risk. It also established loan classification and provisioning requirements. These measures are applied to private and publicly owned banks alike. The Brazilian Securities and Exchange Commission (CVM) independently regulates the stock exchanges, brokers, distributors, pension funds, mutual funds, and leasing companies with penalties against insider trading.

10. COMPETITION FROM STATE-OWNED ENTERPRISES

In the 1990s and early 2000s, the GOB privatized state-owned enterprises across a broad spectrum of industries, including mining, steel, aeronautics, banking, energy, and electricity generation and distribution. While the GOB has divested itself from many of its state-owned companies, it maintains partial control (at both the federal and state level) of some previously wholly state-owned enterprises. Notable examples of partially federally-controlled firms include energy giant Petrobras and power utility Eletrobras. Both Petrobras and Eletrobras include non-government shareholders, are listed on both the

Brazilian and NYSE stock exchanges, and are subject to the same accounting and audit regulations as all publicly traded Brazilian companies.

The 2010 "pre-salt" legislation gives Petrobras sole operator status for the development of the new oil discoveries. The terms and conditions of the new regime favor Petrobras as the sole operator, although foreign firms are still anticipated to play a role in the pre-salt oil fields.

OECD Guidelines on Corporate Governance of SOEs

In addition to major players like Petrobras and Eletrobras, the Brazilian government, at both the federal and state levels, maintains ownership interests in a variety of other smaller enterprises. Typically, corporate governance is led by a board comprised of directors elected by the state or federal government with additional directors elected by non-government shareholders. Brazilian enterprises with state ownership are concentrated in the energy, electricity generation and distribution, transportation, and banking sectors. Many of these firms are also publically traded companies on the Brazilian and other stock exchanges.

Sovereign Wealth Funds

The Sovereign Fund of Brazil (FSB) is the sovereign wealth fund of Brazil, established on December 24, 2008. It is a non-commodity fund that is required to support national companies in their export activities and acts as a mechanism for anti-cyclical development, promoting investment in projects of strategic interest to Brazil domestically and abroad.

11. CORPORATE SOCIAL RESPONSIBILITY

Most state-owned and private sector corporations of any significant size in Brazil pursue corporate social responsibility (CSR) activities. Many corporations support local education, health and other programs in the communities where they have a presence. Brazilian consumers, especially the local citizenry where a corporation has or is planning a local presence, expect CSR activity. It is not uncommon for corporate officials to meet with community members prior to building a new plant or factory to review what types of local services the corporation will commit to providing. Foreign and local enterprises in Brazil often advance United Nations Development Program (UNDP) Millennium Development Goals (MDGs) as part of their CSR activity, and will cite their local contributions to MDGs, such as universal primary education and environmental sustainability.

The U.S. diplomatic mission in Brazil supports American business CSR activities through the +Unidos Group (Mais Unidos), a group of more than 100 American companies established in Brazil. Additional information on how the partnership supports public and private alliances in Brazil can be found on its website: www.maisunidos.org.

OECD Guidelines for Multinational Enterprises

Brazil adheres to the OECD Declaration on International Investment and Multinational Enterprises.

12. POLITICAL VIOLENCE

Strikes and demonstrations occur occasionally in urban areas and may cause temporary disruption to public transportation. Occasional port strikes also impact commerce. Large, spontaneous protests occurred in June 2013 during the Confederations Cup. The protests started in response to a hike in bus fares and later grew to include complaints regarding the government's perceived inability to tackle corruption and improve public services, such as education and healthcare. During the 2014 FIFA World Cup, protests were far smaller. On March 15, 2015, nearly two million Brazilians, principally in Sao Paulo, organized to protest the government of President Rousseff, citing the economic downturn and the Petrobras corruption scandal. Although U.S. citizens have traditionally not been targeted during such events, U.S. citizens traveling or residing in Brazil are advised to take common-sense precautions and avoid any large gatherings or any other event where crowds have congregated to demonstrate or protest. For the latest U.S. State Department guidance on travel in Brazil, please consult www.travel.state.gov.

13. CORRUPTION

In 2013, Brazil ranked 72nd (out of 175 countries) in Transparency International's Corruption Perceptions Index. In South America, Brazil ranked behind Chile and Uruguay, and ranked ahead of Colombia, Peru, Argentina, Suriname, Bolivia, Ecuador, Guyana, Paraguay and Venezuela. With regard to major emerging economies in the BRICS grouping, Brazil ranked ahead of China (80th), India (94th), and Russia (127th), and tied with South Africa (72nd).

Corruption scandals are a regular feature of Brazilian political life. Since 2014, focus has centered on what could be the biggest corruption scandal in Brazil's history, involving Petrobras, the para-statal petroleum company. Known as Operation Car Wash (Lava Jato), more than 103 people have been criminally charged in the scandal, including former Petrobras directors and executives of the biggest private construction companies in Brazil. Nearly fifty politicians are reportedly under investigation as well, including leaders of both houses of Brazil's Congress. In 2015, prosecutors announced "Operacao Zelotes" (i.e. "Operation Zealots"), in which firms are alleged to have bribed tax officials to reduce their assessments. Experts predict that these scandals could take years to unravel, and judicial proceedings usually move quite slowly in Brazil. Still, these investigations are seen as largely independent and a positive step in breaking widespread corruption in Brazil.

UN Anticorruption Convention, OECD Convention on Combatting Bribery

Brazil is a signatory to the OECD Anti-Bribery Convention and a participating member of the OECD Working Group on bribery. It was one of the founders, along with the United States, of the intergovernmental Open Government Partnership, which seeks to help governments increase transparency. Brazil has laws, regulations and penalties to combat corruption, but their effectiveness is inconsistent. Bribery is illegal, and a bribe by a local company to a foreign official is a criminal act. A company cannot deduct a bribe to a foreign official from its taxes. While federal government authorities generally investigate allegations of corruption, there are inconsistencies in the level of enforcement among individual states. Corruption has been reported to be problematic in business dealings with some authorities, particularly at the municipal level. U.S. companies operating in Brazil are subject to the U.S. Foreign Corrupt Practices Act.

Resources to Report Corruption

Contact at government agency or agencies are responsible for combating corruption:

NAME: Roberta Solis
TITLE: International Affairs Advisor
ORGANIZATION: Controloria Geral da Uniao (CGU)
TELEPHONE NUMBER: +55-61-2020-7241
EMAIL ADDRESS: roberta.ribeiro@cgu.gov.br

Contact at "watchdog" organization (international, regional, local or nongovernmental organization operating in the country/economy that monitors corruption:

NAME: Magri Caio
TITLE: Analyst
ORGANIZATION: Ethos Institute
TELEPHONE NUMBER: 11-3897-2400
EMAIL ADDRESS: caio@ethos.org.br

14. BILATERAL INVESTMENT AGREEMENTS

Brazil does not have a Bilateral Investment Treaty (BIT) with the United States. On March 26, 2015, Brazil signed a Bilateral Investment Treaty with Mozambique. In the 1990's Brazil signed BITs with Belgium and Luxembourg, Chile, Cuba, Denmark, Finland, France, Germany, Italy, the Republic of Korea, the Netherlands, Portugal, Switzerland, the United Kingdom and Venezuela, but none of these have been approved by the Brazilian Congress. In 2002, an inter-ministerial working group decided to withdraw the agreements from Congress for approval, so they have not and will not be voted on any time soon. Brazil also has not ratified the Mercosul investment protocol.

BILATERAL TAXATION TREATIES

Brazil does not have a double taxation treaty with the United States, but it does have such treaties with 33 other countries, including, among others, Japan, France, Italy, the Netherlands, Canada, Spain, Portugal, and Argentina. Brazil signed a Tax Information Exchange Agreement (TIEA) with the United States in March 2007, and that agreement entered into force on May 15, 2013, signed by President Dilma Rousseff in Decree 8003/2013.

15. OPIC AND OTHER INVESTMENT INSURANCE PROGRAMS

Programs of the Overseas Private Investment Corporation (OPIC) are fully available, and activity has increased in recent years. The size of OPIC's exposure in Brazil may occasionally limit its capacity for new coverage. Brazil has been a member of the Multilateral Investment Guarantee Agency (MIGA) since 1992.

16. LABOR

The Brazilian Ministry of Labor estimates that in 2014, only 396,993 formal jobs were created, a drop of 64.4 percent compared to 1.1 million in 2013. Job creation results for 2014 were Brazil's worst on record since 1999, when the country created only 196,000 formal jobs. Still, the Brazilian Institute of Geography and Statistics (IBGE) estimated unemployment in the six major metropolitan areas to be 4.3 percent at the end of 2014, the lowest level since the survey began in 2002. Unemployment levels vary significantly across regions.

According to a 2011 IBGE report, the Brazilian labor force has 92.5 million workers. In 2014, roughly 58 percent were located in the services sector, 15 percent in agriculture, and 21 percent in the construction and manufacturing sectors. Brazil has ratified a number of International Labor Organization (ILO) conventions. Brazil is party to the UN Convention on the Rights of the Child and major ILO conventions concerning the prohibition of child labor, forced labor and discrimination.

Brazil's labor code is highly detailed. Formal sector workers are guaranteed 30 days of annual leave and severance pay in the case of dismissal without cause. Brazilian employers are required to pay a "thirteenth month" of salary to employees at the end of the year. Brazil also has a system of labor courts that are charged with resolving routine cases involving unfair dismissal, working conditions, salary disputes, and other grievances. Labor courts have the power to impose an agreement on employers and unions if negotiations break down and either side appeals to the court system. As a result, labor courts routinely are called upon to determine wages and working conditions in industries across the country. The system is tantamount to compulsory arbitration and does not encourage collective bargaining. In recent years, however, both labor and management have become more flexible and collective bargaining has assumed greater relevance.

The Ministry of Labor estimates that there are nearly 11,000 labor unions in Brazil, but officials note that these figures are inexact. Labor unions, especially in sectors such as metalworking and banking, tend to be well-organized and aggressive in advocating for wages and working conditions and account for approximately 19 percent of the official workforce according to a recent IBGE release. Strikes occur periodically, particularly among public sector unions. Unions in various sectors engage in industry-wide collective bargaining negotiations mandated by federal regulation. While some labor organizations and their leadership operate independently of the government and of political parties, others are considered to be closely associated with political parties.

Employer federations, supported by mandatory fees based on payroll, play a significant role in both public policy and labor relations. Each state has its own federation, which reports to the National Confederation of Industries (CNI), headquartered in Brasilia.

17. FOREIGN TRADE ZONES/FREE PORTS/TRADE FACILITATION

The federal government has granted tax benefits for certain free trade zones. Most of these free trade zones aim to attract investment to the country's relatively underdeveloped North and Northeast regions. The most prominent of these is the Manaus Free Trade Zone, in Amazonas State, which has attracted significant foreign investment, including from U.S. companies. In October 2011, President Rousseff signed a constitutional amendment that extends Manaus's status as an industrial zone for another 50 years. Constitutional amendment 83/2014 came into force in August 2014 and extended the status of Manaus Free Trade Zone until the year 2073.

18. FOREIGN DIRECT INVESTMENT AND FOREIGN PORTFOLIO INVESTMENT STATISTICS

Table 2: Key Macroeconomic Data, U.S. FDI in Host Country/Economy

	Host Country Statistical source*		USG or international statistical source		USG or International Source of Data: BEA; IMF; Eurostat; UNCTAD, Other
Economic Data	YEAR	AMOUNT	YEAR	AMOUNT	
Host Country Gross Domestic Product (GDP) ($M USD)	2013	2,243,074	2013	2,243,074	www.worldbank.org/en/country
Foreign DirectINVESTMENT	HOST COUNTRY STATISTICAL SOURCE*		USG OR INTERNATIONAL STATISTICAL SOURCE		USG OR INTERNATIONAL SOURCE OF DATA: BEA; IMF; EUROSTAT; UNCTAD, OTHER
U.S. FDI in partner country ($M USD,	2013	87,500	2013	78,094	http://www.bea.gov

	Host Country Statistical source*		USG or international statistical source		USG or International Source of Data: BEA; IMF; Eurostat; UNCTAD, Other
stock positions)					
Host country's FDI in the United States ($M USD, stock positions)	2014	14,086	2013	1,054	http://www.bea.gov
Total inbound stock of FDI as % host GDP	2013	28%	N/A	N/A	

* **http://www.bcb.gov.br**

Table 3: Sources and Destination of FDI

Results from the IMF's Coordinated Direct Investment Survey (CDIS) are generally consistent with host country data. There is a discrepancy between BCB and IMF calculations for U.S. FDI distribution in Brazil, as well as Brazilian FDI distribution in the United States. According to the BCB, the United States had the highest stock of FDI in Brazil as of 2013. The BCB calculates FDI distribution by ultimate investing country (for which the United States ranks number one), whereas the IMF calculates FDI distribution by immediate investing country (for which the Netherlands ranks number one). The ultimate investor occupies the top of the control chain and does not necessarily coincide with the immediate investor.

Direct Investment from/in Counterpart Economy Data					
From Top Five Sources/To Top Five Destinations (US Dollars, Millions)					
Inward Direct Investment			Outward Direct Investment		
Total Inward	715,182	100%	Total Outward	225,635	100%
Netherlands	182,610	26%	Austria	66,172	29%
United States	107,693	15%	Cayman Islands	38,806	17%
Spain	73,628	10%	Virgin Islands	25,407	11%
Luxembourg	53,254	8%	Spain	19,273	9%
France	36,393	5%	The Bahamas	18,165	8%
"0" reflects amounts rounded to +/- USD 500,000.					

Table 4: Sources of Portfolio Investment

Results from the IMF's Coordinated Portfolio Investment Survey (CPIS) are generally consistent with host country data.

Portfolio Investment Assets
Top Five Partners (Millions, US Dollars)

TOTAL			EQUITY SECURITIES			TOTAL DEBT SECURITIES		
All Countries	29,217	100%	All Countries	15,554	100%	All Countries	13,757	100%
United States	10,661	36%	United States	6,260	40%	United States	4,620	32%
Denmark	3,452	12%	Cayman Islands	2,145	14%	Denmark	3,439	25%
South Korea	2,483	8%	Bermuda	1,630	10%	South Korea	2,483	18%
Cayman Islands	2,263	8%	Switzerland	750	5%	The Bahamas	1,279	9%
Bermuda	1,631	6%	Portugal	612	4%	Spain	860	6%

LAWYERS CONTACTS

CENTRAL

AHARONI, RAHAV
AHARONI LAW OFFICE
10 Herzog, Tel Aviv 62915
Tel: 03-9055478; 050-732-2688; Fax: 153-8-949-4707
Email: ralaw@012.net.il; Website: www.aharonilaw.com
Main Fields of Practice: Succession law — joint estates in Israel and U.S.; probate, wills and trusts; business law; real estate law; business transactions. Family law, immigration, taxes, estates, transportation law, commercial law, collections, civil law, foreign investments, marketing agreements, government relations, contracts.

ALEXANDROVITZ, SHANNI
Liam Schwartz & Associates
12 M. Begin St. (Ground Floor), Ramat Gan, 52521
Tel: 03-753-8600; Fax: 03-751-8201
Email: shanni@lsa-law.com; Website: www.lsa-law.com
Main fields of practice: Family law, U.S. and Israeli immigration and consular law.

ARGAMAN, JOSHUA B.
Argaman Law Offices
17 Kaplan St., Tel Aviv, 64734
Tel: 03-691-8111; Fax: 03-691-5666
Email: jbargaman@012.net.il
Main Fields of Practice: General practice, estates/probate law, commercial/collections, real estate law, civil law, notary services, personal injury law, corporations/banking.
Languages spoken: English, Hebrew

ARUBIN & LUZ
77 Orlov, Petah Tiqva 4934286
Tel: 03-670-0799; Fax: 03-670-2288
Email: law@rbls.co.il; Website: www.rbls.co.il
Main fields of practice: Civil litigation, military, employment, traffic court, commercial, real estate, property

management
Languages spoken: Hebrew, English, French

AZOULAY, CINDY
Kan-Tor & Acco
12 M. Begin Street (Floor 2), Ramat Gan, 52521 Israel
Tel: 03-613-8202; Fax: 03-613-7944
Email: Cindy@ktalegal.com; Website: www.ktalegal.com
Main fields of practice: U.S. corporate and individual immigration and relocation
Languages spoken: English, Hebrew

BAHARAV, RONEN
Preis, Baharav & Co.
39 Montefiore St, Tel Aviv, 6520108
Tel: 03-541-5555; Fax: 03-541-5550
Email: baharav@pnb.co.il; Website: www.pnb.co.il
Main fields of practice: Corporate, banking and investment regulatory and financing transactions.
Languages Spoken: English, Hebrew

BARR, LOUIS
Wimpfheimer, Aronoff & Co.
Ayalon House, 12 Abba Hillel, 16th Floor, POB 3306, Ramat Gan 52136
Phone: 077 667 0783
Fax: 077 667 0711
Email: lbarr@swalegal.co.il ; Website: www.swalegal.co.il
Main Fields Of Practice: Employee benefits & executive compensation, non-profit & tax-exempt organizations and tax law.
Languages Spoken: English, Hebrew.

BEN DROR, YOSSI
Y. Ben-Dror in association with Eitan, Mehulal & SadotAdvocates and Patent Attorneys
10 Abba Eban Blvd., P.O.Box 2081, Herzlia 46120, Israel
Tel: (972) 9-9720801; Mobile: (972) 54-3066637
Email: yossib@ybendror.com
Website: www.ybendror.com
Main field of practice: Insurance, banking/financial, hi-tech and startups, private equity/venture capital, Commercial/business law, foreign investments, marketing agreements, patents/trademarks/copyrights, Contracts, transportation law, corporations and M&A, aeronautical/maritime, foreign claims, taxes, Govt. relations, labor relations, life sciences and pharmaceuticals, international trade, insolvency, receivership
And dissolution, projects and energy, real estate, litigation, dispute resolution, capital, banking and finance,
Investment funds.Languages: Hebrew, English

BENJAMIN, ARI
Benjamin & Co.
38 Chovevei Zion St., Tel Aviv, 63346
Tel: 052-595-7710; Fax: 153-52-595-7710
Email: Benjamin@outlook.co.il
Main fields of practice: IP, commercial, real-estate, civil litigation, estates/probate
Languages spoken: English, Hebrew

BLUM, LISA
3 De Haas Street, Tel Aviv 62666
Tel: 03-605-8180; Cell: 054-205-8180; Fax: 03-602-4464
Email: lisab@inter.net.il
Main fields of practice: Notary, labor law, non-profit organizations, mediation
Languages spoken: English, Hebrew

Buckwald, Yehuda
Buckwald Afek & Co. Law Office
33 Jabutinski Street, Ramat Gan
Tel: 972-3-644-2170 Fax: 072-211-1312
Email: buckwald-law@013.net.il
Main fields of practice: Civil-commercial; corporate; high-tech companies; contract; real estate; labor; family law, including wills, inheritance, guardianship; administrative; white collar offences; litigation and mediation
Languages spoken: English, Hebrew

COHEN, JAMES S.
Cohen, Pex, Brosh Law Offices
Montifiori 17, Petach Tikvah 4949002
Tel: 03-6121511, from the US: 347-436-7672; Fax: 153-36121511
Email:jcohen@lawoffice.org.il; Website: www.lawoffice.org.il
Main fields of practice: U.S. visa and immigration law, immigration to Israel, real estate, business, estates, Israel constitutional law, administrative law, U.S. pension law, congressional practice.
Languages spoken: Among partners — English, Hebrew, Russian, Romanian, Dutch

ASAF DOK LAW FIRM
Criminal & Military Law Office
32 Nakhalat Yitzkhak Street , Tel Aviv 6744824
Tel: 03-550-5995; 052-688-5006; Fax: 077-555-8060
Email: office@dok.co.il; Website: www.dok.co.il
Main Fields of Practice: Criminal law, military law, and U.S. and Israeli immigration and consular law.
Languages Spoken: English, Hebrew

DROR, ARIEL
HaYetzira St
S.H.P. House, Ramat Gan
Tel: 03-6951408; Fax: 03-6951683
Email: droorlawoffice@bezeqint.net
Main Fields of Practice: Family law; inheritance law, divorce, property, rabbinical court, foreign judgments, children's issues, abduction, Hague Convention.

FENSTER, YITZCHAK
Notary Public and Attorney-at-Law
25 HaBarzel St., 5th Fl., Ramat HaChayal, Tel Aviv 69710 (by Lionbird)
Second office in Bnei Brak
Cell phone: 054-548-4004
Email: yitzchak@fenster-law.com
Main fields of practice: Notary, hi-tech, corporate, commercial, investments
Languages: English, Hebrew, Spanish, Arabic

FLANTER, GUY
Criminal & Military Law Office

7 Zabotinski Street, Moshe Aviv Tower, 27th Floor, Ramat Gan 52520
Tel: 03-744-7448; Cell: 050-666-4499; Fax: 03-744-7449
Email: info@flanter-law.co.il; Website: http://www.flanter-law.co.il
Main fields of practice: Criminal law, military law, disciplinary proceedings
Languages spoken: English, Hebrew

FREEDMAN, EDWIN
154 Menachem Begin Road, Tel Aviv, 64921
Fax: 03-609-2266; Tel: 03-696-6611;
Email: Edwin@edfreedman.com ; Webpage: www.edfreedman.com
Main fields of practice: General practice, estates/probate, family
Languages spoken: English, Hebrew, French, Hungarian

FRIEDMAN, MARK
Patent attorneys and advocates
Moshe Aviv Tower, 54th floor, 7 Jabotinsky Street, 52520 Ramat Gan, Israel
Tel: 03-611-4100; Fax: 03-611-4101
Email: rivka_f@friedpat.com; Webpage: www.friedpat.com

HANNER, GABRIEL
HANNER-OFER
242 Ben-Yehuda Street (Ground Floor, Accessible to Handicapped), Tel-Aviv, 6350105 Israel
Tel: 03-546-8888; Fax: 03-546-7536; Cell (for urgencies): 050-552-3333
Email: lawfirm@hanner.co.il; Website: www.hanner.co.il
Main fields of practice: Hi-tech & internet, corporations & banking, claims/investments, general practice, estates/probate law, commercial/collections, real estate law and real estate taxation, civil law litigation, Business Transactions
Languages spoken: English, Hebrew, French

HARELI , RONI
Advocate and notary
4 Berkowitz St., Museum Tower, 6th floor, P.O.B. 33111, Tel Aviv 61330
Tel: 03-693-5200; Fax: 03-693-5287
Email: roni@notary-services.co.il; Website: ronilaw.co.il
Main fields of practice: Corporate; real estate; commercial and notarial services; tax planning; commercial, including domestic and international; notarized life certificates; prenuptial agreement approval; notarial wills and testaments; notarized Hebrew-English translations
Languages: English, Italian

HEIMOVITZ, IRWIN
Heruti, Heimovitz & Co.
64A Shenkin St. POB 14204, Tel Aviv, 61141
Fax: 03-560-5356; Tel: 03-560-1994/5; cell: 054-4536160
Email: Heimw@013.net
Main fields of practice: General practice, immigration law, estates/probate law, family law, real estate/property law
Languages spoken: English, Hebrew, Yiddish

HELLED, AMNON
10 Mikveh Israel POB 2402, Tel Aviv, 65114
Fax: 03-566-1642; Tel: 03-560-1956/7/8

Main fields of practice: General practice, real estate/property law, probate law, family law, notary public
Languages spoken: English, Hebrew, Yiddish

HYMAN, DONN
2B Yehuda Street, Ramat Hasharon, 47311
Tel: 077-523-2095; Cell: 052-615-6078; Fax: 077-555-8011
Email: donnhyman@yahoo.com
Main fields of practice: Notary services, real estate, estates, inheritance, corporate, commercial transactions, Internet; notary public
Languages spoken: English, Hebrew

KREMERMAN, JODI
Notary public and Attorney at law
2 Weizmann Street, Tel Aviv 64731
Tel: 03-609-3295; Cell: 054-530-9309; Fax: 03-696-3213
Email: jodi@kremermanlaw.com; www.kremermanlaw.com
Main fields of practice: Commercial–civil, U.S. immigration Law, duel citizen assistance-translation services, apostille service, real estate/property, Israeli and international corporate, contract, aviation, and marine law
Languages spoken: Fluent English, Hebrew, German and Russian

KOLODNY, NOAM
Law Office
Moshe Aviv Tower, 16th Floor
7 Jabotinsky Road
Ramat Gan, 5252007
Tel: 03-644-1175; Fax: 03-649-1169
Email: noam@kolodnylaw.co.il Website: www.kolodnylaw.co.il
Main fields of practice: Banking/Financial, commercial/business law; foreign investments, marketing agreements, patents/trademarks/copyrights; civil law, contracts, corporations, foreign claims, estates, taxes, govt. relations, labor relations, immigrations.
Languages: English, Hebrew

DAVID KRETZMER AND ASSOCIATES
Advocates and Notaries
35 Jabotinsky street, Twin Towers 2, 13th Floor, Ramat Gan, 52511
Tel: 03-613-6901; Fax: 03-613-6905
Email: david@kretzmerlaw.com; Website: www.kretzmerlaw.com
Main fields of practice: Securities law, company law, tax law, general practice, real estate law, property law, immigration law, international cross jurisdictional litigation and arbitration.
Languages spoken: English, Hebrew

MANN, KENNETH
Libai, Mann & Co., Advocates
8 Boulevard Shaul Hamelech, Tel Aviv
Tel: 03-609-0101; Fax: 03-609-0077
Email: kenneth@libaimann.co.il; Website: www.mann-law.com
Main fields of practice: Criminal law, extradition, government relations, estates
Languages spoken: English, Hebrew

NOVOTNY, PERRY Esq.
Law Office of Perry Novotny
Silver House, 7 Abba Hillel Street, Ramat Gan, Israel 52522

Tel: 03-613-9444; Fax: 03-613-9449
Email: office@usvisa.co.il; Website: www.usvisa.co.il
Main fields of practice: Visa and U.S. & Israel immigration law, criminal law, general practice

PREIS, ZIV
Preis, Baharav & Co.
39 Montefiore Street, Tel Aviv 6520108
Tel: 03-541-5555; Fax: 03-541-5550; 054-7746055
Email: preis@pnb.co.il; Website: www.pnb.co.il
Main Fields of Practice: Corporate, commercial, investments and mergers and acquisitions.
Languages spoken: English, Hebrew

RONISKY, GABRIEL
Ronisky Law
Ehud Manor 13, 9th Floor, Holon, 58670
Tel: 050-991-8383; Fax: 03-761-7476
Email: gabe@roniskylaw.com; Website: www.roniskylaw.com
Main Field of Practice: U.S. immigration & consular law
Languages Spoken: English, Spanish, Hebrew

ROSENTHAL, MICHAEL S.
Rosenthal Law
Licensed US Attorney/Certified Foreign Lawyer
12 HaNatziv St, #5, Tel Aviv
Tel: 052-7334347
Email: Michael@rosenthalimmigration.com; Website: www.rosenthalimmigration.com|
Main fields of practice: Immigration law
Languages spoken: English; Hebrew

ROZEN, STEPHEN
Amit, Pollak, Matalon & Co.
17 Yitzchak Sadeh St., 19th Floor, Tel Aviv 6777517
Tel: 03-568-9035; Cell: 057-766-6438
Email: Sb_rozen@apm-law.com; Website: www.apm-law.com
Main fields of practice: corporate, hi-tech, commercial, regulatory, anti-trust, finance, real estate, litigation, taxation, environment, bankruptcy/liquidation, securities, employment/labor law, infrastructure projects, and energy

ROZENBERG, JACOB
Advocates and Notaries|
52 Rabbi Akiva St, Bnei Brak 5127309
Tel: 03-5783383; Fax: 03-5789466
Webpage: office@goodlaw.co.il
Main fields of practice: Notary services
Languages: Hebrew, French, Dutch

SABA, NICHOLAS
75 Herzel Street, Ramla, Israel, 72100
Tel: 08-922-5431; Fax: 08-922-4413
Email: nicksaba@smile.net.il; Website: www.nicola-saba-law.co.il
Main fields of practice: Notary, translation, family matters, inheritance
Languages spoken: English, Hebrew, Arabic

SOFER, SHAI
32 Sheshet Hayamim St, Hod Hasharon.
or 15 Rothschild St, Rison le Zion
Office: 077-4060213; Fax: 077-604-0301
Email: shai.sofer@gmail.com; Website: www.sofer-law.com
Main fields of practice: Commercial law, land law, business and civil litigation, torts, disability law
Languages spoken: Hebrew, English (and sign language)

SCHWARTZ, LIAM
12 M. Begin St. (Ground Floor), Ramat Gan, 52521 Israel
Tel: 972-3-753-8600; Fax: 972-3-751-8201
Email: Liam@lsa-law.com; Website: www.lsa-law.com
Main fields of practice: U.S. and Israeli immigration and consular law
Languages spoken: English, Hebrew

SEGELOV, LISA
33 Jabotinsky, Floor 5, Migdal Teumim tower
Migdal 1, 5th Floor Room 510, Ramat Gan, 52511
Tel: 03-613-4244; Fax: 03-613-4245
Email: notary@cslaw.co.il; Webpage: www.lawyerscs.com
Main fields of practice: Immigration law, corporations/banking, tax law, general practice, real estate/property law
Languages spoken: English, Hebrew, Yiddish

SHIMONY, ELI
89 Medinat Hayehudim St, Herzliya 4676672
Tel: 052-2769773; 09-8669556; Fax: 09-8664476
Email: office@eshimony-law.com; Website: www.eshimony-law.com
Main Fields of Practice: IP (patent/trademark/copyright), commercial, business transactions, real-estate, civil litigation, corporate, banking and investment – regulatory and financing transactions, succession law – joint estates in Israel and the U.S; probate, wills and trusts.
Languages Spoken: English, Hebrew

SILVER, MONTE
Silver & Co. Attorneys at Law
32B Habarzel Street, 2nd Floor, Ramat Hahayal, 69701
Tel: 03-6444808; 054-4232683; Fax: 03-6444818
Email: ms@silvercolaw.com
Main field of practice: U.S. and Israeli lawyer. Formerly worked with the I.R.S. and U.S. Tax Court. Deals excusively with tax issues, such as U.S. tax (Federal/State/Estate/Income) and FBAR matter.

SKLAR AVNIELI, DALIAH R
DRSI Law Offices
B.S.R. Tower 3, Kinneret 5, Bnei Brak
Tel: 03-516-6505; Fax: 072-215-9478
Email: office@drsi-law.com; Website: www.drsi-law.com
Languages Spoken: Native English Speaker
Main Fields of Practice: Commercial/business law, foreign investment, contracts, corporations, estates, taxes, immigration.

TREITEL, ANDREW
28 Ahad Ha'am St
Tel Aviv-Yaffo 6514107

Tel: 03-629-4601
Email: atreitel@gmail.com
Main fields of practice: Inheritance/Wills/Probate, Trusts & Estates, General Corporate.
Languages spoken: English, Hebrew
Bar Admissions: Israel, New York.

WIMPFHEIMER, JAN
S. Wimpfheimer, Aronoff & Co.|
Ayalon House, 12 Abba Hillel, 16th Floor, POB 3306, Ramat Gan 52136
Tel: 077-667-0700; Fax: 077-667-0711
Email: jan@swalegal.co.il; Website: www.swalegal.co.il
Main fields of practice: Corporate, private equity and investment funds
Languages spoken: English, Hebrew
Bar Admissions: Israel, New York

NORTHERN

FRIEDLAND, JONATHAN
26 Ben Gurion Boulevard, POB 8992, Haifa, 35023
Tel: 04-853-1446; Fax: 04-853-1476
Email: consage@netvision.net.il
Main fields of practice: General practice, corporations/banking, estates/probate law, aeronautical/admiralty; transnational agreements.
Languages spoken: Hebrew, English, Spanish

LIPSCHITZ, MOSHE
64 Hameginim, Haifa, 31002
Tel: 04-814-0500; Fax: 04-855-7038
Main fields of practice: General practice, family law, immigration law, criminal law-narcotics; foreign claims/investment
Languages spoken: Hebrew, English, French, Arabic

RON, AMIT
Yaacov Salomon, Lipschutz & Co
1 Natanzon St POB 303, Haifa 3303473
Tel: 04-814-0500; Fax: 04-855-7038
Email: Amitr@ysl-law.com; Website: www.ysl-law.com
Main fields of practice: Family law, banking/financial, commercial/business law, marketing agreements, patents/trademarks/copyrights, civil law, damages, contracts, transportation, corporations, estates, Government relations.
Languages spoken: Hebrew, Arabic

SOUTHERN

YANIR, BENJAMIN
117 Hehalutz, POB 334, Beersheva, 84102
Tel: 08-627-7484; Fax: 08-627-7493
Main fields of practice: General practice, family law, estates/probate law, corporations; banking, personal injury law; real estate/property law
Languages spoken: English, Hebrew, German, Yiddish

JERUSALEM AREA

WIMPFHEIMER, JAN
S. Wimpfheimer, Aronoff & Co.,
Beck Building, 8 Rehov Hartum, POB 45413, Har Hotzvim, Jerusalem, 91451
Tel: 077-667-0700; Fax: 077-667-0711
Email: jan@swalegal.co.il; Website: www.swalegal.co.il
Main fields of practice: Corporate, private equity and investment funds
Languages spoken: English, Hebrew

CHILE - INVESTMENT AND BUSINESS CLIMATE - STRATEGIC INFORMATION AND CONTACTS FOR STARTING BUSINESS

Chile is a coastal country located in the southwest region of South America. Chile is an attractive destination for investors, boasting an open market economy, well-developed institutions that support financial growth and strong rule of law. The country has a positive disposition toward foreign direct investment (FDI), viewing it as key to sustaining Chile's impressive economic trajectory over the last three decades. Its laws and regulations encourage investment by foreigners and very few restrictions upon FDI exist. Chile's conversion and transfer policies are similar to those found in highly-developed countries like the U.S. The government does not expropriate assets or holdings.

Chile's legal framework for attracting and protecting foreign direct investment (FDI) is solid. Legal disputes can, however, take several years to reach conclusion in the courts, making arbitration and mediation attractive alternatives for resolving business controversies. Chile is a signatory to the 1958 New York Arbitration Convention and a member state to the International Centre for Settlement of Investment Disputes (ICSID); disputes under the U.S.-Chile bilateral Free Trade Agreement (FTA) are resolved under the latter framework. Chile is compliant with its World Trade Organization agreement on Trade-Related Investment Measures (WTO/TRIMS) obligations. Chile does not apply performance requirements in reviewing proposed investment projects.

Rights to the broad range of private ownership and establishment are observed in Chile. Mineral, hydrocarbon, and fossil fuel deposits within Chilean territory are restricted from foreign ownership, but may be licensed by the government to private enterprise. Real and intellectual property (IP) rights are generally respected, but Chile is not fully compliant with the obligations concerning IP set forth in the U.S.-Chile FTA. The regulatory system in Chile is generally transparent.

Chile's capital markets are well-developed and open to foreign portfolio investors. The World Economic Forum's Global Competitiveness Report for 2014-2015 ranks Chile as the most competitive country in South America. CODELCO, which dominates the copper mining industry, is one of only a few state-owned enterprises (SOEs). SOEs generally operate on equal footing with private companies. There is growing awareness of the importance of corporate social responsibility in Chile. Political violence is rare and is unlikely to affect foreign investors. Corruption exists in Chile but on a much smaller scale than is the case with most Latin American countries. Chile has a favorable ranking of 21 out of 175 countries on Transparency International's 2014 Corruption Perceptions Index.

Chile has 40 bilateral investment agreements in force. Moreover, Chile has 27 other investment agreements, including the investment chapters of the FTAs signed by the country, the Latin American Integration treaty and the Protocol of the Pacific Alliance. Additionally, Chile is a party to the convention of the World Bank's Multilateral Investment Guarantee Agency (MIGA). A treaty between the U.S. and Chile to avoid double taxation has been signed, and is currently waiting for ratification in both the Chilean Senate and the U.S. Senate. Some employers view Chile's labor laws as cumbersome, and a labor reform bill currently submitted to Congress proposes to increase the bargaining power of unions. Unemployment is low, at 6.3 percent on average in 2014. Chile has tax-free zones.

According to the UN Conference on Trade and Development (UNCTAD), FDI inflows to Chile in 2012 reached USD 28.5 billion, and fell to USD 20.3 billion in 2013. FDI inflows to Chile from the U.S. amounted to USD 3.4 billion, and total FDI stock from the U.S. stood at USD 39.8 billion in Chile at the end of 2012 (must recent information available).

1. OPENNESS TO, AND RESTRICTIONS UPON, FOREIGN INVESTMENT

ATTITUDE TOWARD FOREIGN DIRECT INVESTMENT

For over three decades, Chile has made FDI an essential part of its national development strategy. Chile's sound, market-oriented policies have created significant opportunities for foreign investors to participate in the country's steady economic growth. Chile's business climate is generally straightforward and transparent. Foreign investors receive treatment similar to Chilean nationals, and there is no overall economic or industrial strategy that has discriminatory effects on foreign investors or foreign-owned investments. A broad political consensus on the advantages of foreign investment means that, despite the currently ongoing replacement of part of its regulatory framework, the favorable orientation of Chile's policies toward FDI is unlikely to suffer significant changes.

OTHER INVESTMENT POLICY REVIEWS

In the past three years, the Government of Chile has not conducted an updated investment policy review through the OECD. The last OECD investment policy review for Chile dates from 1997. It is available at:

http://www.oecd.org/investment/countryreviews.htm

http://www.oecd.org/daf/inv/investment-policy/34384328.pdf

The last Trade Policy Review that the WTO conducted for Chile was in 2009, and is available at:

http://www.wto.org/english/tratop_e/tpr_e/tpr_e.htm

https://www.wto.org/english/tratop_e/tpr_e/tp320_e.htm

Chile is not among the countries for which UNCTAD has done investment policy reviews to date.

In 2013, Chile's Foreign Investment Committee (FIC) commissioned the consulting firm SCL Econometrics to produce an analytical report on the measured impact of FDI in the Chilean economy. The report shed light about direct, spillover ad sector-specific impacts of FDI, and is available at:

http://www.ciechile.gob.cl/wp-content/uploads/2010/10/estudio%20impacto%20de%20la%20ied%20en%20la%20economia%20chilena.pdf

LAWS/REGULATIONS OF FOREIGN DIRECT INVESTMENT

FDI in Chile enters under either the Foreign Investment Statute Decree Law 600 (DL600) or Chapter XIV of the Central Bank's Compendium of Foreign Exchange Regulations (CFER). The minimum investment under DL600 is USD 5,000,000 in currency or USD 2,500,000 in the case of fixed assets, technology, debt capitalization, and profit reinvestments. FDI valued below these levels but above USD 10,000 is made through Chapter XIV of the Central Bank's CFER.

Under DL600, a foreign investor signs a contract with the Government of Chile (GOC) establishing the terms of the investment. The general regulations, terms, interest, and other modalities of foreign credit contracts as well as surcharges related to total costs to be paid by the debtor, including commissions, taxes, and the Central Bank of Chile must also authorize expenses. DL600 allows for capital increases in a given investment. A principal benefit of investing under DL600 is the option to lock in a ten-year, invariable total effective income tax rate (42 percent in 2014).

Chile's Foreign Investment Committee (FIC), the entity responsible for administering DL600, establishes the terms and conditions of investments made under DL600. Applications are typically approved within a matter of days and almost always within a month. The FIC's authority to reject a foreign investment is limited by the Chilean Constitution. The FIC's decision can be appealed if an investment is rejected.

Use of DL600 is optional; a qualifying investor can also choose to go through Chapter XIV of the Central Bank's regulations if so desired. Chapter XIV establishes regulations that govern foreign exchange operations related to credits, deposits, investments, and capital contributions originating abroad. Investments made under Chapter XIV do not involve signing a contract with the Chilean state. Instead, the Central Bank grants authorization for a given investment. FDI made under Chapter XIV must be in a foreign currency and does not convey any special rights to the investor, such as access to a guaranteed tax rate. The investor must inform the Chilean Central Bank of the investment through a commercial bank or other authorized financial institution. FDI valued at less than USD 10,000 does not require Central Bank approval.

Chile's openness and transparency to FDI are embodied in DL600. This law has been the main regulatory norm for FDI in Chile during the last 40 years. However, the most recent tax reform, passed by the Chilean Congress in 2014, mandated its derogation and replacement. DL 600 will remain in force until January 1, 2016. A draft bill, which establishes a new regime applicable to FDI that will replace DL 600 and creates a new Framework Law for Foreign Investment, was submitted to Congress in January 2015. It was approved in April 2015 by the Chamber of Deputies (Lower Chamber), and will next be reviewed by the Senate.

The new Framework Law provides assurances to foreign investors about the enforcement of rights and obligations of contracts signed under DL 600. The new regime will keep a number of guarantees, such as access to the exchange market (including for the remittance of capital and earnings); prohibition of arbitrary discrimination; and exemption from sales tax and services on imports of capital goods. An exceptional right allows foreign investors to request investment authorizations in similar terms to Article 3 of DL 600, and locks in an invariable tax rate of 44.5 percent for up to four years. However, tax invariability will no longer be granted for the then year period of time that DL 600 had permitted. Finally, the bill creates new institutions for FDI attraction. These include a Ministers Committee, intended to advise the President on the definition of long-term FDI strategies, and an Investment Promotion Agency, in charge of implementing the national FDI policy.

In 2002, the Chilean Government launched an Investment Platform Initiative ("the Initiative") aimed at attracting international corporations' Latin American headquarters to Chile. As part of the Initiative, an eligible company can make use of a variety of incentives, including tax exemptions for overseas shareholders based on certain criteria and a lack of restrictions on domestic borrowing by a platform company. The Initiative addresses the problem of three-way taxation by exempting platform companies from Chilean tax on overseas earnings and provides foreign investors with additional incentives to invest in Chile. This Initiative is meant to foster regional joint ventures between foreign investors and Chilean partners. To facilitate the entry of foreign capital into Chile, the Initiative also allows companies that are already established in the region to move their centers of operation to Chile without incurring the transaction costs involved in selling and re-buying assets. In 2011, the Congress passed a new Funds Law that modernizes the regulation of asset management funds and simplifies taxation on foreign investors' earnings from investments made on Chilean funds.

Foreign investors are unlikely to experience government interference in Chile's legal system.

INDUSTRIAL PROMOTION

The Chilean government seeks to attract foreign investment to industrial and mining sectors through tax incentives. For example, subject to approval on a case-by-case basis by the Foreign Investment Committee, a foreign investor can lock in an invariable tax rate (42 percent in 2013) for up to 20 years, as opposed to the maximum ten-year limit afforded to investments in other sectors under DL600; however, as noted previously, the framework proposed to replace DL 600 will limit such invariability periods to four years. For more information about benefits of investing in industrial development and the extractive industries, see DL600, http://unctad.org/sections/dite_dir/docs/wir2013/wir13_fs_cl_en.pdf. See the FIC's "Foreign Investor Guide" for information about tax treatment and foreign investments generally: http://www.ciechile.gob.cl/wp-content/uploads/2010/10/Foreign_Investors_Guide_in_Chile.pdf.

LIMITS ON FOREIGN CONTROL

There are no limits on foreign ownership or control of business entities or assets in Chile. See the "Right to Private Ownership and Establishment" section below for restrictions applicable to all investors.

Certain types of investment projects require additional authorization beyond that of the FIC and the Central Bank. There are no restrictions on foreign investment in telecommunications, but investors must acquire a license, and the number of licenses available is limited in some new sectors of the industry. The requirements for obtaining certain licenses in the telecommunications sector remain unclear as the industry evolves; at least one U.S.-based firm experienced significant delays in 2013 attempting to secure licenses due to opaque license granting requirements. These delays are still ongoing. Projects in the copper mining sector require the Chilean Copper Commission's authorization; investments in the fishing sector require the approval of the Under-Secretariat of Fishing; authorization from the Bank and Financial Institutions Regulatory Agency is required to operate in the banking sector; and the Securities and Exchange Commission must authorize projects related to insurance and investment funds. Additional authorizations are required from the Pension Funds and Private Health Insurance regulatory agencies to participate in those sectors. For projects with a potential environmental impact, authorization is required from the Environmental Evaluation Service, a decentralized service related to but independent from the Ministry of Environment. Chile also maintains national security related restrictions on investments in the areas of nuclear energy, defense, maritime transportation, real estate, and mining.

Profit remitted, withdrawn or distributed to foreign investors is subject to a withholding tax. Dividends paid to foreign shareholders are subject to an additional 35 percent tax on distribution, but a credit of 22.5 percent is given against the additional tax where the amount at issue is subject to Chile's First Category tax. The company must withhold the additional tax. The same tax procedure applies to remittances of profit made to partners and to profit withdrawn by foreigners. As noted, though, the effective tax rate – including taxes on remittances - for foreign investment occurring through DL600 can (for now; see discussion of replacement framework above) be capped at the ten-year invariable rate (42 percent in 2013).

PRIVATIZATION PROGRAM

There are no ongoing privatization programs currently in Chile.

SCREENING OF FDI

FDI is subject to pro forma screening by Chile's FIC. Businesses in general do not consider that such screening mechanisms constitute a barrier to investment, because approval procedures are expeditious and, with the exception of a few sensitive sectors, all investments are approved.

In practice, the entire application and approval process for investments under DL 600 takes approximately 20 days.

The law requires that the government's FIC approve investment proposals. Approval is required for investments exceeding USD 5 million or investments made in certain sectors, including the media and the provision of public services, and investments made by foreign governments or by foreign public entities.

COMPETITION LAW

Foreign investors are not required to seek a ruling before investing on the potential competition implications of a planned investment. Chile's anti-trust law, the Chilean Free Competition Act (1973), prohibits mergers or acquisitions that would prevent free competition in the industry at issue. An investor may voluntarily seek a ruling by an Antitrust Court that a planned investment would not have antitrust implications.

INVESTMENT TRENDS

Chile has recently witnessed a downward trend both in FDI flows and domestic investment. FDI flows to the country fell by 29 percent in 2013 (as compared to 2012), but regained some momentum the following year, growing by 14 percent in 2014 (as compared to 2013). Meanwhile, statistics maintained by the Central Bank of Chile (BCC) recorded four consecutive quarters of contractions in domestic investment in 2014 over the corresponding periods the prior year, the worst cycle the country has witnessed since the 1990s; the final figure for the year was a 6.1 percent decrease in comparison to 2013. Most analysts attributed these trends primarily to the mining sector, where investment has slowed down considerably due to the recent deterioration in global copper prices.

Table 1

Measure	Year	Index or Rank	Website Address
TI Corruption Perceptions index	2014	21 of 175	transparency.org/cpi2014/results
World Bank's Doing Business Report "Ease of Doing Business"	2015	41 of 189	doingbusiness.org/rankings
Global Innovation Index	2014	46 of 143	globalinnovationindex.org/content.aspx?page=data-analysis
World Bank GNI per capita	2013	USD 15,230	data.worldbank.org/indicator/NY.GNP.PCAP.CD

2. CONVERSION AND TRANSFER POLICIES

FOREIGN EXCHANGE

Chile's regulation ensures that capital markets are well developed and open to both foreign portfolio investment and FDI. In May 2000, Chile eliminated the one-year withholding period requirement for foreign capital entering the country under Chapter XIV. This type of investment capital may now be repatriated immediately without penalty.

A second major initiative in 2000 was the discontinuation of the use of the encaje (lock-in), which required foreign investors to deposit 30 percent of foreign-sourced loans and portfolio investment with the Central Bank in a non-interest-bearing account for up two years. However, the Central Bank reserves the right to re-impose the encaje mechanism if needed in the future.

Over a decade ago, the Chilean government delivered important reforms and measures aimed at promoting savings in investment securities, including by exempting capital gains taxes on highly traded stocks of publicly traded companies, lowering taxes for foreign investors on interest payments, and advancing the integration of Chilean capital markets with the international financing market. An important recent step has been the creation and development of the Mercado Integrado Latinoamericano (MILA), an initiative that seeks to connect stock markets of Mexico, Colombia, Peru and Chile.

A second set of reforms enacted in 2005 and 2006 aimed at promoting broader financing alternatives for high growth, emerging companies (small- to medium-sized enterprises, SMEs) and tax incentives for the development of a local risk capital fund management industry. In June 2007, the GOC passed Law 20.190, which introduced tax incentives to promote venture capital. The law improves the availability of financial resources for SMEs and provides tax benefits to public as well as private venture capital funds. Law 20.190 authorizes Chile's Development Promotion Agency (CORFO, www.corfo.cl) to take an equity position of up to 40 percent in specialized venture capital funds. It also allows banks to invest up to the equivalent of one percent of their asset base in venture capital through investment fund administrators and subsidiaries.

A third capital markets reform introduced in 2010 aimed at increasing security levels of financial transactions and reinforcing regulatory and supervision capabilities. This set of reforms enhanced competition in the credit market by increasing available credit instruments and improving consumer information. The reform also increased liquidity, deepened credit markets, improved flexibility for investment funds, created Exchange Traded Funds (ETFs), allowed access to secondary markets, and fostered investment in mutual and investment funds.

Investors, importers, and others are guaranteed access to foreign exchange in the official inter-bank currency market without restriction.

The Central Bank reserves the right to deny access to the inter-bank currency market for royalty payments in excess of five percent of sales. The same restriction applies to payments for the use of patents that exceed five percent of sales. In such cases, firms would have access to the informal market. The Chilean tax service reserves the right to prevent royalties of over five percent of sales from being counted as expenses for domestic tax purposes.

Remittance Policies

Under the Investment Chapter of the U.S.–Chile FTA, the parties must allow transfers of covered investments to be made freely and without delay into and out of its territory. These include transfers of profits, royalties, sales proceeds, and other remittances related to the investment. However, for certain types of short-term capital flows, the chapter allows Chile to impose transfer restrictions for up to 12 months as long as those restrictions do not substantially impede transfers. If restrictions are found to impede transfers substantially, damages accrue from the date of the initiation of the measure.

As a general rule, Chile does not engage in currency manipulation. The IMF classifies Chile's exchange regime as a free-floating exchange rate within an inflation-targeting monetary framework. However, the

Central Bank reserves the right to intervene under exceptional circumstances to correct significant deviations of the currency from its fundamentals.

3. EXPROPRIATION AND COMPENSATION

Chilean law grants the government authority to expropriate property, including property of foreign investors, but only for public or national interests, on a non-discriminatory basis and in accordance with due process of law.

The law requires the payment of compensation without delay at fair market value, in addition to any applicable interest. The government has not nationalized a private firm since 1973.

4. DISPUTE SETTLEMENT

LEGAL SYSTEM, SPECIALIZED COURTS, JUDICIAL INDEPENDENCE, JUDGMENTS OF FOREIGN COURTS

The legal system of Chile is based on civil law. The basis for its public law is the 1980 Constitution which was most recently reformed in 2005. Chile's legal and regulatory framework provides for effective means for enforcing property and contractual rights. Laws governing issues of interest to foreign investors are found in several statutes, including the Commercial Code of 1868, the Civil Code, the Labor Code and the General Banking Act. Chile has specialized courts for dealing with tax and labor issues.

The judicial system in Chile is generally transparent and independent. The likelihood of government intervention in court cases is low. If a state-dependent firm is involved in the dispute, the GOC may become directly involved through the State Defense Council. In cases where courts determine a firm is bankrupt, a receiver is named to distribute the debtor's remaining assets to the creditors.

Judgments of foreign courts and binding international arbitration rulings are generally recognized and enforced by local courts.

BANKRUPTCY

Chile has a new Insolvency and Re-entrepreneurship Law, which entered into force in October 2014, replacing the old Bankruptcy Law. This new law regulates bankruptcy procedures, seeking to avoid the criminalization of bankruptcy.

With the new law, for the first time Chile addresses the issue of trans-border insolvency, establishing as a principle that foreign creditors will hold equal rights to domestic creditors. This provision seeks to facilitate judicial cooperation between Chile and foreign countries.

The World Bank's 2015 Doing Business Report did not capture the effects of the new Insolvency and Re-entrepreneurship Law; Chile's ranking in the report is 70 out of 189 in the category of "resolving insolvency".

INVESTMENT DISPUTES

Disputes involving U.S. investors typically have been settled in negotiations between the investor and the appropriate government entity. Disputes have been referred to the local judicial system although the time required for resolution may make this an unattractive option for foreign investors. Because of the high caseload, understaffing and antiquated case-management procedures, resolution of business disputes in the civil court system can take four to five years. Accordingly, litigants often choose to settle out of court.

Mediation and binding arbitration exist in Chile as alternative dispute resolution mechanisms. A suit may also be brought in court under expedited procedures involving the abrogation of constitutional rights.

The FTA Investment Chapter provides a mechanism for investors to pursue a claim against a host government that is in breach of the FTA's investment obligations, an investment agreement, or an investment authorization. An important exception is that disputes related to investment authorizations under DL600, are not subject to this mechanism. Only agreements that take effect at least two years after the FTA's entry into force may make use of this mechanism. Under this section, the investor pursuing a claim may by right submit a claim under the International Center for Settlement of Investment Disputes (ICSID) Convention or under the United Nations Commission on International Trade Law (UNCITRAL) arbitration rules. Any other mutually agreed upon arbitral institution may also be utilized. Rules agreed upon by the parties will govern the proceedings except to the extent that they are inconsistent with the FTA. An investor must give notice of intent to arbitrate at least 90 days before submitting a claim, and must wait at least six months from the time of the event which gave rise to the claim before initiating a proceeding. All claims must be brought within three years of the date when the claimant acquired knowledge of the breach and/or injury.

The FTA chapter on investments encourages consultations or negotiations before recourse to dispute settlement mechanisms. If the parties fail to resolve the matter, the investor can submit a claim for arbitration. Provisions in Section C of the FTA ensure that the proceedings are transparent by requiring that all documents submitted to or issued by the tribunal be available to the public, and by stipulating that proceedings be public. The tribunal must also accept amicus curiae submissions. The FTA chapter on investments establishes clear and specific terms for making proceedings more efficient and avoiding frivolous claims. Chilean law is generally to be applied to all contracts. However, arbitral tribunals decide disputes in accordance with FTA obligations and applicable international law.

INTERNATIONAL ARBITRATION

Since 1958, Chile has been party to the Convention on the Recognition and Enforcement of Foreign Arbitral Awards (New York Convention). It is also party to (i) the Pan-American Convention on Private International Law (Bustamante Code) since 1934; (ii) the Inter-American Convention on International Commercial Arbitration (Panama Convention) since 1976; and (iii) the Washington Convention on the Settlement of Investment Disputes between States and Nationals of Other States since 1992.

Local courts respect and enforce foreign arbitral awards. Chile has a dual arbitration system in terms of regulation, meaning that different bodies of law govern domestic and international arbitration. International commercial arbitration is governed by the International Commercial Arbitration Act that is modeled on the 1985 UNCITRAL Model Law on International Commercial Arbitration. In addition to this statute, there is also Decree Law Number 2349 that regulates International Contracts for the Public Sector and sets forth a specific legal framework for the State and its entities to submit their disputes to international arbitration. The Judiciary Code and the Code of Civil Procedure govern domestic arbitration.

Under the U.S.-Chile FTA's investment chapter, there have not been any claims that reached beyond the initial consultations stage. No cases where the claimant is from the U.S. and the respondent is Chilean are recorded in the ICSID website.

ICSID Convention and New York Convention

Since 1991, Chile has been a member state to the International Centre for the Settlement of Investment Disputes (ICSID Convention). In 1975 Chile became a signatory to the Convention on the Recognition and Enforcement of Foreign Arbitral Awards (1958 New York Convention).

DURATION OF DISPUTE RESOLUTION

Arbitration and mediation are attractive alternative dispute mechanism for resolving business controversies because litigation can take several years to reach a conclusion. Rule of law and governance are strong within Chile. Generally, judgments and arbitral awards, including international judgments and awards, are recognized and enforced in Chile without issues. However, Chilean courts apply the rules of the International Commercial Arbitration Act, which means that the Supreme Court may refuse to recognize an arbitral award issued abroad if the award has not yet become binding on the parties, or has been set aside or suspended by a court of the country in which, or under the law of which, that award was made.

5. PERFORMANCE REQUIREMENTS AND INVESTMENT INCENTIVES

WTO/TRIMS

Chile does not maintain any measures that are inconsistent with the World Trade Organization agreement on Trade-Related Investment Measures (TRIMS) requirements.

INVESTMENT INCENTIVES

Investment incentives in Chile are in the form of tax credits, tax exemptions, and co-financing of research and development projects and early-stage entrepreneurship, as outlined in the paragraphs below.

Research and Development

Chile does not subsidize foreign investment. There are, however, some incentives linked to isolated geographical zones and to the information technology sector. These benefits relate to co-financing of feasibility studies as well as to incentives for the purchase of land in industrial zones, the hiring of local labor, and the facilitation of project financing. Other important incentives include accelerated depreciation accounting for tax purposes, special tax treatment for retained earnings (which will be derogated in 2017 due to the 2014 tax reform), and legal guarantees for remitting profits and capital.

Chile has other special incentive programs aimed mostly at promoting investment and employment in remote or disadvantaged regions, the development of new businesses, support for micro-, small-, and medium-sized enterprises, and promotion of technological innovation.

Since 2001, the Chilean Economic Development Agency (CORFO) has implemented the "Chile Invests" plan with the goal of fostering FDI in certain sectors outside the Santiago Metropolitan Region in certain sectors. A key objective of the plan is to encourage investment in areas of non-traditional technology such as biotechnology, research and development of new materials, electronics and engineering processes, and new production techniques to increase the value added to natural resource exports. The plan also promotes investment in the energy sector, mainly for non-conventional renewable energy projects. CORFO provides co-financing programs to pre-investment feasibility studies for projects using renewable non-conventional energy resources. See CORFO's website for more information about its investment incentive programs: http://www.english.corfo.cl/programs.

The Arica Law of 2001 grants tax credits to companies in the provinces of Arica and Parinacota. Investment projects amounting to over 2,000 UTM (about USD 148,000) in Arica are eligible for a tax credit of 30 percent of the value of the fixed physical assets (40 percent for tourism projects). Investment projects totaling more than 1,000 UTM (about USD 74,000) in Parinacota are eligible for a tax credit of 40 percent of the value of the fixed physical assets. These incentives are available until December 31, 2030. [Note: The Unidad Tributaria Mensual (UTM) is an inflation-indexed measure of value, adjusted on a monthly basis. On April 9, 2015, 1 UTM was equivalent to about USD 71].

A third investment promotion plan for the province of Tierra del Fuego in Region XII (Magallanes) is available for mining, manufacturing, transport, fishing and tourism companies that produce goods or services made up of at least 25 percent local labor and inputs.

Other investment incentives have been introduced through the "Chile Competes Plan." The Plan includes an exemption from income tax normally paid by institutional investors, such as mutual funds and pension funds, on earnings from the transfer of corporate stock that is publicly traded, or bonds or other publicly offered securities representing debt issued by the Central Bank of Chile, the Chilean Government, or by companies incorporated in Chile.

In January 2011, the Ministry of Economy, through CORFO, established a USD 40 million program called StartUp Chile, whereby selected entrepreneurs receive a USD 40,000 grant and, for foreigners a Chilean work visa, to develop a "startup" business in Chile. Upon admittance into the program, an entrepreneur is given six months to develop a project and then promote it through a series of pitches and seminars at local universities, corporate meetings and other community outreach. In January 2015, the program launched the call for its 12th generation, with 100 new vacancies.

Performance Requirements

Neither Chile's Foreign Investment Committee nor the Central Bank applies performance requirements in its review of proposed investment projects.

The investment chapter in the U.S.–Chile FTA establishes rules prohibiting performance requirements that apply to all investments, whether by a third party or domestic investors. The FTA investment chapter also regulates the use of mandatory performance requirements as a condition for receiving incentives and spells out certain exceptions. These include government procurement, qualifications for export and foreign aid programs, and non-discriminatory health, safety, and environmental requirements.

Data Storage

The Chilean government does not follow "forced localization." Foreign investors are not obliged to use domestic content in goods or technology.

There are no requirements of which Post is aware for foreign IT providers to turn over source code and/or provide access to surveillance.

6. RIGHT TO PRIVATE OWNERSHIP AND ESTABLISHMENT

Except for the limitations in the fisheries and media sectors noted above, Chile does not, in general, restrict the right to private ownership or establishment. Section 24 of Article 19 of the Constitution establishes, however, the "absolute, exclusive, inalienable and permanent domain" of the Chilean state over all mineral, hydrocarbon, and fossil fuel deposits within Chilean territory. Under Chilean law, the government may grant concession rights to individuals and companies for exploration and development of these natural resources for a finite period. There are also national security-related measures regarding the purchase of real estate by foreigners near land borders with Chile's neighbors.

7. PROTECTION OF PROPERTY RIGHTS

Real Property

Secured interests in property, both movable and real, are recognized and generally enforced in Chile. There is a recognized and generally reliable system for recording mortgages and other forms of liens.

Chile ranked 45 out of 183 economies in the World Bank's 2015 Doing Business report for property registration.

INTELLECTUAL PROPERTY RIGHTS

Because of concerns about its commitment to the protection of intellectual property rights (IPR), Chile has been included on the Special 301 Priority Watch List (PWL) since January 8, 2007. The Chilean government has undertaken a number of legislative reforms to strengthen its IPR regime and bring it in line with international commitments, including the U.S.-Chile Free Trade Agreement (FTA). However, there are still substantive deficiencies in Chile's IPR laws and enforcement of existing IPR protections. Of particular concern are inadequate patent and test data protection in the pharmaceutical sector; the lack of an effective system for addressing patent issues expeditiously in connection with applications to market pharmaceutical products; circumvention of technological protection measures; piracy of music and software, particularly over the internet; Chile's failure to protect encrypted program-carrying satellite signals, including its failure to address the sale of pirate satellite decoder boxes; and inadequate protection for plant varieties. The 2014 Special 301 Report on IPR is available on the USTR website at http://www.ustr.gov/about-us/press-office/reports-and-publications/2014.

Chile has been a member of the World Intellectual Property Organization (WIPO) since 1975 and joined the Treaties on Copyright and Performances and Phonograms in April 2001. Chile approved legislation to comply with TRIPS obligations related to industrial property in December 2004. The law provides, among other protections, for expedited court proceedings and the authority to seize illegal copies of patented products. In 2008, Chile ratified the Patent Cooperation Treaty (PCT), which came into force in June 2009.

The U.S. and Chile have committed to making a system available for the resolution of disputes regarding internet domain names. This follows international standards with respect to problems such as the cyber piracy of brands and trademarks for country domain names. Furthermore, both countries committed to creating a database containing information on individuals who have registered higher-level domain names. This database will protect the personal data of those who have registered.

It is generally easy for investors to register intellectual property – including copyrights, trademarks, patents and trade secrets.

For additional information about treaty obligations and points of contact at local IP offices, please see Chile's WIPO country profile at: http://www.wipo.int/directory/en/details.jsp?country_code=CL

Useful information on IP issues in Chile can also be found from the American Chamber of Commerce in Chile, http://www.amchamchile.cl/node/110125.

Resources for Rights Holders

Inquiries regarding intellectual property issues in Chile can be addressed to:
Ted Alexander Bryan
Economic Officer
U.S. Embassy, Santiago
(56)-(2)-2330-3397

BryanAT@state.gov
Contact information for country-specific resources:
Roberto Matus
General Manager
AmCham Chile

(56)-(2)-2290-9760
roberto.matus@amchamchile.cl

8. TRANSPARENCY OF THE REGULATORY SYSTEM

Chilean regulatory systems tend to be transparent, and government regulators generally have little discretion in carrying out their duties. Rulemaking processes do not generally include formal provisions for public hearing or comment. The World Bank's "Doing Business 2015" report ranks Chile 41st of 189 economies (after ranking 39th in 2014) for ease of starting a business. The U.S.–Chile FTA establishes some additional obligations for transparency in regulatory processes.

9. EFFICIENT CAPITAL MARKETS AND PORTFOLIO INVESTMENT

Chile's capital markets are well-developed and open to foreign portfolio investors. Credit is allocated on market terms and is available to foreigners, although the Central Bank does reserve the right to restrict foreign investors' access to internal credit if a credit shortage exists. To date, this authority has not been exercised.

Publicly traded Chilean companies attract substantial international investment.

Under the U.S.-Chile FTA, U.S. insurance firms have full rights to establish subsidiaries or joint ventures for all insurance sectors, with limited exceptions. In 2001, the First Capital Market Reform phased in insurance branching rights and modified Chile's legislation to open cross-border supply of key insurance sectors such as marine, aviation, and transport insurance, and insurance brokerage of reinsurance. The objective was to remove unnecessary restrictions affecting the deepening of the capital market and competition in the insurance market.

U.S. banks and securities firms are allowed to establish branches and subsidiaries and may invest in local firms without restriction, except under very limited circumstances. U.S. financial institutions are also able to offer financial services to citizens participating in Chile's privatized voluntary saving plans, and they have gained increased market access to Chile's mandatory social security system. U.S.-based firms are allowed to offer services in Chile in areas such as financial information, data processing, and financial advisory services, with limited exceptions. Under the measures outlined in "Capital Market Reform III," Chilean mutual funds are permitted to use foreign-based portfolio managers.

In May 2011, the stock markets of Chile, Peru and Colombia merged to become the second largest trading market in Latin America after Brazil. This market alliance, known as the Integrated Latin American Market (MILA), hopes to better expose investors to assets linked to the region's natural resources. Chile's IPSA Index is a total return index and is composed of 40 highly traded stocks. The IPSA has been calculated since 1977 and is revised on a quarterly basis.

The main institutional investors and suppliers of capital to local companies are the pension fund administrators (AFP) as well as insurance companies, mutual funds and banks. Institutional investors hold more than half of the instruments issued in the fixed-income market.

Pension funds are the largest institutional investors followed by insurance companies. As of March 2015, Chile's six AFPs managed a total investment portfolio of USD 170.6 billion, representing about 68 percent of Chile's GDP. The pension funds administered by the AFPs belong to 9.6 million participants, of which 5 million are contributors. The total resources under AFP administration were distributed in five different types of funds of varying degrees of risk.

The GOC has been raising the percentage of pension funds that can be invested overseas. In 2008, Congress approved a reform package for the pension system increasing the threshold for pension fund administrators to invest abroad (from 30 to 60 percent of their funds). In 2014, AFPs invested 44 percent of their resources abroad. The reform package also set the foundation on which to build a "solidarity pillar" to increase coverage among lower-income contributors and self-employed workers and expand social security assistance coverage.

In 2012, insurance companies (including reinsurance companies) in Chile managed nearly USD 50 billion in assets, representing 18 percent of GDP. Insurance companies invest a major share of their portfolio in fixed-income securities. Nine percent of their portfolio is invested abroad.

MONEY AND BANKING SYSTEM, HOSTILE TAKEOVERS

The Chilean banking system is sound, competitive, and meets Basel standards. There are currently 24 banks operating in Chile, and four are foreign-owned representational branches. Only one bank is completely owned by Chilean private economic interests (BCI). The rest have some level of incorporation with foreign institutions. Foreign banks can compete on the same terms as their domestic rivals. There are also seven local savings and loan corporations, and one state-owned bank, Banco Estado, which is the nation's third largest. Private banks manage most corporate business.

The Chilean banking industry is subject to strict limits on lending to a single debtor or group of related companies. This is capped at five percent of the capital and reserves of a bank for collateral-free loans and at 25 percent for collateralized loans (fixed assets).

Summary of Chilean Banking System (February 2015):

Total Loans – USD 209 billion

Deposits – USD 169.1 billion

Total Assets – USD 294.9 billion

Source: Chile's Superintendence of Banks and Financial Institutions

General Information on the Financial Market

Banks and Financial Institutions: 24 participants. Total Loans: USD 209.0 billion

Pension Funds: 6 administrators (3 firms of which are US owned). Funds under management: USD 170.6 billion

Insurance Companies: 60 (28 general insurers, 32 life insurers).

According to the World Economic Forum's Global Competitiveness Report for 2014-2015, Chile is the most competitive country of South America and the fourth most competitive of the Americas after the U.S., Canada, and Puerto Rico. Chile is ranked 33rd in the world.

10. COMPETITION FROM STATE-OWNED ENTERPRISES

Chile has relatively few state-owned enterprises (SOEs), most having been privatized during the military government's economic reforms between 1974 and 1989. Notable SOEs are the national copper company, CODELCO; the national petroleum company, ENAP; the National Postal System (Correos de Chile); and the state-owned bank, Banco Estado.

In general, private enterprise is allowed to compete with public enterprise under the same terms and conditions (e.g., there are many private copper mines and private banks). However, there are specific areas where this does not hold and SOEs enjoy special advantages. For example, ENAP is the only refining company in Chile. SOEs spend a similar portion of their budget on research and development to the portion spent by private sector domestic and foreign companies in the same sector.

Most SOEs in Chile are structured so that the company management reports to a board of directors, which includes the relevant government minister (e.g., the Minister of Mining sits on ENAP's board of directors). Most board members are independent representatives from the private sector and academia, or from that industry's main labor union or trade association. The President of Chile usually designates board members.

Chile passed a law in October 2009 modifying CODELCO's corporate governing structure to its current form. The law removed the Ministers of Finance and Mining and a representative of the military from the board of directors. It also expands the board to nine members, three of whom are designated by the President of Chile, two of whom are nominated by CODELCO's labor unions and approved by the President of Chile, and four of whom are elected by the Consejo de Alta Dirección Pública (Chile's independent committee that makes high-level civil service appointments) and subsequently approved by the President of Chile.

SOEs are subject to the same taxes and the same value added tax rebate policies as their private sector competitors.

OECD Guidelines on Corporate Governance of SOEs

According to the World Bank's 2014 publication, Corporate Governance of State-Owned Enterprises in Latin America: Current Trends and Country Cases, Chile has taken major steps to improve corporate governance of its state-owned enterprises (SOEs). In 2001, the Sistema de Empresas Públicas (SEP) was created. The SEP is a technical advisory body, with authority to centrally oversee management of the SOEs. A nine-member governing council, whose members are nominated by the President, the Ministers of Finance and Economy and the CEO of CORFO, oversees the SEP. Among the 33 SOEs linked to the central government, the SEP exerts ownership representation and responsibilities regarding the control and supervision of 23 of them. The SEP's main functions include nominating and appointing SOEs' directors, approving strategic plans, establishing annual goals and controlling the management of the SOEs under its supervision. However, the largest Chilean SOEs (including CODELCO, ENAP and Banco del Estado de Chile) are not under SEP control and supervision, but operate in a decentralized and autonomous way. Many of these companies have a regulatory framework specifically developed for their operations and approved by special laws, and they are linked to the government through the sector ministries of their line of competency.

The World Bank's report is available at:
http://documents.worldbank.org/curated/en/2014/07/20183864/corporate-governance-state-owned-enterprises-latin-america-current-trends-country-cases

As an OECD member, Chile adheres to the OECD Guidelines on Corporate Governance for SOEs. According to the World Bank's 2014 publication mentioned above, Chile has made significant progress in the harmonization of standards across SOEs in the areas of information disclosure, accounting provisions, and auditing. Each SOE submits an annual report and has the obligation to publish quarterly management reports. All SOEs are required to have internal auditors and are subject to an annual external audit by independent auditing firms. All SOEs are headed by a board of directors and there is a clear definition and division of the roles played by the SOE Board and the CEO.

Allocation of seats on the boards of Chilean SOEs is determined by the SEP, as described above, or outlined by the laws that regulate them. As CODELCO's corporate governance shows (see previous section), there is a mix between seats appointed by recommendation from an independent high-level civil service committee, and seats allocated by political authorities in the government.

Court processes regarding SOEs involved in investment disputes are transparent and non-discriminatory.

SOVEREIGN WEALTH FUNDS

Chile has two sovereign wealth funds constituted principally from state copper revenues. The Economic and Social Stabilization Fund (FEES) was established in 2007 and was valued at USD 14.7 billion in February 2015. The FEES seeks to fund public debt payments and temporary fiscal deficits, in order to keep a countercyclical fiscal policy. The Reserve Pension Fund was established in 2006 and was valued at USD 7.9 billion as of February 2015. The stated purpose of this fund is to anticipate future needs from the Government in order to make payments to those eligible to receive pensions but whose contributions to the private pension system are not enough to reach a minimum guaranteed by the State. A third sovereign wealth fund, called the Bicentennial Fund, encourages Chileans to study abroad through the use of government-funded scholarships.

The Chilean Central Bank, at the direction of the Ministry of Finance, administers the sovereign wealth fund. The Ministry of Finance receives advice on policy related to the funds from an external Finance Committee made up of independent advisors. The Ministry of Finance publishes monthly, quarterly, and yearly reports on the funds.

11. CORPORATE SOCIAL RESPONSIBILITY

The government encourages foreign and local enterprises to follow generally accepted CSR principles, including the OECD Guidelines for Multinational Enterprises and the United Nations Guiding Principles on Business and Human Rights.

There is general awareness of corporate social responsibility among both producers and consumers in Chile. As part of the OECD accession process, Chile passed a law in September 2009 setting out new rules to help bolster corporate social responsibility. Chile maintains and enforces domestic laws concerning labor and employment rights, consumer protections and environmental protections. Labor and environmental laws are not waived in order to attract or retain investments.

Independent NGOs in Chile promote and monitor CSR. Examples include NGO Acci6n RSE (http://www.accionrse.cl) and the Catholic University of Valparaiso's Center for Corporate Social Responsibility.

OECD GUIDELINES FOR MULTINATIONAL ENTERPRISES

The Chilean government encourages foreign and local enterprises to follow generally accepted CSR principles. As an OECD member country, Chile adheres to the OECD Guidelines for Multinational Enterprises. The GOC set up a contact point, which is the head of the OECD Department at the Trade Directorate (Direcon).

Chile also endorses the United Nations Guiding Principles on Business and Human Rights. According to the Chilean government delegation at the third annual U.N. Forum on Business and Human Rights held in Geneva in December 2014, a national plan is being developed to assess the current situation and identify gaps and good practices.

12. POLITICAL VIOLENCE

The incidence of terrorist activity and civil disturbance is generally low in Chile, and the violence that has occurred has had little impact on the Chilean economy. While crime rates are slowly increasing throughout the country, the vast majority of crimes are nonviolent. During the last 10 years there have been relatively few incidents of politically motivated attacks on investment projects or installations. In 2014, there were occasional incidents of vandalism of storefronts and public transport during student protests over education reform, some of which included violent incidents. Incidents of anti-American sentiment and civil disorder are rare, and there have been no attacks known to be attributable to international terrorist organizations.

Since 2007, Chile has experienced approximately 220 small-scale bombings. Anarchist groups have claimed credit for some of the incidents. Beginning in May 2014, anarchist groups expanded their targets to include mass transportation and public places including, on two occasions, the Santiago metro train system during normal operating hours. A bombing on September 8, 2014 in the commercial area above a metro stop injured 14 people and was recognized immediately by the government not only as a terrorist attack but also as a wakeup call demanding forceful action. Arrests were made.

There have also been violent incidents on farms and forestry plantations in south-central Chile, resulting in one death, damage to property, and other related injuries in 2014. Many of these incidents are related to the land claims and other grievances of indigenous people (the indigenous Mapuche group) in regions VIII (Bio-Bio) and IX (Araucania).

13. CORRUPTION

Corruption in Chile is limited. Since 2003, Chile has had laws in place that establish a more efficient and professional civil service through performance-based incentives and a reduction in political appointee positions in public service positions. In 2005, the GOC passed a law to regulate political party and candidate financing to further deter corrupt government practices.

Chile has signed and ratified the Organization of American States (OAS) Convention against Corruption, as well as the UN Anticorruption Convention. Chile is also a signatory to the OECD Convention on Combating Bribery, fulfilling the necessary accession processes, including implementation of its Anti-Bribery Convention obligations. Chile is an active member of the Open Government Partnership (OGP).

In 2007, a new law came into force that provides protection for public employees who denounce irregularities or violations in accountability standards and at the same time, Chile ratified the United Nations Convention against Corruption. In 2009, Chile passed a transparency law obligating government offices to public information about expenditures, employee salaries, and other fiscal data. It also mandates that citizens be provided up-to-date information on how to access government services and request information. The law created an autonomous Transparency Council which is charged with implementing the requirements of the law. The administration of President Piñera (2010-2014) launched a campaign to educate citizens about their right to access public information and created Chile Atiende, an online and in-person platform to streamline access to common government services.

As noted previously, Chile ranked 21nd out of 175 countries in Transparency International's 2014 Corruption Perceptions Index (with 1 being the lowest perception of corruption).

A series of corruption scandals involving a mining firm, a major conglomerate, and a relative of President Bachelet caused great concern in late 2014 and early 2015. As of the publication date of this report, investigation and prosecution of these cases remained ongoing. Authorities have arrested and pursued criminal and civil charges against those implicated where deemed appropriate.

U.S. firms have not identified corruption as an obstacle to FDI.

UN Anticorruption Convention, OECD Convention on Combatting Bribery

Chile has signed and ratified both the UN Anticorruption Convention and OECD Convention on Combatting Bribery.

Resources to Report Corruption

Contact at non-profit organization to report corruption:
Alberto Precht
Executive Director
Chile Transparente (Chile branch of Transparency International)
Avenida Rancagua 535
7501089 Providencia
Santiago, Chile
(+56)-(2)-274-3627
chiletransparente@chiletransparente.

14. BILATERAL INVESTMENT AGREEMENTS

The United States-Chile Free Trade Agreement (FTA) entered into force on January l, 2004. The chapter on investment is modeled on the standards found in agreements throughout the world such as U.S. bilateral investment treaties and customary international law. The main objective of the FTA chapter is to provide stability and security to investors. It provides six basic forms of protection:

Non-discriminatory treatment, based on national treatment and most-favored-nation treatment, for investors from either country;

Freedom from performance requirements;

Free transfer of investment funds;

Expropriation only when consistent with international law;

A minimum standard of treatment in customary international law; and

The ability to hire key managerial and technical personnel without regard to nationality.

In 1991, Chile became a signatory of the Washington Convention of 1965, which created the International Center for Settlement of Investment Disputes (ICSID). Since then, Chile has negotiated numerous Bilateral Investment Treaties (BITs) through which Chile provides additional protection to foreign investment flows. According to information provided by the Government of Chile to ICSID, as of the end of 2014, Chile had signed 55 BITs, of which 41 are in force. There are agreements in force with Argentina, Australia, Austria, Belgium and Luxembourg, Bolivia, China, Costa Rica, Croatia, Cuba, Czech Republic, Denmark, Ecuador, El Salvador, Finland, France, Germany, Greece, Guatemala, Honduras, Iceland, Italy, Malaysia, Nicaragua, Norway, Panama, Paraguay, Peru, Philippines, Poland (2 treaties), Portugal, Romania, Spain, Sweden, Switzerland (1999 treaty), Ukraine, the United Kingdom, Uruguay (2 treaties), and Venezuela. BITs signed but not in force include those with Brazil, Colombia, Dominican Republic, Egypt, Hungary, Indonesia, Lebanon, Netherlands, New Zealand, South Africa, Switzerland (1991 treaty), Tunisia, Turkey and Vietnam.

BILATERAL TAXATION TREATIES

Chile has double taxation treaties in force with: Australia, Belgium, Brazil, Canada, Colombia, Croatia, Denmark, Ecuador, France, Ireland, Malaysia, Mexico, New Zealand, Norway, Paraguay, Peru, Poland, Portugal, Russia, South Korea, Spain, Sweden, Switzerland, Thailand and the United Kingdom.

Chile and the United States have signed the U.S.-Chile Treaty to Avoid Double Taxation, which addresses certain tax-related obligations for U.S. companies operating in Chile. In May 2012 President Obama submitted the treaty to the U.S. Senate for ratification. In March 2014, the Government of Chile submitted the treaty to the Chilean Congress for ratification; at the time of publication of this report, the Chilean Lower Chamber of the Congress (the Chamber of Deputies) had ratified the treaty and submitted to the Senate for its approval, which remains pending. The U.S. Senate has not yet ratified the treaty. Other double taxation treaties signed by Chile but not in force include those with Austria and South Africa.

15. OPIC AND OTHER INVESTMENT INSURANCE PROGRAMS

A Bilateral Investment Agreement between Chile and the United States, through the Overseas Private Investment Corporation (OPIC), took effect in 1984. Chile is a party to the convention of the World Bank's Multilateral Investment Guarantee Agency (MIGA).

16. LABOR

Unemployment in Chile stood at 6.3 percent on average during 2014. The labor participation rate was 60 percent as of December 2014. The size of the total workforce increased by 1.1 percent in December 2014 as compared to the same period in 2013.

Chile has and generally enforces laws and regulations related to these internationally recognized labor rights: freedom of association and collective bargaining; the elimination of forced labor; child labor, including the minimum age for work; discrimination in respect to employment and occupation; and acceptable conditions of work related to minimum wage, occupational safety and health, and hours of work.

Chile has enjoyed generally calm labor relations over the last decade, but strikes do occur. Strikes and public protests have been concentrated in the mining, health, education, transportation, and civil service sectors. Over the past several years, some strikes in Chilean ports have occurred during the summer season, when most of the country's fruits exports are shipped abroad. Arbitration and mediation mechanisms exist to resolve labor-related disputes. Strikes are prohibited in certain essential services sectors prescribed by law. A new labor reform, submitted to Congress in December 2014, is currently under review and will likely be debated by the Chilean congress in the 2015 legislative year.

Union membership is voluntary. According to the GOC's Labor Directorate, 14.2 percent of Chile's workforce belonged to a trade union in 2013. Multiple unions exist in many companies, and management can negotiate collective agreements with any of the unions or with ad hoc groups of workers. Unions can form confederations or nationwide labor centrals and can affiliate with international labor federations. Contracts are normally negotiated at the company level. Multi-company bargaining is permitted on a voluntary basis. Law establishes all overtime, paid annual vacations, and holidays. Women are entitled to state-funded maternity leave for a period of six weeks before and six months after childbirth. Layoffs are not permitted between conception and one year after the female employee has returned from maternity leave. The labor reform mentioned above proposes to strengthen unions' entitlement to engage exclusively in the collective bargaining process.

Top executive salaries are on a par with European countries, although well below those in the United States. Chile allows companies to deduct set training costs (up to one percent of annual payroll) from corporate tax payments. A company can also use 10 percent of the rebate to finance an analysis of its training needs, and 15 percent to run a training department.

The maximum number of labor hours allowed per week in Chile is 45.

Subject to certain exceptions, Chilean nationals must comprise no less than 85 percent of the workforce of companies employing more than 25 persons.

A 2007 subcontracting law defines outsourcing as two different activities: subcontracting and the supply of outside labor. Subcontracting is when a company permanently outsources a specific process to another firm which takes full responsibility for it, carrying it out with its own employees. However, the law does not permit companies to outsource their main economic activity. Retention of outside labor falls within the ambit of subcontracting under the law only where it is temporary in nature, defined as stints of up to 90 (or in some cases 180) days during an emergency. Additionally, only firms that register as suppliers of temporary labor and set up guarantees against their obligations to their own workers are allowed to fulfill this function. The law also sets limits on the number of staff that can be used on short-term jobs.

17. FOREIGN TRADE ZONES/FREE PORTS/TRADE FACILITATION

Chile has two tax-free zones: one in the northern port city of Iquique (Region I) and the other in the southern city of Punta Arenas (Region XII). Merchants and manufacturers in these zones are exempt from corporate income tax, value added taxes (VAT), and customs duties. Businesses can re-export goods without paying taxes but must pay VAT (19 percent) and import duties when goods leave the zone to be used or sold in other regions of Chile. The same exemptions also apply to manufacturers in the Chacalluta and Las Americas Industrial Park in Arica (in the XV Arica and Parinacota Region). Mining, fishing and financial services are not eligible for free zone concessions. Management companies and firms established in the free zone are exempt from payment of tariffs, VAT, other charges on imports, first category income tax under the Income Tax Law, and payment of VAT on goods and services for all their operations in the free zone.

Foreign-owned firms have the same investment opportunities in these zones as Chilean firms.

18. FOREIGN DIRECT INVESTMENT AND FOREIGN PORTFOLIO INVESTMENT STATISTICS

Table 2: Key Macroeconomic Data, U.S. FDI in Host Country/Economy

		Host Country Statistical source*	USG or international statistical source		USG or International Source of Data: BEA; IMF; Eurostat; UNCTAD, Other
Economic Data	Year	Amount	Year	Amount	

Host Country Gross Domestic Product (GDP) ($B USD)	2013	273.6	2012	277.2	www.worldbank.org/en/country
Foreign Direct Investment		Host Country Statistical source*	USG or international statistical source		USG or international Source of data: BEA; IMF; Eurostat; UNCTAD, Other
U.S. FDI in partner country ($M USD, stock positions)	2013	3,42 0	2013	41,110	http://bea.gov/international/factsheet/factsheet.cfm?Area=203
Host country's FDI in the United States ($M USD, stock positions)	N/A		2012	487	http://bea.gov/international/factsheet/factsheet.cfm?Area=203
Total inbound stock of FDI as % host GDP	2013	7.4 %	2013	7.3 %	

*Chilean Central Bank economic statistics are available online in Spanish only: http://www.bcentral.cl/estadisticas-economicas/

Table 3: Sources and Destination of FDI

Direct Investment from/in Counterpart Economy Data					
From Top Five Sources/To Top Five Destinations (US Dollars, Millions)					
Inward Direct Investment			Outward Direct Investment		
Total Inward	199,251	100%	Total Outward	85,732	100%
United States	26,461	13%	Brazil	12,303	14%
Netherlands	19,473	10%	Argentina	6,952	8%
Spain	16,963	9%	Peru	6,314	7%
Canada	11,674	6%	Colombia	5,899	7%
Bermuda	9,423	5%	Spain	4,137	5%
"0" reflects amounts rounded to +/- USD 500,000.					

Source: IMF Coordinated Direct Investment Survey

Table 4: Sources of Portfolio Investment

According to the FIC, between 2009 and 2013, the mining sector attracted 44.9 percent of implemented FDI under DL600, followed by services (17.6 percent); electricity, gas and water (10.2 percent); manufacturing (4.7 percent); transportation and communications (3.4 percent); commerce (1.2 percent); construction (1.0 percent); and agriculture and fishing (0.2 percent). Total implemented FDI through DL600 from 2009-2013 amounted to USD 100.8 billion.

According to its Central Bank, Chile recorded USD 20.3 billion in FDI in 2013, representing a 29 percent decrease from 2012. The top five recipient sectors of FDI in 2013 were: electricity, gas and water (USD 4.9 billion); financial services (USD 3.2 billion); mining (USD 2.3 billion); other services (USD 1.2 billion); and communications (USD 877 million).

Portfolio Investment Assets								
Top Five Partners (Millions, US Dollars)								
Total			Equity Securities			Total Debt Securities		
All Countries	136,764	100%	All Countries	103,036	100%	All Countries	33,729	100%
United States	59,563	44%	Luxembourg	42,695	41%	United States	17,012	50%
Luxembourg	42,782	31%	United States	42,551	41%	Germany	3,626	11%
Germany	4,990	4%	United Kingdom	3,524	3%	Japan	3,227	10%
United Kingdom	4,650	3%	Germany	1,364	1%	Brazil	1,264	4%
Japan	3,435	3%	US Virgin Islands	1,007	1	Switzerland	1,257	4%

Source: IMF Coordinated Portfolio Investment Survey

IMPORTANT CONTACTS

ATTORNEYS PRACTICING IN CHILE

The U.S. Embassy in Santiago, Chile, assumes no responsibility or liability for the professional ability or reputation of, or the quality of services provided by, the following persons or firms. Inclusion on this list is in no way an endorsement by the Department of State or U.S. Embassy in Santiago, Chile. Names are listed alphabetically, and the order in which they appear has no other significance. The information in the list on professional credentials, areas of expertise and language ability are provided directly by the lawyers. You may receive additional information about the individuals by contacting the local bar association (or its equivalent) or the local licensing authorities.

Individuals who cannot afford legal assistance will find Pro-Bono legal assistance services on the last page of this list.

Albagli Zaliasnik
Address: Miraflores 130, 25th floor, Santiago.
Telephone: 56-2-2-4456000.
Website: http://www.english.az.cl/
Fields of law: corporate, tax, litigation, intellectual and industrial property.

Alessandri Abogados
Address: El Regidor 66, 10th floor, Las Condes, Santiago.
Telephone: 56-2-2-7876062.
Website: http://www.alessandrilaw.com/

Fields of law: corporate, intellectual property, mergers and acquisitions, dispute resolution and arbitration, capital markets, tax, labor law, insurance, foreign investment and international business transaction, natural resources and environment.

Barros y Errázuriz
Address: Isidora Goyenechea 2939, 10th Floor, Las Condes, Santiago.
Telephone: 56-2-2-3788900.
Website: http://www.bye.cl/en/
Email: contacto@bye.cl
Fields of law: Antitrust, capital markets, corporate, dispute resolution, energy, environment, financing, foreign investment, real estate, tax, labor, insurance, telecommunications.

Bofill Mir & Alvarez Jana
Address: Andres Bello 2711, 8th and 9th floor, Torre Costanera, Las Condes, Santiago
Telephone: 56-2-2-7577600
Website: http://www.bmaj.cl/eng/
Fields of law: Administrative law, environmental, regulated markets, antitrust, banking, bankruptcy, civil and commercial litigation, international arbitration, energy, corporate, labor, mergers and acquisitions, mining, tax, telecommunications.

Carey
Address: Isidora Goyenechea 2800, 43rd Floor, Las Condes, Santiago.
Telephone: 56-2-2-9282200.
Website: http://www.carey.cl/en/
Email: carey@carey.cl
Fields of law: Antitrust and regulated markets, aviation and maritime law, banking and financial, capital markets, construction, criminal law, energy, environmental law, litigation and arbitration, intellectual property, tax, public law, labor and employment law, immigration, hospitality and gaming, insolvency, bankruptcy and restructuring.

Cariola Diez Pérez-Cotapos
Address: Andres Bello 2711, 19th floor, Las Condes, Santiago.
Telephone: 56-2-2-3604000.
Website: http://www.cariola.cl/
Fields of law: business organization, foreign investment, competition law, taxation, labor and social security system, environmental regulations, intellectual property, visas.

Claro & Cia
Address: Apoquindo 3721, 14th floor, Las Condes, Santiago.
Telephone: 56-2-2-3673000
Website: http://www.claro.cl/en/index.html

Email: claro@claro.cl
Fields of law: Administrative, antitrust, banking, bankruptcy, business organizations, constitutional, criminal law, data protection, economic regulation, energy and natural resources, real estate, insurance, intellectual property, international trade, labor and employment, litigation and arbitration, mining, project finance, tax, telecommunications.

CMC Abogados y Consultores
Address: Avenida Kennedy 5600, 5th floor, Vitacura, Santiago.
Telephone: 56-2-2-3790152.
Website: http://www.cmcabogados.cl/eng/index.html
Email: contacto@cmcabogados.cl
Fields of law: Litigation and criminal defense, extraditions, internal investigations, immigration.

Fernandois & Cia
Address: Nueva Tajamar 481, Torre Norte, suite 708, Santiago.
Telephone: 56-2-2-2036311.
Website: http://www.fermandois.cl/english-site/home.html
Email: abogados@fermandois.cl
Fields of law: Administrative and constitutional litigation, economic regulatory law, corporate and international business law, criminal and labor law.

Grasty Quintana Majlis &Cia
Address: Magdalena 140, 20th floor, Las Condes, Santiago.
Telephone: 56-2-2-4990460.
Website: http://gqmc.cl/en/
Email: gqmc@grasty.cl
Fields of law: Corporate, labor, natural resources, litigation.

Guerrero Olivos
Address: Vitacura 2939, 8th floor, Las Condes, Santiago.
Telephone: 56-2-2-6742900
Website: http://www.guerrero.cl/prontus_guerrero/site/edic/base/port/inicio.html
Email: abogados@guerrero.cl
Fields of law: Banking and finance, project finance, capital markets, insurance, water law, foreign investment, constitutional law, administrative law, tax law, franchising, litigation, arbitration and dispute resolution, telecommunications, energy and natural resources, mining, environmental law, antitrust, intellectual property, sanitary law.

Gutiérrez Waugh Jimeno Asenjo
Address: Isidora Goyenechea 3477, 23rd floor, Santiago.
Telephone: 56-2-2-3792000
Website: http://www.gutierrezabogados.cl/index.php/en/
Email: recepcion@gutierrezabogados.cl
Fields of law: National and international arbitration, lawsuits, capital markets, antitrust, administrative law, banking, bankruptcy.

Horvitz & Horvitz
Address: Huerfanos 770, suite 2303, Santiago.
Telephone: 56-2-2-6380485.
Website: http://www.horvitz.cl/en/index.htm\
Fields of law: Family law, civil, criminal.

Morales y Besa
Address: Isidora Goyenechea 3477, 19th floor, Las Condes, Santiago.
Telephone: 56-2-2-4727000.
Website: http://www.moralesybesa.cl/eng/
Fields of law: Mergers and acquisitions, banking, capital markets, antitrust, litigation and arbitration, intellectual property, real estate and construction, energy and natural resources, environmental.

Palma Abogados
Address: Isidora Goyenechea 3162, 7th floor, Las Condes, Santiago, Chile.
Telephone: 56-2-2-3676500.
Website: http://www.palma.cl/english-site/index.html
Fields of law: Arbitration, labor law, litigation.

Tapia Elorza & Cia
Address: Colo Colo 379, Suite 604, Concepci6n.
Telephone: 56-41-2-851724.
Website: http://www.tapiaelorza.cl/
Email: etapia@tapiaelorza.cl
Fields of law: Insurance, banking, commercial, labor, civil. Damages.
Verónica Waissbluth Weinstein
Address: Benjamin 2935, Suite 601, Las Condes, Santiago.
Telephone: 56-2-2-3345693
Website: http://wmaabogados.cl/index.html
Email: vwaissbluth@wmaabogados.cl
Fields of law: Family law

PRO BONO SERVICES

Fundación Pro Bono
Address: Calle la Concepcion 226, Providencia, Santiago.
Telephone: 56-2-2-3815660.
Website: http://www.probono.cl/english-version/
Email: probono@probono.cl

Corporación de Asistencia Judicial
Address: Agustinas 1419, Santiago
Telephone: 56-2-29371000
Website: http://www.cajmetro.cl/

Fundación de Asistencia Social y Legal de la Familia
Address: San Martin 543, Santiago.
Telephone: 56-2-2-6980603.
Website: http://www.funlegalfamilia.cl/

COLOMBIA INVESTMENT AND BUSINESS CLIMATE - STRATEGIC INFORMATION AND CONTACTS FOR STARTING BUSINESS IN COLOMBIA

CONTACT FOR MORE INFORMATION

U.S. Embassy Bogota
Economic Section
Carrera 45 #22B-45
Bogota, Colombia
(571) 275-2000
BogotaECONShared@state.gov

With increased security, a market of 47 million people, an abundance of natural resources, and an educated and growing middle-class, Colombia is an increasingly enticing destination for foreign investment. The Colombian government has taken significant steps to open the country up to global trade and investment. In 2013, Colombia had the fourth largest GDP in Latin America after Brazil, Mexico, and Argentina, and has sustained an average growth rate over four percent for the past decade and a GDP growth rate of 4.6 percent in 2014. The World Bank's 2015 Ease of Doing Business Report ranked Colombia 34 out of 189 and in first place within Latin America. Colombia was recognized for implementing a number of reforms that have improved the investment climate, including regulatory reforms and securing access to credit. At the same time, the report criticized the high corporate tax burden, as well as the frequently shifting and highly complicated tax framework.

Colombia's legal and regulatory systems are for the most part transparent and consistent with international norms. Colombia has a comprehensive legal framework for business and foreign direct investment (FDI), and the U.S.-Colombia Trade Promotion Agreement (CTPA) that took effect on May 15, 2012, has strengthened trade and investment between our countries. Through the CTPA and several international conventions and treaties, Colombia's dispute settlement mechanisms and intellectual property rights protection are stronger than ever. Nevertheless, piracy and counterfeit products continue to be a major problem, which is the reason why Colombia remains on the U.S. Trade Representative's Special 301Watch List.

The Colombian government has demonstrated great political will to develop efficient capital markets, attract investment, and create jobs. Sound fiscal and macroeconomic management has allowed Colombia to claim the triple crown of seeing its credit ratings increased to 'Investment Grade' level by Standard and Poor's, Moody's, and Fitch Ratings. Market capitalization as of December 2013 was USD 215 billion. Although restrictions to foreign ownership in specific sectors still exist, Colombia received a record USD 16.8 billion in FDI in 2013 but there could be a drop off in 2014 to USD15.8 billion. Colombia has aggressively pursued foreign investment in key sectors, such as infrastructure. Colombia's average annual unemployment rate continued to decrease in 2014 to 9.1 percent. Forty-nine percent of the workforce still works in the informal economy, but Colombia has abundant unskilled and semi-skilled labor throughout the country as well as managerial-level employees who are often bilingual.

In recent years, security in Colombia has improved significantly, with the percentage of kidnappings down by 86 percent since 2003, and the number of homicides falling by 35 percent within the same period. Since November 2012, the Colombian government and the Revolutionary Armed Forces of Colombia (FARC) have been conducting peace negotiations in Havana, Cuba. Even so, an active domestic insurgency is still ongoing, posing a threat to commercial activity and investment, especially in rural zones where government control is weaker. Corruption is also a significant challenge in Colombia. According to the World Economic Forum's Global Competitiveness Index (2013-2014), corruption is the biggest challenge for doing business in Colombia. The Colombian government continues to work on improving its business climate.

The three largest majority state-owned enterprises, Ecopetrol, ISA, and ISAGEN, are considered models of professional management, competition, and excellent corporate governance. Through its numerous investment treaties, free trade agreements, and progress towards accession into the Organization for

Economic Cooperation and Development (OECD), Colombia has shown it is eager to increase international trade and investment.

1. OPENNESS TO, AND RESTRICTIONS UPON, FOREIGN INVESTMENT

ATTITUDE TOWARD FOREIGN DIRECT INVESTMENT

The Colombian government actively encourages foreign direct investment (FDI). In the early 1990s, the country began economic liberalization reforms, which provided for national treatment of foreign investors, lifted controls on remittance of profits and capital, and allowed foreign investment in most sectors. Generally, foreign investors may participate in privatization of state-owned enterprises without restrictions. Colombia imposes the same investment restrictions on foreign investors that it does on national investors. All FDI involving the establishment of a commercial presence in Colombia requires registration with the Superintendence of Corporations ('Superintendencia de Sociedades') and the local chamber of commerce. All conditions being equal during tender processes, national offers are preferred over foreign ones. Assuming equal conditions among foreign bidders, those with major Colombian national workforce resources, significant national capital, and /or better conditions to facilitate technology transfers are preferred.

OTHER INVESTMENT POLICY REVIEWS

The Organization for Economic Cooperation and Development (OECD) reviewed Colombia's investment policy in April 2012 (**http://www.oecd.org/countries/colombia/colombia-investmentpolicyreview-oecd.htm**) in anticipation of making Colombia an offer to start the OECD accession process. The OECD found that Colombia made significant progress in promoting investment liberalization and improving its investment climate through important policy reforms. The World Trade Organization (WTO) conducted a fourth trade policy review of Colombia in June 2012 (**http://www.wto.org/english/tratop_e/tpr_e/tp365_e.htm**), its first in six years. It found that Colombia continued its trade policy of increased openness and emphasized greater integration with Latin America, the Caribbean, and the rest of the world by negotiating preferential agreements to increase external trade and foreign investment flows. Colombia scored 75 percent out of a hundred, or a "C," in the area of investor protection according to the 2014 World Bank Doing Business Report.

LAWS/REGULATIONS OF FOREIGN DIRECT INVESTMENT

Colombia has a comprehensive legal framework for business and FDI. Colombia's judicial system defines the legal rights of commercial entities, reviews regulatory enforcement procedures, and adjudicates contract disputes in the business community. The judicial framework includes the Superintendency of Industry and Commerce, the Council of State, the Constitutional Court, the Supreme Court of Justice, and the various departmental and district courts, which are also overseen for administrative matters by the Superior Judicial Council. The 1991 Constitution provided the judiciary with greater administrative and financial independence from the executive branch. However, except for the Superintendency of Industry and Commerce's efficient exercise of judicial functions, the judicial system in general remains hampered by time-consuming bureaucratic requirements and corruption. Colombia's foreign direct investment legal framework also incorporates binding norms resulting from its membership in the Andean Community of Nations as well as other free trade agreements and bilateral investment treaties.

INDUSTRIAL PROMOTION

The U.S.-Colombia Trade Promotion Agreement (CTPA) entered into force on May 15, 2012. The CTPA improves legal security and the investment environment while eliminating tariffs and other barriers in goods and services traded between the United States and Colombia. The agreement grants investors the right to establish, acquire, and operate investments on an equal footing with local investors as well as investors of other countries with bilateral investment treaties or investment chapters in free trade agreements with Colombia. It also provides U.S. investors in Colombia protections that foreign investors have under the U.S. legal system, including due process and the right to receive fair market value for property in the event of an expropriation.

LIMITS ON FOREIGN CONTROL

Foreign investment in the financial, hydrocarbon, and mining sectors is subject to special regimes, such as investment registration and concession agreements with the Colombian government, but are not restricted in the amount of foreign capital permitted. The following sectors require that foreign investors have a legal local representative and/or commercial presence in Colombia: travel and tourism agency services; money order operator; customs brokerage; postal and courier services; merchandise warehousing; merchandise transportation under customs control; international cargo agents; public service companies including sewage and water works, waste disposal, electricity, gas and fuel distribution, and public telephone service; insurance firms; legal services; and special air services including aerial fire-fighting, sightseeing, and surveying.

Foreign investors face specific exceptions and restrictions in the following sectors:

Media: Only Colombian nationals or legally constituted entities may provide radio or subscription-based television services. For National Open Television and Nationwide Private Television Operators, only Colombian nationals or legal entities may be granted concessions to provide television services. Colombia's national, regional, and municipal open-television channels must be provided at no extra cost to subscribers. Foreign investment in national television is limited to a maximum of 40 percent ownership of the relevant operator. Satellite television service providers are only obliged to include within their basic programming the broadcast of government-designated public interest channels. Newspapers published in Colombia covering domestic politics must be directed and managed by Colombian nationals.

Accounting, Auditing, and Data Processing: In order to practice in Colombia, providers of accounting services must register with the Central Accountants Board; have uninterrupted domicile in Colombia for at least three years prior to registry; and provide proof of accounting experience in Colombia of at least one year. No restrictions apply to services offered by consulting firms or individuals. A legal commercial presence is required to provide data processing and information services in Colombia.

Banking: Foreign investors may own 100 percent of financial institutions in Colombia, but are required to obtain approval from the Financial Superintendent before making a direct investment of ten percent or more in any one entity. Portfolio investments used to acquire more than five percent of an entity also require authorization. Foreign banks must establish a local commercial presence and comply with the same capital and other requirements as local financial institutions. Foreign banks may establish a subsidiary or office in Colombia, but not a branch. Every investment of foreign capital in portfolios must be through a Colombian administrator company, including brokerage firms, trust companies, and investment management companies. All foreign investments must be registered with the Central Bank.

Fishing: A foreign vessel may engage in fishing and related activities in Colombian territorial waters only through association with a Colombian company holding a valid fishing permit. If a ship's flag corresponds to a country with which Colombia has a complementary bilateral agreement, this agreement shall determine whether the association requirement applies for the process required to obtain a fishing license. The costs of fishing permits are greater for foreign flag vessels.

Private Security and Surveillance Companies: Companies constituted with foreign capital prior to February 11, 1994, cannot increase the share of foreign capital. Those constituted after that date can only have Colombian nationals as shareholders.

Telecommunications: Barriers to entry in telecommunications services include high license fees (USD150 million for a long distance license), commercial presence requirements, and economic needs tests. While Colombia allows 100 percent foreign ownership of telecommunication providers, in WTO negotiations it specifically prohibited "callback" services.

Transportation: Foreign companies can only provide multimodal freight services within or from Colombian territory if they have a domiciled agent or representative legally responsible for its activities in Colombia. International cabotage companies can provide cabotage services (i.e. between two points within Colombia) "only when there is no national capacity to provide the service" according to Colombian law. Colombia prohibits foreign ownership of commercial ships licensed in Colombia and restricts foreign ownership in national airlines or shipping companies to 40 percent. FDI in the maritime sector is limited to 30 percent. The owners of a concession providing port services must be legally constituted in Colombia and only Colombian ships may provide port services within Colombian maritime jurisdiction; however, vessels with foreign flags may provide those services if there are no Colombian-flag vessels capable of doing so.

PRIVATIZATION PROGRAM

Colombia has privatized state-owned enterprises under article 60 of the Constitution and Law No. 226 of 1995. This law stipulates that the sale of government holdings in an enterprise should be offered to two groups: first to cooperatives and workers associations of the enterprise, then to the general public. During the first phase, special terms and credits have to be granted, and in the second phase, foreign investors may participate along with the general public. Colombia's main privatizations have been in the electricity, mining, hydrocarbons, and financial sectors. The government has attached a high priority to stimulating private sector investment in roads, ports, electricity, and gas infrastructure concessions. The government is increasingly utilizing public-private partnerships (PPPs) as the favored option for infrastructure development.

The Colombian government has prioritized its fourth generation infrastructure program (4G) focused on highway construction with PPP opportunities valued at more than USD 24 billion. In order to attract investment and promote PPPs, on November 22, 2013, the Colombian government signed a new infrastructure law clarifying provisions for frequently cited obstacles to participate in PPPs including environmental licensing, land acquisition, and the displacement of public utilities. The new law puts in place a civil procedure that facilitates land expropriation during court cases, allows for expedited environmental licensing, and clarifies that the cost to move or replace public utilities affected by infrastructure projects falls to private companies.

Municipal enterprises operate many public utilities and infrastructure services. These municipal enterprises have engaged private sector investment through concessions. There are several successful concessions involving roads. During 2015, the Colombian government has expressed interest in selling one of its majority state-owned power generation companies, ISAGEN, for approximately USD 2.5 billion. The proceeds from this sale will be used to fund part of the 4G program. These kinds of partnerships have helped promote reforms and create an attractive environment for private, national, and foreign investment.

SCREENING OF FDI

According to the Constitution and foreign investment regulations, foreign investment in Colombia receives the same treatment as an investment made by Colombian nationals. Any investment made by a person that does not qualify as a resident of Colombia for foreign exchange purposes will qualify as foreign investment. Foreign investment is permitted in all sectors, except in activities related to defense, national security, and toxic waste handling and disposal. There are no performance requirements explicitly applicable to the entry and establishment of foreign investment in Colombia. However, there are export incentives relating to the operation of free trade zones.

COMPETITION LAW

All FDI involving the establishment of a commercial presence in Colombia requires registration with the Superintendence of Corporations ('Superintendencia de Sociedades') and the local chamber of commerce. All conditions being equal during tender processes, national offers are preferred over foreign ones. Assuming equal conditions among foreign bidders, those with major Colombian national workforce resources, significant national capital, and /or better conditions to facilitate technology transfers are preferred.

INVESTMENT TRENDS

Since 2010, the Santos administration has continued efforts to open up the economy. Liberalization has progressed furthest in telecommunications, accounting/auditing, energy, mining, and tourism, and to a lesser extent in legal services, insurance, distribution services, advertising, and data processing. Colombia received a record USD16.8 billion in FDI in 2013, an increase of seven percent compared to 2012, ranking as the fourth FDI destination in Latin America after Brazil, Mexico, and Chile. Colombia is projected to receive USD15.8 billion in FDI in 2014.

Colombia's exports promotion agency, recently renamed ProColombia (http://www.procolombia.co/), has an official website to promote investment in Colombia (http://www.investincolombia.com.co/). It gathers investment climate information by sector and region and offers free services to new and established investors such as tailored information requests, public and private sector contacts, and suggestions for in-country visits/agendas. ProColombia's investment booklet provides detailed information about the business environment, including the labor market, legal considerations, exchange rate regime, free trade zones, environmental licensing, and private equity fund opportunities (http://www.investincolombia.com.co/publications/investment-booklet.html).

Table 1

MEASURE	YEAR	INDEX OR RANK	WEBSITE ADDRESS
TI CORRUPTION PERCEPTIONS INDEX	2014	94 of 175	transparency.org/cpi2014/results
WORLD BANK'S DOING BUSINESS REPORT "EASE OF DOING BUSINESS"	2015	34 of 189	doingbusiness.org/rankings
GLOBAL INNOVATION INDEX	2014	68 of 143	globalinnovationindex.org/content.aspx?page=data-analysis
WORLD BANK GNI PER CAPITA	2013	USD7590	data.worldbank.org/indicator/NY.GNP.PCAP.CD

2. CONVERSION AND TRANSFER POLICIES

FOREIGN EXCHANGE

No restrictions apply to transferring funds associated with FDI. However, foreign investment into Colombia must be registered with the Central Bank to secure the right to repatriate capital and profits. Except for special exceptions, direct and portfolio investments are considered registered when the exchange declaration for operations channeled through the official exchange market is presented. Colombia does not manipulate its currency to gain competitive advantages.

Remittance Policies

If investments are registered, repatriation is permitted without any limits. The government permits full remittance of all net profits regardless of the type or amount of investment. Foreign investments must be channeled through the foreign exchange market and registered within one year with the Central Bank's foreign exchange office to be able to repatriate or reinvest the proceeds. There are no restrictions on the repatriation of revenues generated from the sale or closure of a business, reduction of investment, or transfer of a portfolio. Colombian law authorizes the government to restrict remittances in the event that international reserves fall below three months' worth of imports, and reserves have been well above that level for decades.

3. EXPROPRIATION AND COMPENSATION

Article 58 of the Constitution governs indemnifications and expropriations and guarantees owners' rights for legally-acquired property. For assets taken by eminent domain, Colombian law provides a right of appeal both on the basis of the decision itself and on the level of compensation. The Constitution does not specify how to proceed in compensation cases, which remains a concern for foreign investors. The Colombian government has sought to resolve such concerns through the negotiation of bilateral investment treaties and strong investment chapters in free trade agreements, such as the CTPA.

4. DISPUTE SETTLEMENT

LEGAL SYSTEM, SPECIALIZED COURTS, JUDICIAL INDEPENDENCE, JUDGMENTS OF FOREIGN COURTS

The judicial system generally operates without government interference. However, since 2012 the legal system has been affected because of frequent strikes from judges and other legal employees. The main complaints are low salaries and poor job conditions. In 2014, the strikes halted 400,000 judicial processes. In 2012, Law 1564 gave the Superintendence of Industry and Commerce, National Copyrights Directorate, and Colombian Agriculture Institute authority to judge civil commercial cases about intellectual property rights (IPR).

BANKRUPTCY

Colombia's 1991 Constitution grants the Colombian government the authority to intervene directly in financial or economic affairs, and this authority provided solutions similar to U.S. Chapter 11 filings for companies facing liquidation or bankruptcy. Colombia's bankruptcy regulations have two major objectives: to regulate proceedings to ensure creditors' protection and monitor the efficient recovery and preservation of still-viable companies. This was revised in 2006 to allow creditors to request judicial liquidation, which replaces the previous forced auctioning option. Now, inventories are valued, creditors' rights are taken into account, and either a direct sale takes place within two months or all assets are assigned to creditors based on their share of the company's liabilities. The insolvency regime for companies was again revised in 2010 to make proceedings more agile and flexible and allow debtors to enter into a long-term payment agreement with creditors, giving the company a chance to recover and continue operating. In 2012, the general code of procedure eliminated one of the first steps of the restructuring proceedings but preserving the core Bankruptcy is not criminalized in Colombia. In 2013, a bankruptcy law for natural people entered into force: for people whose debts surpass fifty percent of their assets value.

Restructuring proceedings aim to protect the debtors from bankruptcy. Once reorganization has begun, creditors cannot use collection proceedings to collect on debts owed prior to the beginning of the reorganization proceedings. All existing creditors at the moment of the reorganization are recognized during the proceedings if they present their credit. Foreign creditors, equity shareholders including foreign equity shareholders, and holders of other financial contracts, including foreign contract holders, are recognized during the proceeding. Established creditors are guaranteed a vote in the final decision. According to the Doing Business 2015 report, Colombia takes 1.7 years (same average as OECD countries) to resolve insolvency.

INVESTMENT DISPUTES

In 2014 there were still three pending investment disputes. First, a case involving a U.S. fast food company operating in Colombia since 1999. The company purchased land to build a restaurant, but the government seized the property during an investigation of the prior landholder for drug trafficking and money laundering. The second case started in 1994 involving a U.S. marine salvage company. The company has sued the Government of Colombia through different venues for not allowing them to access its property in Colombian territory on grounds of national patrimony protection. Lastly is a case involving a U.S plane allegedly abandoned in Colombian territory in 2010. The U.S. owner has been trying to claim back its property since 2012. Colombian authorities sustain that the plane is their property now, according to national regulations on abandoned aircraft.

INTERNATIONAL ARBITRATION

Foreign judgments are recognized and enforced in Colombia once an application is submitted to the Civil Chamber of the Supreme Court. In 2012, Colombia approved the use of the arbitration process when new legislation based on the UNCITRAL Model Law was adopted. The new statute stipulates that arbitral awards are governed by both domestic law as well as international conventions (New York Convention, Panama Convention, etc.). This has made the enforcement of arbitral awards easier for the parties involved. Arbitration in Colombia is completely independent from judiciary proceedings, and once arbitration has begun, the only competent authority is the arbitration tribunal itself. The CTPA protects U.S. investments by requiring a transparent and binding international arbitration mechanism and allowing investor-state arbitration for breaches of investment agreements if certain parameters are met.

ICSID Convention and New York Convention

Domestic law allows contracting parties to agree to submit disputes to international arbitration, provided that the parties are domiciled in different countries, the place of arbitration agreed to by the parties is a country other than the one where they are domiciled, the subject matter of the arbitration involves the interests of more than one country, and the dispute has a direct impact on international trade. The law lets parties set their own arbitration terms including location, procedures, and the nationality of rules and arbiters. Foreign investors have found the arbitration process in Colombia complex and dilatory, especially with regard to enforcing awards. In October 2012, the new National and International Arbitration Statute, modeled after the United Nations Commission on International Trade Law, took effect.

Colombia is a member of the New York Convention on Investment Disputes, the International Center for the Settlement of Investment Disputes, and the Multilateral Investment Guarantee Agency.

Duration of Dispute Resolution

According to the World Bank's Doing Business 2015 report, domestic commercial litigation takes on average 885 days from the pretrial stage until the final hearing and judgment. Traditionally, most court proceedings are carried out in writing and only the evidence-gathering stage is carried out through hearings, including witness depositions, site inspections, and cross-examinations. The Colombian government has accelerated proceedings and reduced the backlog of court cases by allowing more verbal public hearings and creating alternative court mechanisms. The new Code of General Procedure that entered into force in June 2014 also establishes an oral proceeding which is carried out in two hearings, and there are now penalties for not ruling in the time limit set by the law. Enforcement of an arbitral award can take up to two years.

5. PERFORMANCE REQUIREMENTS AND INVESTMENT INCENTIVES

WTO/TRIMS

There are no active measures inconsistent with World Trade Organization's (WTO) Trade Related Investment Measures (TRIMs) requirements.

Investment Incentives

The Colombian government offers investment incentives such as income tax exemptions and deductions in specific priority sectors. During the last decade it has committed to providing more incentives and stability for investors. Investment incentives through free trade agreements between Colombia and other nations include national treatment and most favored nation treatment of investors; establishment of liability standards assumed by countries regarding the other nation's investors including the minimum standard of treatment and establishment of rules for investor compensation because of expropriation; establishment of rules for transfer of capital relating to investment; and specific tax treatment.

The government offers tax incentives to all investors, such as preferential import tariffs, tax exemptions, and credit or risk capital. Some fiscal incentives are available for investments that generate new employment or production in areas impacted by natural disasters, and companies can apply for these directly with participating agencies. Tax and fiscal incentives are often based on regional considerations. Border areas have special protections due to currency fluctuations in neighboring countries, which can harm local economies. National and local governments also offer special incentives, like tax holidays, to attract specific industries.

One of Colombia's most important tax incentives for any investor was the 30 percent deduction of the value of productive fixed-asset investment when paying income tax. A deduction like that was possible thanks to the so called "contracts of juridical stability"; contracts that protected investors from changes in income or asset taxes. However, since January 2013, new contracts of this type are no longer possible; the protection is only maintained to active contracts or those in the process of approval by the time the law ruling this entered into force (tax reform).

Special tax exemptions have existed since 2003 and range between ten to thirty years. Income tax exemptions in tourism cover new hotels constructed between 2003 and December 31, 2017, and remodeled and/or expanded hotels until December 31, 2017, for a period of 30 years, and for ecotourism services through 2023. New forestry plantations and sawmills also benefit from income tax exemptions since 2003. Late yield crops planted through December 31, 2014, are tax exempt for ten years from the beginning of the harvesting. Electricity from wind power, biomass, and agricultural waste are tax exempt until January 1, 2018, as are river based transportation services provided with certain shallow draft vessels and barges. Certain printing and publishing companies can benefit from tax exemptions until December 31, 2033. Software developed in Colombia is also exempt up to for five years since January 1, 2013. To meet exemption requirements the software must have its intellectual property rights protected, a high concentration of national scientific and technological research and Colciencias (Colombia's agency to support science, technology and innovation) must grant its certification. In December 2014, Congress passed and Santos signed a controversial tax reform measure extending the "wealth tax", placing an additional tax on assets beginning at 0.2 percent and reaching as high as 1.15 percent for businesses with a net equity of over 2 billion pesos, to be phased out by 2018. Additionally, the government added a surcharge to the already existing Income Tax for Equality/Contribución Empresarial para la Equidad (CREE), a tax on company profits over 800 million pesos designed to contribute to employment generation and social investments. The CREE, which stood at 9 percent, received an additional surcharge of 5 percent in 2015, and which will increase until it reaches a surcharge of 9 percent in 2018.

Research and Development

Foreign investors can participate without discrimination in government-subsidized research programs. In fact, most Colombian government research has been conducted with foreign institutions. However, the 2014-2018 National Development Plan (NDP), the strategic plan that leads Government of Colombia's action for the remainder of Santos' administration, includes a provision that gives access to intellectual property rights for free for foreign investors who invest in national security. R&D incentives include Value-Added Tax exemptions for imported equipment or materials used in scientific, technology, or innovation projects, and qualified investments may receive tax credits up to 175 percent. A 2012 reform of Colombia's royalty system allocates ten percent of the government's revenue towards science, technology, and innovation proposals executed by subnational governments. Although only subnational governments can submit a project, anyone, including foreigners, can partner with them. Colombia's government R&D funding increased 40 percent to USD 840 million from 2012 to 2014.

Performance Requirements

Performance requirements are not imposed on foreigners as a condition for establishing, maintaining or expanding investments. The Colombian government does not have performance requirements, impose local employment requirements, or require excessively difficult visa, residence, and work permit requirements for investors. Under the CTPA, Colombia grants substantial market access across its entire services sector.

Data Storage

According to the Ministry of Information Technologies, the government enforces only the data storage location for government entities. It does so using its service contract with the private company providing the service.

In Colombia, software and hardware are protected by intellectual property rights (Dirección Nacional de Derecho de Autor – DNDA – http://www.derechodeautor.gov.co/). There is no obligation to submit source code for registered software. However, if the IT provider is contracting with the Colombian Government, through a clause of the service contract, the source code must be provided to the entity.

Currently, the Colombian Superintendence for Industry and Trade is developing the control mechanism to ensure that the management of data storage, data base management and personal information management complies with the requirements requested by the government. Law 1581 refers to personal information management.

6. RIGHT TO PRIVATE OWNERSHIP AND ESTABLISHMENT

The 1991 Constitution explicitly protects individual rights against state actions and upholds the right to private property.

7. PROTECTION OF PROPERTY RIGHTS

Real Property

Secured interests in real property, and to a lesser degree movable property, are recognized and generally enforced after the property is properly registered. In terms of protecting third party purchasers, such as one of the cases cited under investment disputes, existing law is inadequate. The concept of a mortgage, trust deed, and other types of liens exists, as well as a reliable system of recording such secured interests. Deeds, however, have some legal risk due to the prevalence of transactions that have never been registered with the Public Instruments Registry. There are approximately 4 million hectares affected by forced displacement and 2 million for violent usurpation. According to the National Audit Office (Contraloria General de la Nacion), about 48 percent of rural land in Colombia, or about 3.7 million plots, do not have a clear title. The Colombian government is working to title these plots and has started a formalization program for land restitution. Colombia ranked 42 out of 188 economies for the ease of registering property according to the World Bank's 2015 Doing Business Report; twelve positions better than the 2014 ranking.

Intellectual Property Rights

In Colombia, the grant, registration, and administration of intellectual property rights are carried out by four different government entities. The Superintendency of Industry and Commerce acts as the Colombian patent and trademark office. The Colombian Agricultural Institute is in charge of issuing plant variety protections and data protections for agricultural products. The Ministry of Interior administers copyrights through the National Copyright Directorate. The Ministry of Health and Social Protection handles data protection for products registered through the National Food and Drug Institute. Although each of these entities experiences significant financial and technical resource constraints, the Superintendence steps up as the most efficient and the second fastest office in the world for patent applications. Colombia is subject to Andean Community Decision 486 on trade secret protection, which is fully implemented domestically by the Unfair Competition Law of 1996.

The patent regime in Colombia currently provides for a 20-year protection period for patents, a 10-year term for industrial designs, and 20 or 15-year protection for new plant varieties, depending on the species. Data protection applications take up to nine months to adjudicate. U.S. agroindustry companies have expressed concern because enforcement and implementation of Colombia's data protection regime for agrochemicals is still weak. The Colombian Agriculture Institute (Instituto Colombiano Agropecuario or ICA) has no internal data protection regulations. The U.S. pharmaceutical industry has complained about slow judicial process and inability of rights holders to obtain preliminary injunctions before a potentially patent-infringing product enters the market. The U.S. Patent and Trademark Office partnered with the Superintendency of Industry and Commerce to establish a Patent Prosecution Highway (PPH) program. The PPH allows for the mutual recognition of patent examination procedures making the patent granting process faster. The program was extended indefinitely due to the success of the pilot.

Colombia has been on the U.S. Trade Representative's Special 301 Watch List every year since 1991 and is also listed in the notorious markets report. Both reports can be found at https://ustr.gov/about-us/policy-offices/press-office/reports-and-publications. The CTPA improved standards for the protection and enforcement of a broad range of intellectual property rights. Such improvements include state-of-the-art protections for digital products such as software, music, text, and videos; stronger protection for U.S.

patents, trademarks and test data; and prevention of piracy and counterfeiting by criminalizing end-use piracy. Colombia is a member of the Inter-American Convention for Trademark and Commercial Protection. Various procedures associated with industrial property, patent, and trademark registration are available at http://www.sic.gov.co/es/web/guest/propiedad-industrial. In August 2012, Colombia joined the Madrid Agreement Concerning the International Registration of Marks (Madrid Protocol). The Colombian government joined the World Intellectual Property Organization (WIPO) Trademark Law Treaty on January 13, 2012, which entered into force on April 12, 2013. WIPO's 1996 Copyright Treaty has been in force since March 6, 2002, and the Performances and Phonograms Treaty since May 20, 2002. Colombia is not a member of the Patent Law Treaty.

On January 23, 2013, the Constitutional Court declared Law 1520 of 2012 implementing several CTPA-related commitments (including copyrights, TV programming quotas, and IPR enforcement measures) unconstitutional on procedural grounds. In response, the Santos administration decided to present separate bills to Congress. A draft copyrights bill is still circulating internally, including with the U.S. Trade Representative, for comment prior to resubmission to Congress. This CTPA copyrights deadline to establish liability for circumventing technological protections was May 15, 2013, and the deadlines to establish liability for misuse/altering information was November 15, 2014. Because the TV programming quotas bill was not approved in all four debates within the required timeframe, it had to be reintroduced to Congress in September 2014 to recommence debate. More recently, the GOC decided to include a less detailed provision for this in the National Development Plan (Article 40). The CTPA deadline for screen quotas was May 15, 2012.

On enforcement, a decree specifying the list of pre-established compensation for trademark counterfeiting was issued in December 2014. However, Colombia has yet to establish additional criminal procedures for counterfeiting, due May 15, 2013, which it plans to address with the copyrights bill or another law that permits modifying its penal code. The Internet Service Providers (ISPs) legislation, another CTPA requirement, was due May 15, 2013. A bill was introduced in 2011, but was archived because it was approved only in the first debate within the required timeframe.

In terms of investigations, Colombia's success against counterfeiting and IPR violations is limited to specific isolated events and seizures. However, Colombian law continues to limit the ability of law enforcement (police, customs, and prosecutors) to effectively combat counterfeiting because they do not have the requisite authorities to effectively inspect, seize, and investigate smugglers and counterfeiters. Low enforcement capacity for micro-contraband (cases where merchandise is valued under USD 12,000, which is the majority) is also a problem. The anti-contraband bill, still being debated in Congress, would include provisions to decrease the minimum amount for criminalization.

Resources for Rights Holders

Embassy point of contact:

U.S. Embassy Bogota
Economic Section
Carrera 45 #22B-45
Bogota, Colombia
(571) 275-2000
BogotaECONShared@state.gov

Country/Economy resources:

American Chamber of Commerce in Colombia: **http://www.amchamcolombia.com.co/**

Council of American Companies in Colombia: **http://www.ceacolombia.com/es/**

For additional information about treaty obligations and points of contact at local IP offices, please see WIPO's country profiles at **http://www.wipo.int/directory/en/**.

8. TRANSPARENCY OF THE REGULATORY SYSTEM

The Colombian legal and regulatory systems are generally transparent and consistent with international norms. The commercial code and other laws cover broad areas including banking and credit, bankruptcy/reorganization, business establishment/conduct, commercial contracts, credit, corporate organization, fiduciary obligations, insurance, industrial property, and real property law. The civil code contains provisions relating to contracts, mortgages, liens, notary functions, and registries. There are no identified private sector associations or nongovernmental organizations leading informal regulatory processes. The ministries generally consult with relevant actors, both foreign and national, when drafting regulations and proposed laws are typically published as drafts for public comment.

Enforcement mechanisms exist, but historically the judicial system has not taken an active role in adjudicating commercial cases. The 1991 Constitution provided the judiciary with greater administrative and financial independence from the executive branch. Colombia has completed its transition to an oral accusatory system to make criminal investigations and trials more efficient. The new system separates the investigative functions assigned to the Office of the Attorney General from trial functions. Lack of coordination among government entities as well as insufficient resources complicate timely resolution of cases.

9. EFFICIENT CAPITAL MARKETS AND PORTFOLIO INVESTMENT

Market capitalization has risen from USD14 billion in 2003 to USD153 billion as of December 2014. Sound fiscal and macroeconomic management allowed Colombia to claim the triple crown of seeing its credit ratings increased to 'Investment Grade' level by Standard and Poor's, Moody's, and Fitch Ratings. Foreign investors are allowed to participate in capital markets by negotiating and acquiring shares, bonds, and other securities listed by the Foreign Investment Statute. These activities must be conducted via a local administrator, which can be a trust company or a stock brokerage firm that has been authorized to do so by the Financial Superintendent (Superintendencia Financiera). Foreign investment capital funds are not allowed to acquire more than ten percent of the total amount of a Colombian company's outstanding shares. Foreigners have no restrictions to establish a bank account as long as they have a valid visa and government ID (Cedula).

The market has sufficient liquidity for investors to enter and exit sizeable positions. Following the crisis of 1998-99, bailouts for failing banks were partially financed through a controversial tax on financial transactions. The tax was originally set at 0.2 percent but has since been increased to 0.4 percent. The tax on financial transactions is applied to all withdrawals from checking and savings accounts, including accounts with the Central Bank. Savings accounts for the purchase of low-income housing, transactions on the inter-bank market, and the sale or purchase of foreign currency are exempt from the tax. The Central Bank respects IMF Article VIII and does not restrict payments and transfers for current international transactions.

MONEY AND BANKING SYSTEM, HOSTILE TAKEOVERS

In 2005, Colombia consolidated supervision of all aspects of the banking, financial, securities, and insurance sectors under the Financial Superintendent. Colombia has an effective regulatory system that encourages portfolio investment. According to the Financial Superintendent, as of December 2014, the estimated assets of the country's main banks totaled approximately USD 184.7 billion. Sixty percent of all disbursed credits were destined for commercial credits, 28 percent for consumption, nine percent for housing, and three percent for microcredit. Past-due loans accounted for three percent of the total portfolio.

Colombia's financial system is well developed by regional standards. The financial sector as a whole is investing in new risk assessment and portfolio management methodologies. Two private financial groups together own over half of all bank assets: the Sarmiento Group (Grupo Aval) controls about 27 percent and the Sindicato Antioqueño Group (Bancolombia) about 27 percent as of December 2014. Total foreign-owned bank assets account for approximately 28 percent of sector assets.

The principal source of long-term corporate and project finance in Colombia are commercial banks. Loans with a maturity in excess of five years are scarce. Unofficial private lenders play a considerable role in meeting the working capital needs of small and medium-sized companies. Only the largest of Colombia's companies participate in the local stock or bond markets with the majority meeting their financing needs through the banking system, by reinvesting their profits, and through suppliers' credit.

10. COMPETITION FROM STATE-OWNED ENTERPRISES

In principle Colombia's SOEs do not receive preferential treatment, though in practice some issues arise such as political authorities running SOEs and conflicts of interest. In general, Colombian SOEs are subject to the general legal framework and receive special treatment in very few areas. One of these areas is bankruptcy law; SOEs are largely protected from insolvency due to the necessity of providing essential public services. Colombian SOEs are, in general, subject to private law and structured as commercial companies. However, depending on the sector, SOEs may also be subject to specific sector norms, such as the Utilities Law.

Private enterprises generally are allowed to compete with public enterprises under the same terms and conditions, although at the sub-national level private liquor companies face licensing restrictions and other administrative barriers that prevent free competition with local SOEs. Private enterprises are allowed to compete with SOEs under the same terms and conditions with respect to access to markets, credit, and other business operations, such as licenses and supplies. State-owned banks are expected to treat SOEs without any preference. Colombian SOEs generally use the financial markets for financing and do not receive additional support from the government except in very rare cases.

In March 2014, Santos signed a new law requiring all SOEs to make information regarding their operations publicly available. Colombia protects the rights of minority shareholders and allows any group of shareholders with less than a ten percent stake to request the intervention of the regulator if they believe the company is taking measures detrimental to their interests. Since January 1st, 2015, following OECD recommendations, a renewed corporate governance code entered into force for companies issuing securities in Colombia. The new code is aimed at incorporating new trends in capital markets and elevates standards to international levels although it preserves the voluntary approach and the principle of "comply or explain". It is required that all companies submit an annual report on their implementation. The code comprises best practices for shareholders' meetings, boards of directors, disclosure of financial and non-financial information, and dispute resolution. The renewed set of guidelines include more protection for minority investors, guidelines on fair treatment of shareholders, alternative methods to resolution of conflicts, transit methods for shareholders to go from passiveness to activism, among others.

According to the International Financing Corporation, member of the World Bank group, Colombia's OECD accession process has elevated the importance of corporate governance at all levels. The IFC has started to support a range of corporate governance-related actions, including legal and regulatory reforms and state-owned enterprise governance. The project also expects to support efforts toward the establishment of a Colombian Corporate Governance Institute and a component to assist SMEs to increase their sustainability and competitiveness by incorporating better corporate governance practices.

According to the OECD, the three largest SOEs, Ecopetrol, ISA, and ISAGEN, are considered to be good examples of professional management, competition, and excellent corporate governance. Nevertheless, between 2014 and 2015 Ecopetrol has been involved in a corruption probe involving executives from a company that allegedly bribed Ecopetrol staff to secure a multi-million dollar oil-service contract.

OECD Guidelines on Corporate Governance of SOEs

At Colombia's request, the OECD analyzed Colombia's corporate governance practices of State Owned Enterprises (SOEs) against OECD Guidelines and released a report in December 2013 (http://www.oecd-ilibrary.org/governance/colombian-soes-a-review-against-the-oecd-guidelines-on-corporate-governance-of-state-owned-enterprises_5k3v1ts5s4f6-en). The OECD found that Colombia's legal framework is compatible with the OECD standards of corporate governance. Colombian SOEs fall into two broad categories: Industrial and Commercial State Companies that are statutory corporations wholly owned by the state and whose origin and norms are established by law and Mixed-Ownership in which the state has a stake and which can take any legal form and are generally governed by the norms applicable to the private sector. The central government owns 70 SOEs and partial SOEs. SOEs exist in the following sectors: defense article production, regional utility companies, postal service, electricity generation and distribution, hospitals, airports, banking, television, education, regional lotteries, alcohol and spirit distillers, and oil and gas.

Sovereign Wealth Funds

In 2012 Colombia started operating a sovereign wealth fund, called a savings and stabilization fund, using royalties from the extractive industry. The fund can administrate up to 30 percent of annual royalties. The fund's main objective is to promote saving and economic stabilization in the country and it is administrated by the Central Bank. According to the Ministry of Finance, Colombia has saved as of December 2014 around USD 2.5 billion including returns. The fund savings have continuously grown since its establishment when it started with approximately USD500 million. The rest of royalties' resources are administered by other internal funds aimed to boost productivity in Colombia through new technologies and innovation.

11. CORPORATE SOCIAL RESPONSIBILITY

Colombia adheres to the corporate social responsibility (CSR) principles outlined in the OECD Guidelines for Multinational Enterprises. It has a long tradition of CSR across many industries and encourages public and private enterprises to follow OECD guidelines. Beneficiaries of CSR programs include students, children, populations vulnerable to Colombia's armed conflict, victims of violence, and the environment. Larger companies, in particular, structure their CSR programs in line with generally accepted international CSR principles. On several occasions, companies in Colombia have been recognized on an international level, including by the State Department, for their CSR commitments.

Overall, Colombia has adequate environmental laws on the books, is proactive at the federal level in enacting environmental protections, and does not waive labor or environmental regulations to attract investors. However, the Colombian government struggles with enforcement, particularly in more remote areas. Geography, lack of infrastructure, and lack of state presence all play a role, as does a general shortage of resources in its national and regional level institutions. The Environmental Chapter of the CTPA requires Colombia to maintain and enforce environmental laws, protect biodiversity, and promote opportunities for public participation. In October 2014, the Minister of Environment and Sustainable Development signed the modification to decree 2820 on environmental licensing. With this change the Colombian Government expects to streamline and optimize the issuance of permits for exploration and exploitation of natural resources in Colombia.

OECD GUIDELINES FOR MULTINATIONAL ENTERPRISES

The government of Colombia encourages foreign and local enterprises to follow generally accepted CSR principles as outlined in the OECD Guidelines for Multinational Enterprises.

12. POLITICAL VIOLENCE

Violence, including political violence, has diminished significantly in recent years. Colombian government figures show that the number of terrorist acts decreased by 14 percent from 2013 to 2014. Homicides nationally continued a downward trend, with 13,258 in 2014, compared with 15,419 in 2013. The number of kidnappings in 2014 was 288, a 3.7 percent decrease from 299 in 2013, and a 91 percent decrease since 1999 when there were 3,204 kidnappings.

Security in Colombia has improved significantly in the past 15 years. However, there continues to be an active domestic insurgency that threatens commercial activity and investment, especially in rural zones where government control is weaker. The government estimates the Revolutionary Armed Forces of Colombia (FARC) insurgent group has around 8,000 armed members, and the National Liberation Army (ELN) has around 1,500. Both groups attack oil pipelines, mines, roads, and electricity towers to disrupt economic activity and put pressure on the government. Both groups also extort businesses in their area of operation, sometimes kidnapping personnel and destroying the property of operations that refuse to pay.

The extractive sector has been especially hard hit by insurgent attacks. According to the Ministry of Defense, there were 141 attacks on oil pipelines in 2014, a 45 percent decrease compared to 2013. These attacks sometimes temporarily forced oil companies to stop production while pipelines were repaired or to transport oil by more expensive alternate methods.

The Colombian government and FARC have been in peace negotiations in Havana, Cuba since November 2012. They have agreed in principle on three of the five negotiating topics – agriculture and rural development, political participation, and drugs – and discussion on the last two agenda items, victims and end of conflict, is ongoing.

13. CORRUPTION

Corruption is a significant challenge in Colombia. According to the World Economic Forum's Global Competitiveness Index (2014-2015), corruption continues to be one of Colombia's biggest problems for doing business; it ranked 123 out of 144 countries. According to the NGO Transparency International, Colombian citizens' perception on corruption in the country has neither improved nor worsened for the third year running in 2014. Colombia shares the 94th spot worldwide with countries such as Liberia, Egypt and Panama. There was just a slight improvement (an index of 37 out of 100 for 2014, one point better than 2013's and 2012's indexes). Transparency International argues the slight improvement was due to an improvement in the World Economic Forum's 2014 Executive Opinion Survey, which tests the opinion of executives and experts in risk assessment (Colombia improved five positions from 33rd to 28th in 2014).

Despite President Santos' numerous efforts such as the 2011 Anti-Corruption Statute, the "Colombia buys efficiently" initiative, or the anti-corruption observatory created in 2014, concrete results have yet to be seen. High profile corruption cases continue to surface on a frequent basis. In February 2015, the president of the Constitutional Court was involved in a high profile corruption case that obligated him to resign from the judicial body. He was accused of having asked for a USD 200,000 bribe from an oil company, promising that the court would revoke a multi-million-dollar fine.

UN Anticorruption Convention, OECD Convention on Combatting Bribery

Colombia has adopted the OECD Convention on Combating Bribery of Foreign Public Officials and is a member of the OECD Anti-Bribery Committee. It has signed and ratified the UN Anticorruption Convention. Additionally, it has adopted the OAS Convention against Corruption.

The CTPA protects the integrity of procurement practices and criminalizes both offering and soliciting bribes to/from public officials. It requires both countries to make all laws, regulations, and procedures regarding any matter under the CTPA publicly available. Both countries must also establish procedures for reviews and appeals by any entities affected by actions, rulings, measures, or procedures under the CTPA.

Resources to Report Corruption

Useful resources and contact information for those concerned about combating corruption in Colombia include the following:

The Transparency and Anti-Corruption Observatory is an interactive tool of the Colombian government aimed at promoting transparency and combating corruption available at **http://www.anticorrupcion.gov.co/**.

The Presidential Secretariat of Transparency advises and assists the president to formulate and design public policy about transparency and anti-corruption. This office also coordinates the implementation of anti-corruption policies. **http://wsp.presidencia.gov.co/secretaria-transparencia/Paginas/default.aspx/**.

Gerson David Motta Chavarro
Administrative staff of the National Secretary of Transparency
Presidential Secretariat of Transparency
Carrera 8 No.7-26 Bogota, Colombia
(57 1) 562-9300 or (57 1) 5870555
gersonmotta@presidencia.gov.co

14. Bilateral Investment Agreements

Colombia has ten free trade agreements that include investment chapters: the U.S., European Union, Canada, Chile, Mexico, Cuba, Andean Community of Nations (Bolivia, Ecuador, and Peru), European Free Trade Area (only Switzerland and Liechtenstein have ratified), Mercosur (Brazil, Argentina, Paraguay, Uruguay, and Venezuela), and North Triangle (El Salvador, Honduras, and Guatemala). Colombia has also inked trade agreements with South Korea, Israel, Panama and Costa Rica, though they are not yet finalized. The South Korean free trade agreement is expected to come into effect in 2015 and the others will likely be finalized over the next two years. Colombia is also conducting FTA negotiations with Japan and Turkey. Another six agreements are being explored with Australia, China, the Dominican Republic, India, and Singapore.

Additionally, Colombia has stand-alone bilateral investment treaties in force with China, India, Peru, Spain, Switzerland, and UK and a treaty signed but not in force with the Japan. Colombia together with Chile, Mexico, and Peru form the Pacific Alliance, which signed a trade agreement in February 2014 that is expected to take effect sometime in 2015 after final review by the Constitutional Court.

Bilateral Taxation Treaties

Colombia has double taxation treaties with Spain, Chile, Switzerland, Canada, India, Portugal, Mexico, South Korea, France and Czech Republic. Talks for such accords have concluded successfully with Belgium. Colombia is currently negotiating double taxation agreements with Germany, the Netherlands, Japan, and the United States. In October 2014, Colombia and Panama agreed to establish in a year a double taxation treaty.

15. OPIC AND OTHER INVESTMENT INSURANCE PROGRAMS

OPIC made its first investment in Colombia in 1985 and has since made investments totaling over USD 2 billion in a variety of sectors. Additional information can be found at www.opic.gov.

16. LABOR

The labor market reflected positive results in Colombia's healthy economy. The average annual unemployment rate in 2014 continued its downward trajectory to 9.1 percent. Colombia still has one of the highest unemployment rates in the region. About 64.2 percent of the population actively participates in the labor force. Forty-nine percent of the workforce was working in the informal economy at the end of 2013, according to the International Labor Organization. Colombia has abundant unskilled and semi-skilled labor throughout the country, as well as managerial-level employees who are often bilingual.

Pursuant to Colombia's Labor Law, any group of 25 or more workers, regardless of whether they are employees of the same company or not, may form a labor union. Employees of companies with fewer than 25 employees may affiliate themselves with other labor unions. About four percent of the country's labor force is unionized. The largest and most influential unions are composed mostly of public employees, particularly of the majority state-owned oil company and the state-run education sector. The Constitution protects the right to constitute labor unions. Strikes, when held in accordance with the law, are recognized as legal instruments to obtain better working conditions. Strikes in sectors considered essential for some public sector unions are illegal.

Labor rights in Colombia are set forth in its Constitution, the Labor Code, the Procedural Code of Labor and Social Security, sector-specific legislation, and ratified international conventions, which are incorporated into national legislation. Colombia's Constitution guarantees freedom of association and provides for collective bargaining and the right to strike (with some exceptions). It also addresses forced labor, child labor, trafficking, discrimination, protections for women and children in the workplace, minimum wages, working hours, skills training, and social security.

Colombia has ratified all eight of the International Labor Organizations' fundamental labor conventions and all are in force, including those related to freedom of association, equal remuneration, right to organize and collectively bargain, discrimination, minimum working age, forced labor, and prohibition of the worst forms of child labor. Colombia has also ratified conventions related to hours of work, occupational health and safety, and minimum wage. In 2013, Law 1636 was passed to increase protections and opportunities for Colombia's unemployed population. The Ministry of Labor passed a number of resolutions and regulations, covering topics such as social security, occupational safety and health standards, formalization, and labor mediation.

Foreign companies operating in Colombia must follow the same hiring rules as national companies, regardless of the origin of the employer and the place of execution of the contract.

In 2010, Law 1429 eliminated the mandatory proportion requirement for foreign and national personnel; 100 percent of the workforce, including the board of directors, can be foreign nationals. Labor permits are not required in Colombia, except for under-aged workers. Foreign employees have the same rights as Colombian employees.

17. FOREIGN TRADE ZONES/FREE PORTS/TRADE FACILITATION

To attract foreign investment and promote the importation of capital goods, the Colombian government uses a number of drawback and duty deferral programs. One example is free trade zones (FTZ), which the government has used to attract more investment and create more jobs. In 2005, Colombia's Congress passed comprehensive FTZ modernization legislation that opened investment to international companies, allowed one-company/standalone FTZs, and permitted the designation of pre-existing plants as FTZs. This law was updated in 2007 to outline the requirements to be declared a FTZ. Colombia is a leader in FTZs in Latin America. As of January 2015 there were 10 FTZs (between permanent and special –for one enterprise- types) in 20 departments, a tenfold increase since 2005 and twice the average of Central American countries. FTZs account for USD 9.2 billion in investment, around 1,200 companies established and provide around 80,000 direct jobs and 32,000 indirect ones. Job creation is still weak. According to the National Business Association of Colombia (ANDI) the potential is 350,000 and that current figures are far below the Latin American average or the numbers from countries like Nicaragua or Dominican Republic that have fewer FTZs. While the customs authority, DIAN, oversees requests to establish FTZs, the Colombian government is not involved in their operation.

In 2002, Colombia accepted the WTO Committee on Subsidies and Countervailing Measures' decision to phase out all export subsidies in FTZs by December 31, 2006. However, FTZs maintain their special customs and foreign exchange regimes, per Law 1004 passed in 2005, which also grants a preferential 15 percent corporate income tax and exemption from customs duties and value-added taxes on imported materials. In January 2013, a tax reform took effect, grandfathering benefits to existing FTZs while requiring new ones after December 31, 2012 to pay an additional income tax of nine percent until 2015 and eight percent beginning in 2016. In return for these and other incentives, every permanent FTZ must meet specific investment and direct job creation commitments, depending on their total assets, during the first three years of the project. Up to USD 135,000 of assets the investment and job creation can be zero. Between USD135,001 and USD1.3 million of assets, investment requirement is zero but must create 20 jobs. More than USD 1.3 million up to USD 8.1 million of assets, it must invest minimum USD1.3 million and create at least 30 jobs. More than USD 8.1 million of assets requires USD 3.1 million of investment and 50 direct jobs. Special FTZ zones are required to invest and generate more or less direct jobs depending on the economic sector.

18. FOREIGN DIRECT INVESTMENT AND FOREIGN PORTFOLIO INVESTMENT STATISTICS

Table 2: Key Macroeconomic Data, U.S. FDI in Host Country/Economy

	Host Country Statistical Source*		USG or International Statistical Source		USG or International Source of Data: BEA; IMF; Eurostat; UNCTAD, Other
Economic Data	Year	Amount	Year	Amount	
Host Country	2013	367.8	2013	378.4	www.worldbank.org/en/country

	Host Country Statistical source*		USG or International Statistical Source		USG or International Source of Data: BEA; IMF; Eurostat; UNCTAD, Other
Gross Domestic Product (GDP) ($M USD)					
Foreign Direct Investment	Host Country Statistical source*		USG or International Statistical source		USG or international Source of Data: BEA; IMF; Eurostat; UNCTAD, Other
U.S. FDI in partner country ($M USD, stock positions)	2013	2861	2013	7819	www.bea.gov www.banrep.gov.co
Host country's FDI in the United States ($M USD, stock positions)	2013	306.7	2013	609	BEA data available 3/19/14 athttp://bea.gov/international/direct_investment_ multinational_companies_comprehensive_data.htm
Total inbound stock of FDI as % host GDP	2013	6.3%			

www.banrep.gov.co

Table 3: Sources and Destination of FDI

Direct Investment from/in Counterpart Economy Data

From Top Five Sources/To Top Five Destinations (US Dollars, Millions)

Inward Direct Investment			Outward Direct Investment		
Total Inward	16,199	100%	Total Outward	7,650	100%

U.S.A	2,861.5	17.7	Panama	3200	41.8
Switzerland	2,083.7	12.9	Bermuda	769.1	10.1
Panama	2,054.6	12.7	Spain	171.7	9.4
United Kingdom	1,416.4	8.7	Chile	680.3	8.9
Spain	950.6	5.9	Peru	633.5	8.3
"0" reflects amounts rounded to +/- USD 500,000.					

Source: IMF Coordinated Direct Investment Survey

Table 4: Sources of Portfolio Investment

PORTFOLIO INVESTMENT ASSETS TOP FIVE PARTNERS (MILLIONS, US DOLLARS)

TOTAL			EQUITY SECURITIES			TOTAL DEBT SECURITIES		
All Countries	23,913	100%	All Countries	13763	100%	All Countries	10150	100%
U.S.A	15894	66	U.S.A.	9479	69	U.S.A	6417	63
Luxembourg	2042	9	Luxembourg	1728	13	International Organizations	862	8
Chile	1630	7	Chile	1599	12	Germany	510	5
Intl Orgs	862	4	Canada	274	2	Brazil	404	4
Germany	510	2	Cayman Islds	246	2	France	319	3

Source: IMF Coordinated Portfolio Investment Survey

BUSINESS AND LEGAL CONTACTTS

Department of Arauca

Avila & Asociados Office: Carrera 25 No. 18 A 49, Oficina 202 Arauca, Colombia Phone: (577) 885-6751 / 885-7575 Mobile: (57) 310-763-8828 E-mail: avilaleguizamon@yahoo.com ; aaa.abogados.517@gmail.com
Fields: Administrative, civil and commercial law.
Languages: Spanish.

Armenia / Department of Quindío

Leguizamón González Asociados Office: Carrera 14 No. 23-27, Oficina 601 Armenia, Colombia Phone: (576) 748-6522; 748-6522. Mobile: (57) 312-714-7988; 311-709-3203 E-mail: abogada.helena@hotmail.com
Website: http://bufeteabogadosarmenia.blogspot.com/

Members of the firm: Luis Enrique Leguizamón and Maria Helena Gonzalez de Leguizamón. **Fields**: Family law, adoption, child custody, marriage/divorce, civil law, criminal law, damages, narcotics, contracts. Firm may take cases outside the city.
Languages: Spanish

Bogotá, D.C. / Department of Cundinamarca Civil Law

Alberto Preciado & Asociados. Office: Calle 75 # 5-59 Piso 5. Bogotá, D.C., Colombia. Phone: (571) 744-7888; Fax: 489-0769 E-mail: alpre@albertopreciado.com Website: www.albertopreciado.com

Principal members of the firm (established in 1951): Preciado-Peña Alberto, Colombian citizen, born in Bogotá, 1923; National University of Colombia; Preciado-Arbeláez, Alberto: Colombian citizen, born in Bogotá, 1955; Colegio Mayor de Nuestra Señora del Rosario University. **Fields**: Family law, commercial/business law, foreign investments, damages, contracts, corporations, taxes, labor relations, criminal law. Languages: Spanish, English & French.

Alfredo Moreno Dávila International Trade Consultants Office: Calle 90 Bis No. 12-28 Piso 2 Bogotá D.C., Colombia Phone: (571) 271-3995. Mobile: (57) 310-877-8915 Email: alfredomorenodavila@customs-trade.com , gerencia@customstrade.com

Website: www.customs-trade.com , www.alfredomorenodavila.com

Principal member of the firm established in 2010: Alfredo Moreno-Dávila, Lawyer-LL.M (master of laws). University of Los Andes-University of Ottawa-University of Carleton.

Fields: commercial/business law, foreign investments, taxes, commercial law, contracts, transportation law, corporations, aeronautical/maritime, foreign claims.

Firm can provide service of court reporter.
Languages: Spanish, English and French.

Ayerbe Abogados Office: Carrera 7 # 73-55, Oficina 1102 Bogotá, D.C., Colombia Mobile: (57) 315-563-5219 E-mail: rayerbesr@ayerbeabogados.com Webpage: www.ayerbeabogados.com

Principal member of the firm: Rodrigo Vicente Ayerbe, Colombian citizen, born in 1948. Javeriana University in Bogotá Law School 1970; Harvard Law School 1972. He has practiced law for 42 years.

Partners: Felipe Ayerbe, Rodrigo Ayerbe Jr., Andres Florez, Claudia Romero, Laura Castro, Juan Hernandez, Paula Velez, Maria J. Fallofo, Valentina Naranjo.

Fields: Commercial/Business Law, Foreign Investments, Civil Law, Commercial Law, Contracts, Corporations, Estates, Labor Relations.

Firm can provide service of court reporter. Languages: Spanish and English.

Baker & McKenzie Office: Avenida 82 # 10-62, Piso 6 Bogotá, D.C., Colombia Phone: (571) 634-1500; Fax: 376- 2211; Mobile: (57) 315-348-8471 E-mail: office.bogota@bakermckenzie.com

Website: www.bakermckenzie.com /Colombia Principal members of the firm: Trujillo, Jaime Eduardo, Colombian citizen. London School of Economics and Political Science (LL.M. International Business Law) 1994. University de los Andes (J.D.) (1988). **Fields**: Corporate, Energy, Mining & Infrastructure, Dispute Resolution, Labor & Employment,

Taxes, Intellectual property. Firm can take cases outside of the city.
Languages: English and Spanish.

Brigard & Urrutia Abogados Office: Calle 70A No. 4-41 Bogotá, D.C., Colombia Phone: (571) 346-2011; Fax: 310-0609 E-mail: info@bu.com.co Website: www.bu.com.co

Principal members of the firm: Urrutia-Valenzuela, Carlos: Colombian citizen, born 1949. Los Andes University School of Law in Bogotá, JD, 1977; New York University School of Law, MCJ; Michelsen-Jaramillo, Sergio: Colombian citizen, born in Bogotá, 1960. Los Andes University, School of Law in Bogotá, JD, 1984; University of Paris II, Masters in Commercial Law. Umaña-Trujillo, Carlos: Colombian citizen, born in Bogotá, 1960. Colegio Mayor de Nuestra Señora del Rosario University, JD, 1983; New York University School of Law. **Fields**: Commercial/business law, banking/financial, contracts, corporations Insurance, foreign investments, marketing agreements, patents/trademarks/copyrights, estates, taxes, damages, transportation law, aeronautical/maritime/, foreign claims, government relations, labor relations, immigration, civil law, criminal law.

Languages: Spanish English and French.

Chávez- Herrera & Morano International P.A. Office: Avenida Carrera 9 No. 113-52 Oficina 602. Edificio Torres Unidas 2 Bogotá, D.C., Colombia Phone: (571) 745-8546; Mobile: (571) 311-457-9962 E-mail: herreramorano@herrera-morano.com Web site: www.herrera-morano.com

Principal members of the firm established in 1982: Herrera-Ramirez, Fernando Javier: Colombian citizen, born 1954. Externado de Colombia University, School of Law, 1980; Masters in Commercial and Financial Law, Civil and Family Law, Criminal Law (1981-1982). Chávez-Alarcón, Diego Alberto: Colombian citizen, born 1954. Externado de Colombia University, School of Law, 1980; Masters in Commercial and Financial Law at Colegio Mayor de Nuestra Señora del Rosario University (1986).

Fields: Civil, family law, child custody, parental child abduction, child protection, marriage/divorce, insurance, commercial/business law, foreign investments, civil law, damages, commercial law, contracts, corporations, aeronautical/maritime, labor relations, immigration and auto/accidents.

Firm can provide services of a certified translator, court reporter/stenographer or notary. They may take cases outside the city. Languages: Spanish and English

Consultores en Red S.A.S Office: Carrera 7 No. 71 - 21 Torre A, Of. 201

Bogotá, D.C., Colombia Phone: (571) 312-0624; Fax: 3174256 E-mail: bcg@cer.com.co ; gat@cer.com.co Principal member of the firm established in 2001: Bruno Camargo Giraldo, Colombian citizen. Externado de Colombia University, School of Law. JD, University Institute Ortega y Gasset. Masters in Law, Economics and Public Policies.

Fields: Banking/Financial, Commercial/Business Law, Foreign Investments, Marketing agreements, Patents/Trademarks/copyrights, Civil Law, Criminal Law, Commercial Law, Contracts, Corporations, Foreign Claims, Taxes. Firm may take cases outside the city.

Languages: Spanish and English.

Data & TIC Consultores S.A.S Office: Carrera 7 # 26-20, Office 2301 Bogotá, D.C., Colombia Phone: (571) 346-7122 E-mail: rafael.gamboa@dataytic.com

Webpage: www.dataytic.com.co Principal member of the firm, established in 2011: Gamboa-Bernate, Rafael Hernando: Colombian citizen, Pontificia Universidad Javeriana School of Law in Bogota; The John Marshall Law School, Chicago Illinois: LL.M. in intellectual Property (June, 2002), LL.M. in information Technology (2001)

Fields: Information Technology and Privacy Law, Banking/Financial, Commercial/Business Law, Foreign Investments, Marketing Agreements, Patents/Trademarks/Copyrights, Civil Law, Damages,

Collections, Commercial law, Contracts, Transportation Law, Corporations, Aeronautical/Maritime, Foreign Claims, Taxes, Immigration, Auto/Accidents.

Firm can provide services of a certified translator, stenographer or notary. They may take cases outside the city.

Languages: Spanish, English and French.

Diaz Cárdenas Abogados Office: Avenida Carrera 15 # 106-32 Oficina 608 Bogotá, D.C., Colombia Phone: (571) 619-2941; Mobile: (57) 310-8831617 E-mail: jdiaz@colombianattorney.com Website: www.colombianattorney.com Principal member of the firm (established in 1982): Diaz-Cárdenas, Jorge: Colombian citizen, born 1953. Colegio Mayor de Nuestra Señora del Rosario University, Doctor of Jurisprudence, 1977.

Fields: Family law, parental child abduction, child protection, marriage/divorce, insurance, commercial/business law, foreign investments, marketing agreements, civil law, collections, commercial law, contracts, corporations, foreign claims, estates, immigration.

Firm can provide services of a certified translator, court reporter/stenographer or notary. They may take cases outside the city. Languages: Spanish and English

Godoy Cordoba Attorneys at Law, Member of Littler Global. Office: Carrera 7 No. 71-21 Torre B Of. 303 Bogotá, D.C., Colombia Phone: (571) 317-4628; Fax: 317-4637 E-mail: info@godoycordoba.com Website: www.godoycordoba.com Principal member of the firm established in 1988: Carlos Hernan Godoy Fajardo, Colombian citizen born in 1954. Fields: Labor and Immigration Law.

Languages: Spanish and English

González-Rubio Velez, Antonio Office: Carrera 7 # 33-29, Oficina 009 Piso 1 Bogotá, D.C., Colombia

Phone: (571) 5606091; Mobile: (57) 317-4167062 E-mail: gonzalezrubiovelez@yahoo.es Colombian citizen, born in Barranquilla, 1938. Libre University in Bogotá, 1969.

Fields: Civil and commercial law. Languages: English, French, Spanish and Portuguese.

Lloreda Camacho & Co. Abogados. Office: Calle 72 # 5-83, Piso 5 Bogotá, D.C., Colombia Phone: (571) 326-4270, 606-9700; Fax: 606-9701 E-mail: pcorreal@lloredacamacho.com Website: www.lloredacamacho.com

Principal member of the firm, established in 1941: Tamayo-Arango, Gustavo: Colombian citizen, born 1961; Los Andes University in Bogotá. Masters of Procedural Law at Colegio Mayor de Nuestra Señora Del Rosario University (1987). **Fields**: Civil, commercial, administrative, financial, aeronautics, maritime, corporate, tax, labor, contracts, litigation and intellectual property law.

Languages: Spanish and English

MD Mosquera Abogados North Office: Carrera 14 #127 A 48, Office 402 Phone: (571) 696-9229, 696-9230; Fax: 696-8014

Downtown Office: Carrera 8 No. 15-40, Office 1202 Bogota, Colombia.

Phone: (571) 341-3668 – 286-6338; Fax: 334-4181

Mobile: (57) 310-803-8133 – 310-803-8123 E-mail: info@mdmosqueraabogados.com ; eduardo.samek@mdmosqueraabogados.com Web site: www.mdmosqueraabogados.com

Principal member of the firm: Eduardo Samek De la Espriella, Colombian citizen, born in Barranquilla,1935; Javeriana University in Bogotá School of Law, Doctor of Juridical Science.

Partner: Maria Dolores Mosquera Casas de Samek, Colombian citizen, lawyer specialist in Trademarks and Sanitary Registers. **Fields**: Family Law, Marriage/Divorce, Commercial/Business Law, Patents/Trademarks/Copyrights, Sanitary Registers, Civil Law, Canon Law, Commercial Law, Contracts, Corporations, Labor Relations.

Languages: English and Spanish. **Pinilla Plazas y Asociados SAS** Office: Calle 95 No 15 – 33 Of. 404 Bogota, Colombia Phone: (571) 703-0581 - (57) 320-401-3978 Fax: (571) 623-2517 Email: apinilla@pinillalegal.com

Website: http://www.pinillalegal.com/ Principal member of the firm: Pinilla, Luis Alfredo, Colombian Citizen, born in Bogotá, 1978. Rosario University School of law, J.D. 2001; Andes University, Postgraduate. Program in Commercial Law, 2002; New York University School of Law, Master of Laws in General Legal Studies, 2003; Master of Laws in Corporate law, 2006; Admitted to practice law in the State of NY (2004).

He has practiced law in Colombian for 7 years and in New York for 1 year.

Fields: Commercial/Business Law, Foreign Investments, patents/Trademarks/Copyrights, Civil Law, Damages, Commercial Law, Contracts, Corporations.

Firm may take cases outside the city.

Languages: Spanish, English and French.

Philippi Prietocarrizosa & Uria Office: Carrera 9 # 74-08, Office 105 Bogotá, D.C., Colombia Phone: (571) 326-8600; Fax: 326-8610 E-mail: martin.carrizosa@ppulegal.com Website: www.ppulegal.com Principal member of the firm: Carrizosa, Martín, Colombian citizen, born in Bogotá,1964; Los Andes University School of Law in Bogotá, Masters in Commercial Law, 1985. **Fields**: Corporate, competition, banking/financial - capital markets, estates, intellectual property, labor, public, taxes, energy, mining and natural resource, infrastructure and projects, telecommunications and international trade law.

Languages: Spanish and English.

Quantum Consulting Colombia Office: Calle 106 No. 54-93 Oficina 701

Bogotá, D.C., Colombia Phone: (57-1) 300-1267; Fax: 614-5474; Mobile: (57) 310-329-7741 E-mail: jroa@quantumcolombia.com Website: www.quantumcolombia.com

Principal member of the firm established on 2004: Julián Roa Aranda, Colombian citizen born in 1963. Santo Tomas University School of law in Bogota- Colombian Law Specialist **Fields**: Commercial law, Immigration law. Languages: Spanish and English.

Rodriguez, Rincón, Ugeh & Associates

Office: Calle 82 # 14-A-17 Oficina 501
Bogotá, D.C. Colombia

Phone: 57-1-530-7024
Mobile: 57-300-336-9681
E-mail: info@rrulegal.com
Web page: www.rrulegal.com

Principal members of the firm established in 2014: Perez Morales, Marcela. Universidad Autónoma de Colombia Law degree in 2012.

Fields: Commercial/Business law, Immigration, Family law. Firm can take cases out of the city.

Languages: Spanish and English.

Sanclemente Fernández Abogados, S.A. Office: Carrera 9 # 69-70 Bogotá, D.C., Colombia Phone: (571) 310-0555 / 345-2553; Fax 255-9372, 347-0880 Mobile: 57-321-242-1963 E-mail: info@sfa.com.co , dsa@sfa.com.co

Website: www.sfa.com.co Principal member of the firm, established in 1942: Sanclemente Arenas, Diana. LLM 1991 Georgetown University, Washington, D.C.; Undergraduate Degree in Law 1989 at Colegio Mayor de Nuestra Señora del Rosario, Bogota, Colombia.

Fields: Litigation, environment, aviation, labor, immigration and tax law. Languages: Spanish, English and German.

Wiesner & Asociados, Ltda. Office: Carrera 11 A No. 90-16, Of. 403/404 Bogotá, D.C., Colombia Phone: (571) 218-8546, 218-6549 E-mail: jgarcia@wiesnerasociados.com

Website: www.wiesnerasociados.com .

Principal member of the firm, established in 1993: Wiesner, Eduardo A.: Colombian citizen, born 1963. Universidad de los Andes School of Law, Bogotá, Colombia, JD, 1989; London School of Economics and Political Science, London, England, LL.M. with a Merit, 1992. Inter-American Development Bank (IDB) Graduated Scholarship Program Scholar, 1991. Legal Counsel to the Government of Japan. Law

Fields: Foreign investment, telecommunications, antitrust, customs, food and drug, civil, commercial, litigation and mergers & acquisitions. Languages; Spanish and English

Bogotá, D.C. / Department of Cundinamarca Criminal Law

B&B Abogados. Office: Calle 74 No. 10-33, Of. 701 Bogotá, Colombia Phone: (571) 758-9435; Fax: 758-9435 E-mail: consultas@bybabogados.net ; jcbolanos@bybabogados.net

Website: www.bybabogados.net

Principal member of the firm established in 2006: Bolaños, Juan Carlos: Law degree and Insurance specialist from University of La Sabana, 1998; Criminal law specialist from Sergio Arboleda university. **Fields**: Criminal law, contract and intellectual property law. Languages: Spanish and English.

Heraclio Fernandez Abogados Office: Carrera 13 A No. 89-38, Office 528 Bogotá, D.C., Colombia Phone: (571) 616-0865; Mobile: (57) 315-363-7321

E-mail: heracliofs@yahoo.es Members of the firm: Heraclio Fernandez Colombian citizen, born in Tunja, Boyacá, 1932. Externado de Colombia University in Bogotá. Public offices held: Magistrate of the Superior Tribunal of Tunja; Other members: Ulises Fernandez Rojas & Gabriel Fernandez Rojas. **Fields**: Criminal law, Contracts, Estates, Government relations, Auto/Accidents.

Languages: Spanish and English

Muñoz Sotelo, Lauro Vicente
Office: Calle 127D # 56-33
Bogotá, D.C., Colombia
Phone: (571) 271-4838; Mobile: (57) 315-234-8855
E-mail: lauro.vicente@hotmail.com
Colombian Citizen, born in 1935, Universidad Nueva Granada
Fields: Criminal law.
Languages: Spanish and English

Bogotá, D.C. / Department of Cundinamarca Family and Canonic Law

Chávez- Herrera & Morano International P.A. Office: Avenida Carrera 9 No. 113-52 Oficina 602. Edificio Torres Unidas 2 Bogotá, D.C., Colombia Phone: (571) 745-8546; Mobile: (571) 311-457-9962 E-mail: herreramorano@herrera-morano.com Web site: www.herrera-morano.com

Principal members of the firm established in 1982: Herrera-Ramirez, Fernando Javier: Colombian citizen, born 1954. Externado de Colombia University, School of Law, 1980; Masters in Commercial and Financial Law, Civil and Family Law, Criminal Law (1981-1982). Chávez-Alarcón, Diego Alberto: Colombian citizen, born 1954. Externado de Colombia University, School of Law, 1980; Masters in Commercial and Financial Law at Colegio Mayor de Nuestra Señora del Rosario University (1986).

Fields: Civil, family law, child custody, parental child abduction, child protection, marriage/divorce, insurance, commercial/business law, foreign investments, civil law, damages, commercial law, contracts, corporations, aeronautical/maritime, labor relations, immigration and auto/accidents.

Firm can provide services of a certified translator, court reporter/stenographer or notary. They may take cases outside the city. Languages: Spanish and English

MD Mosquera Abogados North Office: Carrera 14 #127 A 48, Office 402 Phone: (571) 696-9229, 696-9230; Fax: 696-8014

Downtown Office: Carrera 8 No. 15-40, Office 1202 Phone: (571) 341-3668 – 286-6338; Fax: 334-4181 Mobile: (57) 310-803-8133 – 310-803-8123 Bogotá, D.C., Colombia. E-mail: info@mdmosqueraabogados.com ; eduardo.samek@mdmosqueraabogados.com Web site: www.mdmosqueraabogados.com

Principal member of the firm: Eduardo Samek De la Espriella, Colombian citizen, born in Barranquilla, 1935; Javeriana University in Bogotá School of Law, Doctor of Juridical Science.

Partner: Maria Dolores Mosquera Casas de Samek, Colombian citizen, lawyer specialist in Trademarks and S**anitary Registers.** Fields: Family Law, Marriage/Divorce, Commercial/Business Law, Patents/Trademarks/Copyrights, Sanitary Registers, Civil Law, Canon Law, Commercial Law, Contracts, Corporations, Labor Relations.

Languages: English and Spanish.

Rivera, Pinilla & Gallón Abogados Office: Calle 67 No. 6-60, Of. 1003. Edificio Torre Ejecutiva Bogotá, D.C, Colombia

Phone: (571) 211-6702 / 2123153; Fax: 2129155 E-mail: juangallon@rpglegal.com Website: www.rpglegal.com Principal member of the firm, Juan Carlos Gallon, Colombian citizen born in 1974. Universidad Javeriana, in Bogota 1999, Master's degree in Communications Law and Family Law and

Master's degree in Family law 2002. Fields: Family law, adoptions, child custody, parental child abduction, child protection, marriage/divorce, civil law. Languages: Spanish and English

Bogotá, D.C. / Department of Cundinamarca

Intellectual Property Law

Álvarez Bernate Asociados Office: Calle 69 A # 4-64 Bogotá, D.C., Colombia Phone: (571) 636-7334; Fax: 636-7650 E-mail: calvarez@alvarezbernate.com Website: www.alvarezbernate.com Principal member of the firm: Álvarez, Camilo: Colombian citizen, born 1953. Colegio Mayor de Nuestra Señora del Rosario University, Doctor of Jurisprudence, 1978; University of Virginia Law School, LL.M., 1981; Columbia Business School, MBA, 1989. **Fields**: Contracts, corporate, maritime and intellectual property law.

Languages: Spanish and English.

B&B Abogados. Office: Calle 74 No. 10-33, Of. 701 Bogotá, Colombia Phone: (571) 758-9435; Fax: 758-9435 E-mail: consultas@bybabogados.net ; jcbolanos@bybabogados.net

Website: www.bybabogados.net

Principal member of the firm established in 2006: Bolaños, Juan Carlos: Law degree and Insurance specialist from University of La Sabana, 1998; Criminal law specialist from Sergio Arboleda university. **Fields**: Criminal law, contract, and intellectual law. Languages: Spanish and English.

Cavelier Abogados Office: Carrera 4 # 72-35 Edificio Siski Bogotá, D.C., Colombia Phone: (571) 347-3611; Fax: 211-8650 Website: www.cavelier.com E-mail: cavelier@cavelier.com Principal member of the firm, established in 1953: Cavelier, Germán: Colombian citizen, born in Chicago, Illinois, 1922. Colegio Mayor de Nuestra Señora del Rosario University, 1946. **Fields**: Commercial, foreign investment, mergers & acquisitions, competition, financial, commercial, contracts, intellectual property, telecommunications, health registrations and international law. Languages: Spanish, French and English.

Data & TIC Consultores S.A.S Office: Carrera 7 # 26-20, Office 2301 Bogotá, D.C., Colombia Phone: (571) 346-7122 E-mail: rafael.gamboa@dataytic.com

Webpage: www.dataytic.com.co Principal member of the firm, established in 2011: Gamboa-Bernate, Rafael Hernando: Colombian citizen, Pontificia Universidad Javeriana School of Law in Bogota; The John Marshall Law School, Chicago Illinois: LL.M. in intellectual Property (June, 2002), LL.M. in information Technology (2001)

Fields: Information Technology and Privacy Law, Banking/Financial, Commercial/Business Law, Foreign Investments, Marketing Agreements, Patents/Trademarks/Copyrights, Civil Law, Damages, Collections, Commercial law, Contracts, Transportation Law, Corporations, Aeronautical/Maritime, Foreign Claims, Taxes, Immigration, Auto/Accidents.

Firm can provide services of a certified translator, stenographer or notary. They may take cases outside the city.

Languages: Spanish, English and French.

Figueroa Sierra & Asociados, Abogados Office: Carrera 9 No. 74-08 Oficina 504 Bogotá, D.C., Colombia Phone: (571) 211-3090; Fax: 611-3018 E-mail: fsa@fsa-law.com Website: www.figueroasierra.com Principal member of the firm, established in 1986: Figueroa-Sierra. Augusto:

Colombian citizen, born in Bogotá, 1950. Los Andes University School of Law in Bogotá; University of Illinois at Urbana-Champaign, Masters of Arts and Ph.D. candidate in Latin American Development.

Fields: Foreign investment, corporate, commercial contracts, competition, taxes, labor law, finance, insurance, oil & gas, mining, real estate, telecommunications and intellectual property law .

Languages: Spanish, French and English.

Jurislegal S.A.S Office: Calle 111 No. 7C-18

Bogotá, D.C., Colombia Phone: (571) 467-4557

Mobile: (57) 314-888-4292, (57) 320-305-6937 E-mail: jurislegal@jurislegal.com Website: www.jurislegal.com Principal member of the firm: Jaramillo-Abuchaibe, Jorge: Colombian citizen, born 1960. Javeriana University in Bogotá, Doctor of Law, 1985, Master's Degree in Commercial Law. **Fields**: Commercial/ Business Law, Contracts, Corporations, foreign investment, Marketing agreements, Patents/trademarks/Copyrights, Taxes, Labor law.

Firm can provide services of a certified translator, court reporter/stenographer or notary. They may take cases outside the city. Languages: Spanish and English

LLoreda Camacho y & Co. Abogados. Office: Calle 72 # 5-83, Piso 5 Bogotá, D.C., Colombia Phone: (571) 326-4270, 606-9700; Fax: 606-9701 / 326-4271 E-mail: pcorreal@lloredacamacho.com Website: www.lloredacamacho.com

Principal member of the firm, established in 1941: Lloreda-Londoño, José Antonio: Colombian citizen, born 1946; Javeriana University in Bogotá School of Law, Masters in Labor Law, 1971; University of Paris, Doctor in European Community Law, 1973. **Fields**: Civil, commercial, administrative, financial, aeronautics, maritime, corporate, tax, labor, contracts, litigation, torts and intellectual property law.

Languages: Spanish and English

Posse, Herrera & Ruiz Abogados Office: Carrera 7 No. 71-52, Torre A, Of. 504 Bogotá, D.C., Colombia Phone: (571) 325-7300; Fax 325-7313 E-mail: phr@phrlegal.com Website: www.phrlegal.com

Fields: Merge & Acquisitions, Competition Law, Corporate Law, Labor and Immigration, Tax Planning and International Commerce, Financial law and Capital Markets, Dispute Resolutions, Natural Resources and Energy, Environmental Law, Real Estate Projects and Trusts, Infrastructure and PPPs, Insurance. , Intellectual Property.

Languages: Spanish, English, French and Portuguese.

Philippi Prietocarrizosa & Uria Office: Carrera 9 # 74-08, Office 105 Bogotá, D.C., Colombia Phone: (571) 326-8600; Fax: 326-8610 E-mail: martin.carrizosa@ppulegal.com Website: www.ppulegal.com Principal member of the firm: Carrizosa, Martín, Colombian citizen, born in Bogotá,1964; Los Andes University School of Law in Bogotá, Masters in Commercial Law, 1985. **Fields**: Corporate, competition, banking/financial - capital markets, estates, intellectual property, labor, public, taxes, energy, mining and natural resource, infrastructure and projects, telecommunications and international trade law.

Languages: Spanish and English.

Bogotá, D.C. / Department of Cundinamarca Tax Law

Alfredo Moreno Dávila International Trade Consultants Office: Calle 90 Bis No. 12-28 Piso 2 Bogotá D.C., Colombia Phone: (571) 271-3995. Mobile: (57) 310-877-8915 Email: alfredomorenodavila@customs-trade.com , gerencia@customstrade.com

Website: www.customs-trade.com , www.alfredomorenodavila.com

Principal member of the firm established in 2010: Alfredo Moreno-Dávila, Lawyer-LL.M (master of laws). University of Los Andes-University of Ottawa-University of Carleton.

Fields: commercial/business law, foreign investments, taxes, commercial law, contracts, transportation law, corporations, aeronautical/maritime, foreign claims.

Firm can provide service of court reporter.
Languages: Spanish, English and French.

Baker & McKenzie Office: Avenida 82 # 10-62, Piso 6 Bogotá, D.C., Colombia Phone: (571) 634-1500; Fax: 376- 2211; Mobile: (57) 315-348-8471 E-mail: office.bogota@bakermckenzie.com

Website: www.bakermckenzie.com /Colombia Principal members of the firm: Trujillo, Jaime Eduardo, Colombian citizen. London School of Economics and Political Science LL.M. International Business Law, 1994. University de los Andes, J.D. 1988. **Fields**: Corporate, Energy, Mining & Infrastructure, Dispute Resolution, Labor & Employment,

Taxes, Intellectual property. Firm can take cases outside of the city.

Languages: English and Spanish.

Data & TIC Consultores S.A.S Office: Carrera 7 # 26-20, Office 2301 Bogotá, D.C., Colombia Phone: (571) 346-7122 E-mail: rafael.gamboa@dataytic.com

Webpage: www.dataytic.com.co Principal member of the firm, established in 2011: Gamboa-Bernate, Rafael Hernando: Colombian citizen, Pontificia Universidad Javeriana School of Law in Bogota; The John Marshall Law School, Chicago Illinois: LL.M. in intellectual Property (June, 2002), LL.M. in information Technology (2001)

Fields: Information Technology and Privacy Law, Banking/Financial, Commercial/Business Law, Foreign Investments, Marketing Agreements, Patents/Trademarks/Copyrights, Civil Law, Damages, Collections, Commercial law, Contracts, Transportation Law, Corporations, Aeronautical/Maritime, Foreign Claims, Taxes, Immigration, Auto/Accidents.

Firm can provide services of a certified translator, stenographer or notary. Firm can take cases outside the city.

Languages: Spanish, English and French.

Figueroa Sierra & Asociados, Abogados Office: Carrera 9 No. 74-08 Oficina 504 Bogotá, D.C., Colombia Phone: (571) 211-3090; Fax: 611-3018 E-mail: fsa@fsa-law.com Website: www.figueroasierra.com Principal member of the firm, established in 1986: Figueroa-Sierra. Augusto: Colombian citizen, born in Bogotá, 1950. Los Andes University School of Law in Bogotá; University of Illinois at Urbana-Champaign, Masters of Arts and Ph.D. candidate in Latin American Development. **Fields**: Foreign investment, corporate, commercial contracts, competition, taxes, labor law, finance, insurance, oil & gas, mining, real estate, telecommunications and intellectual property law .

Languages: Spanish, French and English.

Lloreda Camacho & Co. Abogados. Office: Calle 72 # 5-83, Piso 5 Bogotá, D.C., Colombia Phone: (571) 326-4270, 606-9700; Fax: 606-9701 E-mail: pcorreal@lloredacamacho.com Website: www.lloredacamacho.com

Principal member of the firm, established in 1941: Tamayo-Arango, Gustavo: Colombian citizen, born 1961; Los Andes University in Bogotá. Masters of Procedural Law at Colegio Mayor de Nuestra Señora Del Rosario University (1987). **Fields**: Civil, commercial, administrative, financial, aeronautics, maritime, corporate, tax, labor, contracts, litigation, and intellectual property.

Languages: Spanish and English

Muñoz Tamayo & Asociados Office: Calle 72 # 7-82, Piso 8 Bogotá, D.C., Colombia Phone: (571) 210-0666; Fax: 210-3856 Website: www.mutasoc.com

E-mail: info@mtalegal.co Principal member of the firm, established in 1990: Muñoz-Tamayo, Diego: Born in Bogotá, 1957. University of Paris II, School of Law, Economics and Social Sciences (DEUG, 1977); Los Andes University School of Law in Bogotá, Masters in Commercial Law; London School of Economics & Political Science (LL.M., Masters in International Financial Law, 1985); Oxford University, Saint Anthony's College (M.S.C., Masters in Public Policies in Latin America, 1986). **Fields**: Corporate, financial and capital markets, telecommunications, media and technology, conflict, resolution and litigation, environmental law, real state, labor and tax law. Languages: Spanish, English, German and French.

Payán, Urdaneta & Co. Lozano Villamizar Morales Abogados Office: Calle 59A-Bis # 4A-33 Bogotá, D.C., Colombia Phone: (571) 212-9400; Fax: 217-8440 E-mail: payanur@payanurdaneta.com Website: www.payanurdaneta.com Principal member of the firm: Urdaneta Wiesner, Adolfo: Colombian citizen, born in Bogotá, 1939.

Colegio Mayor de Nuestra Señora del Rosario, Bogotá, J.D. 1965.Education: Mayor de Nuestra Señora del Rosario, Bogotá (LL.B.), Southwestern Legal Foundation, University of Texas, Dallas, Texas. Parker School of Law, Columbia University, New York,

Fields: Corporations, Corporate Governance, Foreign investments, Industry property, Dispute resolution, litigation, labor and taxes law. Languages: Spanish, English and French.

Philippi Prietocarrizosa & Uria Office: Carrera 9 # 74-08, Office 105 Bogotá, D.C., Colombia Phone: (571) 326-8600; Fax: 326-8610 E-mail: martin.carrizosa@ppulegal.com Website: www.ppulegal.com Principal member of the firm: Carrizosa, Martín, Colombian citizen, born in Bogotá,1964; Los Andes University School of Law in Bogotá, Masters in Commercial Law, 1985. Fields: Corporate, competition, banking/financial - capital markets, estates, intellectual property, labor, public, taxes, energy, mining and natural resource, infrastructure and projects, telecommunications and international trade law.

Languages: Spanish and English.

Barranquilla / Department of Atlántico

Blanco-Navarra, María de Jesús Office: Carrera 51-D # 90-144 Barranquilla, Atlántico, Colombia Phone: (575) -357-1815; Mobile: (57)300-815-4945 E-mail: mayito1227@gmail.com Colombian citizen, born in 1940. Externado de Colombia University in Bogotá. Labor law and Budget administration. She has practiced law during 47 years.

Fields: Family law, adoptions, child custody, child protection, marriage/divorce, commercial/business law, civil law, collections, commercial law, contracts, corporations, labor relations.

Lawyer can provide services of a certified translator, court reporter/stenographer or notary. She may take cases in Barranquilla or Cartagena.

Languages: Spanish.

Carvajal Abogados Office: Carrera 53 No. 68 B 57 Oficina 2- 214 Barranquilla, Atlántico, Colombia Phone: (575) 360-2254, 360-4904 E-mail: jcarvajal@carvajalabogados.com

Website: www.carvajalabogados.org Firm established in 1976.

Fields: Family law, adoptions, child custody, parental child abduction, child protection, marriage/divorce, commercial/Business law, Foreign investments, Civil law, damages, contracts, labor relations, auto/accidents. Firm can provide services of a certified translator and can take cases outside of the city.

Languages: Spanish and English & French.

Donaldo del Villar Delgado Office: Calle 39 # 43-123, Piso 8, Office G-4 Barranquilla, Atlántico, Colombia Phone: (575) 344-9823; Mobile: (57) 310-6304863

E-mail: dddvd@hotmail.com Colombian citizen, born 1962. School of law, Universidad del Atlántico 1986. Major in Criminal Law, Universidad Libre 1996. Master in Law, Universidad del Norte 2010. **Fields**: Auto accidents, narcotics, damages and criminal law.

Firm can provide the services of a certified translator, court reporter/stenographer or notary and take cases outside of the city.

Languages: Spanish, **Moreno-Villalba, Daniel** Office: Carrera 52 # 72-114, Office D-52 Barranquilla, Atlántico, Colombia Phone: (575) 358-5615, 368-5512; Mobile: (57) 310-633-3599 E-mail: damorvi@metrotel.net.co ; damorvi@att.net

Colombian citizen, born in Barranquilla, 1950. Los Andes University School of Law in Bogotá, 1975; University of Rochester. He has practiced law during 40 years **Fields**: Family law, Marriage/Divorce, Commercial/ Business Law, Marketing Agreements, Civil Law, Commercial Law, Contracts, Corporations, Estates.

Firm can provide services of a certified translator, court reporter/stenographer or notary. They may take cases in Barranquilla, Santa Marta or Cartagena.

Languages: Spanish and English

Uribe Largacha Abogados S.A. Office: Carrera 51 No. 79-34, Of. 501 Barranquilla, Atlántico, Colombia Phone: (575) 318-5060 Mobile: (57) 321-541-3456, 321-541-3469 E-mail: ruribe@ul.com.co Website: www.ul.com.co

Members of the firm: Rodrigo Uribe Largacha, Colombian citizen. Lawyer with postgraduate studies in tax law, tax management and international taxation. Karina de Sales Gonzalez & David Bedoya Goyes. **Fields**: Commercial/business law, foreign investments, marketing agreements, civil law, commercial law, contracts, corporations, taxes, labor relations and immigration law.

Firm can provide services of a certified translator, court reporter/stenographer or notary. Firm may take cases outside the city. Languages: Spanish, German and English

Bucaramanga / Department of Santander del Sur

Muñoz Zerpa Abogados – Estudio Jurídico Office: Calle 35 No. 25-37, Torre A, Apt. 303 Bucaramanga, Santander, Colombia Phone: (577) 632-2307; 645-1325; Mobile: (57) 314-350-0189 E-mail: munozserpa@hotmail.com Principal member of the firm: Eduardo Hernando Muñoz Serpa, Colombian citizen born in 1931. Universidad Libre, Bogota. He has practiced law during 40 years. **Fields**: Damages, Taxes.

Firm may take cases outside the city.

Language: Spanish

Cali / Department of Valle del Cauca

Alzate Castaño, Humberto Office: Carrera 4 Oeste No. 1-65. Apt 1303

Edificio San Antonio del Peñon

Cali, Valle del Cauca, Colombia Phone: (572) 315-2495, 370-2528; Mobile: 57-315-273-4901 E-mail: halzatec@hotmail.com

Colombian citizen, born in Caicedonia, Valle, 1943. Santiago de Cali University, Doctor of Law, Political and Social Sciences, 1970. **Fields**: Civil, marriage/divorce, Family law.

Firm can provide services of a certified translator, stenographer or notary. Firm may take cases outside the city. Languages: Spanish and English.

ARPE Abogados Asociados Office: Calle 19 Norte No. 3 N 17 Oficina 82 Cali, Valle del Cauca, Colombia Phone: (572) 661-2796; Mobile: (57) 313-766-8789

E-mail: arpe@colombia.com Website: www.arpeasesoresdecobranza.es.tl Principal member of the firm: Felipe Arias Arce, Colombian citizen born in 1987, St. Bonaventure University. **Fields**: Civil, criminal and family law, labor relations and auto/accidents Languages: Spanish and English

Ayerbe Abogados Office: Calle 7-Oeste # 2-63 Barrio Santa Teresita Cali, Valle del Cauca, Colombia Phone: (572) 892-6717; Fax 892-6772; Mobile: (57) 315-563-5219 E-mail: rayerbesr@ayerbeabogados.com

Website: www.ayerbeabogados.com Principal member of the firm: Rodrigo Vicente Ayerbe, Colombian citizen, born in 1948. Javeriana University in Bogotá Law School 1970; Harvard Law School 1972. He has practiced law for 42 years.

Partners: Felipe Ayerbe, Rodrigo Ayerbe Jr., Andrés Flórez, Claudia Romero, Laura Castro, Juan Hernández, Paula Vélez, Maria J. Fallofo, Valentina Naranjo. **Fields**: Commercial/Business Law, Foreign Investments, Civil Law, Contracts, Corporations, Estates, Labor Relations. Firm can provide service of court reporter. Languages: Spanish and English.

Posso Escobar, Gustavo Adolfo Office: Calle 11 No. 4-34, Of 817, Edificio Plaza de Cayzedo Phone: (572) 880-5064; Mobile: (57) 315-570-6829; Cali, Valle del Cauca, Colombia E-mail: gusposso @hotmail.com

Website: www.gustavopossoasesorias.com Colombian citizen, born in 1962, Universidad San Buenaventura, Cali. **Fields**: Family law, child custody, marriage/divorce, commercial/business law, civil law, damages, commercial law, contracts, corporations, estates, taxes, labor relations, auto/accidents

Language: Spanish and English.

Cartagena de Indias / Department of Bolivar

Bossa-Sotomayor, Eduardo Rafael Office: Centro Sector Matuna, Edificio Banco Popular, Oficina 1008 Cartagena, Bolívar, Colombia. Phone: (575) 664-7071; Fax: 660-0001

E-mail: edbossas@gmail.com Colombian citizen, born in Cartagena, Bolívar, 1934. University of Cartagena, law degree, 1965. **Fields**: Civil, commercial, labor and family law Languages: Spanish and English.

Martinez – Arboleda & Eljach Office: Calle 32 No. 5-09 Of. 314

Edificio Andian.

Cartagena, Bolívar, Colombia. Phone: (575) 664-4584; 664-7128 E-mail: e.arboleda@une.net.co ; rmartinez@etb.net.co , rvmt@me.com

Principal member of the firm established in 1986: Rodrigo Martinez, Colombian citizen born in 1947, Universidad de Cartagena 1975. **Fields**: Family Law, adoptions, child custody, marriage/divorce, Commercial/business law, foreign investments, civil law, commercial law, damages, contracts, transportation law, Aeronautical/Maritime corporations, estates and labor relations.

Language: Spanish and English

Romano, Luz Elena Rebolledo de Office: Isla de Manga, Callejón Porto No. 25-47 Cartagena, Bolívar, Colombia. Mobile: (57) 310-610-1772; 301-795-7663

E-mail: luzel8@yahoo.es . Colombian citizen, born in Sincelejo; University of Cartagena **Fields**: Civil, labor and family law.

Language: Spanish and English

Medellin / Department of Antioquia

MOLINA DIAZ & ABOGADOS

Molina Arrubla Carlos Mario Office: Calle 56 No. 47-14 /301

Medellín - Colombia
Phone: (4) 2932700 - Fax (4) 2515530 E-mail: moldi@une.net.co
Website: www.molinadiazabogados.com Principal member of the firm: Molina Arrubla, Carlos Mario. He has practiced law since 1984

Fields: Criminal Law.

Firm can provide the services of a certified translator, court reporter/stenographer or notary. They may take cases outside the city.

Languages: Spanish and English

Parrado Ochoa, Holguin & Cia Abogados Office: Carrera 55 # 40A-20 Edificio Torre Nuevo, Centro La Alpujarra Zona Administrativa, Office 1311 Medellín, Colombia Phone: (574) 262-3601/2323506; Mobile: (57) 310-8318482.

E-mail: abogadosensucasa@hotmail.com Website: www.parradoabogadodonaldo.com Members of the firm: Parrado Ochoa, Gonzalo Anibal, Colombian citizen born in 1973. Law degree from University of Medellín. He has practiced law since 1992.

Rocio Ochoa Holguin. Fields: Family law, adoptions, child custody, parental child abduction, child protection, marriage/divorce, Insurance, commercial/business law, foreign investments, marketing agreements, civil law, criminal law, damages, commercial law.

Firm can provide the services of a certified translator. They may take cases in Medellin, Bogota or Cartagena.

Languages: Spanish and English

Rada Attorneys at law Office: Carrera 40A No. 11B-54 Office 1004

Medellín, Colombia Phone: (574) 268-2435
Mobile: (57) 311-7693976
E-mail: lawyerscolombia@yahoo.com
Website: www.lawyerscolombia.com

Principal member of the firm: Rada Ortega, Esteban; Colombian citizen born 1982. Law degree from Universidad of Medellin and Universidad Pontificia Bolivariana de Medellin. **Fields**: Family Law, Adoptions, Child Custody, Parental Child Abduction, Child Protection, Marriage/Divorce, Banking/Financial, Commercial/Business Law, Foreign Investments, Civil Law, Criminal Law, Commercial Law, Contracts, Corporations, Foreign Claims, Estates, Immigration.

Firm can provide the services of a certified translator, court reporter/stenographer or notary. They may take cases outside the city. Languages: Spanish and English

Pereira / Department of Risaralda

Ocampo-Ossa, Rodrigo Office: Calle 5 # 14-35, Of 102A Pereira, Risaralda, Colombia Phone: (576) 331-4050; Fax: 331-4060 E-mail: rocampo50@yahoo.com Principal member of the firm: Rodrigo Ocampo Ossa. Colombian citizen born 1950. Javeriana University, School of law in Bogotá, Doctor of Law and Economic Sciences, 1971. He has practiced law for 44 years. Other member of the firm: Luisa Ocampo Jaramillo. **Fields**: Family law, marriage/divorce, insurance, banking/financial, commercial/business law, civil law,

Damages, Commercial law, contracts, Transportation law.
Firm can provide the services of a certified translator, court reporter/stenographer or notary.
Languages: Spanish, English

Popayan / Deparment of Cauca

Andrade-Ríos, Luis Hernando Office: Carrera 8 # 2-44, Office 312 Edificio Hormaza Popayán, Cauca, Colombia. Phone: (572) 824-1810, 824-0783; Mobile: (57)311-5327410 E-mail: luisandrade28@hotmail.com ; lhandrade@une.net.co Colombian citizen, born in 1943. University of Cauca, Law and Economic Sciences, 1970; Javeriana University in Bogotá, Labor Law, 1973. **Fields**: Damages, Contracts, Government relations, Labor relations.

Firm can provide the services of a certified translator, court reporter/stenographer or notary. They may take cases outside the city.

Languages: Spanish.

Santa Marta / Department of Magdalena

Caribbean Legal Advisers SAS.

Office: Calle 24 # 4-86
Santa Marta, Colombia.
Phone: (575) 421-4330; 5-422-0665; Mobile: 57-317-378-8870
E-mail: caribelegal@yahoo.com

Principal member of the firm established in 2012: Alonso, Gustavo. Universidad del Norte, specialized in Commercial/Business Law in Universidad Sergio Arboleda.

Fields: Commercial, Business, Civil law. He may take cases outside the city.
Languages: English, German, Spanish.

Tunja / Department of Boyacá

Fernández-Sandoval, Heraclio Office: Calle 20 # 10-36, Office 407 Tunja, Boyacá, Colombia Phone: (578) 742-3011; 742- 4326; Fax: (578) 740-1978 E-mail: heracliofs@yahoo.es; ufernandez@hotmail.com Colombian citizen, born in Tunja, Boyacá, 1929. Externado de Colombia University in Bogotá. Public offices held: Magistrate of the Superior Tribunal of Tunja, Governor of Boyacá. **Fields**: Criminal law, Contracts, Estates, Government relations, Auto/Accidents.

Language: Spanish and English

ECUADOR - INVESTMENT AND BUSINESS CLIMATE - STRATEGIC INFORMATION AND CONTACTS FOR STARTING BUSINESS

Ecuador is a country straddling the equator on South America's west coast. Ecuador is relatively open to foreign investment in most sectors; however, foreign direct investment (FDI) inflows are very low in comparison to other Latin American countries. Economic, commercial, and investment policies are often contradictory and subject to frequent changes. The legal uncertainty resulting from inconsistent application and interpretation of existing laws complicates enforcement of contracts and increases the risks and costs of doing business. Systemic weaknesses in the judicial system and its susceptibility to political or economic pressures are issues for U.S. companies investing in or trading with Ecuador. The existing U.S.-Ecuador Bilateral Investment Treaty (BIT) provides guarantees for national treatment; unrestricted remittances and transfers; prompt, adequate, and effective compensation for expropriation; and the resolution of investment disputes through international arbitration. The Government of Ecuador's (GOE) ongoing actions could lead to the termination of its BITs, placing uncertainty on the future of Ecuador's investment treaties.

Foreign investors may remit 100 percent of net profits and capital, subject to a capital exit tax currently set at five percent. Ecuadorian law requires private companies to distribute 15 percent of pre-tax profits to employees each year.

A number of U.S. companies operating in Ecuador, primarily in regulated sectors such as petroleum and electricity, have filed for international arbitration due to investment disputes.

In April 2015, the United States Trade Representative moved Ecuador from Watch List to Priority Watch List in its annual Special 301 Report on intellectual property. This decision was based on Ecuador's 2014 repeal of its criminal IPR provisions. GOE officials said the criminal IPR provisions would be reinstated to bring Ecuador back in compliance with its international obligations but, as of April 2015, no such legislation had been passed.

U.S embassy recommends exerting caution when considering investment in Ecuador.

1. OPENNESS TO, AND RESTRICTIONS UPON, FOREIGN INVESTMENT

ATTITUDE TOWARD FOREIGN DIRECT INVESTMENT

Ecuador is relatively open to foreign investment (FDI) in most sectors. Its overall investment climate remains challenging and uncertain as Ecuador's economic, commercial, and investment policies are often contradictory and subject to change. The regulatory framework has specifically targeted the banking and media sectors, negatively affecting these industries. Frequent changes in Ecuador's tax code make business planning difficult.

In general, the legal complexity resulting from the inconsistent application and interpretation of existing laws complicates enforcement of contracts and increases the risks and costs of doing business in Ecuador. Business disputes with U.S. companies can become politicized, especially in sensitive areas such as the energy sector. Several high level investment disputes involving U.S. companies, mostly linked to the energy sector, are under international arbitration.

OTHER INVESTMENT POLICY REVIEWS

In the past three years, Ecuador has not conducted an investment policy review with the Organization for Economic Cooperation and Development (OECD), World Trade Organization (WTO), or United Nations Conference on Trade and Development.

LAWS/REGULATIONS OF FOREIGN DIRECT INVESTMENT

The Organic Law for Production Incentives and Tax Fraud Prevention, passed in December 2014, includes provisions to improve tax stability and lower the income tax rate in the mining sector. The law also included provisions intended to increase tax revenues; it eliminated the tax exemption for income derived from the occasional sale of shares in Ecuadorian entities and it limited advertising expenses companies are allowed to deduct for tax purposes to four percent of revenue.

Systemic weakness in the judicial system and its susceptibility to political and economic pressures constitute important problems faced by U.S. companies investing in Ecuador.

The Superintendence of Companies, Securities, and Insurance offers information for registering businesses on its website at http://www.supercias.gob.ec/.

INDUSTRIAL PROMOTION

The Coordinating Ministry of Strategic Sectors publishes a catalogue of investments in strategic sectors on its website at http://www.sectoresestrategicos.gob.ec/. The Coordinating Ministry for Production, Employment, and Competitiveness offers information on investing in Ecuador on its website at http://www.produccion.gob.ec/.

LIMITS ON FOREIGN CONTROL

One hundred percent foreign equity ownership is allowed without the need for authorization or prior screening in the sectors open to domestic private investment. Articles 313 through 315 of the 2008 Constitution establish that the state is responsible for management of strategic sectors through state-owned or controlled companies. The sectors identified include: energy in all its forms, telecommunications, non-renewable natural resources (includes petroleum, natural gas, and mining), transportation, hydrocarbon refining, media, water, biodiversity, and genetic patrimony. In the last few years, new state companies were formed in mining, pharmaceuticals, and to import goods required by the executive branch.

For license and franchise transactions, no limits exist on royalties that may be remitted. All license and franchise agreements must be registered with the Ecuadorian Intellectual Property Institute (IEPI). In addition to registering with the Superintendence of Companies, Securities, and Insurance, foreign investors must register investments with Ecuador's Central Bank for statistical purposes.

Selected Strategic Sectors:

Petroleum

Per the 2008 Constitution, all subsurface resources belong to the state. Ecuador permits investment by foreign oil companies, but has not allowed production sharing agreements since 2009. Only the state is authorized to participate in domestic fuel distribution, refining, and transport activities. Most fuel prices are controlled and subsidized by the central government.

Mining

The mining sector is relatively open to foreign investment, but investment in mining continues to be modest. Foreign companies have the same access to large-scale mining concessions as domestic investors, but are prohibited from investing in small-scale mining operations.

In 2014, the Government of Ecuador introduced several changes to its mining tax regime in an attempt to attract investment in the sector. Presidential Decree 475, published in October 2014, altered the windfall tax calculation. The Organic Law for Production Incentives and Tax Fraud Prevention included provisions to improve tax stability and lower the income tax rate in the mining sector. The Government of Ecuador also created a separate ministry of mines, which was previously within the Ministry of Non-Renewable Resources.

Electricity

The Organic Law for the Public Service of Electric Energy, which took effect on January 16, 2015, permits some private sector participation and foreign investment in Ecuador's electricity sector. Per the 2008 Constitution, the electricity sector is a public service and strategic sector.

Telecommunications

In February 2015, Ecuador's National Assembly passed a telecommunications law that requires telecommunications companies to pay a percentage of revenue to the government. This requirement applies to providers of cellular and fixed line telephone service, internet service, and subscription television with more than 30 percent of market share. The payments range from 0.5 to 9 percent of revenue.

In February 2015, the Government of Ecuador finalized the sale of spectrum rights to the country's two largest cellular service providers. Corporación Nacional de Telecomunicaciones, a public enterprise, is the monopoly provider of landline telephone services and also provides cellular service.

Media

The 2013 Communications Law prohibits partial or total ownership of media businesses by foreign companies or citizens that do not reside permanently in Ecuador. This provision applies to all media owners (radio, subscription video, audio, television, and printed press) with products that reach at least 30 percent of the population. Implementing regulations for the law softened this prohibition to allow citizens or companies from countries that have signed bilateral commercial or economic agreements with Ecuador to own media companies. The United States has no such agreement with Ecuador. The Communications Law also introduced a requirement that advertising disseminated in Ecuador must have 80 percent domestic content. It also requires that television and radio frequencies are distributed 33 percent to private media, 33 percent to public media, and 34 percent to community media.

The government controls a large share of radio, television, and other press holdings. Article 312 of the Constitution prohibits financial institutions, their shareholders, board members, and legal representatives from media ownership. In addition, the Organic Law for Regulation and Control of Market Power, enacted in October 2011, prohibits anyone possessing more than a six percent interest in a media company from investing in any other business sector.

Fishing

Foreign investment in domestic fishing operations is subject to approval by the National Fisheries Development Council. Extractive fishing by foreign companies is permitted provided that the catch is processed in Ecuador.

Privatization Program

Information not available.

Screening of FDI

One hundred percent foreign investment in domestic companies is allowed without prior authorization or screening in sectors open to domestic private investment.

Competition Law

The Superintendence of Control of Market Power reviews transactions for competition-related concerns.

Investment Trends

In 2013, Ecuador received the lowest foreign direct investment (FDI) inflows relative to GDP in South America, and the second lowest in the Western Hemisphere. FDI inflows remained low in 2014. According to the Central Bank of Ecuador, total FDI inflows were USD 774 million in 2014, or .77 percent of GDP of USD 100.5 million, with USD 10 million coming from the United States.

Table 1

Measure	**Year**	**Index or Rank**	**Website Address**
TI Corruption Perceptions index	2014	110 of 175	**transparency.org/cpi2014/results**
World Bank's	2015	115 of	**doingbusiness.org/rankings**

Doing Business Report "Ease of Doing Business"		189	
Global Innovation Index	2014	115 of 143	**globalinnovationindex.org/content.aspx?page=data-analysis**
World Bank GNI per capita	2013	USD 5,760	**data.worldbank.org/indicator/NY.GNP.PCAP.CD**

2. Conversion and Transfer Policies

Not applicable/information not available.

Foreign Exchange

In the year 2000, Ecuador adopted the U.S. dollar (USD) as the official currency. Foreign investors may remit 100 percent of net profits and capital, subject to a five-percent capital exit tax. There are no restrictions placed on foreign investors in transferring or repatriating funds associated with an investment.

Remittance Policies

In 2012, Ecuador recognized Delaware, Florida, Nevada, and Wyoming as pre-eminent corporate tax havens. They also designated Puerto Rico, the U.S. Virgin Islands, American Samoa, and Guam as part of that list. (LLCs based in these locations are excluded from competing for Ecuadorian government procurement contracts.) In February 2015, the Ecuadorian tax authorities published a resolution with a new list of tax havens that included no U.S. states, although some U.S. jurisdictions remained. The resolution introduced the concept of jurisdictions of lower taxation, which are not specifically listed but may be applied on a case by case basis.

The Financial Action Task Force (FATF) released a public statement in February 2015 indicating that Ecuador remains on the list of jurisdictions with strategic anti-money laundering/combating the financing of terrorism (AML/CFT) deficiencies that have not made sufficient progress in addressing the deficiencies. The release also noted that Ecuador has taken steps to improve its AML/CFT regime, including by issuing CFT regulations for the freezing of terrorist assets and AML/CFT regulations for the supervision of credit and savings cooperatives.

3. Expropriation and Compensation

The Constitution establishes that the state is in charge of managing the use and access to land, while recognizing and guaranteeing the right to private property. It also provides for the redistribution of land if it has not in active use for more than two years. Access to land for the landless is a major theme of the government's agricultural policy; to date, however, there have not been any public seizures of private assets under the current administration. The 2010 Organic Code for Commercial Production and Investment (Production Code) includes expropriation as a way to improve the distribution of production factors and enhance opportunities for the rural population. Pending land-reform legislation was delayed given the highly charged political nature of the issue. The 2015 Telecommunications Law does allow expropriation of private land in accordance with the rules and procedures of the law when necessary for the installation of network infrastructure.

Under Ecuador's BIT with the United States, expropriation can only be carried out for a public purpose, in a nondiscriminatory manner, and upon payment of prompt, adequate, and effective compensation.

Some local and foreign mining companies have had their concessions occupied by informal miners, who have subsequently sought a share of the concessions or have carried out mining activities without repercussions.

Property, whether land or mobile assets, jointly owned by several persons or companies, can be seized by Ecuadorian courts through judgments or seizure orders. Resolution and compensation typically require many years and significant legal costs. In addition, the Organic Law for the Defense of Labor Rights, approved in September 2012, allows property to be seized by state entities (tax administrator, state-owned banks, and municipal governments) when debts have not been serviced. The law eliminated the protections provided to LLCs by extending corporate debts to their shareholders, their heirs, or third parties that have a relationship with the debtor. In 2012, the tax authority used the law's mandate to seize the assets of an export-oriented conglomerate. Some of these assets were auctioned off in December 2013 while others, including a banana plantation, were sold to the workers through government-granted loans.

4. Dispute Settlement

Legal System, Specialized Courts, Judicial Independence, Judgments of Foreign Courts

Ecuador has a civil codified legal system. Systemic weakness in the judicial system and its susceptibility to political and economic pressures constitute challenges faced by U.S. companies investing in Ecuador. The local judicial system is hampered by political pressure, delays, and inconsistent rulings in both civil and commercial cases. Enforcement of contract rights, equal treatment under the law, Intellectual Property protections, and unstable regulatory regimes are concerns.

According to the 2014 Rule of Law Index of The World Justice Project, which uses survey data to measure the extent to which countries adhere to the rule of law in practice, Ecuador ranked 77 out of 99 within the countries surveyed.

Bankruptcy

Ecuador is ranked 151 out of 189 in the category of Ease of Resolving Insolvency in the 2015 World Bank's, Doing Business Report.

Investment Disputes

A number of U.S. companies operating in Ecuador, most notably in the petroleum sector, have filed for international arbitration due to investment claims. The GOE has treated these disputes as a political issue, speaking negatively about investors involved these cases.

International Arbitration

U.S Investors guarantees under the U.S.-Ecuador BIT include the access to dispute mechanisms to resolve any investment claim arising out of the treaty. The treaty names the International Centre for the Settlement of Investment Disputes (ICSID) as the venue. In September 2008, Ecuador's constitution was amended to prohibit the ceding of sovereign jurisdiction in disputes with private companies before international tribunals. In January 2010, Ecuador withdrew from the ICSID Convention. In March 2013, President Correa requested that Ecuador's National Assembly terminate the U.S.-Ecuador BIT, arguing it was inconsistent with Ecuador's 2008 Constitution. Efforts to terminate the BIT have progressed slowly, to this day the treaty still remains in place.

ICSID Convention and New York Convention

Ecuador was formally a member state to the International Centre for the Settlement of Investment Disputes (ICSID convention). Ecuador withdrew from the ICSID Convention in 2010. Ecuador is a signatory to the convention on the Recognition and Enforcement of Foreign Arbitral Awards (1958 New York Convention).

DURATION OF DISPUTE RESOLUTION

The Ecuadorian judicial system is influenced by political pressure, delays in the process, and inconsistent rulings. Systemic weakness in the judicial system and its susceptibility to political and economic pressures constitute important problems faced by U.S. companies investing in or trading with Ecuador.

5. PERFORMANCE REQUIREMENTS AND INVESTMENT INCENTIVES

WTO/TRIMS

In 2014, the government negotiated over 900 import substitution agreements with companies. The companies were committed to reducing their imports and to start substituting imported goods with locally producing goods. In exchange, the government relaxed import regulations for those companies to import products that are restricted under quality and standards regulations enacted in December 2013. These contracts have not been publicly released.

Under the Andean Community Common Automotive Policy, Ecuador imposes local content requirements on automobiles assembled in country in order for assemblers to qualify for reduced duties on imports. The WTO Agreement on Trade-Related Investment Measures (TRIMS) prohibits such requirements. Although under the TRIMS Agreement Ecuador was obliged to eliminate local content requirements by 2000, the local content requirement is still in place. In 2012, the requirement was set at 24.3 percent, but current requirements are unclear, as new guidelines are pending.

INVESTMENT INCENTIVES

The Organic Law of Production Incentives and Tax Fraud Prevention, which took effect on December 30, 2014, provides for tax incentives related to depreciation calculations and income tax rates, which could benefit some foreign investors.

The country's Production Code establishes tax incentives to attract both domestic and foreign investment in certain priority sectors: fresh and processed food, forestry, agro-forestry, metalworking, petrochemical products, pharmaceuticals, tourism, renewable energies, logistical services, biotechnology, applied software, and those determined by Ecuador's president to be strategic import substitution sectors. Some incentives, which may take the form of tax exemptions, income tax deductions, as well as a five-year tax holiday, are mostly applicable for investments made outside of Quito and Guayaquil and for new investments. To qualify for the tax incentives, a Technical Secretary of the Sectoral Council for Production must approve an investment proposal. To date, few companies have applied for these incentives. Implementing regulations for the Production Code were published in April 2011.

In May 2011, Ecuador launched the Institute for Export and Investment Promotion (PRO ECUADOR), which to date has focused on export promotion.

Research and Development

Information not available.

PERFORMANCE REQUIREMENTS

Visa and residence requirements are relatively relaxed and do not inhibit foreign investment.

Committee of Foreign Trade (COMEX) Resolution 011-2015, which took effect March 11, 2015, applied tariff surcharges from 5 to 45 percent on almost 3,000 tariff lines. In its notification to the World Trade Organization, Ecuador argued the tariff surcharges were necessary to protect Ecuador's balance of payments in response to decreased oil prices and the appreciation of the U.S. dollar. The tariff surcharges are to remain in effect for up to 15 months.

DATA STORAGE

Information not available.

6. RIGHT TO PRIVATE OWNERSHIP AND ESTABLISHMENT

Foreign and domestic private entities can own business enterprises and engage in almost all forms of business activity.

7. PROTECTION OF PROPERTY RIGHTS

REAL PROPERTY

There have been cases where the judicial system has not adequately protected property owners' rights.

Ecuador currently ranks 80out of 189 in the World Bank's Doing Business Report's category for Ease of Registering Property.

With the goal of protecting consumers and preventing a real estate bubble, the National Assembly approved in June 2012 a law that allows homeowners to default on their first home and car loan without penalty if they forfeit the asset. The provisions do not apply to homes with a market value of more than USD 146,000 or vehicles worth more than USD 29,200.

INTELLECTUAL PROPERTY RIGHTS

Enforcement against intellectual property infringement remains a serious problem in Ecuador. In April 2015, the United States Trade Representative downgraded Ecuador from Watch List to Priority Watch List in its annual Special 301 Report on intellectual property. This decision was based on Ecuador's 2014 repeal of its criminal IPR provisions. Government of Ecuador officials said the criminal IPR provisions would be reinstated to bring Ecuador back in compliance with its international obligations but, as of April 2015, no such legislation had been passed. One of Ecuador's largest outdoor markets, La Bahia in Guayaquil, is listed in the United States Trade Representative's Notorious Markets report.

Piracy of computer software and counterfeit activity in brand name apparel is widespread. Pirated CDs and DVDs are readily available on many streets and in shopping malls. Weak copyright enforcement remains a significant problem, especially concerning sound recordings, computer software, and motion pictures. In contrast, piracy of Ecuadorian music and movies has declined significantly. This is due in part to improvements in legitimate local production and distribution and to government-sponsored public awareness campaigns focused on reducing piracy of Ecuadorian produced content.

The Ecuadorian Intellectual Property Institute (IEPI) was established in January 1999 to handle patent, trademark, and copyright registrations. IEPI reports information on its activities on its website at http://www.propiedadintelectual.gob.ec/. The IEPI website includes little information on seizures of counterfeit goods.

In 2010, Ecuador established compulsory license regimes for pharmaceutical and agrochemical products. At least five compulsory licenses were issued in 2014, including two for medicines that treat non-fatal illnesses. The compulsory licenses allow local firms to import or manufacture patented drugs. IEPI is reviewing additional compulsory license applications.

The Ecuadorian National Police and Customs service are responsible for carrying out IPR enforcement, but do not always enforce court orders. IEPI can take enforcement actions through an administrative process that can result in sanctions and/or confiscation of counterfeit goods.

Resources for Rights Holders

For additional information about treaty obligations and points of contact at local IP offices, please see WIPO's country profiles at http://www.wipo.int/directory/en/.

Embassy point of contact: ecuadorcommercial@state.gov.

Local lawyers list: http://ecuador.usembassy.gov/service/assistance.html

Camara de Comercio Ecuatoriano Americana (AmCham) Quito: http://www.amchamec.org/

Camara Ecuatoriano Americana de Comercio (AmCham) Guayaquil: http://www.amchamgye.org.ec/

8. Transparency of the Regulatory System

Ecuador enacted the Organic Law for Regulation and Control of Market Power in October 2011. The implementing regulations for the law include mechanisms to prevent, control, and sanction market power abuses, restrictive market practices, economic concentration, and unfair competition. The regulatory body, the Superintendence of Control of Market Power, can fine companies found to be in violation of the law up to 12 percent of gross revenue.

9. Efficient Capital Markets and Portfolio Investment

In March 2014, Ecuador enacted the Law to Strengthen and Optimize Business Partnerships and Stock Markets, which reformed nine previous laws governing Ecuador's stock markets. The law created an executive branch regulatory board to oversee the stock markets. Ecuadorian government officials said the new law was also intended to allow businesses to be created more quickly.

Money and Banking System, Hostile Takeovers

The GOE is openly hostile towards private banks and financial institutions, considering them enemies of President Correa's Citizen's Revolution. Between 2012 and 2013, the financial sector was the target of numerous new restrictions. By 2012, most banks had sold off their brokerage firms, mutual funds, and insurance companies to comply with constitutional changes following a May 2010 referendum. The amendment to Article 312 of the Constitution required banks and their senior managers and shareholders with more than six percent equity in financial entities to divest entirely from any interest in all non-financial companies by July 13, 2012. These provisions were incorporated into the Anti-Monopoly Law passed in September 2011.

The Organic Monetary and Financial Code, published in the official registry September 12, 2014, created a five-person Monetary and Financial Policy and Regulation Board of presidential appointees to regulate the banking sector. The law gives the Monetary and Financial Policy and Regulation Board the ability to prioritize certain sectors for lending from private banks. The law also created an electronic currency to be administered by Ecuador's Central Bank and backed by its assets.

Ecuador's Central Bank was established in 1927. Since Ecuador's dollarization in 2000, the Central Bank has played a much smaller role in that it is no longer the lender of last resort.

The Central Bank issued Regulation 29 in July 2012, requiring all financial transfers (inflows and outflows) to be channeled through the Central Bank's accounts. In principle, the regulation increases monetary authorities' oversight and prevents banks from netting their inflows and outflows to avoid paying the five-percent capital exit tax.

In November 2012, the National Assembly passed a law that would severely restrict the operations of private credit risk rating agencies (bureaus). The law has not yet been fully implemented. It grants exclusive rights to credit-related data to a state-run entity. If implemented as written, private credit bureaus, while not prohibited from operating, would be obliged to give up their databases to the government and could no longer receive data directly from the financial sector.

In November 2013, the Banking Committee issued Resolution 2694 setting ceilings on salaries and fringe benefits of financial sector employees, legal representatives, and executives. Resolution 2839, passed in March 2014, partially eased the limitations imposed in November 2013.

10. Competition from State-Owned Enterprises

The 2009 Organic Law of Public Enterprises regulates state-owned enterprises (SOEs). SOEs are most active in areas designated by the 2008 Constitution as strategic sectors, especially non-renewable natural resources, telecommunications, and transportation.

Regulations allow SOEs greater flexibility in the use of public resources. SOEs follow a special procurement regime with greater flexibility and limited oversight. The Law of Public Enterprises requires SOEs to follow generally accepted accounting principles; however, SOEs are not required to follow the same accounting practices as the central government, nor do they have to participate in the electronic financial management system used in most of the public sector for budget and accounting management. SOEs are eligible for government guarantees, and face lower tax burdens than private companies.

The Production Code softened some of the restrictions on the private sector introduced in the Constitution and in the Organic Law of Public Enterprises by allowing private investment in strategic sectors. However, the Production Code is secondary to the relevant laws governing strategic sectors.

OECD Guidelines on Corporate Governance of SOEs

Third-party analysts generally assess that SOEs maintain some degree of independence from the government. Ecuadorian courts generally favor SOEs and court processes are often nontransparent.

Sovereign Wealth Funds

Ecuador does not have a sovereign wealth fund.

11. Corporate Social Responsibility

There is substantial awareness of corporate social responsibility (CSR) among the large businesses operating in Ecuador. Many multinational and large domestic companies maintain corporate social responsibility strategies, following generally accepted CSR principles. They are active in areas such as sustainability, clean environmental practices, and education. Consumer awareness of CSR is less pronounced than producer awareness.

OECD Guidelines for Multinational Enterprises

Ecuador is not included on the list of adherents to the OECD Guidelines for Multinational Enterprises.

12. Political Violence

Ecuador does not have a tradition of frequent violence as a result of demonstrations or political instability. Crime is a serious concern, especially in the larger cities.

Student, labor union, and indigenous protests against government policies have been a regular feature of political life in Ecuador. While disruptive, especially to transportation, violence is usually limited and localized. Protesters often block city streets and rural highways, and public transportation tends to be disrupted during these incidents. Popular protests in 1997, 2000, and 2005 contributed to the removal of three elected presidents before the end of their terms.

Some indigenous communities opposed to development have blocked access by petroleum and mining companies.

13. Corruption

Corruption is a serious problem in Ecuador. Transparency International consistently ranks Ecuador poorly among countries it surveys in the region. Ecuador ranked 110 out of 175 countries surveyed for Transparency International's 2014 Corruption Perceptions Index and received a score of 33 out of 100.

Ecuador has laws and regulations to combat official corruption, but they are inadequately enforced. Illicit payments for official favors and theft of public funds reportedly take place frequently. Dispute settlement procedures are complicated by the lack of transparency and inefficiency in the judicial system.

Offering or accepting a bribe is illegal and punishable by imprisonment for up to five years. The Controller General is responsible for the oversight of public funds and there are frequent investigations and occasional prosecutions for irregularities.

UN Anticorruption Convention, OECD Convention on Combatting Bribery

Ecuador ratified the UN Anticorruption Convention in September 2005. Ecuador is not a signatory to the OECD Convention on Combating Bribery. The 2008 Constitution created the Transparency and Social Control branch of government, tasked with preventing and combating corruption, among other things. In December 2008, President Correa issued a decree that created the National Secretariat for Transparency to investigate and denounce acts of corruption in the public sector. Both entities can conduct investigations into alleged acts of corruption. Responsibility for prosecution remains with the Office of the Prosecutor General.

Resources to Report Corruption

Through the Function of Transparency and Social Control, alleged acts of corruption can be reported by dialing 159 within Ecuador. The Council for Citizen Participation and Social Control also maintains a web portal for reporting alleged acts of corruption: http://www.cpccs.gob.ec.

14. Bilateral Investment Agreements

In 1993, the United States and Ecuador signed a BIT, which entered into force in 1997. This treaty provides for national treatment; unrestricted remittances and transfers; prompt, adequate, and effective compensation for expropriation; and access to international arbitration to resolve any investment dispute. In September 2009, the GOE requested approval from the National Assembly to terminate the treaty, along with the BITs of another 12 nations. The GOE claims the treaties' international arbitration provisions for resolution of investor-state disputes conflicts with the 2008 amended Constitution.

In 2013, the GOE formed a committee, made up of government officials and private citizens, to produce a report on Ecuador's current BITs, playing close attention to the investment dispute mechanism itself. The committee has released some interim findings with no clear impact on the status of Ecuador's BITs and pending international investment arbitration cases.

In 2014, Ecuadorian officials announced the intention to renegotiate Ecuador's BITs to remove aspects of the treaties that conflict with the Constitution. Officials did not announce if negotiations have begun and no negotiations have begun with the United States.

Bilateral Taxation Treaties

Ecuador does not have a bilateral taxation treaty with the United States.

15. OPIC and Other Investment Insurance Programs

Since 1986, Ecuador has had an Investment Guarantee Agreement with the Overseas Private Investment Corporation. Ecuador is also signatory to the Multilateral Investment Guarantee Agreement.

16. Labor

Ecuador's population is about 16 million. Semi-skilled workers are relatively abundant at low wages. The National Wages Council and Ministry of Labor Relations set minimum compensation levels for private sector employees annually. The minimum basic salary for 2015 is USD 354 per month. Mandatory bonuses and other contributions pushed total compensation to over USD 400 per month. Ecuador's Production Code requires that workers be paid a dignified wage, defined as an amount that would enable a family of four with 1.6 wage earners to be able to afford the basic necessities. The cost and the products that are considered basic necessities is determined by Ecuador's Statistics Institute (INEC). In March 2015, the cost of basic necessities was USD 657.68, while the official family wage level is at USD 660.80. As of December 2014, INEC estimated Ecuador's unemployment rate at 3.8 percent and underemployment at 46.69 percent.

The Law for Labor Justice and Recognition of Work in the Home, which included several changes related to labor and social security, took effect April 20, 2015. The law eliminated the requirement that the government contribute 40 percent of pension obligations to Ecuador's Institute of Social Security (IESS). The requirement was replaced with a government guarantee that it will provide funding to IESS in the case that IESS does not have the resources from employee and employer contributions to make the payments. The law also lowered the yearly percentage increase in pension payments to match inflation. The law limited the yearly bonus paid to employees, which is equal to 15 percent of companies' profits and is required by law, to 24 times the minimum wage. Any surplus profits are to be handed over to IESS. The law also limits the tax deduction for salaries companies are allowed to pay top executives to a multiple of the lowest salary paid to a company employee. The multiple will be set considering the size of the company, income, number of employees, sector, and other factors. The law also mandates that employees' thirteenth and fourteenth month bonuses, which are required by law, be paid in installments throughout the year instead of in lump sums. Employees have the option to opt out of this change and continue to receive the payments in lump sums. The law eliminates fixed-term employee contracts and replaces them with indefinite contracts, which shortens the allowable trial period for employees to 90 days. The law also allows participation in social security pensions for non-paid work at home.

Trained financial professionals and engineers can be difficult to attract and many graduates require additional training to reach international standards. Little post-graduate education exists in Ecuador, and scientists and medical professionals are nearly all foreign-trained. Masters-level degrees are widely offered, but relatively few are competitive with international quality levels. Upper-level Ecuadorian business managers have frequently been educated abroad and often in the United States.

The Labor Code provides for a 40-hour work week, 15 calendar days of annual paid vacation, restrictions and sanctions for those who employ child labor, general protection of worker health and safety, minimum wages and bonuses, maternity leave, and employer-provided benefits.

There is special legislation regulating labor in export processing zones. Most workers in export processing zones are hired on temporary contracts, and, while technically covered by the Labor Code, enforcement is weak.

The 2008 Constitution bans child labor, requires hiring workers with disabilities, and prohibits strikes in most of the public sector. Unpaid internships are not permitted in Ecuador.

Most workers in the private sector and at SOEs have the constitutional right to form trade unions and local law allows for unionization of any company with more than 30 employees. Private employers are required to engage in collective bargaining with recognized unions. The Labor Code provides for resolution of conflicts through a tripartite arbitration and conciliation board process. The Code also prohibits discrimination against union members and requires that employers provide space for union activities.

Workers fired for organizing a labor union are entitled to limited financial indemnification, but the law does not mandate reinstatement. The Public Service Law enacted in October 2010 prohibits the vast majority of public sector workers from joining unions, exercising collective bargaining rights, or paralyzing public services in general. The Constitution lists health; environmental sanitation; education; justice; fire brigade; social security; electrical energy; drinking water and sewerage; hydrocarbon production; processing, transport, and distribution of fuel; public transport; and post and telecommunications as strategic sectors. Public workers who are not under the Public Service Law may join a union and bargain collectively since they are governed by the provisions under the Labor Code.

17. Foreign Trade Zones/Free Ports/Trade Facilitation

The 2010 Production Code authorized the creation of Special Economic Development Zones (ZEDEs) that are subject to reduced taxes and tariffs. The government considers the extent to which projects promote technology transfer, innovation, and industrial diversification when granting ZEDE status. The municipality of Quito prioritized development of a ZEDE near Quito's international airport in 2014. Turisfranca and Metrozona are ZEDEs located in Quito. There are also ZEDEs located in Yachay and Manta.

18. Foreign Direct Investment and Foreign Portfolio Investment Statistics

Host country data is from the Central Bank of Ecuador. The Central Bank only publishes FDI calculated as net flows.

Table 2: Key Macroeconomic Data, U.S. FDI in Host Country/Economy

	Host Country Statistical source*		USG or international statistical source		USG or International Source of Data: BEA; IMF; Eurostat; UNCTAD, Other
Economic Data	**Year**	**Amount**	**Year**	**Amount**	
Host Country Gross Domestic Product (GDP) ($B USD)	2013	94.5	2013	94.5	www.worldbank.org/en/country
Foreign Direct Investment	Host Country Statistical source*		USG or international statistical source		USG or international Source of data: BEA; IMF; Eurostat; UNCTAD, Other
U.S. FDI in partner country ($M USD, stock positions)	n/a	n/a	2013	449	BEA data available 3/19/14 at http://bea.gov/international/direct_investment_multinational_companies_comprehensive_data.htm
Host country's FDI in the United States ($M USD, stock positions)	n/a	n/a	2013	8	BEA data available 3/19/14 at http://bea.gov/international/direct_investment_multinational_companies_comprehensive_data.htm
Total inbound stock of FDI as % host GDP	n/a	n/a	2013	0.48%	

* Host country data is from the Central Bank of Ecuador. The Central Bank only publishes FDI calculated as net flows.

Table 3: Sources and Destination of FDI

Direct Investment from/in Counterpart Economy Data

FROM TOP FIVE SOURCES/TO TOP FIVE DESTINATIONS (US DOLLARS, MILLIONS)					
INWARD DIRECT INVESTMENT			OUTWARD DIRECT INVESTMENT		
Total Inward	774	100%	Total Outward	n/a	100%
Canada	229	29.6%			
China	79	10.2%			
Spain	77	9.9%			
The Netherlands	76	9.8%			
Uruguay	62	8.1%			
"0" reflects amounts rounded to +/- USD 500,000.					

IMPORTANT INVESTMENT AND BUSINESS CONTACTS

Contact for More Information

Please contact Embassy Quito at ecuadorcommercial@state.gov

LOCAL ATTORNEYS

LIST OF ATTORNEYS

1. AGUIAR, Dr. Juan J.

Name of Firm: [illegible] E9-15 y Shyris, Ed.Ivsemon Park, of. 13A, Quito. Telephones: 225-0575, ext. 108 (Atn.: Jakie Tindco); 092716688. E-mail address: juan_aguiar@yahoo.com . JD/MBA Willamette University, Oregon, 2002. Attorney Catholic University, Quito, 2010. Specializes in U.S. immigration law (consular practice).

2. ALMEIDA Guzman, Dr. Angel Diego

Name of firm: "Almeida Guzman & Asociados." Address: Ave. Amazonas N39-61 y Pereira, Edificio Centro Financiero, Office 501, Quito. Telephones: 2981-578 to 582. Fax: 2981-584. Born Jan 28, 1957. E-mail address: dalmeida@almeidaguzman.com. [illegible] Social Sciences; Doctor´s Degree in Jurisprudence (Law School, D.J.) Catholic University, Ecuador. Member of the Quito Bar Society. Active member of the Ecuadorian Institute of Tax Law. Member of the International Bar Association. Member of the Interamerican Bar Association. Experience in legal-corporate counseling, as well as in corporate mergers, acquisitions, split-offs, take-overs, privatization projects, and business restructuring. Assessment on stocks market, trust, fiduciary funds, tax, foreign investment, and transfer of technology legislation. Various types of legal undertakings related to professional practice fields; these include counseling regarding project finance, construction projects, international banking, and finance operations. Arbitrator at the Center of Mediation and Arbitration of the Ecuadorian-American Chamber of Commerce.

3. BAQUERO DE LA CALLE, DR. JOSE ANTONIO

ῶϪ ͅϴ ç◀ ώ⃞ Ϫ⃞ Ϫςώ ῶϪϴ Γ ◀ Ϫb !bbϪ ςϪ ςϱt Γ !ώϴώ

Edificio Proinco Calisto, 7th Floor, Office 701 -704, Quito. Telephones: 2522-877, 2520-887. Fax: 2569-514. E-mail address: tmb-abogados@andinanet.net Born July 23, 1915. D. J. Central University, Quito, 1939. Specializes in commercial, civil and labor, patent and trademark, oil and mining law. Handles estate and trade dispute cases, immigration cases.

4. BARRERA Sweeney, Dr. Patrick

ῶϪ ͅϴ ϴ◀ ώϪώ ῶϪ !bώbϪ ↕ ϪOώ !bbϪ !OϪ !ώϴώ tςϱϱ Γ

Juan Pablo Sanz, Edificio Antisana 1, 10mo. Piso. Telephones: 224-5830. Fax: 224-5827. Born Seo 13, 1957. Email address: info@barreramolina.com . Catholic University, Doctor in Jurisprudence, 1984. John Hopkins University, Master in International Relations, 1986. Southwestern Legal Foundation, International and American Law, 1987. Languages: Spanish, English and Italian. Specializes in banking, finances, energy, mines and natural resources.

5. BERMEO Rosales, Dr. Rodrigo

Name of Firm: "Bermeo & Bermeo." Address: Ave. 12 de Octubre N24-528 y Cordero, Edificio World Trade Center, Torre B, 12th Floor, Quito. Telephones: 2545-871, 2556-027, 2556-028, 2231-227, 2231-228, 2231-229. Fax: 2564-620. E-mail address: rbr@bermeolaw.com and bblaw@andinanet.net Born October 7, 1957. LL. B. Catholic University, Quito, 1983. Admitted to Bar, 1983. Special courses: International Law Institute, Rome, 1988. International and Comparative Law Center, Dallas, 1986. Specializes in intellectual property. Handles trademark and patent cases. Carries out a general legal practice that includes commercial, corporate, immigration and labor law.

6. BRITO M, Dr. Eduardo

ῶϪ ͅϴ ç◀ ῶ◀ Ϫ Address: Avenida Coruña 1770 y Ernesto Noboa, 3er. Piso, Edificio Durvilla Quito. Telephone: 2228498. Telefax: 2226-346 . E-mail address: ebritom@britomoranabogados.com Born September 30, 1962. Master of Laws, Harvard Law School, Cambridge, Massachusetss, 1996. Juris Doctor, Catholic University, Quito, Ecuador, 1988. Master of Arts, University of Brasilia, Brazil, 1986. Bachelor of Arts, Catholic University, Quito, Ecuador, 1985. Admitted to Bar, 1988. Languages: English, French, Portuguese and Spanish. Specializes in: admiralty law and maritime matters (maritime finance and litigation, maritime liens, bankruptcy, shipbuilding/conversion/sales disputes, infrastructure development, marine insurance, charter parties disputes, agency agreements, cargo claims, casualty and vessel registration); antitrust and trade regulation; aviation law; banking, capital markets and finance; bids on public contracts; corporate law (corporate governance, mergers, acquisitions and joint ventures); family law (adoptions, divorces); foreign investments in Ecuador; franchising; gas, mining and oil law; handles collections on percentage basis; immigration law; intellectual property law (copyrights, patents, trademarks and licensing); management/labor disputes; negotiation and mediation in trade disputes; privatizations; real estate transactions; resorts and hospitality; tax law; telecommunications law; transfer of technology and personnel. Firm has offices in Guayaquil, Manta, Portoviejo and Quito and process servers in each office.

7. BUSTAMANTE, Dr. Jose Rafael

ὢϪ ͅϴ ҫ̤◄ ▯ ᲂώώ̊Ϫ Γ ◄ ▯ ᲂώώ̊Ϫ Address: Av. Amazonas y Patria, Edificio Cofiec, Piso 10, Quito. Telephones: 256-2739, 256-2740, 256-2680, 256-2681. Tele/fax: 255-9092, 256-4069, 256-4628. Born Nov 29, 1953. Email: jrbustamante@bustamante.com.ec Catholic University of Quito, Doctor in Jurisprudence, 1978. Georgetown University, Master in Comparative Law, 1979. Admitted to Bar, 1978. Specializes in constitutional, corporate, civil, mercantile, admiralty, financial, administrative, tax and labor laws, public and private contracting, insurance, real estate, foreign investment, immigration, oil and gas, mining, environmental, telecommunications, electrification, privatization and intellectual property rights.

8. CASTRO Pazmiño, Dr. Xiomara:

Name ͅϴ ҫ̤↨ Ϫ̤ͤϬϪϴ, !ϛώϦ Address: Av. 12 de Octubre 24-593 y Av. Francisco Salazar, Piso 10, Quito, Ecuador. Tel: 290-6966. Fax: 252-3306. Email: xcastro@coronelyperez.com . Born: November 10, 1969. Catholic University of Guayaquil, Bachelor in Social and Political Sciences, 1991, Attorney at Law, 1994, Family Clinic, 19931994. University of Florida College of Law, LL.M. in Comparative Law, 1999, Certificate of Specialization in International Taxation, 1999. Member of International Bar Association, International Law Organization, Fulbright Alumni. Specializes in Corporate Law, Tax Law and International Commerce and Investments. Language: Spanish and English.

9. CHIRIBOGA Barba, Dr. Enrique

ὢϪ ͅϴ ҫ◄ ▯ ᲂώώ̊Ϫ ͤ◄ ▯ ᲂώώ̊Ϫ ↕ ώ̤ Ϧ̊ώ̤ !ϦϦϪ !ΟϪ̤ !ώϴώ Γ̤ ώώ,

Edificio Cofiec, 4th, 5th, 10th and 11th . Floor, P. O. Box 17-01-02455, Quito. Telephones: 2562-680 and 2562-681. Fax: 2564-069. E-mail address: eschirib@bustamante.com.ec Born January 29, 1942. Admitted to Bar, 1968. Catholic University, Quito (J. D. 1968); Georgetown University; University of Madrid. Specializes in industrial property law (patents, trademarks, licensing, etc.), general business, and corporate law.

10. CHIRIBOGA Vasconez, Dr. Federico

Name of Firm: "Perez, Bustamante y Ponce". Address: Ave. Republica de El Salvador 1082 y Naciones Unidas, Edificio Mansion Blanca, Torre Londres, 9th Floor, Quito. Telephone: 2254323, 2260-666, 2244-466. Fax: 2258-038. E-mail address: fchiriboga@pbplaw.com Web: www.pbplaw.com . Born April 22, 1933. LL. D. University of Salamanca, Spain, 1960. Specializes in foreign investment, corporations, taxes, oil and mining legislation. Handles collection cases on a contingent basis, estate cases, trade dispute cases, and out-of-court commercial dispute settlement (preferable).

11. FALCONI Puig, Dr. Miguel

Name of Firm: "Falconi Puig Abogados" Address: Ave. Amazonas 477 y Roca, Edificio Rio Amazonas, 9th Floor, Office 900, P.O. Box 17-03-0423, Quito. Telephones: 2561-808, 2561

809. Fax: 2567-293, 2504-790. E-mail address: mail@falconipuig.com Born July 18, 1944. Education: Catholic University, Ecuador; University of Cambridge, Course of Foreign Lawyers and Law Students, 1970. Memberships: Ecuadorian Bar. Specialist in privatizations and public contracts, bids and administrative law.

12. GALLEGOS Dominguez, Dr. Carlos

Name of Firm: "Dr. Carlos Gallegos D. Abogados." Address: Ave. 12 de Octubre N24-562, EϦϴҒϦ ώϦϪ ↕ ϪϪ Ϫ ⅃ ϭϰ ϴҒώ ϭϰϴϯ ▯ Telephone: 250-8059. Fax: 250-8062. E-mail address: cgallegos@yahoo.com and cgd@uio.satnet.net Born June 23, 1951, Quito. LL. B. Catholic University, Quito, 1976. B. A. Business Administration, Central University, Quito, 1983. Specializes in commercial, corporate, banking, civil law, oil and mining matters. Handles foreign investment, patent and trademarks, trade disputes and taxation, registration and establishment of foreign firms in Ecuador, real estate matters, divorce and immigration cases. Member of the Interamerican Bar Association, Washington,

D.C.

13. GALLEGOS Dominguez, Dr. Ivan

ὢϪ ϴ ç̦Ḛ̊ ƀ ƀF jὢϪ !ƀƀϪ !OϪ Ϫ ςFὢ ⱡ9c Γ !ὢ EƀϴFio Forum, 6th floor. P.O. Box 17-01-2772, Quito, Ecuador. Telph: + 5932.2521480. Fax: + 5932.2560736. E-mail address: info@ejgallegos.com . Born November 26, 1940. LLB Central University, Quito, 1967. Specializes in Corporate, Commercial, Alternative Dispute Resolution, Government contracts and Real Estate matters. Handles international trade disputes and collection cases. Handles Mergers and Acquisitions. Specializes in complex litigation and administrative matters. Handles immigration matters and Foreign Investment in Ecuador.

14. GUERRERO Bermúdez, Dr. José Edmundo

ὢϪ ϴ ç̦Ḛ̊ ƀ ƀF j ϪϪ ὢϪϴ Address: Av. Jorge Washington 718 y Amazonas, Edificio Rocafuerte, 8th Floor. Tel: 223-5700, 223-5709 and 223-5699. Fax: 223-5709 Email: pepeyoya@uio.satnet.net . Born: October 27, 1934. Admitted to Bar: 1945. Central University of Quito, Bachelor in Social and Political Sciences, Doctor in Jurisprudence and Attorney at Law, Bachelor in Journalism. Member of the International Lawyers Union. Firm has specialists in every kind of legal procedures such as: Criminal, Civil, Transit, etc. Languages: Spanish, English and French.

15. GUERRERO Vivanco, Dr. Walter

Name of Firm: "Estudio Juridico Dr. Walter Guerrero Vivanco." Address: Ave. Republica de El Salvador N35-82 y Portugal, Edificio Twin Towers, Ofice 4A. Telephones: 2443-680, 2443796, 2443-810 and 09-9-700-013. Fax: 2443-796. Home telephone: 2898-329. Born Jan 10, 1937. E-mail address: w.guerrero.v@andinanet.net Specializes in penal and criminal cases. Handles traffic cases. Does not speak English.

16. HELOU Cevallos, Dr. Carlos

Name of Firm: "Carlos Helou Abogados." Address: Ave. Reina Victoria 1539 y Colon, Edificio Banco de Guayaquil, 9th Floor, Office 906, Quito. Telephones: 2565-180. Fax: 224-2568. Born Mar 14, 1952. Email address: carlos_elou@yahoo.com . Born March 14, 1952, Quito. LL. B. Catholic University, Quito, 1977. Specializes in immigration matters, trademarks, patents, banking, registration and establishment of foreign firms in Ecuador.

17. IBARRA Arboleda, Dr. Rigoberto

ὢϪ ϴ ç̦Ḛ̊ ƀ ƀF Mςὢὢ !ƀƀϪ !O Amazonas 21-147 y Ramon Roca., Quito. Telephone: 290-9170, 290-9160 and 290-9161. Fax: 290-9169. Cell: 09-9-442-275. Born Jun 25, 1960. Email address: ibaril@q.ecua.net.ec . Admitted to Bar, 1994. Education: Masters in Criminal Law and Indigenous JusFϪ, OϪƀὢƀ ! ὢ ƀϪ ƀϪ Ambato, June 2004. Attorney at Law-Bachelor in Political Sciences, Central University, Quito, May 1994. Ϫὢ Γ ƀϪὢϪ ὢ ƀϪ ΓϪFϪFὢF ƀὢOὢƀ University, Boston, July 2004. Specialist in Criminal Law, Technical and Business Institute, Lima, Peru, September 2006. ςF DϪϴϪϪ ϪFὢOϪƀὢƀ ὢFὢ ƀϪ j ὢΓὢ ⱡθθϱ ϪςϪ ϴ Ϫ ƀϪ !ςὢƀ ƀϪ FFὢ Specializes in Criminal Law. Does not speak English.

18. JIJON L., Dr. Rodrigo

Name of Firm: "Perez, Bustamante y Ponce". Address: Ave. Republica de El Salvador 1082 y Naciones Unidas, Edificio Mansion Blanca, Torre Londres, 9th Floor, Quito. Telephone: 2260

666. Fax: 2258-038. E-mail address: rjijon@pbplaw.com Born March 14, 1959, Quito. Admitted to Bar, 1983. Education: Catholic University, Quito, (Doctor in Law, 1983); Tulane Law School (M. A. 1984). Member of the Interamerican Bar Association, Tulane Lawyers Association, Asia-Pacific Lawyers Association. Other languages: French. Specializes in immigration law, commercial, tax, companies, labor.

19. LOZA Burgos, Dra. Federica Genoveva

[illegible] cativo Universal Misionero, office 101, Tababela (near the new airport), Quito. Telephones: 2391-766, 095010-353. E-mail address: fglb53@gmail.com . Born May 27, 1980, Quito. Central University of Quito, Bachelor in Political and Social Sciences, Doctor in Jurisprudence, Quito, 2006. Expert in Documentation. Specializes in Real Estate, Civil, Commercial and Labor Law. Speaks some English.

20. MOLINA Novillo, Dr. César

[illegible] Viteri & Andrade Ceval [illegible] Juan Pablo Sanz, Edificio Antisana 1, 10mo. Piso, Quito. Telephone: 224-5830. Fax: 2245827. Born Aug 23, 1959. Email address: info@barreramolina.com . Graduated as Doctor in Jurisprudence at the Catholic University in Quito, 1984. University of Rome,-Roman Law, 1987. Languages: Spanish, English and Italian. Specializes in public and private procurement, foreign investment, immigration, aeronautical law, intellectual and industry property.

21. MUÑOZ Neira, Dr. Luis Alfredo

[illegible]

Edificio Patria, Oficina 903. Telefaxes: 2543-461 and 2523-562. E-mail address: mnlawyers@andinanet.net Born September 28, 1957. Admited to Bar 1982. Specializes in criminal cases. Handles criminal and immigration cases.

22. NEIDL, Dr. Andrew G.

[illegible] Address: P.O. Box 17.01.2772 Ave. Republica 396 y Diego de Almagro, Quito, Ecuador. E-mail: Andrew.neidl@ejgn.com . Specializes in general practice, real estate, corporate, intellectual property and anti-counterfeiting, international IP matters, venture capital, merger and acquisitions, commercial and foreign investments, energy and hydrocarbons, banking & finance, telecommunications and IT, government bids and contracts, ADR & negotiations, aviation and maritime, environmental and translations.

23. ORTEGA DE GRIJALVA, DRA. ALBA LUCIA

[illegible] Address: World Trade Center, Ave. 12 de Octubre N24-562 y Cordero, Torre A, Oficina 1108, Quito. Telephones: 2229-159 and 2228

411. Fax: 2228-831. E-mail address: ogabogad@uio.satnet.net . Born: May 17, 1959. J.D. Catholic University. Admitted to Bar in 1989. Specializes in commercial law, immigration, insurance, banking and labor matters, international rights.

24. PAZ Durini, Dr. Jorge

Name of Firm: "Paz & Horowitz." Address: Whimper #1105 y Diego de Almagro, P.O. Box 1721-1533, Quito. Telephones: 2222-057, 2508-123, 2227-676, 2501-354. Fax: 2501-902, 2222-058. Born 1958, Quito. E-mail address: ph@ph.com.ec Doctorate in Laws from Catholic University, Quito and admitted to Bar in 1982. International Joint Ventures and Investment Treaties at IDLI, Rome, 1988. LL.M. in International Business Transactions and

U.S. Contract and Corporate Law, Temple University, Philadelphia, Pennsylvania, 1991. Vice President of the Mining Chamber of Ecuador. The firm provides legal services in international and national commercial law, with particular emphasis on mining, oil and gas, intellectual and industrial property, telecommunications, transfer of technology and personnel, foreign investment, and management/labor issues. Has process server on staff.

25. PEREZ Arteta, Dr. Jose

Name of Firm: "Perez, Bustamante y Ponce". Address: Ave. Republica de El Salvador 1082 y Naciones Unidas, Edificio Mansion Blanca, Torre Londres, 8th Floor, Quito. Telephone: 2254323, 2260-666. Fax: 2258-038. E-mail address: jperez@pbplaw.com Born May 11, 1934. LL.

B. Catholic University, Quito. Master of Comparative Law, SMU, Dallas, Texas. Specializes in civil and corporate law (including patents), handles collection cases on a percentage basis, estate cases, trade disputes. Other language: French. Member of the Interamerican Bar Association, Washington, D.C.; International Fiscal Association. Handles immigration cases.

26. ROMERO PONCE, Dr. Diego

Name of Firm: "Romero Arteta Ponce Abogados." Address: Ave. 12 de Octubre N26-97 y Abraham Lincoln, Edificio Torre 1492, 8th. Floor, Quito. Telephones: 2986-666 and 2986-667. Fax 2986-664 and 2986-665. E-mail address: rap@law.com.ec & gvillagomez@law.com.ec . Web Page: www.rap.com.ec & www.ecuadorlawyer.com . Born May 1960. LL. B. Central University, Quito, 1968. Post graduate studies: LL. M. Pittsburgh University, Pennsylvania; LL. M. Harvard University, Cambridge, Massachusetts. Specializes in Corporate Law. Foreign investment, negotiations, public and private, oil and mining law, administrative cases, estate cases, intellectual property, immigration law. Member of the International Bar Association (IBA), London; Interamerican Bar Association, Washington, D.C.; Asia-Pacific Layers Association (APLA), Korea; Interamerican Association of Industrial Property (ASIPI); Brazilian Association of Intellectual Property (ABPI).

27. ROMERO Ponce, Dr. Gustavo

Name of Firm: "Romero Arteta Ponce Abogados." Address: Av. 12 de Octubre N26-97 y A. Lincoln, Edificio Torre 1492, 8vo. Piso, P.O. Box 17-03-719, Quito. Telephones: 2986-666, 2986-667 Fax: 2986-664. E-mail address: rap@law.com.ec . Born September 30, 1955. Degrees: Solicitor and Doctor in Law of the Catholic University, Quito. Specializes in commercial law, patents and trademarks, aeronautic law, oil and gas. Member of the Quito Bar Association; Ecuadorian Industrial Property Association (AEPI); American Association of Industrial Property (ASIPI); International Bar Association (IBA); International Association for the Protection of Industrial Property (AIPPI); Asia-Pacific Lawyers Association (APLA);

[illegible]

International Bar Association.

28. SALAZAR B., Dr. Rodrigo

Name of Firm: "Perez, Bustamante y Ponce". Address: Ave. Republica de El Salvador 1082 y Naciones Unidas, Edificio Mansion Blanca, Torre Londres, 9th Floor, Quito. Telephone: 2260

666. Fax: 2258-038. E-mail address: rsalazar@pbplaw.com Born April 7, 1952, Quito. Admitted to Bar, 1979. Education: Catholic University, Quito, Doctor in Law, 1979. Member of the Interamerican Bar Association, Asian-Pacific Lawyers Association. Specializes in corporation and foreign investment, banking, aviation.

29. SANTELICES I., Dr. Waldo

[illegible]

Quito. Telephone: 593-2-223-0236. Cell: 09-857-4015. E-mail address: wsantel@ejsantelices.com . Born July 21, 1963, Santiago de Chile, Chile. Admitted to Bar: August 31, 2005. Education: Catholic University, Quito, Bachelor in Legal and Social

[illegible]

2004. Specializes in criminal cases and commercial law. Speaks some English.

30. SEMPERTEGUI, Dr. Leonardo

[illegible] Alfaro y Ave. 6 de Diciembre esquina, Edificio Monasterio Plaza, Piso 10. Telephone: 593-2-6012-442 & 6012-443, cel phone 084057181. Email: LSV@sempertegui.com Web Page: www.sempertegui.com. The Firm specializes in constitutional law, administrative law, energy law, oil & gas law, taxation, public contracts, litigation, human rights, foreign investment, intellectual property, corporate law, civil law & private contracting, employment labor law, antitrust. Member of ABA and AIPM. Speaks fluent English.

31. SILVA Altamirano, Dr. Walter E.

Address: Espinoza E4-11 and Ave. Colombia, Edificio Avila, Office 301, Quito. Telephone: 2955-191, 2286-583, 09-9449-107. Fax: 2286-583. Home: 2542-226. Born Jul 2, 1939. Central University graduate with experience in foreign countries. Specializes in traffic cases. Does not speak English.

32. TOBAR Carrion, Dr. Bernardo

Name of Firm: "Tobar & Bustamante Abogados." Address: Ave. 12 de Octubre y Lincoln Esq., Edificio Torre 1492, 10th. Floor, Office 1002, P.O. Box 17-03-883, Quito. Telephones: 2986456, 2986-457. Fax: 2986-462. E-mail address: xcalderon@tobarybustamante.com Born August 13, 1965. Attorney at Law and Doctor in Jurisprudence, Catholic University, Quito. Admitted to Bar, 1989. Ph.D. in Advanced International Legal Studies, Dipl. International Business Transactions, University of The Pacific, McGeorge School of Law, Salzburg University, Faculty of Law, and Austro-American Institute of Education. Dipl. Intellectual Property, International Copyright Institute of the U.S. Copyright Office and WIPO. Drafter and lobbyist of the new Ecuadorian Intellectual Property Law. The firm specializes in intellectual property ,including Patent and Trademark Law and Technology Law; and Transnational Business, particularly commerce. The firm is a leader in litigation in IP and IP trade-related matters, and anti-piracy and anti-counterfeiting practices. Member of Ecuadorian Industrial Property Association, Interamerican Institute of Copyrights, Latin-American Institute of Technology, Information and Law.

33. TORRES Gonzalez, Dr. Oswaldo

Name of Firm: "Torres & Asociados." Address: Robles 653 y Ave. Amazonas, Edificio Proinco, 11th

Floor, Office 1109-1112, Quito. Telephone: 256-2914. Fax: 2562-793. E-mail address: otorres@uio.satnet.net Born July 22, 1939. LL. B. Central University, Quito. Admitted to Bar, 1965. Harvard University, 1965. New York University, 1966. Institute of Social Studies, The Hague, 1967. Specializes in commercial, corporate, civil, patent, trademark, and taxation cases. Handles collections on a percentage basis, trade disputes, oil and mining law, and immigration cases.

34. VINTIMILLA Saldaña, Dr. Jaime R.

Name of Firm: [illegible] Address: Ave. Juan Ramírez N 3615 y Germán Alemán. Tele/Fax: 2243-647 and 2240-182. Cell phone: 09-9-461-989 Home: 2503-393. E-mail address: jvintimi@interactive.net.ec and jvintimilla@vgylex.com . Born November 18, 1967, Azogues. Doctor in Jurisprudence, Catholic University, Quito, 1995. Member of the Interamerican Bar Association, Ecuadorian Bar, Roman Law Institute. Other language: French. Specializes in immigration matters, constitutional procedures, registration and establishment of foreign firms in Ecuador, alternative methods of conflict resolution. Handles civil and commercial law.

QUITO LAWYERS SOCIETIES

Colegio de Abogados (Quito Bar Association)

Piedrahita 225 y 6 de Diciembre Quito, Ecuador Telephone: 256-7619, 256-7621 Fax: 256-8567 E-mail address: colabpi@mail.colobpi.pro.ec Website: www.colabpi.pro.ec

PUBLIC ACCOUNTING FIRMS

Deloitte & Touche (deloitteecuador@deloitte.com) Ave. Amazonas 3517 y Pablo Sanz, Edificio Xerox Quito, Ecuador Telephone: 225-1319, 2254412 Fax: 2435-807, 2460-062

Price Waterhouse Coopers (www.pwcglobal.com) Almagro 2054 y Whimper, Edificio IBM Quito, Ecuador Telephones: 2525-440, 2562-288 Fax: 2567-096 **Romero & Asociados** (www.romeroyasociados.com) Ave. Amazonas N33-319 y Rumipamba Edificio Torre Carolina, 8th, 9th, & 10th Floor Quito, Ecuador Telephone: 2267-012 Fax: 2257-013

Credit reports can usually be obtained through banks or through commercial reporting agencies such as Dunn and Bradstreet, Inc. In addition to Ecuadorian government and commercial banks, and branches of several foreign banks, there is a Quito branch of the First National City Bank (Citibank), Republica de El Salvador y Naciones Unidas, Quito, telephones: 297-0052, 297-0053.

There is an organization in Ecuador that conducts genealogical investigations.

You may write to: Centro Nacional de Investigaciones Genealogicas y Antropologicas

P.O. Box 135-B, Quito, Ecuador President: Juan Freile Granizo

QUITO LAW CLINICS

Law Clinics in Quito provide *pro bono services* to individuals who are in need of legal assistance and do not have the economic means to hire an attorney.

Clínica Jurídica de la Universidad Internacional SEK

Calle Fray Francisco Compte y Cruz de Piedra` Guápulo Quito, Ecuador Telephone: 2223688 / 2238385 Fax: (593 2) 2223689

Clinica de Derechos Humanos de la Pontificia Universidad Católica del Ecuador

Avenida 12 de Octubre y Carrión Quito, Ecuador Telephone: 22225782

GUYANA INVESTMENT AND BUSINESS CLIMATE - STRATEGIC INFORMATION AND CONTACTS FOR STARTING BUSINESS IN GUYANA

Contact Point at Post for Public Inquiries

Frisco McDonald
Economic/Commercial Officer
Embassy of the United States of America
100 Duke and Young Streets
Kingston
Georgetown, Guyana
Phone: (011) (592) 225-4900-9 Ext. 4220
Fax: (011) (592)-225-8597
Email: **McDonaldFJ@state.gov**
http://georgetown.usembassy.gov

Wynette Oudkerk
Economic/Commercial Specialist
Embassy of the United States of America
100 Duke and Young Streets
Kingston
Georgetown, Guyana
Phone: (011) (592) 225-4900 Ext:4213
Fax: (011) (592)-225-8497
Email: **OudkerkW@state.gov**
http://georgetown.usembassy.gov

Guyana is a country located in South America's North Atlantic coast. During 2014, Guyana's investment climate showed no signs of recovery from the downward turn of 2013. Political gridlock and infighting hampered the country's development efforts on several fronts. The Amaila Falls Hydropower Project, which would have been the largest capital project in the country's history, fell apart after a decade of planning when U.S. developer and equity partner Sithe Global withdrew from the multinational development team in August 2013. The company had concerns related to political risk following objections to the venture by the country's largest opposition party.

Guyana has failed to crack down on money laundering, and parliament has been unable to pass legislation strengthening Anti-Money Laundering/Countering the Financing of Terrorism (AML/CFT) laws. Consequently in November 2014, the Caribbean Financial Action Task Force (CFATF) recommended that its members implement counter measures to protect their financial systems from the ongoing money laundering and terrorist financing risks emanating from Guyana. CFATF also referred Guyana to its parent body, the international Financial Action Task Force (FATF), for review. Although FATF has not concluded its review of Guyana, consumers and importers are already complaining of increased costs and delays in processing international financial and trade transactions. The government continues to encourage foreign investment but with limited success outside of the gold mining sector. Perceptions of corruption, inefficient government, inadequate infrastructure, and crime remain barriers to attracting foreign investment.

Early general elections were held on May 11, 2015. The APNU-Alliance for Change party won 33 out of 65 seats in the National Assembly and David Granger was sworn in as President on May 16th, 2015.The impending elections slowed down current and prospective investment since implementation of many governmental projects were either put on hold or curtailed, until after the elections. Presentation of the National Budget, which has a constitutional deadline of April 30th, was also affected.

1. OPENNESS TO, AND RESTRICTIONS UPON, FOREIGN INVESTMENT

ATTITUDE TOWARD FOREIGN DIRECT INVESTMENT

Foreign direct investment (FDI) into Guyana is actively encouraged and seen by the Government as critical to its economic development. Numerous incentives are offered to investors in this regard. While its track record in attracting government-to-government development assistance is strong, its long-term record in attracting private-sector investment remains poor. Consequently, investment productivity as measured by the Incremental Capital/Output Ratio (ICOR) is low. In 2007 Guyana's ICOR was around 27, which means that it took USD 27 of investment to generate USD 1 of extra output. Countries using capital effectively generally have an ICOR of 4 or below.

The Government of Guyana supports a traditional investment agency, the Guyana Office for Investment (GO-INVEST). GO-INVEST focuses primarily on agriculture and agro-processing, tourism, manufacturing, information and communication technology, seafood and aquaculture, and wood processing. Potential investors should note that GO-INVEST is the first point of contact to obtain necessary permits and tax concessions. GO-INVEST often determines that many prospective investors' proposals lack sufficient capital; these inquiries generally do not progress further. Due to the state's major role in the domestic economy and the Government of Guyana's tendency to centralize decision-making, relatively large foreign investments receive intense political attention, often from the highest political level. Over the past decade, the government enacted new laws or amended existing ones to encourage foreign direct investment, with mixed levels of success.

In 2009, the GOG launched its Low Carbon Development Strategy (LCDS) as a plan to transform the economy, conserve its forests, and adapt to global climate change while reducing carbon emissions. Initially relying on donor assistance, with plans to eventually draw on private investment in a global market for carbon credits, the GOG intends to channel forest conservation payments into human capital development, climate change adaptation, and strategic investments in low-carbon economic sectors like business process outsourcing, hydropower, sustainable forestry and wood products processing, ecotourism, biofuels, aquaculture, and other high-value, export-oriented agriculture. Guyana established an Office for Climate Change, REDD+ Secretariat, as well as a Project Management Unit within the Office of the President to attract and vet potential foreign investors in sectors complimentary to the LCDS.

Following the launch of the LCDS, the Government of Norway entered into an agreement to protect Guyana's tropical forest for its carbon storage and other ecological services. Depending on Guyana's performance, Norway had planned on contributing a total of up to USD 250 million by 2015 if Guyana demonstrates continued low rates of deforestation and forest degradation. However as of April 2015, they have only contributed USD 115 million. The Government of Guyana believes this financial commitment and inclusion of incentives for forest conservation in the 2009 Copenhagen Accord will lead to higher levels of LCDS investment in coming years. Thus far, however, no other international donors have stepped forward in any substantial way to pay for Guyana's ecosystem services, and the Norway payments are likely to be reduced due to Guyana's increased deforestation rate.

OTHER INVESTMENT POLICY REVIEWS

Guyana has been a World Trade Organization (WTO) member since 1995. Guyana is currently scheduled for a WTO Trade Policy Review in September of 2015.

LAWS/REGULATIONS OF FOREIGN DIRECT INVESTMENT

Sufficient legislation exists in Guyana to enable foreign investment in the country, but implementation of relevant legislation continues to be inadequate. The objectives of the Investment Act of 2004 are to stimulate socioeconomic development by attracting and facilitating foreign investment. Other relevant laws include the Income Tax Act, the Customs Act, the Procurement Act of 2003, the Companies Act of 1991, the Securities Act of 1998, and the Small Business Act. Regulatory actions are still required for much of this legislation to be effectively implemented.

The judicial system is generally perceived to be slow and ineffective in enforcing legal contracts. The 2015 World Bank's Doing Business Report states that it takes 581 days to enforce a contract in Guyana. Suspected corrupt practices and long delays make the courts an unattractive option for settling investment or contractual disputes, particularly for foreign investors unfamiliar with Guyana. In order to redress this obstacle to investment, the Government of Guyana, with support from the Inter-American Development Bank (IADB), established a Commercial Court in June 2006. Given Guyana's growth potential, there is need for expansion and strengthened capacity in the near future.

INDUSTRIAL PROMOTION

Guyana offers potential investors—foreign and domestic alike—a broad spectrum of investment choices, ranging from more traditional industries (such as mining, sugar, rice, and timber), to non-traditional export sectors (such as aquaculture, agro processing, fresh fruits, and vegetables, light manufacturing, value-added forest products), to services exports (such as tourism and Information Technology-enabled services). Many products receive duty-free or reduced-duty treatment in destination markets.

Additionally, Guyana enjoys considerable established commercially-viable mineral reserves principally in gold, diamonds, and bauxite. Smaller deposits of manganese, copper, rare earth elements, and uranium also exist. Their commercial viability, however, has not been definitively determined.

Opportunities can be found on the following websites:

Guyana Office for Investment: **http://goinvest.gov.gy/investment/investment-guide/**
The National Procurement & Tender Administration (NPTA): **http://www.npta.gov.gy/**
National Industrial & Commercial Investment Limited: **http://www.privatisation.gov.gy/**

LIMITS ON FOREIGN CONTROL

In the mining sector there are restrictions with respect to the ownership of property for small and medium-scale mining to citizens of Guyana. Foreigners may enter into joint-venture arrangements under which the two parties agree to jointly develop a mining property. There are no restrictions on the percentage of the investment shouldered by the foreign investor, and these arrangements are strictly governed through private contracts. Since this type of relationship carries a high risk factor, the U.S. Embassy strongly encourages investors to exercise proper due diligence when exploring their options.

PRIVATIZATION PROGRAM

Foreign investors generally have equal access to privatization opportunities, even though the privatization process may not be transparent. For some larger operations, foreign investment is openly preferred.

Since 1992, the GOG has privatized 16 out of 21 state-owned enterprises (SOEs). Only Guyana Oil Company Limited, Guyana National Printers Limited, Guyana Sugar Corporation, the National Communication Network (NCN), and Guyana Power & Light (GPL) remain as SOEs. The head of the Privatization Unit/National Industrial and Commercial Investments Limited also serves as Chairman of Guyana Power and Light.

Most large-scale investments in Guyana's infrastructure are government projects financed by international lending institutions, with the Inter-American Development Bank (IDB) their largest lender. U.S. firms are generally given equal access to these projects.

Screening of FDI

There is no mandatory screening of foreign investment. The government, however, conducts de facto screenings of most investments to determine which businesses are eligible for special tax treatment and access to licenses, land, and approval for investment incentives. In spite of recent efforts to remove discretionary power from the various ministries, ministers still retain significant authority to determine how relevant laws, such as the Investment Act, Small Business Act, and Procurement Act, are applied.

In general, international investors receive the same treatment as local investors in Guyana. One exception is the special approval required for local financing. Foreign borrowers applying for a loan of more than GYD 2 million (USD 10,000) must request permission from the Minister of Finance. This requirement reflects Guyana's preference for foreign investors to bring capital into the country.

Another exception exists in the mining sector, where ownership of property for small- and medium-scale mining is restricted to citizens of Guyana. Foreigners may enter into joint-venture arrangements under which the two parties agree to jointly develop a mining property. There are no restrictions on the percentage of the investment shouldered by the foreign investor; these arrangements are strictly by private contract. However, such relationships are highly risky, and appropriate due diligence of potential joint venture partners is required.

Competition Law

As Guyana strives to improve competition and fair-trading both nationally and internationally, the Government of Guyana enacted the Competition and Fair Trading Act in 2006 to govern matters of this nature. This act seeks to promote, maintain, and encourage competition; to prohibit the prevention, restriction, or distortion of competition and the abuse of dominant positions in trade; and to promote the welfare and interests of consumers and to establish a Competition Commission for connected matters.

In support of the functioning of this Act, a Competition Commission was instituted. The Commission is responsible for reviewing all commercial activities identifying those that adversely affect the economic interest of consumers; investigating such businesses which do not comply with the Act; and conducting inquires in connection with any matter falling within the provisions of the Act.

Investment Trends

The Government of Guyana publicly encourages foreign direct investment (FDI). While its track record in attracting government-to-government development assistance is strong, its long-term record in attracting private-sector investment remains poor. Total FDI in Guyana decreased by 27.1 percent, from USD 293.8 million in 2012 to USD 214.0 million in 2013. However, in March 2015, ExxonMobil began exploratory drilling in the Starbroek block, initially investing roughly USD 300 million into the project. According to a study performed by the U.S. Geological Survey, as much as the equivalent of 15 billion barrels of oil are located in the Guyana-Suriname Basin. If successful, the venture would mean billions in revenue for the country and could potentially transform the social, political, and economic landscape.

Table 1

Measure	Year	Index or Rank	Website Address
TI Corruption Perceptions index	2014	124	transparency.org/cpi2014/results
World Bank's Doing Business Report "Ease of Doing Business"	2015	123	doingbusiness.org/rankings
Global Innovation Index	2014	80	globalinnovationindex.org/content.aspx?page=data-analysis
World Bank GNI per capita	2013	USD 3,750	data.worldbank.org/indicator/NY.GNP.PCAP.CD

Millennium Challenge Corporation Country Scorecard

The Millennium Challenge Corporation (MCC), a U.S. Government foreign aid agency focused on promoting growth in the recipient countries by emphasizing good economic policies such as free markets and low corruption. Developing nations must demonstrate positive performance in three key indicators; ruling justly, investing in people, and fostering economic freedom. A list of countries/economies with MCC scorecards and links to those scorecards is available here:**http://www.mcc.gov/pages/selection/scorecards**. Details on each of the MCC's indicators and a guide to reading the scorecards are available here: **http://www.mcc.gov/pages/docs/doc/report-guide-to-the-indicators-and-the-selection-process-fy-2015**.

2. CONVERSION AND TRANSFER POLICIES

FOREIGN EXCHANGE

The Guyana dollar (GYD) is fully convertible and transferable. According to the 2013 Bank of Guyana Annual Report, the average exchange rate is USD 1 to GYD 206.33 at the end of March 2014, the last reported rate (**http://www.bankofguyana.org.gy/bog/images/statistical_tables/exc_rates.pdf**). However, the exchange rate has been relatively stable, fluctuating between GYD 203 and GYD 209 for more than five years. No limits exist on inflows or repatriation of funds, although there are spot shortages of foreign currency. Regulations also require that all persons entering and exiting Guyana declare all currency in excess of USD 10,000 to Customs authorities at the port of entry.

In practice, many large foreign investors in Guyana use subsidiaries outside Guyana to handle earnings generated by the export of primary products, including timber, gold, and bauxite. Those companies then advance funds to their local entities to cover operating costs.

Guyana has a floating exchange rate that is determined by supply and demand, which is predominantly driven by activities of Guyana's three largest commercial banks. The government has intervened in support of the GYD with some success. The government will likely continue to intervene in defense of the GYD and its international reserves.

The GYD is generally stable, depreciating marginally by 0.37 percent against the USD in 2012. The relative stability of the currency is underpinned by a sufficient flow of foreign exchange to the market. The exchange rate is expected to remain relatively stable since there is more than an adequate supply of foreign exchange in the system to meet balance of payments needs.

Remittance Policies

There is no limit to the acquisition of foreign currency, although the government limits the amount that a number of state-owned firms may keep for their own purchases. Regulations on foreign currency denominated bank accounts in Guyana allow funds to be wired in and out of the country electronically without having to go through cumbersome exchange procedures. Foreign companies operating in Guyana have experienced no government-induced difficulties in repatriating earnings in recent years.

Guyana is neither an important regional nor offshore financial center, nor does it have any free trade zones. Money laundering is perceived as a serious problem and has been linked to drug trafficking (principally cocaine), firearms, corruption, and fraud, as well as to the influx of foreign currency. Guyana has a large informal economy in which cash is preferred by both buyers and sellers for most transactions, making it highly vulnerable to money laundering. On November 20, 2013, the Caribbean Financial Action Task Force (CFATF) issued a statement classifying Guyana among jurisdictions with strategic AML/CFT deficiencies that have not made sufficient progress in addressing the deficiencies or have not complied with their Action Plan developed with the CFATF to address these deficiencies. The CFATF calls on its members to consider implementing counter measures to protect their financial systems from the ongoing money laundering and terrorist financing risks emanating from each jurisdiction.

3. EXPROPRIATION AND COMPENSATION

On August 16, 2001, the National Assembly approved the Acquisition of Lands for Public Purposes Bill 2001.This Act cleared the way for the government to acquire private parcels of land at prices below market value. Since its inception, the government has exercised the Act in a limited capacity, mainly for development purposes deemed to be in the national interest (e.g., clearing the way to build the Berbice River Bridge) and in breach of contract cases.

Evidence of discrimination against U.S. investments, companies, or representatives in the application of expropriation laws has not been identified. Nevertheless, expropriation can occur without proper fair market valuation.

The forestry sector operates at greater risk for expropriation or similar actions. Some forestry companies and individuals have been subject to action under the aforementioned 2001 act, due to alleged breach of contracts with the government, non-use of their concessions, and/or owing debts to the government.

4. DISPUTE SETTLEMENT

LEGAL SYSTEM, SPECIALIZED COURTS, JUDICIAL INDEPENDENCE, JUDGMENTS OF FOREIGN COURTS

Guyana's legal system, like most Commonwealth countries, follows the English Common Law system. Vestiges of the Roman-Dutch legal system remain, especially in the areas of land tenure. In early 2005, Legislative amendments were made to allow Guyana's accession to the Caribbean Court of Justice as its final Court of Appeal.

Guyana's Supreme Court of Judicature hears both criminal and civil matters. Therefore, the Supreme Court in its civil jurisdiction has the standing to hear intellectual property claims. Though the Constitution of Guyana provides for the independence of the judiciary, in practice the Executive has some influence over the judicial branch of the government. The hearing of civil matters is a slothful process and is perceived to be unfair. Judgments of Courts within the Commonwealth are considered judicial precedents where Guyanese laws are silent.

Suspected corrupt practices and long delays make the courts an unattractive option for settling investment or contractual disputes, particularly for foreign investors unfamiliar with Guyana. In order to redress this obstacle to investment, the Government of Guyana, with support from the Inter-American Development Bank (IADB), established a Commercial Court in June 2006. Given Guyana's growth potential, there is need for expansion and strengthened capacity in the near future.

BANKRUPTCY

The 1998 Guyana Insolvency Act provides for the facilitation of insolvency proceedings. According to data collected by Doing Business, resolving insolvency takes 3.0 years on average and costs 29 percent of the debtor's estate, with the most likely outcome being that the company will be sold piecemeal. The average recovery rate is 18 cents on the dollar. Globally, Guyana received a ranking of 141 out of 189 economies for Ease of Resolving Insolvency.

The 2004 Financial Institutions Act gives the Central Bank power to take temporary control of financial institutions in trouble. This Act provides legal authority for the Central Bank to take a more proactive role in helping insolvent local banks.

INVESTMENT DISPUTES

There are two ongoing investment disputes involving U.S. interests in Guyana.

A U.S. firm, which owns 80 percent of Guyana Telephone and Telegraph (GT&T), has expressed concern over the GOG's intentions to terminate GT&T's contractually guaranteed monopoly on land-line and international telecommunications prior to its expiration. The GOG's actions are linked to its desire to introduce legislation that would fully liberalize the telecommunications sector. The U.S firm and the GOG are having ongoing discussions to try and find a mutually acceptable agreement on the issue.

Another U.S company has filed a lawsuit against Guyana Telephone and Telegraph (GT&T), alleging that they engaged in unfair trade practices in order to have Caribbean Telecommunications Ltd.'s license to provide cellular services in Guyana cancelled.

INTERNATIONAL ARBITRATION

Guyana does not have a Bilateral Investment Treaty with the United States. Negotiations began in 1993 but broke down in 1995. Since then, the two nations have not conducted any subsequent negotiations.

Double taxation treaties are in force with Canada (1987), the United Kingdom and Northern Ireland (1992), and CARICOM (1995). Other double taxation agreements remain under negotiation with India, Kuwait, and the Seychelles. The CARICOM-Dominican Republic Free Trade Agreement provides for the negotiation of a double taxation agreement, but no significant developments occurred since March 2009.

International arbitration decisions are enforceable under the Arbitration Act of 1931.

ICSID Convention and New York Convention

Guyana is a member state to the International Centre for Settlement of Investment Disputes (ICSID).

Guyana has ratified the convention on the Recognition and Enforcement of Foreign Arbitral Awards (1958 New York Convention), which went into force in December of 2014.

DURATION OF DISPUTE RESOLUTION

According to the World Bank's Doing Business report, resolving disputes takes 581 days, costs 25.2 percent of the value of the claim, and requires 36 procedures. Suspected corrupt practices and long delays make the courts an unattractive option for settling investment or contractual disputes, particularly for foreign investors unfamiliar with Guyana.

5. PERFORMANCE REQUIREMENTS AND INVESTMENT INCENTIVES

WTO/TRIMS

Guyana has been a World Trade Organization (WTO) member since 1995.

INVESTMENT INCENTIVES

The Status of Aliens Act allows a non-resident of Guyana to acquire and dispose of assets and moveable and immoveable property in the same manner as a citizen of Guyana. The GOG treats domestic and foreign investors alike with regard to investment incentives. Guyana offers incentives based on specific criteria such as location of an investment or investment in specific government-targeted sectors.

The 2003 Fiscal Enactments Act allows the Minister of Finance to grant exemptions from Corporate Tax for a period of five years to an investor if the activity demonstrably creates new employment in certain regions of the country (primarily hinterland regions one, eight, nine, and 10). In the case of new economic activity, the Minister may grant a tax holiday of up to 10 years if the activity falls under the following categories: non-traditional agro processing (excluding sugar refining, rice milling, and chicken farming); tourist hotels or eco-tourist hotels; information and communications technology (excluding retailing and distributing); petroleum exploration, extraction, or refining; and mineral exploration, extraction, or refining. The Minister maintains final discretion over which investors receive corporate tax exemptions.

The Income Tax Act of 1998 provides for accelerated depreciation of plant and equipment pending approval of the Minister of Finance on a case specific basis. The GOG previously utilized the Act to provide export tax allowances for manufacturing or processing of non-traditional products exported to countries outside of the Caribbean Community and tax allowances for research and development.

The Minister of Finance maintains authority to approve exemptions and waivers from customs duty, excise tax, and value added tax on plant, equipment, machinery, and spare parts. Though not required, the government expects investors to submit business proposals to GO-INVEST that outline the proposed project, the value of the investment, and employment to be generated from the investment. GO-INVEST reviews proposals and makes recommendations to the Guyana Revenue Authority (GRA) in accordance with the Customs Duties Order of 2003. The GRA determines whether imports comply with regulation and whether those materials are eligible for tax relief. GRA makes the final recommendation to the Minister of Finance whether to grant exemptions and waivers from customs duty, excise tax, and value added tax.

Similarly, the policy provides for a tax allowance for non-traditional exports to non-CARICOM countries. Traditional products include rice, sugar, bauxite, gold, diamonds, timber, petroleum, lumber, shrimp, molasses, and rum. The allowance ranges between 25 percent and 75 percent, and at least 10 percent of sales must be exported to qualify.

In certain circumstances, Guyana also offers duty-free imports and tax holidays to investors on request. A key factor in the determination of duty-free status and value added tax waiver is value addition. The authorities note that blanket approvals are not given; instead each import consignment is reviewed individually. When granted, GRA lowers or waives the duty and value added tax completely, based on the industry and item. The authorities note that tax holidays are less likely to be granted than duty-free status or a value added tax waiver.

A number of companies, both foreign and domestic, have benefited from investment incentives such as corporate tax exemption, income tax (In Aid of Industry) exemption, export tax exemption on non-traditional exports, and exemption from customs duty, excise tax, and value added tax.

Research and Development

The GOG has not financed research and development programs, but foreign firms are encouraged to initiate research and development initiatives. The GOG does not force foreign investors to use domestic content in goods or technology. Both local and foreign investors, however, have found it useful to purchase from local sources as well as import goods unavailable on the local market.

Performance Requirements

Although no explicit government policy regarding performance requirements exists, some are written into contracts with foreign investors and could include the requirement of a performance bond. Some contracts require a certain minimum level of investment. Investors are not required to source locally, nor must they export a certain percentage of output. Foreign exchange is not rationed in proportion to exports, nor are there any requirements for national ownership or technology transfer.

Data Storage

Foreign investors are not required to establish or maintain a certain amount of data storage within the country.

6. RIGHT TO PRIVATE OWNERSHIP AND ESTABLISHMENT

Guyana's constitution specifically protects the right of foreigners to own property or land in Guyana. Private entities may freely acquire and dispose of interests in business enterprises, although some newly privatized entities have limits on the number of shares that may be acquired by any one individual or entity (domestic or foreign). Similarly, the articles of association of some firms prohibit the issuance of more than a certain number of share transfers to any one individual or company in an effort to prevent attempts to gain control of such companies in the secondary market.

Foreign and domestic firms possess the right to establish and own business enterprises and engage in all forms of remunerative activity. Enterprises in mining, telecommunications, forestry, banking, and tourism sectors require licenses. Obtaining necessary licenses can be a time-consuming task. According to GO-INVEST's Investor's Roadmap, the estimated processing time to obtain the approvals to lease state or government owned lands may take one year; some investors report much longer processing times.

7. PROTECTION OF PROPERTY RIGHTS

Real Property

The country has a dual registry system of property rights with distinct requirements, processes, and enforcement mechanisms. The two types of registry systems are deeds (Deeds Registry) and title (Land

Registry) registries that operate in separate jurisdictions, which in theory help to avoid the problem of double entry and dual registration. But overall Guyana's property rights system is overly bureaucratic and complex, with regulations that are overlapping and competing, overloaded, and nontransparent. This affects the proper allocation, enforcement, and effectiveness of property rights, as well as, the efficiency of all property-based markets such as housing, land, commercial property, and financial markets (especially primary ones such as mortgage markets). The judicial system is generally perceived to be slow and ineffective in enforcing legal contracts. The World Bank's Doing Business Report 2015 says that it takes 581days to enforce such contracts.

The banking system uses the term mortgages, yet these instruments are not backed up by real estate assets, as it is typically done. Instead, the term mortgage is used to define a specific type of consumer loan dedicated to the building of a home.

There are three types of land ownership in Guyana today: a) Public land – 85 percent: made of what used to be known as state and government lands; b) Amerindian land – 14 percent: lands owned by the Amerindians, which are titled, and the alienation was done in the 1970s; and c) Private land – 1–2 percent: land that can be transferred by either freehold or absolute grant. A freehold transfer could use either transport system or a land registration system that is based on the Torrens type registry. An absolute grant is issued to properties that come from agricultural lands. The first step of alienation is for the land to become state lands and to be subsequently titled to an individual. A grant is issued through a presidential decree.

Intellectual Property Rights

Upon independence in 1966, Guyana adopted British law on intellectual property rights (IPR). Guyana's Copyright Act is dated 1956, and its Trademark Act and Patents and Design Act are dated 1973. Numerous attempts to pass comprehensive legislative updates to this legislation have been unsuccessful. Piecemeal modernization amendments contained in the Geographic Indication Act of 2005, the Competition and Fair Trading Act 2006, the Business Names Registration Act 2000, and the Deeds Registry Authority Act 1999 have offered additional protection to local products and companies. No such modern legislation exists to protect the foreign-registered rights of investors. Guyana joined the World Intellectual Property Organization (WIPO) and acceded to the Berne and Paris Conventions in late 1994. Guyana has not ratified a bilateral intellectual property rights agreement with the United States.

Registering a patent or trademark can take six months or longer, but no effective enforcement mechanisms exist to protect intellectual property rights. Patent and trademark infringement continues to be common. Local television stations, including the state-owned and operated National Communication Network (NCN), pirate and rebroadcast TV satellite signals with impunity. Most music, videos, and software for sale are pirated. Book piracy is also rampant, especially foreign textbooks; some estimates say illegally photocopied textbooks account for nearly one-third of local sales.

Additionally, it was reported by the head of the leading e-governance authority in Guyana that more than one-third of the computers used in government offices utilize pirated software.

In September 2012, both local and international media reported that the Education Ministry invited seven pre-selected local firms to supply photocopies of primary and secondary level textbooks published by Trinidad and Tobago-based Royards Publishing Company. In response, Royards Publishing submitted a bid to supply the government with the original textbooks. Following threats of legal action by the copyright holder, the Government came to terms to purchase the textbooks legally. However, the government's initial willingness to sanction textbook piracy generated international and local criticism for its apparent indifference to IPR. Guyana does not have a ratified intellectual property rights agreement with the United States.

The Ministry of Foreign Trade and International Cooperation and the Ministry of Legal Affairs drafted Trade Related Intellectual Property Rights (TRIPS) legislation in 2001, but the draft still lies dormant and unused.

For additional information about treaty obligations and points of contact at local IP offices, please see WIPO's country profiles at **http://www.wipo.int/directory/en/**.

Resources for Rights Holders

Frisco McDonald
Economic/Commercial Officer
Embassy of the United States of America
100 Duke and Young Streets
Kingston
Georgetown, Guyana
Phone: (011) (592) 225-4900-9 Ext. 4220
Fax: (011) (592)-225-8597
Email: **McDonaldFJ@state.gov**
http://georgetown.usembassy.gov

Wynette Oudkerk
Economic/Commercial Specialist
Embassy of the United States of America
100 Duke and Young Streets
Kingston
Georgetown, Guyana
Phone: (011) (592) 225-4900 Ext:4213
Fax: (011) (592)-225-8497
Email: **OudkerkW@state.gov**
http://georgetown.usembassy.gov

8. TRANSPARENCY OF THE REGULATORY SYSTEM

Guyana does not possess anti-trust legislation. In April 2006, Parliament passed the Competition and Fair Trading Act, which targets offenses such as price fixing, conspiracy, bid-rigging, misleading advertisements, anti-competitiveness, abuse of dominant position, and resale price maintenance. A Competition Commission with authority to review anti-competitive business practices has been established but remains understaffed.

Historical factors, Guyana's small population, and limited economy have led many sectors to be dominated by one or two firms. Bureaucratic procedures appear cumbersome and often require the involvement of multiple ministries. Investors often receive conflicting messages from various officials, causing difficulty in determining where the authority for decision-making lies. In the absence of adequate legislation, much decision-making remains centralized. An extraordinary number of issues continue to be resolved in Cabinet or in the Office of the President, a process that is commonly perceived as non-transparent and often results in delays. Attempts to reform Guyana's many bureaucratic procedures have failed to reduce red tape.

Generally, draft pieces of legislation are available in the Parliament Library for public review.

9. EFFICIENT CAPITAL MARKETS AND PORTFOLIO INVESTMENT

In Guyana, interest rates on capital loans typically range from 10 percent to 20 percent. The Minister of Finance must grant permission for a foreign investor to borrow more than USD 10,000 (GYD 2 million) from a local bank. The GOG sells Treasury Bills at auction to finance the public debt. Past attempts at private bond financing have failed, and private companies have not made any large bond offers in recent years.

The banking system in Guyana is liquid. Local bank statements reveal that deposits continue to increase even as loans remain flat; a trend that suggests the existence of a large informal, cash-only economy. Analysts estimate that the informal economic activity accounts for 50 percent or more of Guyana's total economic activity. Eager to lend money, but skeptical of Guyana's legal system, banks claim an inability to find suitable local applicants for loans at prevailing interest rates.

Guyana adopted the Credit Reporting Act No. 9 of 2010, which guarantees consumers' right to access their data. The first credit reporting bureau license was granted to Creditinfo, which went into effect on July 15, 2013 and was open for business to the public starting December 1, 2013. The credit-reporting bureau has been working with banks and utility companies to compile reliable credit information for use by lenders. Lack of access to capital remains a serious barrier to entrepreneurship and business expansion in the country.

The Guyana Association of Securities Companies and Intermediaries Inc. (GASCI) was formed in 2003 and operates the Guyana Stock Exchange. GASCI consists of four member firms, all of which trade on the stock exchange. The Guyana Stock Exchange trades shares in companies that are either listed on the primary list or on the secondary list. Inclusion on the primary list is both time consuming and an expensive process. Thus far, only one company, Trinidad Cement Ltd., has been able to register on the primary list. The secondary list is composed of 16 companies and consists of those companies that are registered with the Guyana Securities Council (GSC) and eligible to trade. In 2014, total market capitalization was USD 749 million. Trade volume on the Guyana Stock Exchange remains very light due both to the limited number of companies and shares on offer.

The Guyana Securities Council (GSC) is the regulatory body for the securities industry. Since its creation in 2001, it has struggled to obtain required disclosure information from listed, local firms.

MONEY AND BANKING SYSTEM, HOSTILE TAKEOVERS

The Central Bank of Guyana was established by virtue of the 1965 Bank of Guyana Ordinance. Guyana's banking system remains underdeveloped. Inefficiencies and delays periodically plague the foreign currency market. Businesses report that currency shortages can result in significant delays in converting Guyana dollars to U.S. dollars at some banks. Because Guyana has yet to develop an effective interbank trading system, some banks may be short of foreign exchange while others have currency available.

The six commercial banks are by far the most important financial institutions in Guyana with assets worth GYD 421 billion (USD 2 billion) in 2014 – equivalent to 70 percent of the Gross Domestic Product (GDP).

10. COMPETITION FROM STATE-OWNED ENTERPRISES

Private enterprises compete with state-owned enterprises (SOEs) under the same terms and conditions for market access, credit and other business operations, and licenses. Currently there are seven SOEs in Guyana: Guyana Sugar Corporation (GUYSUCO), Guyana Gold Board, Guyana Oil Company Limited, Guyana Power and Light Inc., National Communications Network, the Guyana National Printers, and Georgetown's new Marriott Hotel. The corporate governance structure of Guyanese SOEs requires that the senior management report to the chief executive officer, who reports to the board of directors, who in turn report to a government minister. Political interventions occur in the management of SOEs, since their boards of directors are filled through political appointments directed by the Office of the President.

The National Industrial and Commercial Investments Limited (NICIL), a private limited company, acts as subscriber and manager of the government's shares, stocks, and debentures of any company, cooperative societies, or other corporate body. It also manages government-owned real estate properties, including their acquisition, disposal, or rental. Managing the government's shareholdings and minimizing conflict of interests is NICIL's main function.

During the 1900s, Guyana underwent a significant privatization process, divesting many of its holdings in the banking, telecommunications, agriculture, and manufacturing sectors. Since then the pace of privatization has slowed. Since 2003, the government has privatized only two entities: National Bank for Industry and Commerce, which now does business as Republic Bank; and National Edible Oil Company, acquired by a biofuels company. Furthermore, the state reduced its participation in two of Guyana's leading bauxite mining companies, the Aroaima Mining Company and Linmine Bauxite.

The Public Corporation Act requires public corporations to publish an annual report no later than six months after the end of the calendar year. These financial reports must be audited by an independent auditor.

11. CORPORATE SOCIAL RESPONSIBILITY

Compared to corporate social responsibility (CSR) norms in North America and Europe, Guyana-based businesses lag in adopting CSR policies and activities. Though many businesses engage in charitable acts, the totality of these deeds does not constitute good CSR practices. Guyanese consumers generally are not aware of CSR principles and do not demand them from local businesses they patronize. The Guyanese government has expressed the hope that large multinational companies will lead the way on CSR practices, setting an example for smaller local firms to follow, particularly in the extractive industries sector.

12. POLITICAL VIOLENCE

Political violence has occurred in Guyana. Political protests in Guyana have a history of turning violent. In March 2013, police used force to clear protestors (mostly Brazilian nationals) in the Marudi mining district. Police allegedly used whips and sticks to beat local miners protesting their alleged unlawful removal from the area they claimed for their own use. Several protestors required medical attention at a local hospital. In August 2013 hundreds of persons gathered outside of Parliament to protest a range of political and social issues, ranging from Amerindian land title rights to the removal of the Town Clerk in the Mayor of Georgetown's office. The protest became mildly violent between the protestors and police on guard.

Increased violence between the Indo-Guyanese and Afro-Guyanese communities has historically occurred at the time of national elections. The 2011 national elections, however, were the second successive iteration in which such communal violence was greatly reduced. The 2011 election period saw one incident in which the police used force to quell a peaceful march, but no one was seriously injured.

13. CORRUPTION

Allegations of corruption remain common. According to Transparency International's 2014 Corruption Perceptions Index (CPI), Guyana is ranked 124th out of 175 countries for perceptions of corruption– rising by nine slots from 133 the previous year. Guyana ranks 30th out of 45 in the Western Hemisphere.

Guyana has ratified the IACAC, and bribery is established as a criminal offense under Guyanese law. Although the government passed legislation in 1997 that requires public officials to disclose their assets to an Integrity Commission prior to assuming office, the Integrity Commission has never been constituted and remains inoperative. Public Officials' compliance with the legislation has therefore been uneven.

The Procurement Act of 2003 provides for the establishment of an oversight body, a Public Procurement Commission and the National Procurement and Tender Administration Board (NPTAB), which handles day-to-day operations. The Minister of Finance appoints the members of this Board. The Commission's job is to ensure transparency and accountability throughout the government procurement process including in regards to the NPTAB's operations, has never been established.

Widespread concerns about inefficiencies and corruption at the ministerial, regional, or national level exist regarding the awarding of contracts particularly with respect to concerns of collusion and non-transparency. In his annual report, the Auditor General has noted continuous disregard for the procedures, rules, and the laws that govern public procurement systems.

The Criminal Law Act classifies both corruption and bribery as illegal. Offences carry a penalty of GYD 390,000 (USD 2,000) and three to seven years imprisonment.

On April 16, 2008, Guyana ratified the United Nations Convention against Corruption. Guyana is neither a member of the Organization for Economic Cooperation and Development (OECD) nor a signatory to OECD Anti-Bribery Convention. Guyana is a member of the Organization of American States (OAS) and ratified the Inter-American Convention against Corruption on December 11, 2000.

The World Economic Forum, "Global Competitiveness Report 2014-2015," identified corruption as the largest obstacle, followed by tax rates, to doing business in Guyana. Corruption discourages potential foreign direct investments and foreign investors, and it also undermines economic development and growth.

UN Anticorruption Convention, OECD Convention on Combatting Bribery

On April 16, 2008, Guyana ratified the United Nations Convention against Corruption. Guyana is neither a member of the Organization for Economic Cooperation and Development (OECD) nor a signatory to OECD Anti-Bribery Convention. Guyana is a member of the Organization of American States (OAS) and ratified the Inter-American Convention against Corruption on December 11, 2000.

Resources to Report Corruption

Transparency International
George Fraser
Transparency International Guyana
157 Waterloo Street,
592-231-9586
infotransparencygy@gmail.com

14. BILATERAL INVESTMENT AGREEMENTS

Guyana does not have a bilateral investment treaty with the United States. Guyana has bilateral investment treaties with the United Kingdom, Germany, Cuba, China, Switzerland, South Korea, and Indonesia.

BILATERAL TAXATION TREATIES

Double taxation treaties are in force with Canada (1987), the United Kingdom and Northern Ireland (1992), and CARICOM (1995).

15. OPIC AND OTHER INVESTMENT INSURANCE PROGRAMS

The Overseas Private Investment Corporation (OPIC) renewed its support for U.S. investors in Guyana in 2000 following the settlement of a long-standing dispute between an OPIC client and the GOG.

The Export-Import Bank of the United States (EX-IM) offers insurance and financing to support American exports to Guyana. EX-IM will consider the financing projects in which the total term of the financing is either less than one year or between one or seven years.

16. LABOR

The World Bank estimates that in 2013 Guyana's labor force comprised 313,815 persons. The unemployment rate for 2013 was estimated at 23.9 percent; however, the government does not track either unemployment or job creation rates (**http://data.worldbank.org/indicator/SL.UEM.1524.ZS**).

Approximately 22 percent or 69,039 workers are unionized. Guyana currently has 18 trade unions. Thirteen of these unions fall under the umbrella of the Guyana Trade Union Congress. Four of these unions are members of the Federation of Independent Trade Unions of Guyana. The Trade Union Recognition Act of 1997 requires businesses operating in Guyana to recognize and collectively bargain with the trade union selected by a majority of its workers. Guyana adheres to the International Labor Organization (ILO) Convention protecting worker rights.

Guyana provides education and skills development through primary, secondary, and technical schools, as well as at the University of Guyana and privately-owned institutions of higher learning. Individual companies mount various programs to develop human resources specific to their needs.

Emigration, particularly of skilled labor, poses a serious problem to employers in Guyana. Guyana's net emigration rate in 2014 was estimated at 9.67 percent – the seventh highest in the world. An International Monetary Fund study in 2005 found that 89 percent of university-educated Guyanese eventually leave the country due to better employment options abroad; this represents the highest percentage of "brain drain" of any country. Large private sector companies report a turnover of about 20 percent to 25 percent of their workforce annually and experience difficulty in recruiting and retaining qualified employees. Skilled workers generally migrate to the United States, Canada, the Caribbean, and Europe.

17. FOREIGN TRADE ZONES/FREE PORTS/TRADE FACILITATION

Guyana currently does not maintain any duty-free zones, although the Government of Guyana announced the possibility of establishing such zones in the Lethem area, on the border with Brazil.

18. FOREIGN DIRECT INVESTMENT AND FOREIGN PORTFOLIO INVESTMENT STATISTICS

Table 2: Key Macroeconomic Data, U.S. FDI in Host Country/Economy

	Host Country Statistical source*	USG or International Statistical	USG or International Source of Data: BEA; IMF; Eurostat; UNCTAD, Other

	SOURCE*		SOURCE		
ECONOMIC DATA	YEAR	AMOUNT	YEAR	AMOUNT	
HOST COUNTRY GROSS DOMESTIC PRODUCT (GDP) ($B USD)	2013	2.9	2013	2.9	www.worldbank.org/en/country
FOREIGN DIRECT INVESTMENT	HOST COUNTRY STATISTICAL SOURCE*		USG OR INTERNATIONAL STATISTICAL SOURCE		USG OR INTERNATIONAL SOURCE OF DATA: BEA; IMF; EUROSTAT; UNCTAD, OTHER
U.S. FDI IN PARTNER COUNTRY ($M USD, STOCK POSITIONS)	2013	214	2013	240	http://bea.gov/international/factsheet/factsheet.cfm?Area=257
HOST COUNTRY'S FDI IN THE UNITED STATES ($M USD, STOCK POSITIONS)	N/A		N/A		http://bea.gov/international/factsheet/factsheet.cfm?Area=257
TOTAL INBOUND STOCK OF FDI AS % HOST GDP	N/A		N/A		

*Provide sources of host country statistical data used

A list of local attorneys is available on Embassy Georgetown's emergency services page:**http://georgetown.usembassy.gov/emergency-services.html**.

PARAGUAY

INVESTMENT AND BUSINESS CLIMATE - STRATEGIC INFORMATION AND CONTACTS FOR STARTING BUSINESS

Paraguay has a small but rapidly growing open economy with a strong macroeconomic position and the potential for continued growth over the next decade. Major drivers of economic growth in Paraguay are the agriculture, retail, and construction sectors. The Government of Paraguay encourages private foreign investment. Paraguayan law grants investors tax breaks, permits full repatriation of capital and profits, supports assembly plant operations, and guarantees national treatment for foreign investors. Standard & Poor's (BB-), Fitch (BB), and Moody's (Ba1) all upgraded Paraguay's credit ratings in the last two years.

Paraguay scores at the mid-range or lower in most competitiveness indicators, judicial insecurity hinders the investment climate, and trademark infringement and counterfeiting are a major concern. Recent Government of Paraguay measures to improve the investment climate include passing laws addressing competition, public sector payroll disclosures, and access to information. President Cartes Administration also has escalated the importance of intellectual property enforcement.

Paraguay's export and investment promotion bureau, REDIEX, prepares comprehensive information about business opportunities in Paraguay. The Investor's Route Map is REDIEX's guide for exporters and investors (**http://www.rediex.gov.py/guia-de-inversiones-inv20**).

1. OPENNESS TO, AND RESTRICTIONS UPON, FOREIGN INVESTMENT

ATTITUDE TOWARD FOREIGN DIRECT INVESTMENT

The Government of Paraguay (GOP) encourages private foreign investment. Paraguay guarantees equal treatment of foreign investors under law 117/91 and permits full repatriation of capital and profits under Law 60/90. Paraguay has historically maintained the lowest tax burden in the region, with a 10% corporate tax rate and a 10% Value-added Tax (VAT) on most goods and services.

The GOP recognizes the need to improve Paraguay's infrastructure. In 2013 Paraguay passed legislation governing public-private partnerships (PPP), with the expectation of prompting an infrastructure boom and launching a new phase in the country's economic development. The GOP is expected to announce in 2015 PPPs for infrastructure modernization projects for the international airport in Asuncion and several highways. Large infrastructure projects are usually open to foreign investors.

Paraguay's export and investment promotion bureau, REDIEX, provides useful information for foreign investors, including business opportunities in Paraguay, registration requirements, and laws, rules, and procedures. Information is available online at **http://www.rediex.gov.py/atraccion-de-inversiones**.

OTHER INVESTMENT POLICY REVIEWS

Not applicable.

LAWS/REGULATIONS OF FOREIGN DIRECT INVESTMENT

Not applicable.

INDUSTRIAL PROMOTION

The Government of Paraguay seeks increased investment in the maquila sector and Paraguayan law grants investors a number of incentives. In addition to tax exemptions, inputs are allowed to enter Paraguay tax free, and up to 10% of production is allowed for local consumption after paying import taxes and duties. Assembly plant (Maquila) operations are not restricted geographically.

LIMITS ON FOREIGN CONTROL

Not applicable.

PRIVATIZATION PROGRAM

Not applicable.

SCREENING OF FDI

Not applicable.

COMPETITION LAW

Paraguay passed a Competition Law in 2013, which entered into force in April 2014. Law 4956/13 explicitly prohibits anti-competitive acts and created the National Competition Commission (CONACOM) as the government's enforcement arm.

INVESTMENT TRENDS

Not applicable.

Table 1

Measure	Year	Index or Rank	Website Address
TI Corruption Perceptions index	2014	150 of 175	**transparency.org/cpi2014/results**
World Bank's Doing Business Report "Ease of Doing Business"	2015	92 of 189	**doingbusiness.org/rankings**
Global Innovation Index	2014	89 of 143	**globalinnovationindex.org/content.aspx?page=data-analysis**
World Bank GNI per	2013	USD [illegible]	**data.worldbank.org/indicator/NY.GNP.PCAP.CD**

capita		1,01010	

Millennium Challenge Corporation Country Scorecard

The Millennium Challenge Corporation, a U.S. Government entity charged with delivering development grants to countries that have demonstrated a commitment to reform, produced scorecards for countries with a per capita gross national income (GNI) or USD 4,125 or less. A list of countries/economies with MCC scorecards and links to those scorecards is available here: **http://www.mcc.gov/pages/selection/scorecard**s. Details on each of the MCC's indicators and a guide to reading the scorecards are available here: **http://www.mcc.gov/pages/docs/doc/report-guide-to-the-indicators-and-the-selection-process-fy-2015**.

2. Conversion and Transfer Policies

Foreign Exchange

No restrictions exist in Paraguay on the conversion or transfer of foreign currency. Law 60/90 permits the repatriation of capital and profits. There are no controls on foreign exchange transactions, apart from bank reporting requirements for transactions in excess of USD USD 10,000.

Remittance Policies

Paraguay is a member of the Financial Action Task Force against Money Laundering in South America (GAFISUD), a Financial Action Task Force (FATF)-style regional body.

3. Expropriation and Compensation

Private property has historically been respected in Paraguay as a fundamental right. However, there have been several cases in recent years of expropriations of land without prompt and fair compensation. In recent years, groups of squatters have occupied several farms in order to press for agrarian land reform.

4. Dispute Settlement

Legal System, Specialized Courts, Judicial Independence, Judgments of Foreign Courts

Paraguay has a Civil Law legal system based on the Napoleonic Code. A new Criminal Code went into effect in 1998, with a corresponding Code of Criminal Procedure following in 2000. A defendant has the right to a public and oral trial. A three judge panel acts as a jury. Judges render decisions on the basis of (in order of precedence) the Constitution, international agreements, the codes, decree law, analogies with existing law, and general principles of the law.

Bankruptcy

Paraguay has a bankruptcy law (154/63) under which a debtor may suspend payments to creditors during the evaluation period of the debtors' restructuring proposal. If no agreement is reached, a trustee may liquidate the company's assets. In the World Bank's 2015 Doing Business Report, Paraguay ranks 106 out of 189 economies in regards to the Ease of Resolving Insolvency. The report states that on average it takes 3.0 years to reach a resolution regarding insolvency cases .At a cost of 9.0% of the debtor's estate, with the most likely outcome being that the company will be sold as piecemeal sale. The average recovery rate is 20.8 cents on the USD.

Investment Disputes

Under Paraguayan Law 194/93, foreign companies must demonstrate just cause to terminate, modify, or decide not to renew contracts with Paraguayan distributors. Severe penalties and high fines may result if a court determines that a foreign company ended the relationship with its distributor without first establishing just cause. This sometimes compels Paraguayan distributors to seek expensive out-of-court settlements first. Nevertheless, cases are infrequent and courts have upheld the rights of foreign companies to terminate representation agreements after finding the requisite showing of just cause.

Under two laws, Article 195 of the Civil Procedural Code and Law 1376/1988, a plaintiff pursuing a lawsuit may seek reimbursement for legal costs from the defendant calculated as a percentage (not to exceed 10 percent) of claimed damages. In larger suits, the amount of reimbursed legal costs often far exceeds the actual legal costs incurred.

International Arbitration

Law 117/91 guarantees national treatment for foreign investors. This law allows international arbitration for the resolution of disputes between foreign investors and the Government of Paraguay. Foreign decisions and awards are enforceable in Paraguay.

ICSID Convention and New York Convention

Paraguay is a member of the International Center for the Settlement of Investment Disputes (ICSID). Paraguay is also a signatory to The Convention on the Recognition and Enforcement of Foreign Arbitral Awards (New York Convention).

Duration of Dispute Resolution

In the World Bank's, 2015 Doing Business Report, Paraguay ranks 90 out of 189 in the category dealing with the Ease of Enforcing Contracts.

5. Performance Requirements and Investment Incentives

WTO/TRIMS

Paraguay has been a World Trade Organization (WTO) member since 19945. They have not signed on to the Agreement on Government Procurement. Paraguayan law (4558/11) gives preference in government bids to locally produced goods even if they are up to 20% more expensive than imported goods. Public institutions in charge of large infrastructure projects historically pose difficulties for foreign investors. The Dirección Nacional de Contrataciones Públicas (DNCP or National Directorate for Public Contracts) exists to ensure transparency and fairness in public bids that exceed USD 150,000. American investors have described significant frustration during bidding attempts. Of the 13,445 bids held by the DNCP in 2014, only 103 were open to international companies. Of those, 25 were awarded to international companies, and only one to a U.S. company. President Cartes Administration, which entered office in 2013, has expressed interest in increasing international participation in infrastructure projects and passed a PPP law to attract higher levels of international participation.

Regarding customs procedures, Paraguay requires that specific documentation for each import shipment (e.g., the commercial receipt, certificate of origin, and cargo manifest) be certified by either the Paraguayan consulate in the country of origin or, by paying an additional fee, at the Ministry of Foreign Affairs in Paraguay. Paraguay also requires all companies operating in the country to contract the services of a customs broker. Customs broker fees are standardized by Paraguayan law.

Investment Incentives

Paraguay grants investors a number of tax breaks under Law 60/90, including exemptions from corporate income tax and value-added tax. Paraguay also has a temporary entry system, which allows duty free admission of capital goods such as machinery, tools, equipment, and vehicles to carry out public and private construction work. The government also allows temporary entry of equipment for scientific research, exhibitions, training or testing, competitive sports, and traveler or tourist items.

Research and Development

Not applicable.

Performance Requirements

Paraguay does not mandate local employment or have excessively onerous visa, residence, work permit or similar requirements inhibiting mobility of foreign investors and their employees. However, the bureaucratic process to comply with these requirements can be lengthy. Voting board members of any company incorporated in Paraguay must have legal residence, which takes a minimum of 90 days to establish, posing a potential obstacle to foreign investors.

Data Storage

Paraguay does not suscribe to a "forced localization" policy which requires foreign investors to use domestic content in goods or technology. There are no requirements for maintaining a certain amount of data storage within Paraguay or for foreign IT providers to turn over source code and/or provide access to surveillance. Paraguayan law requires internet service providers to retain IP address for six months for certain commercial transactions.

6. Right to Private Ownership and Establishment

Foreign and domestic private entities may establish and own business enterprises. Foreign businesses are not legally required to be associated with Paraguayan nationals for investment purposes.

There is no restriction on repatriation of capital and profits. Private entities may freely establish, acquire, and dispose of business interests.

7. Protection of Property Rights

Real Property

The 1992 constitution guarantees the right of private property ownership. While it is common to use real property as security for loans, the lack of consistent property surveys and registries often makes it impossible to foreclose. In some cases, acquiring title documents for land can take two years or more. The World Bank's 2015 Business Report ranks Paraguay 60 of 189 for ease of "registering property," noting the process requires 6 procedures, averages 46 days, and costs 1.9% of the property value.

Intellectual Property Rights

Paraguay is on the Watch List and under Section 306 monitoring in the U.S. Trade Representative's (USTR) 2015 Special 301 Report. Issues that affect U.S. firms include: the level of enforcement against piracy and counterfeiting, particularly under the criminal laws, in areas such as Ciudad del Este; judicial inefficiency in intellectual property rights (IPR) cases; lack of protection against unfair commercial use of undisclosed test or other data submitted to the government by agrochemical or pharmaceutical companies; and the use of unlicensed software by the government.

The Government of Paraguay has taken positive steps toward strengthening IPR, particularly since President Cartes took office in August 2013. In October 2013, President Cartes signed the implementing regulation (Decree 460) for Law 4798 of 2012 that created the National Directorate of Intellectual Property (DINAPI). DINAPI is now the Paraguayan government authority responsible for the issuance and protection of copyrights, trademarks, patents, industrial designs, and geographical indications. Additionally, the law authorizes DINAPI's enforcement arm, the General Enforcement Directorate, to conduct administrative investigations and initiate proceedings at customs checkpoints and businesses. During the past 18 months, the Cartes Administration, primarily through DINAPI and partner law enforcement agencies, has escalated enforcement efforts. In December 2013, DINAPI granted pharmaceutical patents to two U.S. companies, the first patents reportedly granted since 2005. DINAPI has also undertaken outreach to the public and signed inter-institutional cooperative agreements to improve IPR protection and enforcement.

Ciudad del Este has been listed in either the USTR Notorious Market List report or the Special 301 Report over the last 15 years. The border crossing at Ciudad del Este and the city itself reportedly serve as a hub for the distribution of counterfeit and pirated products in the tri-border region of Brazil-Argentina-Paraguay and beyond. Paraguayan government agencies track and report on seizures of counterfeit goods. DINAPI reported 93 seizures of counterfeited goods in 2014 with an estimated Manufacturer Suggested Retail Price (MSRP) of USD 131 million. However, the figures are an estimate since DINAPI does not always receive data regarding seizures conducted by other agencies.

Customs officers have the authority to seize, but not destroy, counterfeit goods. Customs must contact the IP prosecutor to obtain a judicial order for the destruction. Property owners have the right to defend their case before the court. Counterfeit goods are held in government storage at no cost to the rights holder. While the rights holder is not legally obligated to pay for the destruction of the counterfeit good, it is common practice in order to ensure prompt destruction. The government should conduct the destruction, but lacks funding to do it in a timely fashion.

Concerns remain about inadequate protection against unfair commercial use of proprietary test or other data generated to obtain marketing approval for agrochemical or pharmaceutical products and the shortcomings in Paraguay's patent regime. Law 3283 from 2007 and Law 3519 from 2008, (1) require pharmaceutical products and agrochemical products to be registered first in Paraguay to be eligible for data protection; (2) allow regulatory agencies to use test data in support of similar agricultural chemical product applications filed by third parties; and (3) limit data protection to five years. Additionally, Law 2593/05 that modifies Paraguay's patent law has no regulatory enforcement. Because of this, foreign pharmaceutical companies have seen their patented products openly replicated and marketed under other names by Paraguayan pharmaceutical companies.

For over a decade the United States maintained a Memorandum of Understanding (MOU) with Paraguay pertaining to IPR protection and enforcement. This MOU expired in April 2012, and negotiations were re-launched in March 2014.

Paraguay has ratified all of the Uruguay Round accords, including the Agreement on Trade Related Aspects of Intellectual Property Rights (TRIPS), and has ratified two World Intellectual Property Organization (WIPO) copyright treaties. For additional information about treaty obligations and points of contact at local IP offices, please see WIPO's country profiles at **http://www.wipo.int/directory/en/**.

Resources for Rights Holders

Albert Keyack
Regional IP Attaché
U.S. Consulate General - Rio de Janeiro
+ 55 (21) 3823-2499

Albert.Keyack@trade.gov

Natalie van der Horst
Deputy Political and Economic Counselor
U.S. Embassy Asuncion
+ 595 (21) 213-715
CommercialAsuncion@state.gov

National Intellectual Property Directorate: **http://www.dinapi.gov.py/**

Paraguayan-American Chamber of Commerce: **http://www.pamcham.com.py**

Local Lawyers: **http://photos.state.gov/libraries/paraguay/5/Consular/Attorneys%20at%20Law.pdf**

8. Transparency of the Regulatory System

Proposed Paraguayan laws and regulations, including those pertaining to investment, are usually available in draft form for public comment after introduction into Senate and Chamber of Deputies committees. In most instances, there are public hearings where members of the general public or interested parties can provide comments.

Historically, regulatory agencies supervisory functions over telecommunications, energy, potable water, and the environment are inefficient and opaque. Politically motivated changes in the leadership of regulating agencies negatively impact firms and investors. Corruption has historically been common in these institutions as time consuming processes provide opportunities for front-line civil servants to seek bribes to accelerate the paperwork. President Cartes Administration, which entered into office in 2013, voiced its commitment to combating corruption and has taken positive steps to promote transparency.

The business registration process was modified in 2006 with U.S. assistance. The GOP instituted a coordinated system among all the offices involved, reducing the number of steps and the time to open a business to 7 procedures, 35 days and lowering the cost to 39.9% of income per capita, according to the World Bank. This is an improvement; however, some aspects of opening a business are still lengthy and costly, such as building health inspections and environmental licenses.

9. Efficient Capital Markets and Portfolio Investment

Credit is available but expensive. High collateral requirements are generally imposed. The high cost of capital makes the stock market an attractive, although underdeveloped option. Paraguay has a relatively small capital market that began less than 20 years ago. As of December 2014, the Asuncion Stock exchange consisted of 133 companies, totaling USD 177 million in transactions. Many family-owned enterprises fear losing control, dampening enthusiasm for public offerings.

In 2011, Banco Bilbao Vizcaya Argentaria (BBVA) Paraguay raised USD 100 million through a private offering of 9.75 percent bonds that will mature on February 11, 2016. BBVA Paraguay will use the proceeds for long-term investment in agribusiness and reforestation in Paraguay. In 2012, Banco Continental S.A.E.C.A., one of the largest banks in Paraguay, issued debt for USD 200 million due in 2017. In January 2014, Banco Regional, the largest private local bank in Paraguay, issued debt for USD 300 million. These transactions are very important to the banking sector in Paraguay and its ability to access the international capital market.

The Government of Paraguay issued Paraguay's first sovereign bonds in 2013 for USD 500 million to accelerate development in the country. In August 2014, Paraguay issued USD 1 billion worth of 30-year bonds. Proceeds are to finance key infrastructure development programs designed to promote economic and social development and job creation. Standard & Poor's, Fitch, and Moody's all upgraded Paraguay's credit ratings in the last two years.*

MONEY AND BANKING SYSTEM, HOSTILE TAKEOVERS

Paraguay's banking system includes 17 banks with a total USD 18.1 billion in assets and USD 13.3 billion in deposits. Non-performing loans in the banking sector totaled just 1.8% of total loans in 2014. The banking system is generally sound but remains overly liquid. Long term financing for capital investment projects is scarce. Most lending facilities are short term. Banks and finance companies are regulated by the Banking Superintendent, which is housed within, and is under the direction of, the Central Bank of Paraguay.

The Paraguayan capital markets are essentially focused on debt issuances. As the listing of stock is limited, with the exception of preferred shares, Paraguay does not have clear rules regarding hostile takeovers and shareholder activism.

10. COMPETITION FROM STATE-OWNED ENTERPRISES

Paraguay's State Owned Enterprises (SOEs) are active in the petroleum distribution, cement, electricity (distribution and generation), water, and land-line and cellular telecommunication sectors. In general, SOEs are monopolies with no private sector participation. Most operate independently but maintain an administrative link with line ministries, namely the Ministry of Public Works & Communications. SOEs have audited accounts and the results are published online.

SOEs' corporate governances are weak. Only the Itaipú and Yacyretá bi-national hydroelectric dams have a board of directors. Other SOEs operate with politically appointed advisors and executives. Only the two bi-national dams are required to have an independent audit. The SOEs are often overstaffed and are an outlet for patronage, resulting in poor administration and services. Some SOEs burden the country's fiscal position, running deficits most years.

OECD GUIDELINES ON CORPORATE GOVERNANCE OF SOES

Not applicable.

SOVEREIGN WEALTH FUNDS

Paraguay does not have a sovereign wealth fund.

11. CORPORATE SOCIAL RESPONSIBILITY

Corporate Social Responsibility (CSR) is growing with the support of Paraguay's largest firms. Additionally the private sector is taking measures to institutionalize ethical business conduct under initiatives such as the Pacto Etico Comercial (Business Ethics Pact). An initiative sponsored by the U.S. Department of Commerce, the Pacto Etico Comercial includes over 100 local, U.S., and international companies that committed to creating a code of ethics and undergoing a rigorous auditing process to reach certification.

OECD GUIDELINES FOR MULTINATIONAL ENTERPRISES

Not applicable.

12. Political Violence

Paraguay has not traditionally been affected by political violence. While Paraguay has been spared the large number of kidnappings that occur in neighboring Latin American countries, a few high profile cases have occurred in recent years, most of them attributed to purported members of the leftist Paraguayan People's Army (EPP). The GOP has responded to the EPP threat with combined military and police operations. Land invasions, marches, and organized protests occur, mostly by rural and indigenous communities making demands on the government, but these events rarely turn violent.

13. Corruption

Paraguayan law provides criminal penalties for official corruption; however, impunity impedes effective implementation. Historically, officials in all branches and at all levels of government have engaged in corrupt practices. Judicial insecurity and corruption in the judicial system hinders Paraguay's investment climate. Many investors find it difficult to enforce adequately contracts and are frustrated by lengthy bureaucratic procedures, limited transparency and accountability, and impunity.

Under President Cartes Administration, the GOP has taken several steps to combat corruption, including the creation of a transparent, internet-based government procurement system; the appointment of respected apolitical officials to key posts; and increased civil society input and oversight. In October 2013, the National Procurement Agency, the Civil Service Secretariat, the Auditor General, the Anticorruption Secretariat, and the Solicitor General signed an MOU to strengthen coordination among key players in the fight against corruption and collaborate on a National Anticorruption Plan.

In May 2014, President Cartes signed Law 5189, mandating the disclosure of all government payroll information. By September, 40 government institutions, including the presidency, ministries, judicial branch, state-owned companies, and local and state entities, had disclosed information on the names of employees, salaries, bonuses, and extraordinary compensation. In September 2014, President Cartes signed an access to information law guaranteeing public access to government information. The new law established a legal framework regarding processing times, fees, criminal or administrative sanctions for noncompliance, appeals mechanism for reviews of disclosure denials, and lists of exceptions outlining the grounds for nondisclosure.

The constitution requires all public employees, elected officials and employees of independent government entities, to disclose their sources of income and their assets no later than 15 days after taking office or being reappointed. A new law that went into effect in January 2014 further requires that the employee additionally include information on the assets and income of spouses and dependent children. The new law does not require officials to file periodically when changes occur in their holdings. Following the August 2013 inauguration of the new government, the president, vice president, the 10 ministers of the executive branch and 22 other minister-rank and high-ranking employees of the Cartes administration filed their financial disclosure forms in compliance with the constitution.

UN Anticorruption Convention, OECD Convention on Combatting Bribery

Paraguay signed and ratified the United Nations Anticorruption Convention in 2005.

Resources to Report Corruption

General Auditors Office
Bruselas 1880, Asuncion, Paraguay
+ 595 21 620 0260
atencion@contraloria.gov.py

Public Ministry
Nuestra Señora de la Asunción c/ Haedo, Asuncion, Paraguay
+ 595 21 454 611
http://www.ministeriopublico.gov.py/contenidos/menu/institucion/denunciar/index.php

Anti-Corruption Secretariat
El Paraguayo Independiente esquina Río Ypané, Asunción, Paraguay
+ 595 21 450-001/2
http://www.senac.gov.py/

Seeds for Democracy
Roma 1055 casi Colón, Asuncion, Paraguay
+ 595 21 420 323
semillas@semillas.org.py

14. Bilateral Investment Agreements

Paraguay has bilateral investment agreements or treaties with the following countries: Austria; Belgium; Chile; Costa Rica; Cuba, Czech Republic, El Salvador; France; Germany; Hungary; Italy, Korea; Luxembourg; the Netherlands; Peru; Portugal, Romania; South Africa; Spain; Switzerland; Taiwan; the United Kingdom; and Venezuela.

Paraguay is a founding member of the MERCOSUR common market, formed in 1991. MERCOSUR has investment protocols for internal and external investment. MERCOSUR's full members are Argentina, Brazil, Paraguay, Uruguay, and Venezuela. MERCOSUR has investment agreements with Canada, Egypt, India, Israel, Mexico, Palestine, Peru, and the Southern African Customs Union (SACU).

Bilateral Taxation Treaties

The United States and Paraguay do not have a Bilateral Investment Treaty, a Free Trade Agreement, or a Bilateral Taxation Treaty.

15. OPIC and Other Investment Insurance Programs

The United States and Paraguay signed a 1992 investment guaranty agreement, allowing OPIC to begin full operations in Paraguay. OPIC has financed telecommunications, forestry, and various renewable energy projects. OPIC has also partnered with Citibank to support loans for small and medium sized enterprises (SMEs) and micro finance loans.

Paraguay is a member of the World Bank's Multilateral Investment Guarantee Agency (MIGA).

16. Labor

With a population growth rate above 3% per annum and 70% of the population below the age of 35, job creation to meet the large and growing labor force is one of the most pressing issues for the Government of Paraguay. However, the weak education system limits the supply of well-educated workers and is an obstacle to growth.

Paraguay's labor code provides for increased protections for full-time employees who have completed ten consecutive years of employment. Firms often periodically renew "temporary" work contracts instead of hiring through long-term contracts.

Paraguayan law provides for the right of workers to form and join independent unions (with the exception of the armed forces and the police), bargain collectively, and conduct legal strikes. The law prohibits binding arbitration. The law prohibits anti-union discrimination, including retribution against union organizers and strikers, and sets a financial penalty. Employers are not, however, required by law to reinstate workers fired for union activity, even in cases where labor courts fine firms for anti-union discrimination.

The minimum age for formal, full-time employment is 18. Adolescents between the ages of 14 and 17 may work if they have a written authorization from their parents, attend school, do not work more than four hours a day, and do not work more than a maximum of 24 hours per week. Adolescents between the ages of 16 to 18 who do not attend school may work up to six hours a day, with a weekly ceiling of 36 hours. The law also permits "light work" for children between the ages of 12 and 14. The government has not formally defined what constitutes permitted light work for children between ages 12 and 14.

17. Foreign Trade Zones/Free Ports/Trade Facilitation

Paraguayan Law 523/95 (which entered into force in 2002) permits the establishment of Free Trade Zones. Paraguay has two Free Trade Zones in Ciudad del Este. Paraguay is a landlocked country with no seaports but has numerous private and public inland river ports. About three-fourths of commercial goods are transported by barge on the Paraguay-Parana river system that connects Paraguay with Buenos Aires, Argentina and Montevideo, Uruguay. Paraguay has agreements with Uruguay, Argentina, Brazil, and Chile on free-trade ports and warehouses for the reception, storage, handling, and trans-shipment of merchandise.

18. Foreign Direct Investment and Foreign Portfolio Investment Statistics

Table 2: Key Macroeconomic Data, U.S. FDI in Host Country/Economy

	Host Country Statistical source*		USG or International Statistical Source		USG or International Source of Data: BEA; IMF; Eurostat; UNCTAD, Other
Economic Data	**Year**	**Amount**	**Year**	**Amount**	
Host Country Gross Domestic Product (GDP) ($M USD)	2014	30,062	2013	29,000	**www.worldbank.org/en/country**
Foreign Direct Investment	**Host Country Statistical source***		**USG or International Statistical Source**		**USG or International Source of Data: BEA; IMF; Eurostat; UNCTAD, Other**
U.S. FDI in	2013	2,095	2013	2,369	**www.bea.gov**

PARTNER COUNTRY ($M USD, STOCK POSITIONS)					
HOST COUNTRY'S FDI IN THE UNITED STATES ($M USD, STOCK POSITIONS)					Information not available.
TOTAL INBOUND STOCK OF FDI AS % HOST GDP	2013	7.3%	2013	8.2%	

Table 3: Sources and Destination of FDI

IMF Coordinated Direct Investment Survey (CDIS) statistics are for 2013. Outward Direct Investment data is not available.

Direct Investment from/in Counterpart Economy Data					
From Top Five Sources/To Top Five Destinations (US Dollars, Millions)					
Inward Direct Investment			Outward Direct Investment		
Total Inward	5149	100%	Total Outward	Not available	100%
United States	2110	41%			
Brazil	841	16%			
Argentina	525	10%			
Spain	239	5%			
United Kingdom	193	4%			
"0" reflects amounts rounded to +/- USD 500,000.					

Table 4: Sources of Portfolio Investment

IMF's Coordinated Portfolio Investment Survey (CPIS) data are not available for Paraguay.

INVESTMENT AND BUSINESS CONTACTS

Contact for More Information

Natalie van der Horst
Deputy Political and Economic Counselor
U.S. Embassy Asuncion
+ 595 21 213 715
CommercialAsuncion@state.gov

LOCAL LAWYERS

ABENTE BRUN, Victor
Office: El Dorado 212 c/Brasilia Phone: (021) 232-330/2 Asuncion, Paraguay Fax: (021) 214-100 E-mail: vab@abentestewart.com.py
Born in Asuncion, Paraguay on September 26, 1946. Graduated from the National University of Asuncion as Attorney at Law in 1969. Specializes in trademarks and patents. Handles civil and commercial cases. Languages: Spanish, French and English.
ALLEN, Hugo
Office: Carlos A. López 837 y Dr. Coronel Phone: 420-365; 225-646 Sajonia/Asuncion, Paraguay Fax: 420-365
Born in Asuncion, Paraguay on March 5, 1929. Graduated from the National University of Asuncion as Attorney at Law and Social Sciences in 1957. Served as a Judge in the Commercial and Civil Courts and as a member of the Court of Appeals. Specializes in civil and commercial cases. Handles real estate and collection cases. No criminal cases or notarial services. Languages: Spanish, English and Portuguese.
ALVARADO, Marcelo
Office: Avda. Peru 708 c/ Tte. Genaro Ruiz Telefono: (595-21) 205-052
Asuncion, Paraguay Fax: (595-21) 610-240/222-486
Home: 607-412
E-Mail: alfio@supernet.com.py
Born in Asuncion, Paraguay on December 13, 1953. Graduated from the National University of Asuncion as Attorney at Law in 1976, and graduated as Master of Laws from Tulane University, New Orleans, Louisiana. Member of the International Bar Association. Specializes in civil and commercial cases. Languages: Spanish and English.

BASSANI, Ruben
Office: O'Leary 966 e/ Manduvira y Piribebuy Phone: 491-305 / 443-802 Asuncion, Paraguay Born in Asuncion, Paraguay on March 22, 1930. Graduated from the National University of Asuncion as Attorney at Law in 1955. Served in the Civil, Criminal and Commercial Courts. Specializes in civil, labor and commercial cases. Handles notarial and collection cases. Languages: Spanish, English and Portuguese.
BERKEMEYER, Hugo (Sr.)
Office: Benjamin Constant 835, Piso 4 Phone: 446-706/443-213 Asuncion, Paraguay Fax: 496-179 E-mail: law@berke.com.py
Born in Asuncion, Paraguay on April 9, 1924. Graduated from the National University of Asuncion as Attorney at Law and Social Sciences in 1949. Specializes in trademarks and patents, industrial property. Handles civil, administrative and commercial cases. Languages: Spanish, English and German.

BERKEMEYER, Hugo T. (Jr.)
Office: Benjamin Constant 835, Piso 4 Phone: 446-706/443-213

Asuncion, Paraguay Fax: 497-085
Home: 606-665
E-mail: law@berke.com.py
Born in Asuncion, Paraguay on October 11, 1958. Graduated from the National University of Asuncion as Attorney at Law and Social Sciences in 1983. Graduated from the University of San Diego (Master of Law) in 1985. Specializes in trademarks and patents, industrial property, government relations, banking/financial, investments, taxes, immigration, labor relations. Languages: Spanish, English and German.

BURT, Esteban
Office: Calle Eulogio Estigarribia 4846 (ex-Boggiani) Phone: 663-536/542
Asuncion, Paraguay Fax: 600-448/ Home: 507-274
Cell Phone: 0971 229-400
E-mail: esteban.burt@pstbn.com.py
Born in Asuncion, Paraguay on May 18, 1954. Graduated from the Catholic University of Asuncion as Attorney at Law in 1982, and graduated as Master of Law from Harvard University Law School in 1984. Legal consultant for Bank of Boston, Boston, Massachusetts from June to December 1984. Member: Colegio de Abogados del Paraguay, International Bar Association, American Society of International Law. Specializes in civil, administrative, labor and commercial cases. No criminal cases. Languages: Spanish and English.

BREUER, Ramiro
Office: Mayor Fleitas 256 e/ Eligio Ayala y Mcal. Estigarribia Phone: 221-096/222-862/201843
Asuncion, Paraguay Fax: 221-096
Cell Phone: 0981 410368
E-mail: breuerra@telesurf.com.py
Born in Detroit , Michigan, U.S.A. on May 13, 1964. Graduated from the National University of Asuncion as Attorney at Law in 1992. Specializes in civil, administrative, labor and commercial cases. Also handles criminal cases. Languages: English, Spanish and French.

BREUER, Raul
Office: Mayor Fleitas 256 Phone: 201-843
Asuncion, Paraguay Fax: 200-016
Cell Phone: 0981-407-168
E-mail: rb@webmail.com.py
Born in Detroit, Michigan, U.S.A. on October 10, 1967. Graduated from the National University of Asuncion as Attorney at Law . Specializes in civil, administrative, labor and commercial cases. Handles criminal cases. Languages: Spanish and English.

DE GASPERI ZAVALA, Gustavo
Office: 18 de Julio 2629 c/ Felix Bogado Phone: 312-376 /331-790 Asuncion, Paraguay Fax: 310-642
Born in Asuncion, Paraguay on March 3, 1930. Graduated from the National University of Asuncion as Attorney at Law in 1953. Specializes in civil and commercial cases. No criminal cases. Languages: Spanish, English and French.

ENCINA MARIN, Alejandro
Office: Ind. Nacional 1145 c/ Rca. de Colombia Phone: 441-117/445-407/442-229 Asuncion, Paraguay Fax: 495-726 E-mail: aencinamarin@hotmail.com
Born in Asuncion, Paraguay on April 9, 1931. Graduated from the National University of Asuncion as Attorney at Law in 1953 and as a Doctor of Law and Social Sciences in Madrid, Spain in 1955. Appointed as District Attorney in 1954. Author of Paraguayan law concerning narcotics and dangerous drugs.

Specializes in criminal cases, except narcotics and dangerous drugs. Languages: Spanish, English, Portuguese and German.

ESTIGARRIBIA, Hugo E.
Office: Oliva No. 1019 c/ Avda. Colón Phone: 441-204
Piso 10 Ofic. 104 E-mail: estigarribiayasociados@gmail.com
Asuncion, Paraguay Web: www.estigarribiayasociados.com
Graduated from the National University of Asuncion as Attorney at Law in 1990 and as a Notary Public in 1991. Master of Laws in International Legal Studies, August 2002. Field of Specialization: International Business Law and International Organizations. Master of Laws in Law and Government, February 2003. Field of Specialization: Constitutional Law and Civil Rights. Languages: Spanish, English and Portuguese (fluent both written and oral).

GOROSTIAGA, Jose Emilio
Office: Eligio Ayala 1036 c/ EE.UU. Phone: 207-668/ 445-678 Asuncion, Paraguay Fax: 445-678 E-mail: gorost@rieder.net.py
Born in Asuncion, Paraguay on March 4, 1931. Graduated from the National University of Asuncion as Attorney at Law and Social Sciences in 1955. Specializes in criminal cases, except narcotics and dangerous drugs. Languages: Spanish, English, and French.

GUANES- Mersan, Alejandro
Office: Ricardo Brugada 196 e/ Brasilia y Luis Morales Phone: 203-030/206-938 Asunción, Paraguay Fax: same numbers
Born in New Orleans, Louisiana, U.S.A. on Sept. 6, 1969. Graduated from the National University of Asuncion as Attorney at Law and Social Sciences in 1993. LL.M., University of Arizona, James
E. College of Law (1999). Specializes in Foreign Investments, Government Relations, Patents/Trademarks/Copyrights, Contracts. Also handles International Trade Law, Electronic Commerce, internet, domain names. Languages: Spanish, English, and Portuguese.

GROSS BROWN, Jorge R.
Office: Benjamin Constant 624 esq. 15 de Agosto Phone: 444-426
Casilla de Correo 730 Fax: 498-169
Asuncion, Paraguay Web: www.grossbrown.com.py
Born in Asuncion, Paraguay on September 24, 1947. Graduated from the National University of Asuncion as Attorney at Law and Social Sciences in 1971. Specializes in civil, administrative, labor and commercial cases. Handles corporate and tax law. Languages: Spanish, English, German, French and Portuguese.

GWYNN SAFSTRAND, Carlos Ramon
Office: Mayor Bullo 590 esq. Azara Phone: 215-115 Asuncion, Paraguay Fax: 215-115
Born in Asuncion, Paraguay on February 15, 1942. Graduated from the National University of Asuncion as Attorney at Law and Social Sciences in 1972. Specializes in civil, administrative, labor and commercial cases. Maintains offices in New York, Washington, Paris and London. Languages: Spanish and English.

LOIZAGA FRANCO, Nestor Gabriel
Office: Acá Carayá 271, Phone: (595-21) 210-376
Asuncion, Paraguay Fax: (595-21) 227-086
E-mail: nloizaga@ferrere.com
Web site: www.ferrere.com
Born in Asuncion, Paraguay on April 21, 1974. Graduated from the Catholic University of Asuncion as Attorney at Law and Social Sciences in 1999. With a Master in George Washington University in 2003. Specializes in Corporative law, International Business Transaction and Trade Mark and Patent law. Languages: Spanish and English and Portuguese.

MERSAN Galli, Oscar A.
Office: Fulgencio R. Moreno 509 esq. Mexico, or. Phone: 496-403 / 449-052
Casilla de Correo 693 447-739 / 492-573
Asuncion, Paraguay Fax: 496-402 496-039
Efax: +(1.425).795.5947 -USA E-mail: oscar@mersan-abogados.com.py Web: www.mersan-abogados.com.py
Born in Asuncion, Paraguay on July 8th, 1945. Graduated from the National University of Asuncion as Attorney at Law and Social Sciences in 1970. Specializes in administrative, fiscal and commercial cases. General taxation practice. Languages: Spanish, English, Portuguese and Italian.

MERSAN, HUGO R.

Office: Fulgencio R. Moreno 509,
Edif. La Colina- Piso 1
Asuncion, Paraguay
Phone: 496-403 / 449-052
447-739 / 492-573
Fax: 496-038/039- 448-380
E-mail: hugo@mersan-abogados.com.py

Born in Asuncion, Paraguay on April 1, 1956. Graduated from the National University of Asuncion as Attorney at Law and Social Sciences in 1979. Specializes in civil and commercial law. Handles Patents/trademarks/Copyrights, Marketing agreements. Languages: Spanish, English and Portuguese

NARVAJA J., Graciela
Phone: (595) 21 – 663-536/43
Office: Eulogio Estigarribia 4846 Fax: (595-21) 600-448 esq. Monseñor Bogarín - Villa Morra E-mail: graciela.narvaja@pstbn.com.py Asuncion, Paraguay
Born in Villarrica, Paraguay on May 4, 1951. Graduated from the National University of Asuncion as Attorney at Law and Social Sciences. Specializes in Immigration, Foreign Investment and Corporation matters. Languages: Spanish, English.

OVIEDO., Hector
Phone: (595) 21 450-324
Office: Ntra Sra. de la Asuncion 719 Fax: (595-21) 451-156 c/ E. V. Haedo. 4 Piso Cell: 0981-411-204 Asuncion, Paraguay
Born in Asuncion, Paraguay on January 5, 1969. Graduated from the National University of Asuncion as Attorney at Law and Social Sciences in 1993. Specializes in Business and Commercial cases. Languages: Spanish, English.

PARQUET V., Javier Maria
Office: Azara 1595 c/ Cnel. Irrazabal Asuncion, Paraguay
Phone: 224-497 /200-255 Fax: 229-952 Cellular: 0981-401-576 E-mail: javpar@conexion.com.py
Born in Asuncion, Paraguay on November 10, 1962. Graduated from the National University of Asuncion as Attorney at Law and Social Sciences in 1987. Graduated from Harvard Law School: Master at Law (LL.M) at 1989. Specializes in civil, administrative, and commercial cases. Languages: Spanish, English, French and Portuguese.

PERONI, Guillermo F.
Office: Av. Jose Estigarribia 4846 (ex Boggiani) Phone: 663-536/42 Asuncion, Paraguay Fax: 600-448 E-mail: psa@infonet.com.py
Born in Asuncion, Paraguay on April 9, 1937. Graduated from the National University of Asuncion as Attorney at Law and Social Sciences in 1961. Received a fellowship from the Eisenhower Foundation in

1970. Specializes in investment promotion, corporate law, administrative, fiscal and commercial cases. Languages: Spanish and English.

PERONI de ZUBIRI, Mariana
Office: Av. Jose Estigarribia 4846 (ex Boggiani) Phone: 663-536/42 Asunción, Paraguay Fax: 600-448 E-mail: mariana.peroni@pstbn.com.py
Born in Buenos Aires, Argentina on August 2, 1962. Graduated from the Catholic University of Asuncion as Attorney at Law and Social Sciences. Handles Patents/Trademarks/Copyrights. Languages: Spanish, and English.

PERONI, LILIANA G.
Office: Av. Jose Estigarribia 4846 (ex Boggiani) Phone: 663-536/42 Asunción, Paraguay Fax: 600-448 E-mail: psa@pstbn.com.py
Born in Asunción, Paraguay on January 22 , 1967. Graduated from the Catholic University of Asuncion as Attorney at Law and Social Sciences. Specializes in Banking/Financial cases and Corporate Law. Languages: Spanish, English and Portuguese.

RIQUELME JR., Armindo
Office: Avda. Perú 708 c/ Tte. Genaro Ruiz Tel. 595 21 205-052
Asunción, Paraguay Fax: 595-21 610-240/222-486 Cell Phone: (0971) 221-870 E-mail: armindoriquelme@yahoo.com E-mail: alfio@supernet.com.py
Born in Buffalo, New York, U.S.A on August 3, 1967. Graduated from the National University of Asunción as Attorney at Law in 1992. Pursued a Masters of Business Adminstration (MBA) in 1999. Masters of Laws in Comparative and International Law in May 2002 in Dallas, Texas. Specializes in Civil, Administrative and International law. Languages: Spanish, English and Portuguese.

SEALL – SASIAIN, Jorge
Office: Pte. Franco 493 Phone: 447-930
1er. Piso Fax: 444-816
Asuncion, Paraguay E-mail: jseall@sce.cnc.una.py
Born in Asuncion, Paraguay on October 20, 1952. Graduated from the National University of Asuncion as Attorney at Law in 1978, and from the Catholic University of Asuncion as a Sociologist in 1979. Graduated as Master of Law from Harvard Law School in 1984 and Doctor of Jurisprudence in 1987. Practiced law in Washington D.C. from 1987 to 1993. Specializes in international, civil, labor, tax and commercial cases. Languages: Spanish, English, French, Italian and Portuguese.

STIMSON, THEODORE
Office: Juan de Salazar 657 y Prof. Ramirez Phone: 202-049 Asuncion, Paraguay Fax: 230-101 Cell: 0991-764-946 Office email: tstimson@vouga-olmedo.com.py Email: tdstimson@yahoo.com
Born in Asunción, Paraguay, April 4, 1967. Graduated from the National University of Asunción, as Attorney at Law, 1992. Graduated from the University of Chicago, The Law School, as Masters of Law, 1994. Specializes in administrative law. Handles foreign investment, corporate, tax, and environmental matters. Languages: Spanish and English.

VARELA, DANIEL
Office: Gral. Santos 710 c/ Siria Phone: 210-058/210-070 Barrio Las Mercedes, Asuncion Fax: 228-353 Cell Phone: 0981- 577-028 E-mail: varelayasociados@webmail.com.py
Born in Asuncion, Paraguay on April 13, 1969. Graduated from the National University of Asuncion as Attorney at Law in 1996, Postgraduate Studies in Diplomacy and International Affairs at the Consular and Diplomatic Academy of the Ministry of Foreign Relations of Paraguay. Attorney at Law and Public Translator. Specializes in Children's issues. Child custody disputes, child support and also in civil, immigration and labor cases. Languages: Spanish, Guaraní, English and German.

VARGAS TALAVERA, Manuel
Office: Av. Ygatimi 655 or Phone: 441-038
Casilla de Correo 4 Fax: 496-811
Asuncion, Paraguay
Born in Caacupe, Paraguay on March 12, 1927. Graduated from the National University of Asuncion as Attorney at Law 1953. Handles trademark and patent cases. Specializes in industrial property regulations. Languages: Spanish, English, French and German.

VOUGA MULLER, Rodolfo
Office: Av. Perú esq. Av. España Phone: 207-185/7 230-100/1 213-598
Asuncion, Paraguay 224-630
Fax: 214-556
Home: 660-656
E-mail: rvouga@pla.net.py
Born in Asuncion, Paraguay on January 4, 1950. Graduated from the National University of Asuncion as Attorney at Law in 1974. Graduated from Georgetown, University Law Center as Master at Law (Common Law Studies). Handles trademark, patent and investment cases. Specializes in commercial, fiscal and labor law. Languages: Spanish, English and German.

ZAVALA SERRATI, Diego Manuel
Office: Fulgencio R. Moreno 509 esq, Mexico Phone: 492-573 / 449-052 Edif. La Colina- Piso 1 447-739 / 496-403 Asuncion, Paraguay Fax: 496-038/039- 448-380
E-mail: diegozavala@mersanlaw.com
Born in Asuncion, Paraguay on October 15, 1967. Graduated from the Catholic University of Asuncion as Attorney at Law and Social Sciences in 1991. LL.M, Yale Law School (1994). Specializes in civil law. Handles Government relations, Foreign Investments, Insurances and general taxation practice. Languages: Spanish, English and Portuguese.

PERU INVESTMENT AND BUSINESS CLIMATE - STRATEGIC INFORMATION AND CONTACTS FOR STARTING BUSINESS

Peru has been one of the fastest growing Latin American economies over the past decade. Between 2003 and 2013 the Peruvian economy grew an average of 6% per year. Though the trend did not continue in 2014, Peru's 2.35% growth was still higher than the 2.0% average growth in Latin America. The government's counter-cyclical stimulus spending, consumption, and private investment are the main driving forces of this growth. Investment grew by 8.3% year-on-year to a value of USD 33.5 billion in 2013. The Ministry of Economy and Finance set a target of 30% growth in public investment, and pledged a total of USD 30 billion over the next five years to address Peru's infrastructure gap, estimated at USD 80 billion. As the economy has grown, poverty in Peru has steadily decreased falling by half from 56% in 2005 to 23.9% in 2013 according to the World Bank. HSBC describes Peru could eventually "be a bigger economy than Chile, Colombia, or even South Africa in the long term."

The steady economic growth began with the pro-market policies enacted by former President Alberto Fujimori in the 1990s. All subsequent governments have continued these policies, including the current administration inaugurated in July 2011 for a five-year term. President Ollanta Humala pledged to encourage private and public investment in infrastructure projects in transportation, telecommunications, energy, sanitation, airports, and maritime ports. Congruent with his other campaign goals to reduce poverty and narrow the nation's socioeconomic gap, President Humala has increased social spending and raised taxes on mining companies.

Peru's local currency, the Nuevo Sol (PEN), has been among the least volatile within Latin American over the past few years. In 2014, it did depreciate close to 10% in comparison to the USD. Since the mid-1990's, the PEN's exchange rate with the USD has fluctuated between 1.25 and 3.55 per USD. The exchange rate, as of March 16, 2015, was PEN 3.097 per USD.

The Government of Peru (GOP) has encouraged integration with the global economy by signing a number of free trade agreements, including the United States-Peru Trade Promotion Agreement (PTPA), which entered into force in February 2009. In 2014, trade between the United States and Peru totaled USD 16.1 billion up from USD 9.1 billion in 2009 the first year of entry into force. From 2009 to 2014, Peruvian exports to the United States jumped from USD 4.2 billion to USD 6.1 billion (a 45% increase) while U.S. exports to Peru jumped from USD 4.9 billion to USD 10.1 billion (a 106% increase). Peru has preferential trade agreements with 49 countries and unions, including the United States, Argentina, Brazil, Uruguay, Paraguay, Bolivia, Colombia, Ecuador, Canada, Chile, China, Mexico, Japan, Singapore, South Korea, Norway, Iceland, Liechtenstein, Switzerland, Thailand, Panama, and the European Union.

In the 2015 World Bank's Ease of Doing Business report, Peru ranked 35 out of 189.

1. OPENNESS TO, AND RESTRICTIONS UPON, FOREIGN INVESTMENT

Attitude toward Foreign Direct Investment

The GOP seeks to attract investment -- both foreign and domestic -- in nearly all sectors of the economy. Several high level Peruvian officials, including President Ollanta Humala, the Minister of Economy and Finance, and the Central Bank President, attended global business conferences and toured several countries in 2014 in an effort to attract foreign investment. Some of these tours were organized and sponsored by In Peru, a private industry organization (**http://inperu.pe**). Peruvians and Americans benefit from the United States-Peru Trade Promotion Agreement (PTPA) which entered into force on February 1, 2009. Since entry into force, total trade (exports and imports) between Peru and the United States expanded significantly from USD 9.1 billion to USD 16.1 billion. The PTPA establishes a secure, predictable legal framework for U.S. investors operating in Peru. The PTPA protects all forms of investment. U.S. investors enjoy in almost all circumstances the right to establish, acquire and operate investments in Peru on an equal footing with local investors.

Other Investment Policy Reviews

Peru aspires to become a member of the Organization for Economic Cooperation and Development (OECD). On February 5, 2015 the GOP announced the start of an 18-month study to identify economic, social, and political "bottle necks" that could hamper Peru's OECD membership aspirations. The government noted that the study would act as a "roadmap" for Peru's goal to achieve membership by 2021 and highlighted education as an example of a key area that Peru must improve. According to the OECD, Peru dedicates only 2.8% of GDP towards education compared to the OECD average of 5.6% of GDP. As a result, Peruvian 15 year olds achieve education results equivalent to 12 year olds in OECD member countries. The result of this lack of investment in education is a chronic shortage of skilled labor in Peru.

Laws/Regulations of Foreign Direct Investment

The 1993 Constitution grants national treatment for foreign investors and permits foreign investment in almost all economic sectors. Under the Constitution, foreign investors have the same rights as national investors to benefit from any investment incentives, such as tax exemptions. In addition to the 1993 Constitution, Peru has several laws governing foreign direct investment (FDI) including the Foreign Investment Promotion Law (Legislative Decree (DL) 662 of September 1991) and the Framework Law for

Private Investment Growth (DL 757 of November 1991). Other important laws include the Private Investment in State-Owned Enterprises Promotion Law (DL 674), the Private Investment in Public Services Infrastructure Promotion Law (DL 758), and specific laws related to agriculture, fisheries and aquaculture, forestry, mining, oil and gas, and electricity. Article 6 of Supreme Decree No. 162-92-EF (the implementing regulations of DLs 662 and 757) authorizes private investors to enter all industries except investments in natural protected areas and manufacturing of weapons.

The GOP has passed several laws and related implementing regulations aimed at encouraging more private investment, such as two important decrees in 2008. The first was a legislative decree containing the Law on Public-Private Partnerships (PPPs). The second decree presents a priority list of projects for PPPs. Congress passed a law to reform regulations that would make PPPs less bureaucratic and more transparent, thus more attractive to foreign companies, in March 2014. Among these public-private partnerships are major infrastructure projects of national importance and upgrades to existing projects: Salaverry maritime port project, Quillabamba thermal power plant (Cusco region), liquid petroleum gas (LPG) transport system (from Pisco to Callao), lines three and four of the Lima and Callao Metro system, water supply to Lima and related headwater works, distribution system of natural gas via pipeline networks (Apurimac, Ayacucho, Huancavelica, Junin, Cusco, Puno, and Ucayali regions), rural broadband installation (optical fiber transportation networks and access networks), and connections to three existing 220 kV power transmission lines. Project opportunities are available on ProInversion's Project Portfolio page, available at:**http://www.proyectosapp.pe/modulos/JER/PlantillaProyectoEstadoSector.aspx?are=1&prf=2&jer=5892&sec=30**.

Although all Peruvian administrations since the 1990s have vowed to support private investment and abide by Peruvian laws, the GOP occasionally has passed measures that some observers have regarded as contravening legal principles. For example, the Garcia Administration in 2011 rescinded a Canadian company's rights to operate a silver mining project in Puno after violent protests opposing the project. The Canadian company delivered to the Peruvian Minister of Economy and Finance a Notice of Intent to submit a claim to arbitration under the terms of the Canada-Peru Free Trade Agreement in February 2014. Furthermore, President Ollanta Humala signed into law a 10-year moratorium on the entry into Peru of live genetically-modified organisms (GMOs) to be used for cultivation in December 2011. Peru also has implemented two inconsistent sets of rules for importing pesticides, one for "regular" importers, which is extremely restrictive and requires importers to file a full dossier with technical information, and another for farmers, which is rather loose and only requires a written affidavit.

The GOP created the Private Investment Promotion Agency, ProInversion, in 2002, based on an existing similar agency. ProInversion has completed both privatizations and concessions of state-owned enterprises and natural resource-based industries. Major recent concession areas include ports, power generation facilities, electrical transmission lines, oil and gas distribution, and telecommunications. In July 2014 the Peruvian Congress passed legislation to reform the public-private concessions process and require more oversight by the Ministry of Economy and Finance. The Ministry of Economy and Finance is working on the implementing regulations, and expects a final draft before the end of 2015.

Industrial Promotion

ProInversion also aims to attract investment in the following sectors: agricultural, construction, ground transportation, energy and mining, finance, health technologies, telecommunications, and travel. Information can be found on ProInversion's website: **http://www.proyectosapp.pe/modulos/JER/PlantillaProyectoEstadoSector.aspx?are=0&prf=2&jer=5351&sec=22**.

Limits on Foreign Control

The Constitution (Article 6 under Supreme Decree No. 162-92-EF) authorizes foreign investors to carry out any economic activity provided investors comply with all constitutional precepts, laws and treaties. Exceptions exist, including exclusion on foreign investment activities in natural protected reserves and manufacturing of war weapons, pursuant to Article 6 of Legislative Decree No. 757. While long-term concessions are granted, the law states Peruvians must maintain majority ownership in certain strategic sectors: media; air, land and maritime transportation infrastructure; and private security surveillance services.

Prior approval is required in the banking (for regulatory reasons, and also applies to domestic investment) and defense-related sectors. Foreigners are also legally prohibited from owning a majority interest in radio and television stations in Peru; nevertheless, foreigners have in practice owned controlling interests in such companies. Under the Constitution, foreign interests cannot "acquire or possess under any title, mines, lands, forests, waters, or fuel or energy sources" within 50 kilometers of Peru's international borders. However, foreigners can obtain concessions and rights within the restricted areas with the authorization of a supreme resolution approved by the Cabinet and the Joint Command of the Armed Forces.

PRIVATIZATION PROGRAM

The GOP initiated an extensive, but not yet complete, privatization program in 1991 in which foreign investors were encouraged to participate. Since 2000, the GOP has promoted multi-year concessions as a means of attracting investment in major projects. In 2000, the government granted a 30-year concession to a private group (Lima Airport Partners) to operate the Lima airport. In 2006, the government granted a 30-year concession to Dubai Ports to build and operate a new container terminal in the Port of Callao. The terminal's first phase became operational in May 2010. In 2006, the Swiss-Spanish-Peruvian consortium Swissport received a 25-year concession to manage nine of Peru's northern airports. In 2011, the GOP awarded the Argentine-Peruvian consortium Aeropuertos Andinos a 25-year concession to manage six of Peru's southern airports. Also in 2011, the government granted a 30-year concession to a Danish-Peruvian consortium led by the Danish-based A.P. Moller-Maersk Group to operate and modernize the multipurpose northern terminal at the Port of Callao. On June 30, 2014 the GOP awarded a multi-billion USD concession for the Southern Gas Pipeline to a consortium led by Brazilian company Odebrecht. The GOP continues to award multi-year concessions for various energy, natural gas, hydro-energy and irrigation, telecommunications, ports, sanitation, roads, and tourism projects.

The concessions process is challenging for U.S. and other international companies interested in bidding on projects. ProInversion, the government agency responsible for drawing up and competing public-private-partnership (P3) concession projects, has come under considerable criticism for its bidding process, deadlines, and ambitious timetables. As a result, U.S. and other international companies have shown limited interest in Peruvian P3 projects.

SCREENING OF FDI

The GOP does not screen, review, or approve foreign direct investment outside of those sectors that require a governmental waiver (see Limits on Foreign Control).

COMPETITION LAW

The Institute for the Protection of Intellectual Property, Consumer Protection, and Competition (INDECOPI) is the GOP agency responsible for reviewing competition-related concerns of a domestic nature.

INVESTMENT TRENDS

Peru has made significant strides in various rankings within the World Bank's Doing Business report, including reformed procedures on starting a business, securing construction permits, registering property, and closing a business. Although Peru's efforts to reform business start-up procedures has made significant strides, according to the 2011 report, Peru declined by three places in the World Bank's business start-up ranking from 60th in 2013 to 63rd in 2014. At the same time, Peru lowered the average amount of time it takes to start a business from 41 days (in 2010) to 25 days (in 2014). Although the 2013 report noted Peru's efforts to strengthen investor protections through a new law regulating the approval of related-party transactions and making it easier to sue directors when such transactions are prejudicial, the 2014 does not show any relevant legal modifications for Peru.

Table 1

Measure	Year	Index or Rank	Website Address
TI Corruption Perceptions Index	2014	85 of 175	transparency.org/cpi2014/results
World Bank's Doing Business Report "Ease of Doing Business"	2015	35 of 189	doingbusiness.org/rankings
Global Innovation Index	2014	73 of 143	globalinnovationindex.org/content.aspx?page=data-analysis
World Bank GNI per capita	2013	USD 6,270	data.worldbank.org/indicator/NY.GNP.PCAP.CD

Millennium Challenge Corporation Country Scorecard

In 2008, Peru received USD 35.6 million from the Millennium Challenge Corporation Threshold funding for health and anti-corruption programs. In 2009 Peru reached upper-middle income country status and is officially ineligible for further Millennium Challenge Corporation assistance.

2. Conversion and Transfer Policies

Foreign Exchange

There are no reported difficulties in obtaining foreign exchange. Under Article 64 of the 1993 Constitution, the GOP guarantees the freedom to hold and dispose of foreign currency. The GOP has eliminated all restrictions on remittances of profits, dividends, royalties, and capital, although foreign investors are advised to register their investments with ProInversion to ensure these guarantees. Exporters and importers are not required to channel foreign exchange transactions through the Central Reserve Bank of Peru (BCR) and can conduct transactions freely on the open market. Anyone may open and maintain foreign currency accounts in Peruvian commercial banks. U.S. firms have reported no problems or delays in transferring funds or remitting capital, earnings, loan repayments or lease payments since Peru's economic reforms of the early 1990s. Under the PTPA, portfolio managers in the United States are able to provide portfolio management services to both mutual funds and pension funds in Peru, including funds that manage Peru's privatized social security accounts.

The 1993 Constitution guarantees free convertibility of currency. However, limited capital controls still exist as private pension fund managers (AFPs) are constrained by how much of their portfolio can be invested in foreign securities. The maximum limit is set by law (currently 50% since July 2011), but the BCR sets the operating limit AFPs can invest abroad. Over the years, the BCR has gradually increased the operating limit, which reached 40% in July 2014. Several additional increases were made between October 2014 and January 2015, bringing the current operating limit up to 42 percent.

The BCR is an independent institution, free to manage monetary policy to maintain financial stability. The BCR's primary goal is to maintain price stability, via inflation targeting. Inflation at year-end in Peru reached 3.9% in 2007, 6.7% in 2008, 0.3% in 2009, 2.1% in 2010, 4.7% in 2011, 2.7% in 2012, 2.8% in 2013, and 3.2% in 2014.

The GOP has implemented policies to de-dollarize the economy, but in the last few years market forces have been more effective in reducing dollarization as the Peruvian Nuevo Sol had trended (until 2014) to appreciate vis-à-vis the U.S. dollar. U.S. dollars account for a decreasing share of banking system transactions, according to the Peruvian Banking Superintendence (SBS). In 2001, U.S. dollars accounted for 82% of loans and 73% of deposits. As of February 2015, U.S. dollars accounted for 42.6% of loans.

The foreign exchange market operates freely, for the most part. To quell "extreme variations" of the exchange rate, the BCR intervenes through purchases and sales in the open market without imposing controls on exchange rates or transactions. In the last few years, the BCR has consistently purchased U.S. dollars to mitigate the risk that spillover from expansionary U.S. monetary policy might result in over-valuation of the Peruvian Nuevo Sol relative to the U.S. dollar. This policy is likely to continue for the foreseeable future, until U.S. economic recovery begins to tighten credit conditions.

Remittance Policies

Peru is neither a major regional financial center nor an offshore financial center. Currently, businesses involved in the transfer of funds only need prior authorization by the Peruvian Banking Authority (SBS) while cash couriers need a signed agreement with the Ministry of Transportation and Communication. The GOP's Financial Intelligence Unit (FIU) is an independent agency that monitors and investigates financial institutions and cash transfers (physical and electronic for money laundering and other financial crimes.

Peru's cash-based and heavily-dollarized economy, large informal sector (estimated to be 70% of GDP), and deficient regulatory supervision of designated non-financial businesses and professions (DNFBPs), such as informal money exchanges and wire transfer services, make the economy vulnerable to money laundering and other financial crimes. The informal remittance businesses remain unsupervised and vulnerable to money laundering, including travel agencies and small wire transfer businesses. Peru would benefit from expanded supervision and regulation of financial institutions and DNFBPs. Progress was made in monitoring and regulating notaries, pawn shops, and exchange houses. Peru is a member of the Financial Action Task Force on Money Laundering in South America (GAFILAT).

A U.S. company complained to the Embassy that their pension plans, issued in the United States and registered under the Texas Commissioner, have been excluded by the SBS from being used by their clients to demonstrate provisional coverage within the funds transfer abroad procedure, despite the company having certified compliance with the coverage requirements. This is notwithstanding the AFPs (pension funds) accepting private voluntary plans from other countries.

3. EXPROPRIATION AND COMPENSATION

The Peruvian Constitution states that the GOP can only expropriate private property on the bases of public interest, such as public works projects or for national security. In order to expropriate Congress is required to pass a decree. The Government of Peru has expressed its intention to comply with international standards concerning expropriations. On January 12, 2012, Congress approved legislation to expropriate a number of homes and other real estate adjacent to the Lima Airport for an airport expansion project. Compensation for expropriations is based on fair market value. Notably, concessionaires have complained that the government has been extremely slow in implementing expropriations, which have caused delays to their investment commitments.

4. DISPUTE SETTLEMENT

LEGAL SYSTEM, SPECIALIZED COURTS, JUDICIAL INDEPENDENCE, JUDGMENTS OF FOREIGN COURTS

The PTPA includes a chapter on dispute settlement, which applies to implementation of the Agreement's core obligations, including labor and environment provisions. Dispute panel procedures set high standards of openness and transparency through the following measures: open public hearings; public release of legal submissions by parties, enlisting special labor or environment expertise for disputes in these areas, and opportunities for interested third parties to submit views. The Agreement emphasizes compliance through consultation and trade-enhancing remedies. The Agreement also encourages arbitration and other alternative dispute resolution measures for disputes between private parties.

Peru is a party to the 1958 Convention on the Recognition and Enforcement of Foreign Arbitral Awards (New York Convention) and to the International Center for the Settlement of Investment Disputes (ICSID convention). Disputes between foreign investors and the GOP regarding pre-existing contracts must still enter national courts, unless otherwise permitted, such as through provisions found in the PTPA. In addition, investors who enter into a juridical stability agreement may submit disputes with the government to national or international arbitration if stipulated in the agreement. Several private organizations -- including the American Chamber of Commerce, the Lima Chamber of Commerce, and Universidad Catolica – operate private arbitration centers. The quality of such centers varies, however, and investors should choose arbitration venues carefully.

BANKRUPTCY

Peru has a creditor rights hierarchy similar to that established under U.S. bankruptcy law, and monetary judgments are usually made in the currency stipulated in the contract. However, administrative bankruptcy procedures under INDECOPI (the Antitrust, Unfair Competition, Intellectual Property Protection, Consumer Protection, Dumping, Standards and Elimination of Bureaucratic Barriers Agency) have proven to be slow and subject to judicial intervention. Compounding this difficulty are occasional laws passed to protect specific debtors from action by creditors that would force them into bankruptcy or liquidation.

INVESTMENT DISPUTES

The 1993 Constitution allows disputes among foreign investors and the government or state-controlled enterprises to be submitted to international arbitration. In 2005, in order to reinforce the constitution, the Supreme Court ruled that all arbitration awards are final and are not subject to appeal.

INTERNATIONAL ARBITRATION

The Constitution permits international arbitration of disputes between foreign investors and the government or state-controlled enterprises. Although Peruvian law stipulates the GOP must accept binding arbitration, parastatal companies and government ministries disregarded unfavorable judgments several times over the past three years. Previously, the Government of Peru turned these arbitration cases over to the judiciary, where they were bureaucratically delayed until the companies conceded the cases. Peru's Supreme Court ruled that effective July 2005 all arbitration findings and awards are final and not subject to appeal.

Peru is a party to the 1958 Convention on the Recognition and Enforcement of Foreign Arbitral Awards (New York Convention), and to the 1965 International Center for the Settlement of Investment Disputes (ICSID convention). Disputes between foreign investors and the GOP regarding pre-existing contracts must still enter national courts. However, investors who conclude a juridical stability agreement for additional investments may submit disputes with the government to national or international arbitration if stipulated in the agreement. Several private organizations -- including the Universidad Catolica, the Lima Chamber of Commerce and the American Chamber of Commerce -- operate private arbitration centers. The quality of these centers varies, and investors should choose arbitration venues carefully.

ICSID Convention and New York Convention

Peru became a signatory to the Convention on the Settlement of Investment Disputes between States and Nationals of Other States (ICSID Convention) since September 4, 1991. Peru ratified the 1958 New York Convention on the Recognition and Enforcement of Foreign Arbitral Awards on July 7, 1988.

DURATION OF DISPUTE RESOLUTION

Dispute settlement remains problematic in Peru; although in 2004 the GOP took steps to improve the dispute settlement process by establishing commercial courts to rule on investment disputes, including two courts of appeal. Prior to the existence of the commercial courts, it took an average of two years to resolve a commercial case through the civil court system. With their specialized judges, these courts have reduced the amount of time to resolve a case to just two months. The appeals level resolves most of these cases.

The criminal and civil courts of first instance and appeal are heard at the provincial level. The Supreme Court is located in Lima. In principle, Peruvian law recognizes secured interests in property, both movable and immovable. With the exception of the commercial courts, the judicial system is extremely slow to hear cases and to issue decisions. A large backlog of cases further complicates decision-making. Court rulings and the degree of enforcement have been difficult to predict. The competence of individual judges varies, and allegations of corruption, political interference, and outside interference in the judicial system are common. Frequent use of appellate processes as a delay tactic leads to the belief among foreign investors that contracts can be difficult to enforce in Peru. The 1997 Law of Conciliation (DL 26872) requires disputants in many types of civil and commercial matters to consider conciliation before a judge can accept a dispute for litigation. Private parties often resort to arbitration to resolve business disputes, avoiding involvement in judicial processes.

Peru has a creditor rights hierarchy similar to that established under U.S. bankruptcy law, and monetary judgments are usually made in the currency stipulated in the contract. However, administrative bankruptcy procedures under INDECOPI (the National Institute for the Defense of Free Competition and the Protection of Intellectual Property) have proven to be slow and subject to judicial intervention. Compounding this difficulty are occasional laws passed to protect specific debtors from action by creditors that would force them into bankruptcy or liquidation.

The 1993 Constitution permits international arbitration of disputes between foreign investors and the government or state-controlled enterprises. Previously, the Government of Peru appealed arbitration cases to the judiciary, where they were typically delayed until the international companies conceded the cases. To reinforce Peruvian law, the Supreme Court ruled that effective July 2005, all arbitration findings and awards are final and not subject to appeal.

5. PERFORMANCE REQUIREMENTS AND INVESTMENT INCENTIVES

WTO/TRIMS

The PTPA has resulted in benefits to U.S. enterprises seeking to invest in Peru. Under the PTPA, Peru has made concessions beyond its commitments to the World Trade Organization (WTO) eliminating investment barriers, such as the requirement for U.S. firms to hire nationals rather than U.S. professionals, and measures requiring the purchase of local goods.

INVESTMENT INCENTIVES

Peru offers both foreign and national investors legal and tax stability agreements to stimulate private investment. These agreements guarantee that the statutes on income taxes, remittances, export promotion regimes (such as drawbacks, or refunds of duties), administrative procedures, and labor hiring regimes in effect at the time of the investment contract will remain unchanged for that investment for 10 years. To qualify, an investment must exceed USD 10 million in the mining and hydrocarbons sectors or USD 5 million within two years in other sectors. An agreement to acquire more than 50% of a company's shares in the privatization process may also qualify an investor for a legal or tax stability agreement, provided that the added investment will expand the installed capacity of the company or enhance its technological development.

Research and Development

Promoting science, innovation, and technology and improving Peru's education system remain priorities for the Humala Administration. Peru ranked last out of 65 surveyed countries in the OECD's 2013 Program for International Student Assessment (PISA). The OECD noted the high inequity of quality between urban and rural schools and low levels of Peruvian students meeting PISA standards in mathematics, science, and reading. The Humala Administration increased spending on education for 2015, including USD 1 billion to build and renovate schools and USD 450 million to hire more teachers. In 2014, the GOP launched an ambitious national plan to promote innovation, science, and technology jobs.

PERFORMANCE REQUIREMENTS

There are no performance requirements that apply exclusively to foreign investors. Peruvian civil law applies to legal stability agreements, which means the GOP cannot unilaterally alter agreements. Notwithstanding these protections, investors should be aware that government officials have delivered negative remarks to the press regarding companies exercising their contractual rights and obligations.

Laws specific to investment in the petroleum and mining sectors provide assurances to investors in those sectors. However, a history of tightening of benefits has occurred in these industries. In 2000, the government modified the General Mining Law, reducing some benefits to investors in that sector. Among the changes were reductions in the term concessionaires are granted to achieve the minimum annual production, increases in fees for holding non-productive concessions, increases in fines for not achieving minimum production within the allotted time, reductions in the maximum allowable annual accelerated depreciation, and revocation of the income tax exemption for reinvested profits.

After a growing number of local communities demanded a share of mining profits from operations in their areas, the incoming Garcia Administration and mining companies agreed in 2006 to a voluntary contribution system whereby companies agreed to provide funding to the government (in addition to the regular corporate income tax) for community infrastructure projects. This voluntary contribution averted adoption of exacting taxes. The agreement allowed mining companies to control where their contributions were invested and did not apply if the prices of metals or minerals drop below certain levels. As the voluntary contribution agreement was to expire at the end of 2011 during a period of windfall profits for extractive industries, the incoming Humala Administration and mining companies agreed in August 2011 to replace it with a new tax regime on mining profits called the "gravamen minero." It produced tax revenues (including the royalty tax) of USD 1.97 billion in 2012; but with declining metals prices the contribution in the January-November tax 2013 period was USD 1.48 billion.

With regard to licensing arrangements, private parties may freely negotiate contractual conditions related to licensing arrangements and other aspects of technology transfer, needing no prior governmental authorization. Registration of a technology transfer agreement with INDECOPI is required for a payment of royalties to be counted against taxes.

Current law limits foreign employees to 20% of the total number of employees in a local company (whether owned by foreign or national interests). The combined salaries of foreign employees are limited to no more than 30% of the total company payroll. However, DL 689 from November 1991 provides a variety of exceptions to these limits. For example, a foreigner is not counted against a company's total if he or she holds an immigrant visa, has a certain amount invested in the company (approximately USD 4,000), or is a national of a country that has a reciprocal labor or dual nationality agreement with Peru. The United States and Peru tolerate dual nationality, but do not have a formal agreement. Furthermore, the law exempts foreign banks, and international transportation companies from these hiring limits, as well as all firms located in free trade zones. Companies may apply for exemption from the limitations for managerial or technical personnel.

The GOP does not maintain any measures that are inconsistent with Trade-Related Investment Measure (TRIM) requirements, according to a WTO Committee on Trade-Related Investment Measure notification dated August 19, 2010.

Although there are no discriminatory or onerous visa requirements, residence, or works permit requirements that inhibit foreign investors' mobility, the application and approval process can be cumbersome and lengthy.

DATA STORAGE

Peru adopted the Personal Data Protection Law (N° 29733) in July 2011 and went into effect on March 22, 2013. The Law is available here in English: **http://web.ita.doc.gov/ITI/itiHome.nsf/1dd3c7c4faeeff0585256ccb00657bab/112a1a2f4d01989c85257a78004dd2ec/$FILE/Peru%20Data%20Protection%20Law%20July%2028_EN.pdf**.

The implementing regulations are available in Spanish here: **http://spij.minjus.gob.pe/normas/textos/220313T.pdf**.

A data controller who processes personal data must notify the National Authority for Personal Data Protection (ANPDP for its Spanish acronym), which keeps a public register of data processors and the type of data they collect. Personal data is defined by the Law as any information on an individual which identifies or makes him/her identifiable through means that may be reasonably used. Sensitive personal data means any of the following: biometric data, data concerning the racial and ethnic origin; political, religion, philosophical or moral opinions or convictions, personal habits, union membership and information related to health or sexual life. Unless otherwise exempted by statute, data controllers are generally required to obtain the consent of data subjects for the processing of their personal data. Consent must be prior, informed, expressed, and unequivocal. In the case of sensitive personal data, consent must also be given in writing, which may be done digitally. Even without the consent of the subject, sensitive data may be processed when authorized by law, provided that it in in the public interest.

Data controllers may process personal data without consent:

When the personal data are compiled or transferred for public entities in control of the personal data and in the performance of its duties;

When personal data is accessible to the public or is intended to be accessible to the public;

To comply with other laws related to financial solvency and credit;

In the case of a law for the promotion of competition in regulated markets under certain circumstances;

When necessary to perform a contract to which the data subject is a party;

For personal data related to health, under certain circumstances;

When processing is carried out by non-profit organizations with political, religious or union purposes, under certain circumstances; or

In an anonymization or disassociation procedure.

A data controller may transfer personal data to places outside of Peru only if the recipients have adequate protection measures. The ANPDP supervises compliance with this requirement. That provision does not apply in the following cases:

When the data subject has given his/her prior, informed, express and unequivocal consent;

Agreements under international treaties to which Peru is a party;

International judicial cooperation;

International cooperation between intelligence agencies for the fight against terrorism, illegal drug trafficking, money laundering, corruption, human trafficking and other forms of organized crime;

When necessary to implement a contract to which the data subject is a party;

To comply with laws concerning the transfer of bank or stock exchanges; or

When the transfer is for the prevention, diagnosis or medical or surgical treatment of the data subject; or when necessary to carry out epidemiological or similar studies (provided that adequate disassociation procedures are applied).

Data controllers must adopt technical, organization and legal measures to guarantee the security of personal data and avoid their alteration, loss, unauthorized processing or access. Peru's law does not require any notifications to any data subject or any other entity upon a breach. Peru does not mandate special regulations be enacted for the processing of personal data of minors. The ANPDP is responsible for enforcement and can issue the following administrative sanctions/fines based upon whether the violation is mild, serious or very serious. The law provides a "Principle for availability of recourse for the data subject" stating that any data subject must have the administrative and/or jurisdictional channel necessary to claim and enforce his rights when they are violated by the processing of his personal data.A

6. RIGHT TO PRIVATE OWNERSHIP AND ESTABLISHMENT

Peruvian law generally grants foreign and domestic entities the right to establish and own business enterprises and to engage in most forms of remunerative activity. Subject to the restrictions listed earlier in this document, both foreign and domestic entities may invest in any legal economic activity -- including foreign direct investment, portfolio investment, and in real estate. Private entities may generally freely establish, acquire, and dispose of interests in business enterprises. In the case of some privatized companies deemed important by the government, the privatization agency ProInversion has included a so-called "golden share" clause in the sales contract, which allows the government to veto a potential future purchaser of the privatized assets.

7. PROTECTION OF PROPERTY RIGHTS

REAL PROPERTY

The GOP recognizes and enforces secured interests in property, both movable and immovable. The GOP is working on improving the registry of those rights, which will further enable the government's enforcement capabilities.

Peru's legal framework provides for easy registration of trademarks, and inventors have been able to patent their inventions since 1994. Peru's 1996 Industrial Property Rights Law provides an effective term of protection for patents and prohibits devices that decode encrypted satellite signals, along with other improvements. Peruvian law does not provide pipeline protection for patents or protection from parallel imports. Peru's Copyright Law is generally consistent with the TRIPS Agreement.

INTELLECTUAL PROPERTY RIGHTS

While the legal framework for protection of intellectual property (IP) in Peru has improved over the past decade, including the law enacted in 2011 to criminalize the sale of counterfeit medicines, enforcement mechanisms remain weak. However, Peru has remained on USTR's Section 301 "Watch List" since 1992 because of continued high piracy rates, inadequate enforcement of IP laws, and weak or unenforced penalties for IP violators.

Under the PTPA, Peruvian law should treat U.S. companies at least as well as Peruvian companies in all IP categories. The PTPA provides for improved IP protection on a broad range of intellectual property rights. Such improvements include protections for digital products such as U.S. software, music, text, and video; protection for U.S. patents, trademarks and pharmaceutical and agrochemical test data; legal penalties to deter piracy; and an electronic system to register and maintain trademarks.

Despite PTPA implementation and recent legal code amendments creating stricter penalties for some types of IP theft, the judicial branch has failed to impose sentences that adequately deter future IP theft. Prosecutors do not pursue piracy cases through the entire process to final judgment. Furthermore, the Peruvian public lacks motivation to change perceptions regarding IP theft. The public continues to purchase pirated software, CDs, DVDs, pharmaceutical products, and books from vendors in public. The purchases continue openly since most Peruvians realize their government will not prosecute this theft.

Some GOP institutions, sometimes with the support of the U.S. Embassy in Lima, sponsor public awareness campaigns to raise awareness about the damage that IP theft causes the Peruvian economy and Peruvians consumers. Peruvian newspapers complain about piracy, including pirated versions of Peru's Nobel Laureate Mario Vargas Llosa's books. While the GOP occasionally has carried out raids against small-time vendors of pirated goods, piracy remains a significant problem for legitimate owners of copyrights in Peru.

The International Intellectual Property Alliance (IIPA) estimates that the piracy level in Peru for recorded music is at 98% and 100% for video content and books. The Business Software Alliance estimates that software piracy level is at 65%, costing the industry USD 60 million in 2014.

The U.S. pharmaceutical industry advises that the GOP fails to provide data exclusivity protection for all pharmaceutical products and does not provide patent linkage or "second use" medical patents. The pharmaceutical industry also advises that the GOP does not offer any extension of the patent term for pharmaceutical products to compensate for processing delays at the patent office. There has also been at least one instance of GOP initiatives creating a backdoor for domestic companies to avoid complying with IP laws. This backdoor can be seen in the pharmaceutical sector in the registration of biosimilar products of biologics, drugs made from organic material that infringe upon patented U.S. biological products.

The GOP agency charged with promoting and defending intellectual property rights is the Antitrust, Unfair Competition, Intellectual Property Protection, Consumer Protection, Dumping, Standards and Elimination of Bureaucratic Barriers Agency (INDECOPI, www.indecopi.gob.pe), established in 1992. Peru belongs to the World Trade Organization (WTO) and the World Intellectual Property Organization (WIPO). It is also a signatory to the Paris Convention on Industrial Property, Geneva Convention for the Protection of Sound Recordings, Bern Convention for the Protection of Literary and Artistic Works, Brussels Convention on the Distribution of Satellite Signals, Phonograms Convention, Satellites Convention, Universal Copyright Convention, the World Copyright Treaty, and the World Performances and Phonographs Treaty and the Film Register Treaty. In December 1994, the Peruvian Congress ratified the World Trade Organization's Agreement on Trade-Related Aspects of Intellectual Property (TRIPs).

Pursuant to the terms of the PTPA, Peru has ratified or acceded to the following agreements: the Convention Relating to the Distribution of Program-Carrying Signals Transmitted by Satellite; the Budapest Treaty on the International Recognition of the Deposit of Microorganisms for the Purposes of Patent Procedure; the WIPO Copyright Treaty; the WIPO Performances and Phonograms Treaty; the Patent Cooperation Treaty; the Trademark Law Treaty; and, the International Convention for the Protection of New Varieties of Plants (UPOV Convention). Although Peru has ratified or acceded to several of the above agreements as part of its implementation of the PTPA, it has not yet fulfilled its PTPA commitments by ratifying or acceding to the following agreements: the Patent Law Treaty; the Hague Agreement Concerning the International Registration of Industrial Designs; and, the Protocol Relating to the Madrid Agreement Concerning the International Registration of Marks.

The GOP does not have a single database that tracks seized counterfeit goods. Moreover, the various Peruvian agencies/ministries do not share information, which results in conflicting and/or an imperfect survey. This information is not available to the public.

Customs officials have the authority to seize counterfeit goods. There is a process of rights holders to be notified for an inspection of the seized goods, but implementation of the process is inconsistent.

Piracy remains a prevalent problem in Peru. GOP officials recognize that the country will not achieve its full economic potential if IPR laws are not implemented more robustly to protect legitimate owners of trademarks, copyrights, and patents. Even Peruvian businesses complain that piracy is biting into their bottom lines, and are joining U.S. and foreign companies to engage the GOP on the economic costs of IPR violations. The World Economic Forum ranked Peru 119 out of 144 countries in its Global Competitiveness Index 2014-2015 (an improvement of one point from last year), significantly behind fellow Pacific Alliance members Chile (56), Mexico (82), and Colombia (96).

INDECOPI reports that hundreds of millions of dollars-worth of pirated goods are sold with impunity in notorious markets like "Polvos Azules," "El Hueco," and "Fronteras Unidas" in Lima. For example, El Hueco is full of shoppers buying the latest pirated movies even though it is located just a few blocks away from the national PNP headquarters. In the outer Andean and Amazon regions, notorious markets for pirated goods operate even more openly with little fear of interference from law enforcement (ref B).

Piracy is so common that notorious markets have fragmented into specializations. For instance, Lima's "Capon Center Mall" specializes in selling low-priced counterfeit medicines. During a July 2014 raid, PNP and SUNAT agents discovered that over 50% of all medicines sold at Capon were counterfeit. Gamarra, a district in Lima, is home to large notorious markets ("Galeria Azul," "Galeria Santa Lucia," "Galeria San Miguel," "Galeria Markata," and "Galeria Senor de Chacos") that specialize in counterfeit clothing. Even upscale districts in Lima like La Molina and Miraflores are home to well-known notorious markets like "La Esquina" and "La Quinta" where hawkers sell fake Gucci, Louis Vuitton, and other high-end merchandise.

GOP and private sector interlocutors note that piracy groups are utilizing internet tools to expand their business. Notorious markets are becoming more adept at using social media to promote and sell their goods, with Facebook being the social media of choice. For instance, "Fronteras Unidas'" Facebook page (**http://www.facebook.com/pages/galeria-fronteras-unidas-grau/173545512699294**) promotes the latest sales and discounts for new merchandise, looking as professional as legitimate companies that use Facebook. MINSA is concerned over the growth of counterfeit medicine moving towards online distribution and sales. One MINSA interlocutor noted that her office has insufficient resources to adequately monitor the ever growing number of unregistered websites offering deeply discounted and counterfeit medicines to the public.

Piracy in Peru is most rampant in software, music, and video content. The International Intellectual Property Alliance estimates that the piracy level for music is around 98% and nearly 100% for video content. The Software Business Alliance estimates that the piracy level for software is 65%, costing copyright holders an estimated USD 60 million in 2014. The Peruvian market is so saturated with pirated movies that there is no legitimate rental market for movies and few legitimate venues to buy legal DVDs of music and movies. Pirated movies sell for three to five Peruvian Nuevo Soles (PEN) (USD 1.00-1.65) per DVD while pirated books sell for less than a third of the price of licensed editions. Novels by noted Peruvian author Mario Vargas Llosa sell in stores for PEN 70 (USD 23.00) while illegal book venders sell it for PEN 25 Soles (USD 8.30). Customers can even use their cell phones to pay for downloading pirated movies. For example, PeliculaSONL (www.peliculasonl.com) allows customers to pay for weekly subscriptions through their Claro and Movistar (the two largest and legitimate cellular network providers) accounts to pay for illegal video downloads.

Resources for Rights Holders

Contact at Mission:

Benjamin Yates
Economic Officer
+51-1-618-2414
YatesBA@state.gov

A list of lawyers can be requested from the Embassy's Commercial Service Office (**Office.Lima@trade.gov**).

Country/Economy resources:

The American Chamber of Commerce in Peru can be contacted via this link:**http://www.amcham.org.pe/contactenos/escribanos.php**.

8. TRANSPARENCY OF THE REGULATORY SYSTEM

Regulatory transparency and independence have become central issues for foreign investors in Peru. Although many of the central government regulators related to foreign investment have relatively transparent and predictable procedures, delays and the lack of predictability in the rulings of these institutions, have been impediments to doing business in Peru.

The Securities Market Superintendence (SMV) maintains the company registry and supervises the securities market. ProInversion handles privatization and most concessions. INDECOPI handles competition policy, bankruptcy, and intellectual property matters. The Superintendence of Banking and Insurance (SBS) regulates banks, insurance companies, and private pension funds, including determination of whether potential market entrants qualify to operate in Peru.

When the GOP privatized state-owned monopolies in the areas of telecommunications, energy, and the hydrocarbons sector in the late 1990s, it also established regulatory institutions to oversee the new private sectors – among them OSIPTEL for telecom, and OSINERGMIN for energy, mining and hydrocarbons – the GOP created the Environmental Enforcement Organism (OEFA) in 2008 which is progressively taking over the environmental enforcement functions previously held by OSINERGMIN and other agencies.

In 2010, OSIPTEL established a "glide path" plan to continuously lower the mobile termination rates for all carriers by October 2013. This created a more favorable and competitive environment for the smaller carriers. In July 2014, OSIPTEL introduced number portability—which allows consumers to keep their mobile phone number despite changing service providers—and cut interconnection fees by 68% to spur competition and facilitate new entrants into the market. OSIPTEL also lowered costs for rural operators to facilitate mobile penetration. Since these changes, over 200,000 Peruvian consumers have switched providers.

U.S. and other non-Peruvian firms and investors have complained about the reinterpretation of rules and the imposition of disproportionate fines coupled with usurious interest charges on unpaid taxes or fines by the Peruvian tax agency, SUNAT. U.S. firms and other investors allege SUNAT's capricious behavior and reinterpretation of tax laws are often contrary to the spirit of the law and intent of government policies, thereby complicating and making normal business operations costlier. This situation may be at least be partly explained by the fact that the remuneration of SUNAT employees is partially determined by the theoretical tax liability they assess in audits. The U.S. Embassy continues to hear that this perverse incentive leads to overzealous tax collection practices.

Businesses point out that SUNAT's retroactive reinterpretation of regulations and laws, levying of disproportionate fines, usurious interest rates on the alleged assessments and below market interest rates on payable tax rebates, lengthy resolution processes, and initiation of full company audits when companies request a refund or legal revaluation of assets for depreciation purposes, create additional investment and trade barriers. In one case, a U.S. firm requested, by clerical mistake, an improper drawback of USD 1,345, only to face SUNAT fines of USD 645,000. Although the case was resolved, legislation now allows for an independent tax tribunal to serve as a check on alleged abuses by SUNAT. However, when SUNAT exercises its right of appeal against unfavorable tax tribunal rulings, the disputed assessments and liabilities on companies' balance sheets are prolonged. As a balance to this tendency, a tax ombudsman must approve SUNAT's request to appeal adverse tax tribunal decisions. At times, the ombudsman has also acted to end unwarranted litigation of disputed assessments. For example, in 2005, a U.S. company won long-standing tax cases against SUNAT as a result of these improvements. Nevertheless, the U.S. Embassy has heard of cases of companies deciding to pay long-disputed assessments in order to eliminate liabilities from their books. A conspicuous case was that of a Canadian bank, which in late-February 2014 decided to pay under protest approximately USD 170 million in tax liabilities, most of it accumulated interest. In recent years a number of companies have opened international arbitration cases against the GOP.

Businesses also complain about high health insurance and pension tax rates, and state that these tax policies hinder investment capital flows. The lack of a U.S.-Peru treaty on double taxation is also a disincentive to foreign investment.

9. EFFICIENT CAPITAL MARKETS AND PORTFOLIO INVESTMENT

Credit is allocated on market terms and the banking industry in Peru is generally considered competitive in offering services to business customers. Private pension funds have keenly competed in recent years with financial companies for bonds issued locally by companies and the GOP. These entities compete because the supply of local securities is insufficient given the small size of the market. Under the PTPA, U.S. financial service suppliers have full rights to establish subsidiaries or branches for banks and insurance companies.

The private sector has access to a variety of credit instruments. In 2013, firms placed USD 1.75 billion on the local bond market, 3.7% below the year earlier. Mutual funds managed USD 5.9 billion in December 2013, a large 16.3% decrease from the December 2013 level. Private pension funds managed a total of USD 36.2 billion in December 2013. (Full 2014 Statistics are not yet available.)

The Securities Market Superintendence (SMV) is the GOP entity charged with regulating the securities and commodities markets. Following the IMF's recommendations, the GOP passed a law reforming the SMV's predecessor, CONASEV (the National Commission for the Supervision of Companies, Securities and Exchanges). SMV's mandate includes controlling securities market participants, maintaining a transparent and orderly market, setting accounting standards, and publishing financial information about covered companies. SMV requires stock issuers to report events that may affect the stock, the company, or any public offerings. This requirement promotes market transparency, and aims to prevent fraud. Trading on insider information is a crime, with some reported prosecutions in past years. One case at the end of 2010 involved three (government-owned health care provider) ESSALUD employees, a stock brokerage firm and an employee of the stock brokerage firm. CONASEV fined these individuals and the stock brokerage firm, and their cases are moving through the Peruvian court system. SMV must vet all firms listed on the Lima Stock Exchange (Bolsa de Valores de Lima) or the Public Registry of Securities. SMV also maintains the Public Registry of Securities and Stock Brokers. SMV is studying ways to improve the regulatory system to encourage and facilitate portfolio investment.

MONEY AND BANKING SYSTEM, HOSTILE TAKEOVERS

The banking system is considered generally sound, thanks to lessons learned during the 1997-1998 Asian crises, and continues to revamp operations, increase capitalization, and reduce costs. Under the SBS's conservative criteria, non-performing loans rose in the last two years, to 2.14% of total loans as of December 2013, yet down from a high of 11% in early 2001. Able bank supervision and strong GDP growth over the last decade through 2014 also helped banks weather the 2008-2009 global financial crises with little trouble.

Economic opening since the 1990s, coupled with competition, has led to banking sector consolidation. Sixteen commercial banks comprise the system, with assets accounting for 88.9% of Peru's financial system. Three banks account for 73% of local loans and deposits among commercial banks. Of USD 93.2 billion in total banking assets at the end of December 2013, assets of the three largest commercial banks amounted to USD 67.3 billion. As of December 2013, foreigners had significant shares in thirteen banks, of which they were majority owners of eleven (including one of the country's largest ones) and operator of one of the largest commercial banks. Notably, two of the four banks that are majority-owned by residents account for 45.1% of commercial banks' assets.

Peru's financial system has 12 specialized institutions ("financieras"), 31 thriving micro-lenders and savings banks (although several large banks also lend to small enterprises), two leasing institutions, two state-owned banks, and one state-owned development bank. In 2013, the Economist Intelligence Unit again ranked Peru number one worldwide on microfinance business environment for the sixth consecutive year because of its sophisticated legal and regulatory framework and competitive microfinance sector. Nevertheless, Peru's over 150 savings and loan cooperatives operate in an environment almost devoid of government oversight.

Peruvian law and regulations do not authorize or encourage private firms to adopt articles of incorporation or association to limit or restrict foreign participation. There are no private or public sector efforts to restrict foreign participation in industry standards-setting organizations. However, larger private firms often use "cross-shareholding" and "stable shareholder" arrangements to restrict investment by outsiders -- not necessarily foreigners -- in their firms. As close families or associates generally control ownership of Peruvian corporations, hostile takeovers are practically non-existent. In the past few years, several companies from the region, China, North America, and Europe have actively been buying local companies in power transmission, retail trade, fishmeal production, and other industries.

10. COMPETITION FROM STATE-OWNED ENTERPRISES

Several electricity, water and sewage, bank, and oil companies remain state-owned and state-operated. The most notable area of SOE activity pertains to the petroleum sector, where the state-owned petroleum company PetroPeru is an oil refiner and operator of an underutilized oil pipeline. Congress passed several laws since which purport to strengthen PetroPeru and free it from bureaucratic controls, so that it can enter into all stages of the petroleum and petrochemical sectors, especially upstream. In 2008, PetroPeru took center stage in a corruption scandal related to oil and gas concessions. The scandal led to the resignation of the Minister of Energy and Mines and the PetroPeru President and forced the GOP to implement a number of changes in PetroPeru's management. Over the last two decades, PetroPeru has experienced significant attrition in managerial and technical expertise. This, coupled with its limited financial resources, cast into doubt the company's ability to implement its long-held plans to expand and upgrade its aging Talara refinery – which continues to produce dirty gasoline and diesel fuel, a situation the government permits by not enforcing regulatory standards. Limited resources and expertise also downplay expectations following repeated announcements from its leadership regarding entrance to upstream, and participation in a proposed gas pipeline and petrochemical complex in southern Peru. Up until recently, PetroPeru's leadership's plans even included a return to oil production through participation in tenders of oil producing blocks that the GOP was set to auction in 2013, with a requirement to partner with PetroPeru. Limited or no interest shown by oil companies in that auction and in several exploration blocs' pending auctions, have left those plans up in the air.

Significant SOEs have audited accounts that are made public. In addition, the accounts are monitored by a board of directors. The majority of the country's SOEs is corporately managed by FONAFE and is listed on FONAFE's website along with their audited accounts (**http://www.fonafe.gob.pe/portal/empresas?accion=transparenciaNew&m=6&Contenidoid=32**). Petroperu, which is managed independently from FONAFE, publishes a report that includes the audited financial statements of the company, such as those of comprehensive income, changes in equity, and cash flows, as well as a summary of significant accounting policies and other explanatory notes included in Petroperu's financial statements. The report is produced annually and is publicly available on Petroperu's website (**http://www.petroperu.com.pe/transparencia/ley27806.asp**).

11. CORPORATE SOCIAL RESPONSIBILITY

Peruvian businesses participate in Corporate Social Responsibility (CSR) programs, primarily on a voluntary basis. For the energy and mining sector, certain regulations do exist to promote social responsibility. Supreme Decree No. 042-2003-EM promotes social responsibility within the mining sector, encouraging local employment opportunities, support to communities' projects, development activities, and purchase of local goods and services. The decree requires mining companies to publish an annual report on sustainable development activities. The Ministry of Energy and Mines has prepared a guidebook for community relations, as well as public information on social measures related to the mining and energy sectors. In February 2011, INDECOPI adopted the Peruvian Technical Regulation of Social Responsibility ISO 26000 that serves as a voluntary guide to CSR activities.

On February 15, 2012, Peru was listed as a compliant country under the Extractive Industries Transparency Initiative (EITI), as the GOP and extractive industries openly publish all company payments and government revenues from oil, gas, and mining. Peru is the only EITI-compliant country in Latin America.

Peru continues to implement its 2013-2017 National Strategy to Combat Forced Labor, which emphasizes the state's role to protect and promote labor rights. The plan simultaneously prioritizes building capacity and empowering vulnerable groups to transform their environment and enforce their rights. The plan addresses both medium and long-term multi-sector plans to eliminate or reduce conditions that enable forced labor. Despite these efforts, the government did not effectively enforce labor laws in all cases. Child labor, particularly in informal sectors, forced labor, and employers engaging in antiunion practices remain significant problems.

12. POLITICAL VIOLENCE

Although political violence against investors is rare, protests, sometimes violent, have taken place in or near communities with extractive industry operations. Environmental concerns were often the cited pretext. Protestors often object to the fact that environmental impact assessments are reviewed by the Ministry of Energy and Mines, rather than the Ministry of Environment, when in fact, the Ministry of Environment along with other national agencies do participate in assessment reviews. In many cases, protestors sought public services not provided by the government. Ideological opposition to foreign mining firms, not opposition to mining itself, often leads to protest in communities incited by NGOs. In some cases, organizers from outside the local community are brought in to foment protests against the companies. Groups blocked roads and an airport in 2014 to protest extractive industry operations; hydroelectric projects; restrictions on informal gold mining, gas exports, and the Government's coca eradication policies. In several of these protests, police and civilians were injured or killed. As of February 2015, the Ombudsperson's Office reported 211 conflicts in Peru; 67% of these conflicts involve socio-economic concerns, usually linked to extractive industries.

Politically motivated movements at times have opposed large extractive projects. In some cases, these movements have been successful in delaying large investments, as occurred in the USD 4.8 billion Conga mine project in Cajamarca in August 2012. In other cases, protests have stopped such investments entirely.

The National Office of Dialogue and Sustainability is actively engaged in mitigating social conflict connected to the extractive industry in Peru. This office addresses conflict in a broader community development context, rather than only responding to social conflicts after they have already erupted. To this end, the government is providing more education, infrastructure, and health care services in areas where extractive industry projects are planned or under development, which will increase government presence and reduce potential for conflict in those (historically underserved and often remote) areas.

Peru's Prior Consultation Law was signed in 2011, and its implementing regulations were approved in 2012. The law requires the GOP to consult with indigenous communities before enacting any legislation, administrative measures, or development projects that could affect communities' rights of territorial demarcation. There have been several successful prior consultation processes related to the extractive industry, but the law remains controversial. Critics believe it creates burdensome processes and results in delays. The industry association Peruvian Society of Hydrocarbons alleges that work on 30 oil exploration blocks is paralyzed due to lengthy permit processing. The National Society of Mining, Electricity and Petroleum (SNMPE) and the government have become involved in assisting local governments to access the extractive industry "canon" (tax revenue-sharing scheme with funding for public works projects) as a way to both stimulate local development and prevent conflicts. Although these efforts have been effective in some mining regions, in others, conflicts have continued or expanded.

Violence remains a concern in coca-growing regions. The government reported that through October 2014, the Shining Path conducted 18 terrorist acts, resulting in the death of two soldiers and two civilians, as well as injuries to six soldiers, seven civilians, and one police officer in the Apurimac, Ene, and Mantaro River Valleys (VRAEM) emergency zone, which includes parts of Ayacucho, Cusco, Huancavelica, Huanuco, and Junin regions. A separate emergency zone in the Upper Huallaga Valley (UHV) includes parts of San Martin and Ucayali regions. There were reports that the Shining Path abducted children to work for the terrorist organization during the year. The Humala government continues the longstanding practice of authorizing separate 60-day states of emergency in two areas where the Shining Path operates – the Apurimac, Ene, and Mantaro River Valleys (VRAEM) and the Upper Huallaga Valley. On September 11, 2014 the GOP declared a new emergency zone in the Loreto region due to drug trafficking activity. The state of emergency authorization suspends some civil liberties and gives the security forces additional authority to maintain public order.

There is little government presence in the remote coca-growing zones of the VRAEM and Upper Huallaga Valley, although significant ramp-up of government presence and programs is underway. The U.S. Embassy in Lima restricts visits by official personnel to these areas because of the threat of violence by narcotics traffickers and columns of the Shining Path. Information about insecure areas and recommended personal security practices can be found at **http://www.osac.gov** or**http://travel.state.gov**.

13. CORRUPTION

It is illegal in Peru for a public official or employee to accept any type of outside remuneration for the performance of his or her official duties. Peru has ratified both the UN Convention against Corruption and the Organization of American States Inter-American Convention against Corruption. Peru is not a member of the Organization of Economic Cooperation and Development (OECD), but it signed a Country Program agreement in December 2014 to provide an anchor for policy reforms aimed at meeting OECD standards and practices. It has not signed the OECD Convention on Combating Bribery, although it has participated as an observer in the Working Group. The Contraloría General is the responsible government agency for overseeing proper procedures in public administration, thus ends up being responsible in combating corruption.

U.S. firms have reported problems resulting from corruption, usually in government procurement processes and in the judicial sector, with defense and police procurement generally considered among the most problematic in spite of PTPA's stipulations and of Peru's Government Procurement Law (Legislative Decree No. 1017, DL 1017, one of several laws passed with the specific intention to implement PTPA). Transparency International ranked Peru 85th out of 175 countries in its 2014 Corruption Perceptions Index, two points lower than 2013.

At the end of 2014, three former regional presidents – roughly equivalent to U.S. state governors – were in jail awaiting trial on corruption charges while a fourth was a fugitive from justice. Three newly elected regional presidents – sworn into office January 1, 2015 – were facing legal problems: two had been sentenced to jail for crimes they committed prior to assuming office but remained at their posts while they appealed; the third was barred from assuming office for failure to pay a USD 333,000 fine associated with a prior bribery conviction. A study published in May of 2014 by the office of the anti-corruption solicitor reported that 92 percent of the over 1,800 district-level mayors in office between 2011 and 2014 had been investigated for criminal activity. Ten percent of sitting members of congress had been suspended for ethical violations since taking office in 2011.

The Peruvian armed forces and national police continue to prefer to execute government-to-government procurements (i.e., purchases by a GOP agency from a foreign government agency or government-owned company). This practice has impeded the participation of U.S. companies in GOP procurement, mainly with the Ministries of Defense and Interior. The Embassy is currently trying to reach an agreement with the Ministry of Interior that could be acceptable for both parties. In July 2012, the Government Procurement Supervisory Agency ruled that government-to-government procurements do not fall under the government procurement law (DL 1017). An article in the 2013 Budget Law also specified that procurements by the GOP from another state are not under the scope of DL 1017. Since then, there have been a number of local media reports of overvalued prices in several government-to-government purchases, of goods or services for the police or the armed forces. Cases include purchases of a satellite, planes, helicopters, and technical assistance training. Overvaluation has apparently occurred even in the case of open tenders, as in the notorious recent case of the purchase of 591 binoculars by the Interior Ministry for the National Police in December 2013. El Comercio, Peru's paper-of-record, published a report in January 2014 alleging the Interior Ministry bought 591 binoculars at a price more than ten times the market rate. In early-March 2014, local media reported that the Public Prosecutor's Office would investigate a technical assistance-training procurement made in 2009 by the Armed Forces Joint Command. This probe comes after the Comptroller General found irregularities and circumstantial evidence of collusion, embezzlement and other crimes. During 2014, the press published articles alleging that Peruvian Air Force officers had accepted kickbacks for illegally selling fuel on the open market.

UN Anticorruption Convention, OECD Convention on Combatting Bribery

Peru signed the UN Anticorruption Convention on December 10, 2003 and ratified it on November 16, 2004.

Peru is not a participating country of the OECD Convention on Combating Bribery of Foreign Public Officials in International Business Transactions.

Resources to Report Corruption

Contact at government agency or agencies are responsible for combating corruption:

Sara Arobes
a.i Technical Secretary
High Commission to Fight Corruption (CAN)
Jr. Carabaya Cdra. 1 S/N - Lima,
(51) (1) 219-7000, ext. 7202
sarobes@pcm.gob.pe

Soraya Altabas
Officer of Technical Cooperation
General Comptroller's Office
Jr. Camilo Carrillo 114, Jesus Maria, Lima

(51) (1) 330-3000, ext.
faltabas@contraloria.gob.pe

Contact at "watchdog" organization (international, regional, local or nongovernmental organization operating in the country/economy that monitors corruption, such as Transparency International):

Samuel Rotta
a.i Executive Director
ProEtica, the Peruvian chapter of Transparency International
Calle Manco Capac 816, Miraflores, Lima
(51) (1) 446-8581, 446-8941, 446-8943
srotta@proetica.org.pe

14. BILATERAL INVESTMENT AGREEMENTS

The United States-Peru Trade Promotion Agreement (PTPA) eliminated the need for a bilateral investment agreement between the United States and Peru. Peru also has free trade agreements with Canada, Chile, China, Colombia, Costa Rica, the European Free Trade Association (which includes Iceland, Liechtenstein, Norway and Switzerland), Japan, Mexico, Panama, Singapore, South Korea, and Thailand. It has Framework Agreements with MERCOSUR countries (Argentina, Brazil, Paraguay, Uruguay, and Venezuela). It has a partial preferential agreement with Cuba. More agreements have been signed and are awaiting full implementation, including with Guatemala, and the Pacific Alliance (Mexico, Colombia, Chile, and Costa Rica).

Peru has bilateral investment agreements in force with Argentina, Bolivia, Canada, Chile, China, Colombia, Costa Rica, Czech Republic, Denmark, Ecuador, El Salvador, Finland, Italy, Korea, Netherlands, Norway, Paraguay, Portugal, Romania, Spain, Sweden, Switzerland, Thailand, United Kingdom, Venezuela, and the European Union.

BILATERAL TAXATION TREATIES

Peru does not have a bilateral taxation treaty with the U.S.

15. OPIC AND OTHER INVESTMENT INSURANCE PROGRAMS

The Overseas Private Investment Corporation (OPIC), an independent U.S. Government agency, offers medium-to-long-term financing and political risk insurance. From 2010 thru 2014, OPIC supported solar power plants, consumer lending, operation and expansion of retail stores, microfinance, installation/operation of stereotactic radiosurgery equipment, consulting services, export services, import-export logistical services, and portfolio expansion of SME, micro-credit and consumer loans, in the form of commitments totaling more than USD 21 million.

Because of the free convertibility of currency, the U.S. Embassy purchases Peruvian currency for expenses on an as-needed basis at the market exchange rate. The USD averaged PEN 2.84/USD in 2014. Peru is a member of the Multilateral Investment Guarantee Agency.

It is unlikely that the GOP would either devalue or revalue the Nuevo Sol. The foreign exchange market mostly operates freely. However, the Peruvian BCR intervenes in the foreign exchange market to prevent significant exchange rate variations – at times day after day. To many observers, this regime has succeeded in avoiding traumatic foreign exchange adjustments to the economy.

16. LABOR

Labor is abundant, although several large investment projects in recent years led to localized shortages of highly skilled workers in some fields. While the legal framework to uphold international labor standards is well-defined, the government did not effectively enforce the law in all cases.

Mining sector contacts praise the technical knowledge and professional dedication of Peruvian engineering graduates. Since the 1960s, the number of jobs created by the Peruvian economy was consistently below the number of new entrants to the labor market. The situation meant underemployment or seeking work in the informal economy. According to the National Bureau for Statistics (INEI), 74.3% of the labor force is informal.

The statutory monthly minimum wage is PEN 750/month (approximately USD 242). INEI estimated the poverty line to be PEN 292/month (USD 92) per person, although it varied by region due to different living costs. The Ministry of Labor (MOL) enforces the minimum wage only in the formal sector. Many workers in the unregulated informal sector, most of them self-employed, make less than the minimum wage. Wages are sometimes higher than U.S. wages in the mining sector for management positions and consulting services. Workers in Peru are paid by the month, not by the year. Some workers, like formal miners, are highly paid and also (per statute) receive a share of company profits up to a maximum total annual amount of 18 times their base monthly salary. Current labor law provides for a 48-hour work week and one day of rest, and requires companies to pay overtime for more than eight hours of work per day and additional compensation for work at night. Noncompliance with the law is a punishable infraction. There is no prohibition on excessive compulsory overtime. Micro-enterprise workers are entitled to social security and pensions.

Peruvian labor law requires that employees provide advance notice to the MOL before holding a strike, with the new legislation not being as permissive as before. According to the MOL, 95 strikes took place in the private sector in 2014, just 1.1% above 2013, but person-hours lost almost doubled, for a total of 3.153 million work hours. Unions in what the government determines are "essential public services" are permitted to call a strike but must provide 10 working days' notice, receive the approval of the MOL, be approved by a simple majority of workers, and provide a sufficient number of workers during a strike to maintain operations, as jointly determined by the union and labor authorities on an annual basis. As of September 2014, the MOL registered 53 total strikes during 2014, 48 of which were declared illegal. According to labor leaders permission to strike was difficult to obtain. The MOL justified its decisions by citing failure of unions to fulfill the legal requirements necessary to strike.

The labor procedure (No.29497) law requires that labor conflicts be resolved in less than six months, allows unions or their representatives to appear in court on behalf of workers, requires proceedings to be conducted orally and video-recorded, and relieves the employee from the burden of proving an employer-employee relationship. At year's end, the labor procedure law was in effect in at least 25 of the 31 judicial districts in Peru.

July 2014 labor reforms to the Occupational Safety and Health (OSH) Law and inspection law allow employers to outsource the management of health and safety to third-party service providers. Employers are now responsible for conducting one health exam every two years, rather than every year, which labor NGOs and unions were concerned leaves short-term contracted workers exposed to industrial illness. These reforms narrow the justification for a criminal penalty to only those cases where employers have "deliberately" violated safety and health laws and where labor authorities have previously notified employers who have chosen not to adopt measures in response to a repeated infraction. Labor experts and NGOs expressed concern about what they considered an unreasonably high threshold for holding employers accountable for workplace injuries and for not maintaining health and safety standards. The law reduces the sentence for employers found guilty of health and safety violations from four-to-eight years' to one-to-four years' imprisonment. In the case of a serious or fatal accident where a worker is found to be solely responsible for noncompliance with OSH rules, the employer is exempted from responsibility.

Six percent of the labor force in the private sector was organized in 2014, with unionization highest in electricity, water, construction, and mining (from 39% to 22%) and generally low in the rest of economy. Unemployment in Lima officially stood at 6.9%% during the first quarter of 2014. A 2012 GOP survey showed that 41.1% of Lima's labor force was underemployed in the same period (versus 58.3% in the same period of 2011). The average nominal monthly salary increased 8.0% year-on-year in the fourth quarter of 2013, INEI reported. The ILO's Global Wage Report 2012/2013 released in December 2012 stated that average real wages in Peru grew at over 3% per annum between 2004 and 2011.

The law forbids businesses from hiring subcontracted workers as a simple provision of personnel, requires businesses to monitor their contractors with respect to labor rights, and imposes liability on businesses for the actions of their contractors, and created a national registry of contracting companies. The PTPA requires Peru to adopt and maintain fundamental labor rights as stated in the ILO Declaration on Fundamental Principles and Rights at Work. In January 2010, the GOP and U.S. Government established the bilateral Labor Affairs Council as mandated in Article 17.5 of the PTPA.

According to labor leaders, the current labor law has weakened unions in part because companies create competing unions that are seen as more favorable to management. Workers in probation status or on short-term contracts are not eligible for union membership. Bargaining agreements are considered contractual agreements, valid only for the life of the contract. Productivity provisions must be included in any collective bargaining agreement. The amount of time union officials may devote to union work is limited to 30 days per year. Unless there is a pre-existing labor contract covering an occupation or industry as a whole, unions must negotiate with each company individually.

The government did not effectively enforce the law in all cases. Penalties for violations of freedom of association and collective bargaining exist, but were rarely enforced. Workers faced prolonged judicial processes and lack of enforcement following trade union activity-related dismissals. For instance, NGOs reported that emblematic cases of labor arbitration dating from 2013 remained in limbo, with the implementation of arbitrators' decisions delayed by ongoing judicial appeals processes.

In practice, workers faced some challenges in exercising their rights of freedom of association and collective bargaining. Unions were generally independent of government and political parties. Employers continued to dismiss workers for exercising the right to strike. Dismissal of striking workers and delays in reinstatement of these workers, in both legal and illegal strikes, was the main tactic used by employers to dissuade workers from going on strike. Labor leaders and the ILO argue that current labor laws erode labor protections and encourage outsourcing in ways that undercut union activity.

Either unions or management can request binding arbitration in contract negotiations. Strikes can be called only after approval by a majority of all workers (union and non-union), voting by secret ballot, and only in defense of labor rights. Unions in essential public services, as determined by the government, must provide a sufficient number of workers during a strike to maintain operations.

The government created in April 2014 the National Labor Superintendence (SUNAFIL, for its Spanish acronym) and opened nine regional offices to represent the labor inspectorate nationally.

All labor in the (very small) export processing zones (EPZs) is subcontracted. With the exception of enjoying greater flexibility in hiring temporary labor, there are no special laws or exemptions from regular labor laws in EPZs.

Foreign employees may not comprise more than 20% of the total number of employees of a local company (whether owned by foreign or Peruvian persons) or more than 30% of the total company payroll. However, under the PTPA, Peru has agreed not to apply most of its nationality-based hiring requirements to U.S. professionals and specialty personnel. Peru also has bilateral agreements with Spain and Argentina, for example, so that Spaniards and Argentines working in Peru do not count as foreigners and vice versa.

17. FOREIGN TRADE ZONES/FREE PORTS/TRADE FACILITATION

Peruvian law currently covers two types of trade zones: export, transformation, industry, trade and services zones (CETICOS), and a free trade zone (ZOFRATACNA) in Tacna. The rules and tax benefits applying to these zones are the same for foreign and national investors. These zones have failed to attract any sizeable investment, and their importance for Peru's economy is negligible.

CETICOS exist at Ilo, Matarani and Paita. One CETICO is authorized in Loreto department, but is not operational. There is concern that the GOP does not have the proper WTO waivers to validate the CETICOS export requirement. The U.S. automotive industry has expressed a specific concern that U.S. brands are unable to compete with used Japanese vehicles that enter the Peruvian market duty-free through the CETICOS. The Ministry of Transportation and Communications banned the importation of right-hand drive vehicles in 2013, citing environmental and safety concerns. Imports of used cars more than five years old and used buses and trucks more than two years old are prohibited.

18. FOREIGN DIRECT INVESTMENT AND FOREIGN PORTFOLIO INVESTMENT STATISTICS

The stock of foreign direct investment in Peru stood at USD 73.6 billion in December 2013 according to the BCR, up from USD 63.4 billion at the end of 2012. According to the most recent data from the BCR, the largest investors in Peru are the United States, Canada, Spain, and Chile. By industry, the main investment destinations are mining (29%), services (24%), oil and gas (17%), manufacturing (10%), finance (13%), and energy (6%).

U.S. foreign direct investment in Peru amounted to USD 10.9 billion in 2012, a 21.4% increase from 2011, according to the U.S. Department of Commerce Bureau of Economic Analysis. Of that sum, USD 4.1 billion was invested in mining, USD 1 billion in manufacturing, and USD 319 million in wholesale trade.

Major foreign direct investments included Xstrata (Switzerland), Hunt Oil (U.S.), Newmont Mining Corporation (U.S.), BHP Billiton (Australia), Cencosud Internacional Limitada (Chile), Endesa Latinoamericana (Spain), Freeport-McMoRan (U.S.), Golds Fields Corona (South Africa), SN Power Peru (Norway), Compania Minera Latino-Americana (Chile), Sempra Energy (U.S.), Citibank (U.S.), Southern Peru Copper (Mexico), Pluspetrol (Argentina), Scotiabank (Canada), Telefonica (Spain), Repsol (Spain), Gerdau (Brazil), Anglo American (United Kingdom), Invercale (Chile), Asa Iberoamerica (Spain), Fraport AG Frankfurt Airport Services Worldwide (Germany), Aeropuertos Andinos del Peru (Argentina), Odebrecht (Brazil), and the Falabella Group (Chile). When completed, Glencore-Xstrata's USD 5.2 billion Las Bambas copper mine project in Apurimac will rank as Peru's largest foreign direct investment ever. The multi-year Hunt Oil-led investment is part of a consortium that invested USD 3.8 billion to develop a natural gas liquefaction plant, maritime terminal, and pipeline in southern Peru.

Peru's direct investment abroad amounts to USD 2.1 billion, according to the BCR. Peruvian investment in Chile, Brazil, the United States, and Bolivia comprised the vast majority of Peru's direct investment abroad.

Table 2: Key Macroeconomic Data, U.S. FDI in Host Country/Economy

	Host Country Statistical source*		USG or International Statistical source		USG or International Source of Data: BEA; IMF; Eurostat; UNCTAD, Other
Economic Data	Year	Amount	Year	Amount	
Host Country Gross Domestic Product (GDP) ($M USD)	2013	193,214	2013	202,350	www.worldbank.org/en/country
Foreign Direct Investment	Host Country Statistical source*		USG or International Statistical source		USG or International Source of data: BEA; IMF; Eurostat; UNCTAD, Other
U.S. FDI in partner country ($M USD, stock positions)	2013	No data	2013	10,061	BEA data available at http://www.bea.gov/iTable/iTable.cfm?ReqID=2&step=1#reqid=2&step=7&isuri=1&202=1&203=30&204=10&205=1,2&200=1&201=1
Host country's FDI in the United States ($M USD, stock positions)	2013	No data	2013	100	BEA data available at http://www.bea.gov/iTable/iTable.cfm?ReqID=2&step=1#reqid=2&step=7&isuri=1&202=1&203=22&204=10&205=1,2&200=2&201=1
Total inbound stock of FDI as % host GDP	2014	No data	2014	No data	N/A

*Peruvian statistical sources: **http://www.mef.gob.pe/index.php?option=com_content&view=article&id=1116&Itemid=100233&lang=es**; **http://elibrary-data.imf.org/DataReport.aspx?c=11666795&d=33061&e=171392**; **http://www.bea.gov/international/di1usdbal.htm**

Table 3: Sources and Destination of FDI

(The chart does not reflect committed investment yet to be executed, for example China Minmetals' Las Bambas project.)

Direct Investment from/in Counterpart Economy Data
From Top Five Sources/To Top Five Destinations (US Dollars, Millions)

INWARD DIRECT INVESTMENT			OUTWARD DIRECT INVESTMENT		
Total Inward	38,841	100%	Total Outward	1,239	100%
United States	9,199	24%	Chile	367	30%
Canada	4,710	12%	United States	267	22%
Spain	3,700	10%	Panama	212	17%
Panama	2,803	7%	Jamaica	194	16%
Cayman Islands	2,590	7%	Bolivia	116	9%
"0" reflects amounts rounded to +/- USD 500,000.					

Source: IMF Coordinated Direct Investment Survey

INVESTMETN AND BUSINESS CONTACTS

CONTACT FOR MORE INFORMATION

Benjamin A. Yates
Economic Officer
U.S. Embassy, Av. La Encalada Cdra. 17 s/n, Monterrico, Lima 33, Peru
(51-1) 618-2410
econlima@state.gov

LOCAL LAWYERS

CRIMINAL LAW - NARCOTICS Garcia de Piccetti, Consuelo

Jr. Carabaya 1011 of. 208 Lima Tel: 428-1647; Fax 424-0566 Cellular: 9-630-2029 e-mail:cpiccetti@yahoo.com

Bobadilla Rojas, Jaime

Jr. Miroquesada 376 of 503 Lima Tel y Fax: 427-9993; 428-3308 Cellular: 9-302-4355.

Obregon Ramirez, Rina

Pso. De La República 589 of 504 La Victoria Tel: 337-6239 Cel: 99995-4714

Albrecht Mas, César Raúl

Calle Daniel Alcides Carrión Nº 186 San Isidro, Lima 27, Tel: 221-2172 Cel: 98103-3450.
calbrecht@estudioangulo.com

Angulo Portocarrero, José Carlos

Calle Daniel Alcides Carrión Nº 186 San Isidro, Lima 27, Tel: 221-2172 Cel: 99415-8201
jangulo@estudioangulo.com

ESTATES / PROBATE LAW / GENERAL PRACTICE/BUSINESS LAW, CONSUMER PROTECTION, UNFAIR COMPETITION Garcia de Piccetti, Consuelo

Jr. Carabaya 1011 of. 208 Lima Tel: 428-1647; Fax: 424-0566 Cellular: 9-630-2029 e-mail:cpiccetti@yahoo.com www.geocities.com/egarpic

Del Mar Abogados

Rivera Navarrete 765, piso 5 San Isidro Tel: 444-6400 e-mail: www.delmarabogados.com

ESTATES / PROBATE LAW / GENERAL PRACTICE/BUSINESS LAW, CONSUMER PROTECTION, UNFAIR COMPETITION Echeandia, Manini, Padron y Asociados

Av. Los Castaños 335 San Isidro 442-6283/442-2730 Fax: 221-1688 e-mail: estudio@estuem.com.pe

Oscar Renato Carrera Dongo

Los Aromos 165, el Remanso La Molina Tel: 9-788-1969 e-mail: rcarrera@pat-abogados.com

FAMILY LAW Garcia de Piccetti, Consuelo

Jr. Carabaya 1011 of. 208, Lima Tel: 428-1647; Cellular: 9-630-2029 e-mail:cpiccetti@yahoo.com

Albrecht Mas, César Raúl

Calle Daniel Alcides Carrión Nº 186 San Isidro, Lima 27, Tel: 221-2172 Cel: 98103-3450. calbrecht@estudioangulo.com

Cok Pita, Lucía Meilú Siulián

Calle Daniel Alcides Carrión Nº 186 San Isidro, Lima 27, Tel: 221-2172 Cel: 99410-0135 lcok@estudioangulo.com

Del Mar Abogados

Rivera Navarrete 765, piso 5 San Isidro Tel: 444-6400 e-mail: www.delmarabogados.com

Fishman, Emilia

Pasaje Los Pinos 190, of 502 Miraflores Tel: 445-9380 / 446-4842 Fax: 446-4198 Celular: 9-348-5760

GENERAL PRACTICE Angulo Portocarrero & Abogados

Calle Daniel Alcides Carrión Nº 186 San Isidro, Lima 27, Tel: 221-2172 Fax: 441-4566 info@estudioangulo.com

Benites, Forno y Ugaz

Guillermo Marconi 165 San Isidro Tel: 615-9090 Fax: 447-5022 E-mail:bmu@bmu.com.pe www.bmu.com.pe

Del Mar Abogados

Rivera Navarrete 765, piso 5 San Isidro Tel: 444-6400 e-mail: www.delmarabogados.com

Piccetti Garcia, Cosuelo

Jr. Carabaya 1011, of 208 Lima. Tel: 428-1647:Fax: 424-0566 Cellular: 9-900-3494 cpiccetti@yahoo.com

Del Castillo Abogados

Santa Luisa 178 San Isidro Tel: 421-4765, 422-5773 Fax: 440-8645

IMMIGRATION LAW

Estudio Julio Cesar Villegas Abogados Law Palmeras 445 San Isidro Tel: 441-9273, 422-8640 Fax: 442-7707 Main Fields of Practice: Immigration Law, Personal Injury Law, General Practice Languages Spoken: English, Spanish

PERSONAL INJURY LAW

Benites, Forno & Ugaz Guillermo Marconi 165 San Isidro Tel: 615-9090 Fax: 615-9091 E-mail:bmu@bmu.com.pe www.bmu.com.pe

TAX LAW

Estudio Julio Cesar Villegas Abogados Law Palmeras 445 San Isidro Tel: 441-9273, 422-8640 Fax: 442-7707

SURINAME - INVESTMENT AND BUSINESS CLIMATE - STRATEGIC INFORMATION AND CONTACTS FOR STARTING BUSINESS

The Government of Suriname officially supports and encourages business development through foreign and local investment. Currently, mining and crude oil attract the vast majority of large scale investment. U.S. multinational Newmont will invest close to USD 1 billion to construct a gold mine scheduled to become operational by the end of 2016, and U.S. companies participate in offshore oil exploration projects. The overall investment climate favors U.S. investors with experience working in developing countries. In addition to mining and oil, opportunities for U.S. businesses exist in agriculture. Issues to watch include the government's lack of capacity, corruption, and a lack of highly skilled labor. While the government does not officially discriminate against foreign investment, a non-transparent screening mechanism for investment, foreign and domestic alike, does constitute a barrier to all investment.

1. OPENNESS TO, AND RESTRICTIONS UPON, FOREIGN INVESTMENT

ATTITUDE TOWARD FOREIGN DIRECT INVESTMENT

The Government of Suriname (GOS) officially considers foreign direct investment an important contribution towards developing the country. The GOS Development Plan 2012-2016 identifies bilateral and multilateral partners as well as private foreign investors as important means to develop the economy. The GOS created the Investment Development Corporation in April 2014 but it appears to be a marketing vehicle without any policy or regulatory role at present.

Suriname has no investment laws or policies which discriminate against foreign investors by prohibiting, limiting or conditioning foreign investment in most sectors. Oil is the exception where the state-owned oil company, Staatsolie, maintains sole ownership of all oil-related activities. Foreign investment is possible through exploration and production sharing agreements with Staatsolie. Staatsolie executes oil exploration agreements with foreign firms through a fair and competitive bidding process.

OTHER INVESTMENT POLICY REVIEWS

The Government of Suriname conducted a Trade Policy review through the WTO in 2013. OECD and UNCTAD did not conduct investment policy reviews within the past three years; however, the Inter-American Development Bank produced a Framework for Private Sector Development in Suriname report in December 2013 (www.idbdocs.iadb.org/wsdocs/getdocument.aspx?docnum=38571795).

LAWS/REGULATIONS OF FOREIGN DIRECT INVESTMENT

Suriname does not have major laws/regulations affecting incoming foreign investment through acquisitions, mergers, takeovers, purchases of securities (including debt, equity, hybrid, and derivative securities) and other financial contracts, and greenfield (start-up) investments, and there are no judicial decisions affecting incoming foreign investment.

The judicial system is largely independent. Article 31 of the Constitution prohibits interference with active court cases and this is generally followed in practice. Judges are considered impartial. However, the judicial system is backlogged and commercial cases can drag on for years.

The Ministry of Trade and Industry last published an official Suriname Investment Guide in 2010: www.gov.sr/ministerie-van-hi/investeerders/investors.aspx.

INDUSTRIAL PROMOTION

Although the GOS focuses on developing the energy, mining, travel and agribusiness sectors it maintains no specific public programs aimed at attracting foreign investment.

LIMITS ON FOREIGN CONTROL

There are no statutory, de facto, or other limits on foreign ownership or control, and no laws require domestic nationals to own a set percentage of domestic companies, or hold seats on the board, or that the percentage of foreign ownership be capped at a certain level or reduced over time.

In general there are no sector-specific restrictions on foreign investment, with the exception of the petroleum sector. Within the petroleum sector, ownership is limited by law to the state oil company (Staatsolie). Staatsolie maintains sole ownership of all petroleum-related activities. Caribbean Single Market and Economy (CSME) countries do enjoy favored status over other sources of foreign investment, but in practice large international firms are not denied investment opportunities. The Economic Partnership Agreement (EPA) with the European Union provides European companies better market access to the CARIFORUM countries.

PRIVATIZATION PROGRAM

The GOS has identified privatization programs mainly in the agribusiness sector. Also, the GOS is considering privatizing two of the many state-owned commercial banks but has not established a time line. Foreign investors can participate in privatization programs. In 2014 Belgian multinational Univeg acquired 90 percent of the state-owned banana company through a public, international bidding process.

SCREENING OF FDI

Foreign direct investments are screened or reviewed by each ministry that oversees major investments in that sector. Special commissions screen all necessary financial and legal documentation; however, the process is not transparent and therefore not understood, constituting a barrier to investment. Screening criteria varies depending on the nature of the investment but are primarily meant to assure the investment is within the legal parameters of trade legislation. The screening procedures usually take place at the beginning of the investment process.

It is unknown why potential investments fail review since the process is not transparent and investment criteria are not public.

Foreign investors must submit an investor's petition which includes the name of the company, representative, company activity, markets, the sector the company wants to invest in, the amount of the investment, and the method of financing. The petition must include copies of business bylaws and other founding documents, a project proposal, and a statement from the investor that it will maintain an updated registration, including of its investment activities, at the tax department.

Competition Law

There is no competition law. A draft law exists, but the National Assembly has not yet passed it.

Investment Trends

The government has expressed a desire to attract foreign direct investment to further develop the economy. However, it has yet to pass legislation beneficial to the investment climate or make improvements to energy or infrastructure development necessary to support additional investment.

Table 1

Measure	Year	Index or Rank	Website Address
TI Corruption Perceptions index	2014	100 of 175	transparency.org/cpi2014/results
World Bank's Doing Business Report "Ease of Doing Business"	2014	162 of 189	doingbusiness.org/rankings
Global Innovation Index	2014	x of 143	globalinnovationindex.org/content.aspx?page=data-analysis
World Bank GNI per capita	2013	USD 9,370	data.worldbank.org/indicator/NY.GNP.PCAP.CD

2. CONVERSION AND TRANSFER POLICIES

Foreign Exchange

There are no legal limitations on foreign investors converting or repatriating funds associated with an investment, but we are aware of at least one case in which a person of Surinamese birth who later became a foreign national experienced years of delay and a seemingly arbitrary bureaucratic process which prevented repatriation of funds derived from the sale of shares of Surinamese holdings. Nominally, funds associated with investments can be converted into a freely usable currency at a legal market clearing rate with the permission of the Foreign Exchange Commission, but the criteria for obtaining permission is opaque.

Suriname has a fixed exchange rate. The official national currency rate is pegged to the U.S. dollar. The Central Bank of Suriname takes measures to maintain the currency peg but a parallel black market exists.

Remittance Policies

There are no recent changes or plans to change investment remittance policies. The waiting period on remittances can be relatively short for dividends, return on investments, principal and interest on private foreign debt, lease payments, royalties, and management fees. The time needed to process the request depends on the sector and the amount transferred. Transfers through the banking system can range from same-day to one week contingent upon approval from the Foreign Exchange Commission.

The Foreign Exchange Commission experiences delays due to a lack of capacity. Very large remittances may experience further delays due to concerns over possible destabilizing effects on the monetary system. Foreign Investors can remit through the legal parallel market. A source of origin must be declared in cases where the incoming or outgoing amount exceeds USD 5,000 or EUR 5,000. There is no limitation on the inflow or outflow of funds for remittance of profits or revenues.

Suriname does not engage in currency manipulation.

Suriname is a member of the Caribbean Financial Action Task Force (CFATF), a FATF-style regional body. The latest information can be found at www.cfatf-gafic.org.

The INCR 2014 report designates Suriname as a jurisdiction of concern. Further information is available in the Bureau of International Narcotics and law Enforcement's 2014 International Narcotics Control Strategy Report (INCSR) at:**http://www.state.gov/j/inl/rls/nrcrpt/2014/database/index.htm**.

3. EXPROPRIATION AND COMPENSATION

Article 34 of Suriname's constitution states that expropriation will take place only for reasons of public utility and with prior compensation. In practice, the government has no history of expropriation. There is no indication that policy regarding expropriation will shift in the near future. However, Article 41 of the Constitution specifically refers to all natural resources as property of the nation, and states that the nation has inalienable rights to take complete possession of all natural resources in order to utilize them for the economic, social, and cultural development of Suriname. Mining and large land holdings present the most risk for expropriation. Successive governments awarded many large land holdings based on political affiliations.

4. DISPUTE SETTLEMENT

LEGAL SYSTEM, SPECIALIZED COURTS, JUDICIAL INDEPENDENCE, JUDGMENTS OF FOREIGN COURTS

Suriname's system of codified law resembles the Dutch system. Laws are laid down in criminal, civil, and commercial codes and verdicts are based on the judge's interpretation of those codes. The commercial code includes property rights and contractual legislation, but there are no specialized courts such as commercial law or civil courts that specialize in intellectual property rights.

The judicial system is generally considered to be independent from government interference, however, depends on the Ministry of Justice and Police (an executive agency) for its budget. Judges are generally considered impartial. The lack of judges and support personnel creates delays in the system.

Judgments of foreign courts are accepted and enforced by the local courts only if Suriname has a legal treaty of jurisprudence with the foreign country involved. If not, the foreign judgement can be brought before the Surinamese court for consideration as long as the court determines it has jurisdiction and doing so does not otherwise violate Surinamese laws.

There are no recent examples of foreign investment problems handled within the legal system.

BANKRUPTCY

Suriname applies commercial and bankruptcy laws. Companies have the right to file for bankruptcy in cases where at least two or more creditors have claims. Creditors have the right to file for liquidation of the debtor's assets due to insolvency. In cases where there is a loan from a commercial bank, repayment of the bank's loan takes precedence. Bankruptcy in principle is not criminalized; however, courts have viewed cases where a board of directors encourages a company to pursue bankruptcy to avoid creditors as a criminal offense.

INVESTMENT DISPUTES

Every effort is made to settle investment disputes outside the court system or via arbitration. There have been no publicly known investment disputes over the past ten years involving U.S. or other foreign investors in Suriname.

INTERNATIONAL ARBITRATION

There is no Bilateral Investment Treaty or Free Trade Agreement with an investment chapter between Suriname and the United States.

Suriname's civil law includes options for arbitration. The government reactivated the Suriname Arbitration Institute (SAI) in August 2014 to offer arbitration and mediation services. The court recognizes foreign arbitral awards only if it is stipulated in the contract or agreement and it does not contradict local law. International arbitration is an accepted means of settling disputes between private parties, but only if local alternatives are exhausted.

ICSID Convention and New York Convention

Suriname is not a party to the Convention on the Settlement of Investment Disputes between States and Nationals of Other States (ICSID). Suriname has been a member of the New York Convention of 1958 on the Recognition and Enforcement of Foreign Arbitral Awards since 1964, when the country was still a colony of The Netherlands. At independence in 1975, Suriname automatically continued its membership in international conventions and treaties.

DURATION OF DISPUTE RESOLUTION

Local dispute resolution proceedings typically last between one month and three years, depending on the complexity of the case and the willingness of parties to cooperate. A shortage of judges increases the time needed to resolve dispute cases.

Suriname is a member and participant in the Caribbean Court of Justice (CCJ) therefore local courts recognize CCJ judgements. Plaintiffs have successfully filed suit against Suriname in the Inter-American

Court of Justice of the Organization of American States. The Surinamese legal system upheld these verdicts but enforcement is not always certain.

5. PERFORMANCE REQUIREMENTS AND INVESTMENT INCENTIVES

WTO/TRIMS

Suriname is a member of the World Trade Organization and does not maintain measures inconsistent with Trade Related Investment Measures (TRIMs) requirements.

INVESTMENT INCENTIVES

Under current regulations foreign investors can benefit from both tax-and non-tax-based incentives. Tax-based incentives include a nine-year tax holiday that can be extended by one year if the investment is at least USD 13 million, accelerated depreciation of assets, and tax consolidation. Under the Raw Minerals Act the government grants an exemption of duties for the import of raw materials from CARICOM member countries. Exemptions are also granted in the food industry, the soft drinks industry and the fruit juice industry. In 2011, the government eliminated import duties on computers and related items. The law accords special consideration on investments exceeding US 50 million and investments in the exploration and exploitation of bauxite, hydrocarbons, gold, and radioactive minerals. Large investments in the mining sector are subject to extensive negotiations between the government and investors. The government maintains the ability to grant incentives that depart from the provisions in investment law, e.g. incentives related to the provision of infrastructure.

Research and Development

The government does not finance and/or subsidize research and development programs, but U.S. and other foreign firms are welcome to initiate research and development. Foreign investors including ALCOA's subsidiary Suralco have contributed to the establishment and maintenance of research facilities at the Anton de Kom University.

PERFORMANCE REQUIREMENTS

The government does not impose performance requirements. The government does mandate that Surinamese citizens be hired if they are available on the labor market for a specific type of work, but such restrictions do not apply to senior management and boards of directors. Visa, residence, and work permit requirements are not excessively onerous.

DATA STORAGE

Foreign investors are not required to use domestic content in goods or technology. Foreign IT providers are not required to turn over source code and/or provide access to surveillance. No mechanisms are used to enforce any rules on maintaining a certain amount of data storage within Suriname.

6. RIGHT TO PRIVATE OWNERSHIP AND ESTABLISHMENT

Foreign and domestic private entities have the right to establish and own business enterprises and engage in all forms of remunerative activity. Once private entities register a business with the Chamber of Commerce (KKF) they have the right to freely acquire and dispose of assets as they see fit.

7. PROTECTION OF PROPERTY RIGHTS

REAL PROPERTY

Secured interest in property, both movable and real, is recognized and enforced. Mortgages and liens are common. Mortgages are registered with the Mortgage Office; however, no effective registration system exists for other types of liens.

No clear definitions and protections of traditional use rights of indigenous peoples, tribes or farmers exist. In 2007 the Inter-American Court on Human Rights ordered Suriname to recognize the collective land rights of tribal people, draft legislation that complies with international treaties, establish a development fund, and provide the Saramaka Maroon People with their own land. The GOS continues to ignore the ruling with no immediate prospect to grant land rights to the Saramaka Maroon People.

It is unknown what percentage of land does not have clear title. There is no sustained effort by the government to identify property owners and register land titles nor is there a publically-accessible land title office. Article 1-1 of the L-1 Decree Principles of Land Policy states that "all land, to which others have not proven their right to ownership, is domain of the State." Furthermore, article 41 of the Constitution states that wealth and resources are property of the nation and shall be used to promote, economic, social and cultural development.

INTELLECTUAL PROPERTY RIGHTS

Suriname is a member a member of the World Trade Organization and the World Intellectual Property Organization, however has not ratified the Trade Related Aspects of Intellectual Property Rights (TRIPS) Agreement. Even though Suriname is party to multiple agreements, IPR protections are not enforced. The current legal framework mentions protection of copyrights, trademarks and patents, however legislation dates back to 1912 (amended in 2001) and 1941. Although the National Assembly passed amendments to the Music Copyright Law of 1913 in March 2015, enforcement remains non-existent.

At present the Bureau of Intellectual Property Rights registers only trademarks. Trademark registration requires approximately one week to complete, but enforcement might take a year due to a backlog at the Bureau of Intellectual Property Rights. Patents and copyrights must be registered abroad since proper legislation does not exist. There is no protection for trade secrets and layout design.

IP protections are not improving. Counterfeit goods enter the country and are sold on the local market, however, Suriname does not track or report on seizures of counterfeit goods. There is little indication of government interest in enforcing prohibitions on counterfeit goods.

Suriname is not listed in the USTR's Special 301 report and is not listed in the notorious market report.

For additional information about treaty obligations and point of contact at local offices please see WIPO's country profiles at http://www.wipo.int/directory/en/.

Resources for Rights Holders
Lorenzo New
Political/Economic Officer
(597) 472-900 ext 2208
newlb@state.gov
List of lawyers: htttp://surinameusembassy.gov/service/list-of-attorneys.html
American Chamber of Commerce of Suriname
Wyndham Garden Paramaribo, Unit 5
Domineestraat 7-9

Phone (597) 521-465
amchamsuriname@sr.net

Transparency of the Regulatory System

The government does not use transparent policies and has no effective laws in place to foster competition and establish "clear rules of the game." Suriname has a draft competition law; however, the National Assembly has yet to vote on the measure. The Competitiveness Forum Suriname coordinates and monitors national competitiveness and is working towards establishing policies and suggesting effective legislation to foster competition. Current legislation such as tax, labor, environment, health and safety, or other laws are not purposely used to impede investment, but may still form obstacles. Employment protection legislation is among the most stringent in the world. Labor laws, for instance, prohibit employers from firing an employee without the permission of the Ministry of Labor once the employee has fulfilled his or her probationary period, which by law is limited to two months. Tax laws are criticized as overburdening the formal business sector while there is a large informal sector that goes untaxed. The government continues to postpone implementation of a value-added tax (VAT), with a revised VAT law tentatively set for introduction in 2016. There are also plans to modernize and lower direct-tax rates with assistance from the Inter-American Development Bank (IDB).

Legal, regulatory, and accounting systems are outdated and therefore not transparent and consistent with international norms. There is no overarching accounting and auditing legislation to set a national accounting standard, regulate the accountancy profession or enforce requirements for financial reporting. Currently, there is neither a requirement for specific accounting standards nor a requirement for auditing unless specifically mentioned in the articles of association of the company. Most financial statements prepared in Suriname are based on The Netherlands Generally Accepted Accounting Principles (NL GAAP). However, Suriname's major domestic corporations and multinational companies operating in Suriname often apply their own standards. Some larger firms use one of the resident international firms such as Deloitte Consulting or BDO international, Ltd., for their accounting needs.

Laws and regulations including investment laws are drafted in consultation with relevant stakeholders but are not made available for public comment. There are no nongovernmental organizations or private sector associations that manage informal regulatory processes. There are no private sector and/or governmental/authority efforts to restrict foreign participation in industry standards-setting consortia or organizations.

9. EFFICIENT CAPITAL MARKETS AND PORTFOLIO INVESTMENT

The government does not promote portfolio investment nor is there an effective regulatory system. There is a small, self-regulating stock market with eleven companies registered which meets twice a month, but no electronic exchange. In 2008, the State Oil Company Suriname (Staatsolie) raised funds through a local bond issuance to expand its refinery.

Sufficient policies do exist for the free flow of financial resources into the product and factor markets. As an IMF article VIII member, Suriname has agreed not to impose restrictions on payments and transfers for current international transactions. Credit is allocated on market terms and at market rates. Foreign investors that establish businesses in Suriname are able to get credit on the local market, usually with a payment guarantee from the parent company. The private sector has access to a variety of credit instruments. Larger companies can obtain customized credit products. There is, however, a Central Bank regulation that limits a commercial bank's credit exposure to any single client.

MONEY AND BANKING SYSTEM, HOSTILE TAKEOVERS

The banking system is considered healthy, with oversight provided by the Central Bank of Suriname. The IMF cites credit risk as a result of rapid credit growth and substantial exposure to the real estate market and government as concerns. The IMF recommends Suriname draft regulations for banks to enhance capital requirements and provisioning and monetary and prudential measures to dampen credit growth, and institutional reforms to strengthen central bank supervisory and crisis resolution powers.

There are no restrictions on the establishment of bank accounts by foreigners. Banks require U.S. citizens to provide information required to comply with the Foreign Affairs Tax Compliance Act (FATCA).

10. COMPETITION FROM STATE-OWNED ENTERPRISES

SOEs operate in the agribusiness, energy and mining, information and communication, finance, and travel sectors. All state-owned entities that conduct commercial activities are listed by the Investment Development Corporation Suriname and meet the same criteria regardless of industry. They enjoy advantages over their private sector counterparts, such as preferential access to land and raw materials and no hard budget constraints. Most do not finance research and development (the state-owned oil company is the major exception). SOEs purchase goods and services from private sector and foreign firms, and pay the same taxes as their private sector competitors.

In some cases the government awards contracts to the private sector over SOEs. For example, in 2011 telecom provider Digicel offered the government a lower quote for services than parastatal Telesur; although Telesur protested, Digicel retained the contract.

Private enterprises can compete with SOEs on the same terms and conditions with respect to market share, products/services and incentives. Private enterprises have the same access to financing as SOEs at commercial banks. However, SOE's may get access to government guarantees or government loans that are not available to private enterprises.

Suriname is not a signatory to the WTO Government Procurement Agreement.

OECD Guidelines on Corporate Governance of SOEs

Every SOE has its own by-laws that structure corporate governance. By-laws also indicate if the Central Auditing Bureau (CLAD) or an independent consultant is responsible for auditing financial records. In practice, the vast majority of SOEs do not publish annual reports and do not appear to be subject to effective external financial oversight. Staatsolie, the largest SOE, publishes annual reports.

The government does not yet adhere to the OECD Guidelines on Corporate Governance for SOEs. SOE Senior management in most cases report to a board of directors and in some instances directly to a line minister. The board of directors (representing the government) is involved in all business decisions. Board seats are allocated to senior government officials and politically-affiliated individuals.

3rd party market analysts regard SOEs' ties to the government as an impediment with the exception of Staatsolie (the state-owned oil company) which is the only SOE to publish audited financial statements and routinely conduct public tenders in a fair and transparent manner.

Regarding investment disputes, court processes are transparent and non-discriminatory.

Sovereign Wealth Funds

The Supreme Audit Institution of Suriname (Rekenkamer) is an independent institute that exercises control of government transparency and accountability and publishes reports on management of state finances. The Rekenkamer traditionally briefs the National Assembly and the public about its findings; however, the current government severely restricts its ability to perform its mission.

There is no sovereign wealth fund. The Central Bank prepared draft legislation to establish an SWF but the government withdrew it without explanation in 2014.

11. CORPORATE SOCIAL RESPONSIBILITY

There is a growing awareness of corporate social responsibility (CSR) among consumers and producers. Historically, ALCOA subsidiary Suralco took the lead on CSR in Suriname, and other companies followed suit. Locally-owned companies that stand out for their CSR are Staatsolie, Surinam Airways, Telesur, and the Fernandes Group of Companies (which includes the Coca Cola soft drinks bottler and McDonald's restaurants). Several foreign corporations have active social responsibility programs.

The government realizes the benefits of CSR and incorporates it in some of its partnerships and agreements. For example, recent agreements between Staatsolie and foreign companies for off-shore oil drilling include stipulations on CSR spending.

The Labor Inspection Department of the Ministry of Labor supervises and enforces the observance of legal regulations regarding conditions of employment and the protection of employees performing duties. The government is drafting consumer protection and environmental protection laws.

There is no legislation for corporate governance, accounting, and executive compensation standards to protect shareholders. There is no legislation regarding public disclosure. There are no NGOs or business associations currently promoting or monitoring CSR.

OECD GUIDELINES FOR MULTINATIONAL ENTERPRISES

The government does not encourage foreign and local enterprises to follow OECD or United Nations Guiding Principles on Business and Human Rights. Companies are allowed to develop their own policies and standards.

12. POLITICAL VIOLENCE

Suriname endured a civil war fueled by narcotics trafficking and racism, the so called "Bush War," during the 1980s. In that conflict, the current president, Desire Bouterse, led a military junta against the "Jungle Commando" led by current legislator Ronnie Brunswijk. The parties have since transferred their conflict to the political arena. There are no examples of damage to projects and/or installations over the past ten years. Suriname is highly politicized; however, elections continue to be mostly free and fair.

13. CORRUPTION

Suriname's corruption laws are outdated, not enforced, and the National Assembly has yet to debate updated draft legislation. The Attorney General and the Ministry of Justice and Police apparently do not investigate frequent, credible allegations of corruption. There are no known significant prosecutions for alleged high-level corruption during the current government. The government established an Anti-Corruption Working Group at the ministerial and technical level to assist the police in combating corruption. Suriname does not have special anti-corruption legislation in place but the penal code penalizes corruption. The current and previous governments each sent draft anti-corruption legislation to the National Assembly, however, neither passed into law. Anti-corruption measures in the penal-code are not consistently enforced, and the majority of those prosecuted to date have been civil servants. Existing laws do not extend to family members of officials or to political parties.

The government does not encourage or require private companies to establish internal codes of conduct. Private companies don't use internal controls, ethics, and compliance programs to detect and prevent bribery of government officials.

Suriname has signed and ratified the Inter-American Convention against Corruption. There are no NGO's involved in corruption issues. U.S. firms have identified corruption as an obstacle to FDI. Corruption is most pervasive in government procurement, the award of licenses and concessions, customs, and taxation.

UN Anticorruption Convention, OECD Convention on Combatting Bribery

Suriname has not yet signed and ratified the UN Anticorruption Convention, and is not party to the OECD Convention on Combating Bribery.

Resources to Report Corruption
Fraud Department
Suriname Police Force (Korps Politie Suriname)
Havenlaan, Paramaribo, Suriname
(597) 404-943

14. BILATERAL INVESTMENT AGREEMENTS

Suriname has signed bilateral investment protection agreements with Indonesia, Cuba and the Netherlands. Suriname has not signed a bilateral investment treaty or an FTA with an investment chapter with the U.S.

BILATERAL TAXATION TREATIES

There is no bilateral taxation treaty with the U.S.

15. OPIC AND OTHER INVESTMENT INSURANCE PROGRAMS

Although Suriname signed an Investment Incentive Agreement with the Unites States in 1993 there are no OPIC programs in operation. The government is party to the Multilateral Investment Guarantee Agency (MIGA) Convention.

16. LABOR

In general, skilled and unskilled labor are available in the labor market. Some sectors are more prone to labor shortages than others, such as the agricultural, construction, medical, and service sectors. According to the International Labor Organization's 2014 report the unemployment rate is approximately 12 percent. The true rate of unemployment is somewhat difficult to determine because many find employment in the large informal sector. The unemployment rate among the youth is estimated at 22 percent.

Some sectors in Suriname, such as the agricultural, medical, and service sectors, experience labor shortages. Heavy equipment operators and repairmen in extractive industries are in high demand. The service sector lacks certified accountants. Government-procured physicians and ER nurses from the Philippines work in hospital emergency rooms. The state oil company Staatsolie recruited welders and other construction workers from the Philippines and Vietnam for the expansion of its refinery.

There are no government policies that require the hiring of nationals, however, the Work Permits Act prohibits employers to employ foreigners without a work permit granted by the Ministry of Labor.

Legislation makes it difficult for employers to adjust employment due to market conditions. The Dismissal Permits Act prohibits employers from dismissing employees without permission of the Minister of Labor. Collective redundancy for organizational or economic reasons is permitted in cases such the close-down or decline of a business that makes reducing staff unavoidable. Suriname has no special economic zones, foreign trade zones, or free ports with alternative labor policies, therefore all entities are subject to existing legislation.

Labor unions are independent from the government but play an active role in politics. There are labor dispute resolution mechanisms in place and they are used to mediate disputes. According to the Labor Dispute Act, only labor disputes concerning a collective bargaining agreement can be brought before a review board. Collective bargaining takes place in both the public and private sector.

The Labor Inspection Department supervises observance of labor abuses, health and safety standards, and enforcement appears sufficient. Suriname is a member of the International Labor Organization (ILO) and recognizes international labor rights in its domestic legislation. Freedom of association, the elimination of forced labor, the elimination of child labor, occupational safety and health, and weekly work hours are incorporated in the labor law. Labors laws are not waived in order to retain investments.

The government introduced a minimum wage in January 2015.

17. FOREIGN TRADE ZONES/FREE PORTS/TRADE FACILITATION

There are no duty-free import zones in Suriname.

18. FOREIGN DIRECT INVESTMENT AND FOREIGN PORTFOLIO INVESTMENT STATISTICS

Table 2: Key Macroeconomic Data, U.S. FDI in Host Country/Economy

	HOST COUNTRY STATISTICAL SOURCE*		USG OR INTERNATIONAL STATISTICAL SOURCE		USG OR INTERNATIONAL SOURCE OF DATA: BEA; IMF; EUROSTAT; UNCTAD, OTHER
ECONOMIC DATA	YEAR	AMOUNT	YEAR	AMOUNT	
Host Country Gross Domestic Product (GDP) ($M USD)	2013	5,400	2013	5,299	www.worldbank.org/en/country
Foreign Direct Investment	Host Country Statistical source*		USG or international statistical		USG or international Source of data: BEA; IMF; Eurostat; UNCTAD, Other

			source		
U.S. FDI in partner country ($M USD, stock positions)	N/A		2013	115	http://bea.gov/international/factsheet/factsheet.cfm?Area=260
Host country's FDI in the United States ($M USD, stock positions)	N/A		2013	8	http://bea.gov/international/factsheet/factsheet.cfm?Area=260
Total inbound stock of FDI as % host GDP	N/A		2013	18%	Source: UNCTAD

*Central Bank of Suriname

Table 3: Sources and Destination of FDI

Suriname does not release foreign direct investment position data publically, but IMF's Coordinated Direct Investment Survey appears consistent. There are no tax havens sources of inward FDI.

INVESTMENT AND BUSINESS CONTACTS

Contact for More Information

Lorenzo New
Economic Officer
U.S. Embassy Paramaribo
(597) 472900
newlb@state.gov

LOCAL LAWYERS

BIHARIESINGH, USHA R.
Address: Henck Arronstraat 75-79, Paramaribo, Suriname. Telephone (office): 477000/477665/08533323
Fax: 421095
Email Address: ubihariesingh@gmail.com orubihariesingh@hotmail.com.
Education – University Degree in Law
FIRM: Attorney at Law Office
Legal Specialty: Civil Law

Types of cases handled: Marriage/Divorce, Adoptions, Car Accidents, Civil Damages, Collections, Estates, Labor Relations, Child Custody
Language: Dutch and English

BLUFPAND, RUTH JUDITH
Address: Virolastraat 53, Paramaribo, Suriname.
Telephone (office): 492925
Mobile: 08754726
Fax: 437655
Email Address: blufpandadv@sr.net
Education - Graduated from the University of Leiden, The Netherlands.
FIRM: Law Office Blufpand
Legal Specialty: Trademark Registration
Types of cases handled: labor related, family related, collections, general judicial advice
Language: Dutch, Surinamese and English

BRANDON, KATHLEEN JUANITA
Address: Weidestraat 63
Telephone (office): 478580/477729
Fax: 477920
Home Telephone: 456628
Mobile phone: 08559790
Email: kjbrandon@kraaglawyers.sr; kjbrandon@sr.net Education: Degree in Law (Anton de Kom University of Suriname)
Firm: Law Firm Kraag
Partners: Mr. J. Kraag, Mr. H. Boldewijn, Mr. D. Kraag
Type of cases handled: Adoptions, Aeronautical/Maritime, Car Accidents, Banking/Financial, Child Custody, Civil Damages, Collections, Contracts, Estates, Immigration, Labor Relations, Marriage/Divorce, Theft/Fraud/Embezzlement
Language: Dutch, English and Spanish (Limited)

KRAAG, DWIGHT SPENCER
Address: Weidestraat 63
Telephone (office): 478580/477729
Fax: 477920
Home telephone: 08810023
Email Address: dskraag@kraaglawyers.sr
Education: Law School Erasmus University Rotterdam
Firm: Advocatenkantoor Kraag/ Law Firm Kraag
Partners: Mr. J. Kraag, Mr. H. Boldewijn, Mr. K. Brandon
Type of cases handled: car accidents, child custody, civil damages, collections, contracts, corporations, estates, insurance, Labor Relations, Marriage/Divorce, Narcotics, Patents/Trademarks/Copyrights, Theft/Fraud/Embezzlement Language: Dutch, English and Sranan Tongo

LIM A PO ADVOCATENKANTOOR
Address: Mr. F.H.R. Lim A Postraat 14, P.O. Box 92, Paramaribo,Suriname.
Telephone (office): 473514, (home): 497127
Mobile: 08781399

Fax: 745394
Email Address: limapo@sr.net;
Education- Graduated University of Suriname.
FIRM: Lim A Po Law Firm
Partners: Bernard A. Halfhide, Hans R. Lim A Po, Marja I. Vos, Nicole Tjin A Djie, R.C. Bleu, E.A. v. der Hilst
(General and Private Practice).
Type of cases handled: collections, estates, trade disputes and marketing agreements, adoptions, child custody, civil damages, government relations, marriage/divorce, aeronautical/maritime, banking/financial, contracts, corporation, foreign claims, insurance, labor relations, mining/petroleum, car accidents, immigration. Language: Dutch and English.

RAIJMANN, FRANK E.M.
Address: Mr. Jaggernath Lachmonstraat 132, Paramaribo, Suriname
Telephone (office): (597) 493464, (home): (597) 0370040
Fax: (597) 494423
Email Address: frank.Raijmann@bdo.sr or info@bdo.sr Website: http://www.bdo.sr
Education – Graduated from the University of Amsterdam, The Netherlands.
FIRM: BDO (Abrahams Raijmann & Partners)
Types of cases handled: Tax, contract and commercial, financial, succession, labor, corporate, mergers and acquisitions. Language: Dutch and English

SCHURMAN, HUMPHREY RICHENEL
Address: Watermolenstraat #32, Paramaribo, Suriname.
Telephone (Office): 476558/476593, cell: 08816809
Fax: 411007
Email Address: hums@sr.net
Website: www.schurman-advocaten.com
Education: Law study at the Faculty of law of the University of Suriname
Degree in Law (MSc), Diplomatic training, Environmental training, telecommunication training.
FIRM: Law Firm Schurman
Legal Specialty: Intellectual Property Specialist, environment, telecommunication, business, trade and advisory
Types of cases handled: intellectual property - trademarks, telecommunications, business and trade – contracts/agreements, licensing, branch registration, insurance, collections, foreign claims, mining and oil industry, land use and planning, environment, health, labour law and regulations-contracts, immigration and work permits, mediation, litigation, family law - marriage/divorces, adoptions, public (car accidents), civil and criminal law, collection, projects-consultancy and management, procedures international companies and donor organizations
Language: Dutch, English

TJON, JANE PEGGY
Address: Costerstraat 7, Paramaribo, Suriname.
Telephone (office): 421113/473358/421137
Fax: 477035
Email address: jtjon@costeradvocaten.net
Education - Graduated from the University of Suriname.

Practiced law: 7 years for the Surinamese Government and
2 years private practice.
FIRM: Coster Advocaten
Partners: Yvonne Engkar, Edward Naarendorp, Sieglien Sewdien
Types of cases handled: adoptions, child custody, civil damages, collections, contracts,estates, immigration, labor relations, marriage/divorce, patents/trademarks/copyrights.
Language: Dutch and English.

TJON JAW CHONG, MAUREEN
Address: Wagenwegstraat 21 ben., Paramaribo, Suriname.
Telephone (office): 425000/ 08865917
Fax: 470744
Email address: mavalo@yahoo.com
Education – University Degree in Law
FIRM: Advocatenkantoor Maureen Tjon Jaw Chong
Legal Specialty: Civil-Criminal Law
Types of cases handled: civil damages, estates, foreign investments, government relations, labor relations, personal law, family law, narcotics, etc.
Language: Dutch and English.

CAROL-ANN TJON-PIAN-GI
Address: Pardolaan 20, Paramaribo, Suriname.
Telephone (office): 492257/ 08861200
Fax: 492257
Email address: catpg@yahoo.com
Education – Master's Degree in Law, Bachelor Degree in English language
FIRM: Advocatenkantoor Carol-Ann Tjon-Pian-Gi
Legal Specialty: Corporate Law, Legal translation
Types of cases handled: company formation, all types of commercial contracts (labor, purchase, lease), franchises, joint ventures, trademarks, translation of all types of legal documents (e.g. contracts, legislation, court documents)
Language: Dutch, English (sworn translator), Sranan Tongo (fluent), Spanish and French (elementary).

NACATIA BRIGITTE SAN A JONG
Address: Sterappelstraat 12, Paramaribo, Suriname.
Telephone (office): 473480/08536785
Fax: 473480
Email address: nbsanajong@hotmail.com
Education – University Degree in Law
FIRM: Advocatenkantoor N.B. San A Jong
Legal Specialty: Criminal cases, private and domestic cases, International law
Types of cases handled: private and domestic, family law cases, litigate free of charge cases, interim injuction proceedings, juvenile affairs, alien affairs, (immigration, residence permits) Language: Dutch, English, Sranan Tongo

SUSILKUMAR GYANDATH RUDREPERSAD KHOEN KHOEN
Address: Monizstraat 18, Paramaribo, Suriname.
Telephone (office): 440058/08504323
Fax: 440058

Email address: acharya.advocaten@gmail.com
Education – Graduated in Law - University of Suriname
FIRM: Law Firm Acharya Advocaten
Legal Specialty: civil law
Types of cases handled: adoptions, insurance, car accidents, child custody, labour relations, civil damages, collections, marriage/divorces, contracts, estates, copyrights
Language: Dutch, English, sarnami, Sranan Tongo

MICHELLA DENISE LAU-KERSSENBERG
Address: Florastraat 65, Paramaribo, Suriname.
Telephone (office): 478866/476868/08630888
Fax: 479977
Email address: legal-aid@outlook.com
Education – Graduated in Law - University of Suriname
FIRM: Law Firm Legal Aid Advocatenkantoor
Legal Specialty: civil law
Types of cases handled: adoptions, car accidents, banking/financial, child custody, civil damages, collections, contracts, foreign claims, government relations, insurance, immigration, labor relations, marriage/divorces, narcotics, copyrights, theft/fraud/embezzlement
Language: Dutch, English, Spanish, Sranan Tongo

SIEGLIEN TJANDERWATIE SEWDIEN
Address: Costerstraat 7, Paramaribo, Suriname.
Telephone (office): 421113/473358/421137
Fax: 477035
Email address:ssewdien@costeradvocaten.net/tssewdien@yahoo.com Education – Graduated in Law - University of Suriname
FIRM: Law Firm Coster Advocaten
Legal Specialty: civil law
Types of cases handled: law of persons, family law cases, obligations, properties, corporate law, division of matrimonial property and parental estate
Language: Dutch, English, sarnami, Sranan Tongo

ELOA FANITA VAN DER HILST
Address: Julianastraat 63, Paramaribo, Suriname.
Telephone (office): 421600, (home); 550303
Fax: 25511
Email address: evanderhilst@4justiceadvocaten.net
Education – Graduated in Law - University of Suriname
FIRM: Law Firm 4 Justice Advocaten
Partners: Anne-Marel Linger
Legal Specialty: civil law
Types of cases handled: adoptions, car accidents, child custody, civil damages, collections, contracts, estates, foreign claims, labor relations, marriage/divorce, theft/fraud/embezzlement, civil and criminal cases
Language: Dutch, English, Sranan Tongo

URUGUAY - INVESTMENT AND BUSINESS CLIMATE - STRATEGIC INFORMATION AND CONTACTS FOR STARTING BUSINESS

The Government of Uruguay recognizes the important role foreign investment plays in economic development and maintains a favorable investment climate that does not discriminate against foreign investors.

Uruguay has a stable legal system in which foreign and national investments are treated alike, most investments are allowed without prior authorization and investors may freely transfer abroad their capital and profits from their investment. There are also significant tax incentives for investors which, together with strong economic growth and booming commodities prices, have contributed to a strong increase in foreign and local investment over the past decade.

Uruguay is a stable democracy. Political risk is low and there have been no recent cases of expropriation. U.S. firms have not identified corruption as a problem for investment. The World Bank's 2014 "Doing Business" Index, which ranks countries according to the ease of doing business, placed Uruguay 9th out of thirty-two Latin American and Caribbean countries.

Uruguay has free trade agreements with its Mercosur partners (Argentina, Brazil, Paraguay and Venezuela), as well as Chile, Bolivia, Colombia, Ecuador, Mexico and Peru. Its strategic location (in the center of Mercosur´s wealthiest and most populated area) and its special import regimes (such as free zones and free ports) also make it a well-situated distribution center for U.S. goods into the region. Several U.S. firms warehouse their products in Uruguay´s tax free areas and service their regional clients effectively. With a market of 3.3 million high-income consumers, Uruguay is a good test market for U.S. products.

Investors can choose between arbitration and the judicial system to settle disputes.

Uruguay has bilateral investment treaties with over 30 countries, including the United States. Both countries also have agreements on Open Skies, Trade and Investment, Cooperation in Science and Technology, Promotion of Small and Medium Firms and Customs Mutual Assistance. As of March 2015, both governments are negotiating an agreement on social security. The United States does not have a double-taxation treaty with Uruguay.

With the fourth largest stock of foreign investment in 2013, the United States is an important investor in Uruguay. Currently about 130 U.S. firms operate locally and distribute their investments amongst a wide array of sectors, including forestry, tourism and hotels, other services, and telecommunications.

1. OPENNESS TO, AND RESTRICTIONS UPON, FOREIGN INVESTMENT

Attitude toward Foreign Direct Investment

The Government of Uruguay (GOU) has traditionally recognized the important role that foreign and local investment plays in economic and social development and works to maintain a favorable investment climate.

Uruguay and the United States signed a Bilateral Investment Treaty (BIT) in November 2005, which entered into force on November 1, 2006. Uruguay and the United States also signed an Open Skies Agreement in late 2004 (ratified in May 2006), a Trade and Investment Framework Agreement (TIFA) in January 2007, and a Science and Technology Cooperation Agreement in April 2008. Under the TIFA, both countries signed two additional protocols on business facilitation and on the environment in 2008. In

2014, Uruguay and the United States signed agreements to foster scientific and technological exchange, promote Small and Medium Firms, and facilitate the mutual assistance of their Customs. As of March 2015, both governments are negotiating an agreement on social security that would, among other things, facilitate the temporary stay of expats and workers in each country. The United States does not have a double-taxation treaty with Uruguay.

Local and foreign investors are treated equally. There are no preferential tax deferrals, grants, or special access to credit for foreign investors. Foreign investors are not required to meet any specific performance requirements. Moreover, foreign investors are not inhibited by discriminatory or excessively onerous visa, residence, or work permit requirements. The government does not require that nationals own shares or that the share of foreign equity be reduced over time, and does not impose conditions on investment permits.

In tenders for private sector participation in state-owned sectors, foreign investors are treated as nationals and allowed to participate in any stage of the process. Bidders on tenders should be prepared for a lengthy adjudication process. Although U.S. firms have not encountered major obstacles in Uruguay's investment climate, some have been frustrated by the length of time it takes to complete bureaucratic procedures and tenders. In addition, the ease by which losing parties may ask for annulment of bid results and force a rebid can result in significant delays in the process.

OTHER INVESTMENT POLICY REVIEWS

The most recent investment policy review on Uruguay was done by the World Trade Organization (WTO) in 2012 and is available at **http://www.wto.org/english/tratop_e/tpr_e/tp363_e.htm**

LAWS/REGULATIONS OF FOREIGN DIRECT INVESTMENT

Investors may choose between arbitration and the judicial system to settle disputes. Uruguay's legal system is based on a civil law system derived from the Napoleonic Code, and the Judiciary is transparent and remains independent of the executive branch.

Law 16,906 (passed in 1998) declares promotion and protection of investments made by national and foreign investors to be in the nation's interest. The law states that: (1) foreign and national investments are treated alike; (2) investments are allowed without prior authorization or registration; (3) the government will not prevent the establishment of investment in the country; and (4) investors may freely transfer abroad their capital and profits from the investment. Decree 002/12 (passed in January 2012 superseding Decree 455/007 from 2007) regulates Law 16,906 and provides significant incentives to investors, which have contributed to a strong increase in foreign and local investment.

Uruguay's Investment and Promotion agency's website helps potential investors navigate the laws, rules and incentives available to both foreign and local investors. **http://www.uruguayxxi.gub.uy/index_en.html**. In 2010 the GOU created a program to create firms in 24 hours, **http://empresaeneldia.portaldelaempresa.gub.uy/Apia/index.htm**

INDUSTRIAL PROMOTION

Uruguay has special regimes to promote tourism, communications, call centers, production of electronics and electronic equipment, software exports, biotech, printing activity, naval and aeronautic industries, forestry, production of vehicles or auto parts, and construction of agricultural machinery. The exploration and exploitation of hydrocarbons is also incentivized, as well as the production of biofuels and the generation of renewable energies. None of the promotion systems described above differentiates between foreign and national investors.

LIMITS ON FOREIGN CONTROL

Aside from a few limited sectors involving national security and limited legal government monopolies in which foreign investment is not permitted, there is neither de jure nor de facto discrimination toward investment by source or origin, with national and foreign investors treated equally. In general, the GOU does not require specific authorization for firms to set up operations, import and export, make deposits and banking transactions in any particular currency, or obtain credit. Screening mechanisms do not apply to foreign or national investments, and special government authorization is not needed for access to capital markets or to foreign exchange.

PRIVATIZATION PROGRAM

Uruguay has not undertaken any major privatization program in the recent past. While some previously government-run monopolies have been opened to private-sector competition, the government continues to have a monopoly in several key sectors (please refer to section 10 for more information).

Private-Public Partnerships are governed by Law 18,786, which was passed in Parliament by consensus in July 2011. Implementing agencies established relevant regulations in January 2012 by Decree 07/12, but as of March 2015 only three projects have been developed.

SCREENING OF FDI

Screening mechanisms do not apply to foreign or national investments, and special government authorization is not needed for access to capital markets or to foreign exchange.

COMPETITION LAW

Uruguay has policies and laws to foster competition. The two pillars are Law 18,159 and Decree 404, both from 1997. The Ministry of Economy has a special division to promote and defend competition.

Two regulatory agencies for telecommunications (URSEC) and water and energy (URSEA) were created in 2001 to, among others things, regulate and control their respective markets. In 2010, the Executive Branch transferred URSEC's policy-design capacity to the National Telecommunications Directorate (DINATEL), leaving it only with control attributes.

The Audiovisual Communications Law, known locally as the media bill, which, as of April 2015, is pending regulation, includes provisions on market caps for cable TV providers that could limit competition.

INVESTMENT TRENDS

Uruguay´s traditionally low inflow of Foreign Direct Investment (FDI) surged in the last decade with a seven-fold growth from about USD 0.4 billion in 2003 to USD 2.8 billion in 2013. Except for a drop in 2008, FDI has not been hit by the global economic and financial crisis. In 2005-2013, Uruguay ranked second in South America after Chile in its FDI to GDP ratio, but has a level two-and-a-half times that of neighboring Brazil or Argentina

The sectors that receive the greatest amount of FDI are pulp mills, construction (real estate in Punta del Este, hotels, and office buildings), agriculture (forestry, ranching, farming, and slaughterhouses), and industry (food and beverages and chemicals).

In recent years, Uruguay has received unusually large-scale investments. In 2005-06, the Finnish firm UPM (ex-Botnia) made Uruguay's largest-ever foreign investment with the construction of a USD 1.2

billion pulp mill. In 2011-14, Finnish-Swedish-Chilean Montes del Plata invested an even larger projected sum –USD 1.9 billion in plant and USD 0.7 billion in land– in another pulp mill project.

U.S. investment in Uruguay has risen to an annual average of USD 77 million in 2009-2013 from an annual average of USD 58 million in 2004-2008. About 130 U.S. firms operate in Uruguay and directly employ over 15 thousand workers. Major firms include Weyerhaeuser (forestry), Conrad Hotels (tourism and gambling), Sabre (call center), McDonald's (restaurants) and Pepsi (syrups).

Table 1

Measure	Year	Index or Rank	Website Address
TI Corruption Perceptions index	2014	21 of 175	transparency.org/cpi2014/results
World Bank's Doing Business Report "Ease of Doing Business"	2015	82 of 189	doingbusiness.org/rankings
Global Innovation Index	2014	72 of 143	globalinnovationindex.org/content.aspx?page=data-analysis
World Bank GNI per capita	2013	15,180	data.worldbank.org/indicator/NY.GNP.PCAP.CD

2. CONVERSION AND TRANSFER POLICIES

FOREIGN EXCHANGE

Uruguay maintains a long tradition of not restricting the purchase of foreign currency or the remittance of profits abroad. Free purchases of foreign currency and remittances were preserved even during the severe 2002 banking and financial crisis.

Uruguay does not engage in currency manipulation to gain competitive advantage. Since 2002, the peso has floated freely, albeit with intervention from the Central Bank aimed at reducing the volatility of the price of the dollar. Foreign exchange can be freely obtained at market rates and there is no black market for currency exchange. The U.S. Embassy uses the official rate when purchasing local currency.

Remittance Policies

Uruguay maintains a long tradition of not restricting remittance of profits abroad.

Article 7 of the U.S.-Uruguay BIT provides that both countries "shall permit all transfers relating to investments to be made freely and without delay into and out of its territory." The agreement also establishes that both countries will permit transfers "to be made in a freely usable currency at the market rate of exchange prevailing at the time of the transfer."

Uruguay is considered a Jurisdiction of Primary Concern for money laundering in the US Department of State's International Narcotics Control Strategy Report (INCSRII).

3. EXPROPRIATION AND COMPENSATION

Uruguay's Constitution declares property rights an "inviolable right" subject to legal determinations that may be taken for general interest purposes, and states that no individuals can be deprived from this right –except in case of public need and with a previous and fair compensation.

Article 6 of the U.S.-Uruguay BIT rules out direct and indirect expropriation or nationalization, except under certain very specific circumstances. The article also contains detailed provisions on how to compensate investors, should expropriation take place.

There have been no cases of expropriation of investment –neither from the United States nor from other countries– in the past five years.

4. DISPUTE SETTLEMENT

LEGAL SYSTEM, SPECIALIZED COURTS, JUDICIAL INDEPENDENCE, JUDGMENTS OF FOREIGN COURTS

Uruguay's legal system is based on a civil law system derived from the Napoleonic Code and includes written commercial law. Two courts specialized on Organized Crime deal with intellectual property claims.

The Judiciary is transparent and remains independent of the executive branch. However, it has sometimes been criticized for being slow. The executive branch rarely interferes directly in judiciary matters, but at times has voiced its dissatisfaction of court rulings.

BANKRUPTCY

A Bankruptcy Law passed in 2008 (No. 18,387) sought to expedite bankruptcy procedures, encouraged arrangements with creditors before a firm goes definitively bankrupt, and provided the possibility of selling the firm as a single productive unit.

The World Bank's 2014 Doing Business Report ranks Uruguay 6th out of 29 countries in Latin America and the Caribbean for its ease of "resolving insolvency."

INVESTMENT DISPUTES

Over the past 10 years, no U.S. citizens or corporations have been involved in an investment dispute.

In February 2010, the tobacco company Philip Morris International sued the Government of Uruguay, arguing that new health measures involving cigarette packaging amounted to unfair treatment of the firm. The case was filed under the Uruguay-Switzerland Bilateral Investment Treaty and, as of April 2015, remains before ICSID. The United States does not support Philip Morris International, its position on this issue or the sales of its product.

INTERNATIONAL ARBITRATION

Investors may choose between arbitration and the judicial system to settle disputes. Local courts recognize and enforce foreign arbitral awards

The U.S.-Uruguay BIT devotes over ten pages to establish detailed and expedited dispute settlement procedures. There have been no claims under the agreement.

ICSID Convention and New York Convention

Uruguay became a member of the International Center for the Settlement of Investment Disputes (ICSID) in September 2000 and is also a signatory of the 1958 New York Convention on the Recognition and Enforcement of Foreign Arbitral Awards.

DURATION OF DISPUTE RESOLUTION

Uruguay's Judiciary is independent, albeit sometimes slow according to private sector representatives. Courts' decisions are enforced and international arbitration awards are respected.

5. PERFORMANCE REQUIREMENTS AND INVESTMENT INCENTIVES

WTO/TRIMS

The WTO's Trade Policy Review on Uruguay (2012) does not mention any measures that are inconsistent with Trade Related Investment Measures (TRIMs) requirements.

INVESTMENT INCENTIVES

The investment promotion regime is regulated by Law 16,906 (passed in 1998) and Decree 002/12 (passed in January 2012) that grants significant tax incentives to investors in a wide array of sectors and activities.

Law 16,906 grants automatic tax incentives to several activities including personnel training; research, scientific and technological development; reinvestment of profits; and investments in industrial machinery and equipment. Other benefits provided exclusively to industrial and agricultural firms by Law 16,906 have in practice been superseded by the regulating decree.

On top of the referred automatic tax incentives, there are special regimes to promote specific sectors (please refer to Industrial Promotion section).

Certain activities –such as the purchasing of land, real estate or private vehicles– are not eligible for the benefits. The principal incentive consists of the deduction from corporate income tax of a share of total investment (up to 100%) over a certain period. The amount of the deduction depends on the score the project gets in a matrix of pre-defined criteria. The matrix takes into account the project's: (1) generation of jobs (quantity and quality); (2) contribution to research and development and innovation, or increase in the usage of clean technologies; (3) increase of exports; (4) contribution to geographic decentralization away from the capital Montevideo; and (5) sectoral indicators that vary according to the nature of the investment (e.g. capital market development, hiring of workers from vulnerable groups or contribution to tourism services and infrastructure).

Other incentives include: 1) exoneration from tariffs and taxes (including VAT) on imports of capital goods and materials for civil works that do not compete against local industry; 2) exoneration from the patrimony tax on personal property and civil works; 3) refunding of VAT paid on local purchases of materials and services for civil works; and 4) special tax treatment of fees and salaries paid for research and development.

A government decree establishes that government tenders will favor local products or services, provided they are of equal quality and not more than 10 percent more expensive than foreign goods or services. U.S. and other foreign firms are able to participate in government-financed or subsidized research and development programs on a national treatment basis.

Research and Development

U.S. and other foreign firms are able to participate in government financed or subsidized research and development programs. However, given the relatively infrequent nature of such funding opportunities, examples of U.S. firms actual receiving funding are quite rare.

PERFORMANCE REQUIREMENTS

Foreign investors are not required to meet any specific performance requirements, and are not inhibited by discriminatory or excessively onerous visa, residence, or work permit requirements. The government does not require that nationals own shares or that the share of foreign equity be reduced over time, and does not impose conditions on the number of foreign workers or on investment permits.

Article 8 of the U.S.-Uruguay Bilateral Investment Treaty bans both countries from imposing seven forms of performance requirements on new investments, or tying the granting of existing or new advantages to performance requirements.

DATA STORAGE

Uruguay does not require foreign investors to use local content in goods or technology in order to invest. However, local content may be required in some sectors in order to become eligible for special tax treatment or government procurements. For instance, the state-owned electric utility recently offered a number of long-term purchase agreements for wind and solar generated electricity that included 20% local content requirements.

Uruguay does not require foreign IT providers to turn over source code or provide access to surveillance.

6. RIGHT TO PRIVATE OWNERSHIP AND ESTABLISHMENT

Private ownership does not restrict a firm or business from engaging in any form of remunerative activity, except in two areas: national security interests and legal government monopolies (see Competition from State Owned Enterprises). One hundred percent foreign ownership is permitted except where restricted for national security purposes.

A 2014 law (No. 19,283) bans foreign States' public companies or their sovereign funds (directly or indirectly) from purchasing land locally.

7. PROTECTION OF PROPERTY RIGHTS

REAL PROPERTY

Secured interests in property and contracts are recognized and enforced. Mortgages exist and Uruguay has a recognized and reliable system of recording such securities. Uruguay's legal system protects the acquisition and disposition of all property, including land, buildings and mortgages.

Traditional Use Rights are not applicable as there is no relevant indigenous community in Uruguay. The vast majority of land has clear property titles.

Since 2005, there has been a debate over the government´s and unions´ position to consider occupations of workplaces as an extension of workers' right to strike – thus enabling workers to lawfully occupy workplaces – which has been opposed by business chambers. (See Labor Section for further information)

INTELLECTUAL PROPERTY RIGHTS

Uruguay is a member of the World Intellectual Property Organization (WIPO), and a party to the Bern and Universal Copyright Conventions, as well as the Paris Convention for the Protection of Industrial Property.

The quality of IP protection and level of enforcement within Uruguay has gradually improved over time and in 2006 the Office of the U.S. Trade Representative (USTR) removed Uruguay from its Special 301 Watch List due to progress in enforcing Intellectual Property Rights, especially with respect to copyright enforcement (which represented a significant improvement over the previous 1937 law).

Patents are protected by a 1999 Law (No. 17,164). Invention patents have a twenty-year term of protection from the date of filing. Patents for utility models and industrial designs have a ten-year term of protection from the filing date and may be extended for an additional five years. The law defines compensation as "adequate remuneration" to be paid to the patent-holder. Some industry groups criticize the slowness of the patent-granting process as well as the lack of data protection.

A 1999 trademark law (No. 17,011) upgraded trademark legislation to TRIPS standards. Registered trademarks last ten years and the license can be renewed as many times as desired. The law provides prison penalties of six months to three years for violators, and requires proof of a legal commercial connection to register a foreign trademark. While enforcement of trademark rights has improved in recent years, local citizens have sometimes managed to register trademarks without owners' prior consent.

Uruguay was included in USTR's 2014 Notorious Markets Report for an increase in reports of counterfeiting and piracy from its free trade zones. The report specifically mentions two of the twelve free trade zones as being of concern. A recent Customs Decree will grant Uruguay's National Customs Agency the authority to operate within free trade zones.

Customs officers have ex officio authority to seize and destroy counterfeit goods but they usually act upon right holders' request. Right holders are responsible for paying for the storage and destruction of the counterfeit goods.

Uruguay tracks and reports on Custom's seizures of goods, some of which are counterfeit. Information is available at**http://www.aduanas.gub.uy/innovaportal/v/10500/1/innova.front/incautacion_de_mercaderias.html**. Notwithstanding there is no centralized reporting system on seizures of counterfeit goods.

For additional information about treaty obligations and points of contact at local IP offices, please see Uruguay's country profile at WIPO at **http://www.wipo.int/directory/en/details.jsp?country_code=UY**

Resources for Rights Holders

Post's Economic Officer covering IP issues is:

Mr. Andrew Winkelman
Chief of the Economic-Commercial Section
Tel: (5982) 1770-2429
e-mail: **winkelmanag@state.gov**

8. TRANSPARENCY OF THE REGULATORY SYSTEM

Transparent and streamlined procedures regulate local and foreign investment.

Uruguay has transparent legislation and a special Commission at the Ministry of Economy to foster competition. The main legal pillars (Law No. 18,159 and decree 404, both passed in 2007) are available at the Commission's website:**https://www.mef.gub.uy/578/5/areas/defensa-de-la-competencia---uruguay.html**

Accounting, legal, and regulatory procedures are transparent and consistent with international norms. Proposed laws and regulations are only occasionally published in draft form for public comment. It is common that parliamentary commissions receive stakeholders while discussing a bill. There are no informal regulatory processes managed by non-governmental organizations or private sector associations

Article 10 of the Uruguay-U.S. BIT mandates both countries to publish promptly or make public any law, regulation, procedure or adjudicatory decision related to investments. Article 11 sets transparency procedures that govern the accord.

9. EFFICIENT CAPITAL MARKETS AND PORTFOLIO INVESTMENT

A capital markets law (No. 18,627) was passed in 2009 to try to jumpstart the local capital market. However, as of 2015, the local capital market remains underdeveloped and highly concentrated in sovereign debt, making it difficult to finance through the local equity market. Trading in shares and commercial paper is virtually non-existent (only six firms are registered with BVM to issue shares), severely limiting market liquidity. However, in early 2015 the state-owned electric power company (UTE) had a successful bond issuance in which demand greatly exceeded supply and the value of the bonds immediately rose over 10 percent, indicating an unmet need for investment opportunities.

As a result of such underdevelopment and the lack of enough liquidity in the markets to enter and exit sizeable positions, Uruguay regularly receives “active” investments oriented to establishing new firms or gaining control over existent ones, but lacks “passive” investments from investment funds.

The government maintains an open attitude towards foreign portfolio investment but there is no effective regulatory system to encourage and facilitate it. Uruguay does not impose any restrictions on payments and transfers for current international transactions.

Bearer shares, which had been widely used, were banned in 2012 as part of the process of complying with OECD requirements (see Bilateral Investment Agreements section). Private firms do not use "cross shareholding" or "stable shareholder" arrangements to restrict foreign investment, nor do they restrict participation in or control of domestic enterprises.

Money and Banking System, Hostile Takeovers

The banking system is generally sound. After undergoing a massive crisis in 2002, the local system has been largely unaffected by the 2008 global financial crisis and has good capital, solvency and liquidity ratios.

With over 40 percent of the market, government-owned Banco de la Republica is the nation’s largest and only Uruguayan-owned bank. The rest of the banking system is comprised of ten international banks.

Credit is allocated on market terms, but long-term banking credit has traditionally been difficult to obtain. Foreign investors can access credit on the same market terms as nationals.

10. COMPETITION FROM STATE-OWNED ENTERPRISES

Uruguay is not a party to the WTO’s Plurilateral Agreement on Government Procurement.

Uruguay maintains state monopolies in a number of areas where direct foreign equity participation is prohibited by law. These include the importing and refining of oil, workers' compensation insurance, and landline telephony. Water sanitation, which had been opened to private-sector participation in the mid-1990s, returned to government control in 2004 after a referendum determined that water is a natural resource to be administered exclusively by the State.

Some traditionally government-run monopolies were opened to private-sector competition in recent decades. Cellular and international long distance services, insurance, and media services are now open to local and foreign competitors. Despite competition, state-owned companies have the largest market share in all the aforementioned sectors. Private-sector generation of power is allowed and increasing, especially in renewable energies, but the state-owned power company UTE holds a monopoly on wheeling rights.

State-run monopolies sometimes contract with foreign-owned companies to provide specific services over a period of time under Build-Operate-Transfer (BOT) systems. Road construction and maintenance, and the construction and operation of both Montevideo's port container terminal and the international airport, are examples of BOT projects. The state-owned oil company ANCAP has also established associations with foreign partners for off-shore and on-shore exploration.

In an attempt to address its major infrastructure shortage while preserving fiscal balance, in 2011 Uruguay passed a Public-Private-Partnerships (PPP) law (No. 18,786). The law, passed in Parliament by consensus and regulated in January 2012 by Decree 07/12, formalizes the procedures, responsibilities, and obligations from the State and private investors.

The law allows various kinds of contracts that enable private sector companies to design, build, finance, operate and maintain certain infrastructures, including brownfield projects. With some exceptions (such as medical services in hospitals or educational services in schools) PPPs can also be applied to social infrastructure. The return for the private sector company may come in the form of user payments, government payments or a combination of both. The procurement process is clear in the law and requires fair and open competition. Interested PPP bidders must demonstrate the background and financial strength asked for in the terms of reference of the PPP procurement process.

The PPP law was launched with high hopes that it would attract private sector participation in major infrastructure projects such as highway and railway construction and operation, waste disposal, and energy. However, as of April 2015, only three PPP projects are underway.

State-owned firms are required by law to publish an annual report, and their balances are audited by independent firms.

OECD Guidelines on Corporate Governance of SOEs

Most state-owned firms are defined as autonomous but in practice coordinate certain issues, mainly tariffs, with their respective ministries and the Executive Branch. SOE boards are appointed by the Executive Branch, require Parliamentary ratification and remain in office for the same term as the Executive Branch.

Sovereign Wealth Funds

There are no Sovereign Wealth Funds in Uruguay.

11. CORPORATE SOCIAL RESPONSIBILITY

The concept of Corporate Social Responsibility (CSR) is relatively new to producers, consumers and the government, but many companies do abide by the principles of CSR as a matter of course.

Many multinational companies find it advantageous to stake out a CSR strategy and have made significant contributions in promoting safety awareness, better regulation, a positive work environment and sustainable environmental practices. U.S. companies have proven to be leaders in promoting a greater awareness of and appreciation for CSR in Uruguay.

Consumers tend to pay attention to the CSR image of companies, especially as it relates to a firm's work with local charity or community causes.

OECD Guidelines for Multinational Enterprises

The government does not play an active role in promoting generally accepted CSR principles.

12. POLITICAL VIOLENCE

Uruguay is a stable democracy in which respect for the rule of law is the norm and the majority of the population is committed to non-violence.

There have been no cases of political violence or damage to projects/installations over the past decade.

A 2013 Latinobarometro study (available at **http://www.latinobarometro.org/latContents.jsp**) pointed to Uruguay as the country that is most supportive of democracy (among 18 Latin American countries) and the one with the civic and political culture most similar to European countries.

13. CORRUPTION

Overall, U.S. firms have not identified corruption as an obstacle to investment.

Together with Chile, Uruguay was ranked as the least corrupt country in Latin America in the 2014 edition of Transparency International's Corruption Perception Index.

Uruguay signed and ratified the UN's Anticorruption Convention and has laws to prevent bribery and other corrupt practices. A law against corruption in the public sector was approved in 1998 and acceptance of a bribe is a felony under Uruguay's penal code. Some high level Uruguayan officials, from the Executive, Parliament and the Judiciary, have been prosecuted for corruption in recent years.

Laws 17,835 and 18,494 (passed in 2004 and 2009) and Decree 226/10 establish a strong framework against money laundering and terrorism finance and include corruption as a preceding crime. Money laundering is penalized with sentences of up to ten years (and also applies to Uruguayans living abroad). Prosecutions have been gradually increasing since 2005.

The Transparency and Public Ethics Committee (**http://www.jutep.gub.uy/**) is the government office responsible for combating public sector corruption.

UN Anticorruption Convention, OECD Convention on Combating Bribery

Uruguay is not a member of the OECD and therefore not party to the OECD's Convention on Combating Bribery.

Resources to Report Corruption

Contact at government agency or agencies responsible for combating corruption:

Name: Mr. Luis Yarzabal
Title: President
Institution: Junta de Transparencia y Etica Publica
Address: Rincon 528, 8th floor, ZC 11000
Tel: (598) 2917 0407
e-mail: **secretaria@jutep.gub.uy**

The local branch of Transparency International is **http://www.uruguaytransparente.org.uy/**

14. BILATERAL INVESTMENT AGREEMENTS

In November 2005, Uruguay and the United States signed a Bilateral Investment Treaty (BIT) to promote and protect reciprocal investments that entered into force on November 1, 2006. The full text of the agreement is available at**www.ustr.gov/Trade_Agreements/BIT/Section_Index.html**.

The BIT grants national and most-favored-nation treatments to investments and investors sourced in each country. The agreement also includes detailed provisions on compensation for expropriation, and a precise procedure for settling bilateral disputes. The annexes include sector-specific measures that are not covered by the agreement and specific sectors or activities which governments may restrict further.

Besides the United States, Uruguay has Bilateral Investment Agreements with the following countries: Armenia; Australia; the Belgium-Luxembourg Economic Union (BLEU); Canada; Chile; China; Czech Republic; El Salvador; Finland; France; Germany; Hungary; India; Israel; Italy; Japan; South Korea; Malaysia; Mexico; Netherlands; Panama; Poland; Portugal; Romania; Spain; Sweden; Switzerland; United Kingdom; United States of America; Venezuela and Vietnam. Uruguay also has BIT with Argentina, Brazil and Paraguay (a general agreement signed in MERCOSUR in 1994).

In 2009, the GOU reacted to its inclusion by the OECD in a grey list of jurisdictions that had not "committed to implement the internationally agreed tax standard." Since then, the government has endorsed OECD standards on transparency and exchange of information and upgraded several regulations to meet such standards. Main measures include signing several tax information exchange agreements, relaxing bank secrecy provisions, and modifying its bearer shares system. In October 2012, the OECD acknowledged the GOU's progress and allowed Uruguay to move on to the second phase of the review process, consisting of a survey of the practical implementation of the standards.

According to the OECD's Global Forum on Transparency and Exchange of Information for Tax Purposes, as of March 2015 Uruguay had signed 31 TIEAs, 16 of which include double taxation provisions. Ten of the TIEAs, three of which include double taxation provisions, are pending parliamentary ratification as of March 2015.

Uruguay has TIEAs with double taxation provisions with Ecuador, Finland, Germany, Hungary, India, Liechtenstein, Malta, Mexico, Portugal, Romania, South Korea, Spain and Switzerland. Agreements with Belgium, United Arab Emirates and Vietnam are pending parliamentary ratification.

Uruguay also has TIEAs in effect –without double taxation provisions– with Argentina, Australia, Canada, Denmark, France, Greenland, Iceland and Norway. TIEAs with seven other countries are pending parliamentary ratification (Brazil, Chile, Faroe Islands, Guernsey, The Netherlands, Sweden and the United Kingdom).

BILATERAL TAXATION TREATIES

Uruguay and the United States do not have double taxation or tax information agreements in place.

15. OPIC AND OTHER INVESTMENT INSURANCE PROGRAMS

Overseas Private Investment Corporation (OPIC) programs are active in Uruguay, though few U.S. companies/projects request their services as due to the country's stability, access to foreign currency, etc., they see little need for them. The GOU signed an investment insurance agreement with OPIC in December 1982. In 2014, the average exchange rate was USD 23.15 Uruguayan Pesos to the Dollar.

16. LABOR

Over the past couple of years, the labor market has operated at virtually full employment, and there has been a shortage of labor in some sectors. Unemployment is structurally higher among youth, especially young women.

Salary Councils - consisting of a three party board including representatives from unions, employers, and the government - are responsible for setting wage increases at a sectoral level that are then applied by individual firms in the sector. If unions and employers fail to reach an agreement to determine the wage increase to be applied for sectors, the government makes the final decision. Labor costs have been increasing over time.

Social security payments are approximately 30 percent of workers' basic salary. Private sector employers are prohibited from firing workers for discriminatory or anti-union reasons. It is not uncommon that dismissals result in labor conflicts. The employer must pay the worker one month for each year of work, with a cap of six months.

Despite its very high literacy rate and tradition of quality public education, Uruguay is currently experiencing a high dropout rate in high school and poor performance in the OECD's Program for International Student Assessment (PISA) that have the potential to reduce the number of qualified workers available over the mid-term. In 2008, the government launched a special institute, INEFOP, to help train the workforce.

Some foreign investors have also reported concerns about the productivity level of Uruguay's workforce. Productivity is usually not included in the negotiations that take place in the salary councils. Given the strong economic growth over the past decade, very low current unemployment (that limits future growth based on labor accumulation) and inflationary pressures, the government is concerned about fostering productivity and intends to include productivity measures in upcoming wage negotiations.

Unionization has tripled from about 110,000 in 2003 to over 350,000 in 2013 (approximately 21 percent of employed workers), and is particularly high in the public sector and some private sectors, such as construction and banks.

Since 2005, the government has introduced several changes to the labor market, including:

In 2005, the government rescinded a decree that enabled employers to request police action to evict occupying workers.

In December 2010, the government passed a decree providing expedited procedures for evicting occupants of public-sector workplaces.

The law on the "Promotion and Protection of Labor Unions," passed in 2006, provides for the immediate reinstatement of the employee if any infringement of the law is proven.

Law 18,099, passed in 2007, on outsourcing increased employers' responsibility for labor violations by third-party firms that were contracted by the employers.

A September 2009 law on Collective Bargaining (No. 18,566) which established a bargaining system structured at three levels: national scope; branch of activity or productive chain; and bipartite collective bargaining at the company level.

Law 19,196, passed in March 2014, provides penal sanctions ranging from three months to two years imprisonment for those employers or their representatives who fail to adopt labor safety standards and thus generate a grave and concrete danger to the life or physical integrity of workers.

Uruguay has ratified numerous International Labor Organization (ILO) conventions that protect worker rights, and generally adheres to their provisions. The Uruguayan constitution guarantees workers the right to organize and strike, and union members are protected by law against dismissal for union activities. Sympathy strikes are legal.

In labor trials, the Judiciary tends to rule in favor of the worker, as s/he is considered to be the weaker party. Labor unions are nominally independent from the government but in practice have a close affinity with the ruling Frente Amplio party.

17. FOREIGN TRADE ZONES/FREE PORTS/TRADE FACILITATION

Twelve free trade zones (FTZs) are located throughout the country. Most FTZs host a wide variety of tenants performing various services (e.g., financial, software, call centers, warehousing and logistics). One FTZ was created exclusively for the development of pharmaceuticals, and two for the production of paper pulp. Since MERCOSUR regulations treat products manufactured in most member states' FTZs (with the exception of Tierra del Fuego and Manaus located in Argentina and Brazil) as extra-territorial – and hence charge them the common external tariff upon entering any member country– industrial production in local FTZs is destined to non-MERCOSUR countries.

Goods, services, products, and raw materials of foreign and Uruguayan origin may be brought into the FTZs, held, processed, and re-exported without payment of Uruguayan customs duties or import taxes. Firms operating in FTZs are also exempted from national taxes.

Government monopolies are not honored within FTZs. Local and foreign-owned industries alike enjoy several advantages in an FTZ, including exemption from all domestic taxes. Additionally, the employer does not pay social security taxes for non-Uruguayan employees who have waived coverage under the Uruguayan social security system. However, Uruguayans must comprise at least 75 percent of a company's labor force to qualify for FTZ tenancy. Goods of Uruguayan origin entering into FTZs are treated as Uruguayan exports for tax and other legal purposes.

Key regulations of free zones:

The operation of free trade zones (FTZs) is regulated by Law 15,921 (from 1987) and the Ministry of Finance's Free Trade Zone Directorate.

Decree 344/010 passed in November 2010 introduced some changes in the free zone regime in order to discourage the establishment of shell or "paper" corporations in free zones for tax evasion purposes. The

Decree requires companies to submit a business plan and limits the term of the authorization to ten years, which is renewable upon GOU review.

Article 309 of Law 18,996 (passed in November 2012) regulates the kind of activities that FTZ users can perform outside the FTZs. For instance, the law prevents them from performing commercial activities of substantial nature (e.g. selling, exhibiting or delivering) related to goods destined to Uruguay's regular (i.e. non-free zone) territory. The law also requires users to request a GOU permit to perform non-substantive activities outside FTZs.

In July 2013, the Executive Branch submitted a bill introducing changes to the FTZ regime –including authorization for Customs´ inspections in FTZ, newly permitted industrial and services-related activities, and new regulations on transfer prices. The bill was not voted in the 2010-2015 parliamentary term and, should the Executive insist with the changes, it would have to submit a new bill. Customs´ inspections in FTZs were subsequently authorized by Decree 97/015 from March 2015.

Law 17,547 passed in August 2002 allows for the establishment of Industrial Parks. Several decrees signed since 2007 have made Industrial Parks more attractive and since then a number, some of which are sector-specific, have been created. Advantages include fiscal exemptions and tax benefits. Industrial Parks can be established by the private sector or the national or local governments.

Uruguay has other special import regimes in place, including Temporary Admission, Private Customs Deposits and Free Ports. The Temporary Admission regime allows manufacturers to import duty-free the raw materials, supplies, parts and intermediate products they will use to manufacture products that will later be exported. The system requires a government authorization and that final products be exported within a period of 18 months. Firms do not have to be located in a specific location to benefit from Temporary Admission.

The Free Port and Bonded Warehouses are special areas where goods that are kept within the premises are exempted from all import-related duties and tariffs. While in the premises, merchandise may be labeled, fractioned and re-packaged. The two differences between the Free Ports and the Bonded Warehouses regimes are that goods can stay for an unlimited amount of time in Free Ports (Bonded Warehouses restrict the stay to one year), and processes done in Free Ports cannot modify the nature of the good (industrialization is allowed in Bonded Warehouses).

The GOU has been increasingly promoting Uruguay as a regional world-class logistics and distribution center. In December 2010, it created the National Logistics Institute (INALOG by its Spanish acronym), a public-private sector institution that seeks to coordinate efforts towards establishing Uruguay as the leading MERCOSUR distribution hub. Uruguay's Investment Promotion Agency, Uruguay XXI, has several reports on Uruguay's role and advantages as a logistics hub.

18. FOREIGN DIRECT INVESTMENT AND FOREIGN PORTFOLIO INVESTMENT STATISTICS

Table 2: Key Macroeconomic Data, U.S. FDI in Host Country/Economy

	Host Country Statistical source*		USG or International Statistical Source		USG or International Source of Data: BEA; IMF; Eurostat; UNCTAD, Other
Economic	Year	Amount	Year	Amount	

Data					
Host Country Gross Domestic Product (GDP) ($M USD)	2014	57.6 billion	2013	55.7 billion	www.worldbank.org/en/country
Foreign Direct Investment	Host Country Statistical source*		USG or International Statistical Source		USG or International Source of data: BEA; IMF; Eurostat; UNCTAD, Other
U.S. FDI in partner country ($M USD, stock positions)	2013	899	2013	1,307	BEA data available 3/19/14 athttp://bea.gov/international/direct_investment_multinational_companies_comprehensive_data.htm
Host country's FDI in the United States ($M USD, stock positions)	N/A	N/A	2013	327	BEA data available 3/19/14 athttp://bea.gov/international/direct_investment_multinational_companies_comprehensive_data.htm
Total inbound stock of FDI as % host GDP	2013	34%			

*** http://www.bcu.gub.uy/Estadisticas-e-Indicadores/Paginas/Default.aspx**

Table 3: Sources and Destination of FDI

Five countries accounted for half of total FDI in 2009-13. Argentina was the largest investor with 30 percent of total FDI, followed by Brazil (7 percent), Spain (6 percent), The Netherlands (5 percent) and the United States (4 percent). Annual average U.S. investment rose to USD 77 million in 2009-2013 from USD 58 million in 2004-2008.

Uruguay's Central Bank reports that the United States held the 4th largest stock of investment in 2013 – USD 899 million (the U.S. Department of Commerce's Bureau of Economic Analysis indicates an investment stock of USD 1.3 billion). U.S. investment is distributed among a wide array of sectors, including forestry, tourism and hotels, services (e.g. call centers or back office) and telecommunications.

DIRECT INVESTMENT FROM/IN COUNTERPART ECONOMY DATA					
FROM TOP FIVE SOURCES/TO TOP FIVE DESTINATIONS (US DOLLARS, MILLIONS)					
INWARD DIRECT INVESTMENT			OUTWARD DIRECT INVESTMENT		
Total Inward	17,547	100%	Total Outward	N/A	100%
Argentina	4,717	27%			
Brazil	1,338	8%			
Spain	1,173	7%			
United States	894	5%			
Netherlands	738	4%			
"0" reflects amounts rounded to +/- USD 500,000.					

Source: IMF Coordinated Direct Investment Survey

Table 4: Sources of Portfolio Investment

PORTFOLIO INVESTMENT ASSETS								
TOP FIVE PARTNERS (MILLIONS, US DOLLARS)								
TOTAL			EQUITY SECURITIES			TOTAL DEBT SECURITIES		
All Countries	4,456	100%	All Countries	667	100%	All Countries	3,789	100%
United States	1,410	32%	United States	157	24%	United States	1254	33%
Brazil	318	7%	Luxembourg	156	23%	Brazil	306	8%
Luxembourg	272	6%	U.K.	126	19%	Cuba	190	5%
U.K.	250	6%	Spain	83	12%	Sweden	168	4%
Cuba	190	4%	Bermuda	80	12%	Netherlands	151	4%

Source: IMF Coordinated Portfolio Investment Survey

IMPORTANT BUSINESS CONTACTS

CONTACT FOR MORE INFORMATION

Mr. Andrew Winkelman
Chief of Economic-Commercial Section
Lauro Muller 1776

Tel: (5982) 1770-2429
e-mail: **winkelmanag@state.gov**

Uruguay's Investment Promotion Agency, Uruguay XXI, also provides relevant information on the investment and trade regimes to potential investors.

LOCAL LAWYERS

COLEGIO DE ABOGADOS DE URUGUAY
Av. 18 de Julio 1006, Apto 401 / Montevideo, Uruguay 11100
TEL: +598 2900 2065
FAX: +598 2902 3778
EMAIL: colabog@adinet.com.uy

DRA. ESC. ANDREA ALTERWAIN BRÜCK
WTC – Luis A de Herrera 1248, Torre 3 Piso 4 Of. 474, Montevideo, Uruguay.
TEL: +598 2626 0184
CEL: +598 99662030
EMAIL: estudio.juridicoab@yahoo.es
WEB SITE: www.estudioab.com.uy

ALS GLOBAL LAW & ACCOUNTING
Soriano 1124 / Montevideo, Uruguay 11100
TEL.: +598 2900 9730
FAX: +598 2903 0095
EMAIL: mloinaz@alsuruguay.com
WEB SITE: www.alsuruguay.com
FIELDS OF SPECIALIZATION: Family Law, Adoptions, Child Custody, Parental Child Abduction, Child Protection, Marriage/Divorce, Insurance, Banking/Financial, Commercial/Business Law, Foreign Investments, Marketing Agreements, Patents/Trademarks/Copyrights, Civil Law, Criminal Law, Damages, Narcotics, Collections, Commercial Law, Contracts, Transportation Law, Corporations, Aeronautical/Maritime, Foreign Claims, Estates, Taxes, Government Relations, Labor Relations, Immigration and Auto/Accidents.

BADO, KUSTER, ZERBINO & RACHETTI
Treinta y Tres 1269/71 / Montevideo, Uruguay 11000
TEL: +598 2916 0310
FAX: +598 2915 5669
EMAIL: mbonino@bkzr.com.uy; estudio@bkzr.com
WEBSITE: www.bkzr.com.uy
FIELDS OF SPECIALIZATION: Commercial/Business Law, Foreign Investments, Foreign Claims, Civil Law, Damages, Collections, Contracts, Transportation Law, Corporations, Estates, Immigration, Accidents.

Name: Baker Tilly Uruguay
Address: Juncal 1305 piso 13
Phone(s): +598 2917 0045
Fax: +598 2916 6907
E-mail: fernandop@bakertillyuruguay.com.uy
Website: www.bakertillyuruguay.com.uy

Fields of Specialization: Family Law, Inheritance Law, Commercial and Corporative Law, international and local Tax and Accounting, Criminal Law, Contracts and Civil Law, Labor Relations, Residency and Immigration

BAKER TILLY URUGUAY
Juncal 1305 piso 13 / Montevideo, Uruguay 11000
PHONE(S): +598 2917 0045
FAX: +598 2916 6907
E-MAIL: fernandop@bakertillyuruguay.com.uy
WEBSITE: www.bakertillyuruguay.com.uy

FIELDS OF SPECIALIZATION: Family Law, Inheritance Law, Commercial and Corporative Law, international and local Tax and Accounting, Criminal Law, Contracts and Civil Law, Labor Relations, Residency and Immigration

BRAGARD & DURÁN ABOGADOS
Yamandú Rodríguez 1321 / Montevideo, Uruguay 11500
TEL./FAX: +598 2600 4447
EMAIL: bda@bda.com.uy
WEBSITE: www.bda.com.uy
FIELDS OF SPECIALIZATION: Banking/Financial, Commercial/Business Law, Foreign Investments, Contracts, Corporations, Estates, Taxes, Government relations, Labor Relations and Immigration.

BRUM / COSTA ABOGADOS
Costa Rica 1667, Second Floor, Carrasco / Montevideo, Uruguay 11500
TEL: +598 2601 7777
EMAIL: obrum@brumcosta.com
WEBSITE: www.brumcosta.com
FIELDS OF SPECIALIZATION: Marriage/Divorce, Insurance, Banking/Financial, Commercial/Business Law, Foreign Investments, Foreign Claims, Marketing Agreements, Civil Law, Criminal Law, Damages, Collections, Contracts, Corporations, Transportation Law, Estates, Taxes, Government Relations, Labor Relations, Immigrations, Accidents.

ESTUDIO BERGSTEIN
Av. 18 de Julio 1117, 5th floor / Montevideo, Uruguay 11100
Tel: +598 2901 2448
FAX: +598 2902 6181
EMAIL: attorneys@bergsteinlaw.com
WEBSITE: www.bergsteinlaw.com
FIELDS OF SPECIALIZATION: Insurance, Banking/Financial, Commercial/Business Law, Foreign Investments, Marketing Agreements, Contracts, Corporations, Taxes.

ESTUDIO RUIZ LAPUENTE
Colonia 810, Office 502 / Montevideo, Uruguay 11100
TEL: +598 2902 1440
FAX: +598 2902 1440
EMAIL: carlos@ruizlapuente.com.uy
WEBSITE: www.ruizlapuente.com.uy

FIELDS OF SPECIALIZATION: Banking/Financial, Commercial/Business Law, Foreign Investments, Patents/Trademarks/Copyrights, Contracts, Corporations, Taxes.

FERRERE ABOGADOS
Edificio Ferrere. Juncal 1392 / Montevideo, Uruguay 11000
TEL: +598 2900 1000
FAX: +598 2900 5000
EMAIL: ferrere@ferrere.com
WEBSITE: www.ferrere.com and www.cpaferrere.com
FIELDS OF SPECIALIZATION: Family Law, Child Custody, Marriage/Divorce, Insurance, Banking/Financial, Commercial/Business Law, Foreign Investments, Marketing Agreements, Patents/Trademarks/ Copyrights, Civil Law, Damages, Collections, Contracts, Transportation Law, Corporations, Aeronautic/Maritime, Foreign Claims, Estates, taxes, Government Relations, Labor Relations, Immigration.

FISCHER & SCHICKENDANTZ
Rincón 487, 4th floor / Montevideo, Uruguay 11100
TEL: +598 2915 7468
FAX: +598 2916 1352
EMAIL: info@fs.com.uy
WEBSITE: www.fs.com.uy
FIELDS OF SPECIALIZATION: Corporate/ Mergers & Acquisitions/ Banking, Real Estate, Commercial/Contracts, Agribusiness & Farmland Investment, Mining, Company Incorporations / Offshore Corporations, Tax & Accounting, Litigation & Arbitration, Labor & Employment, Administrative & Public Law, Residency & Immigration.

GUYER & REGULES
Dr. Luis Bonavita 1294 / Office. 807 - WTC Free Zone / Montevideo, Uruguay 11300
TEL: (598) 2626 1515
FAX: (598) 2626 1515 ext. 213
EMAIL: post@gr.com.uy
WEBSITE: www.guyer.com.uy
FIELDS OF SPECIALIZATION: Family Law, Insurance, Banking/Financial, Commercial/Business Law, Foreign Investments, Marketing Agreements, Patents/Trademarks/Copyrights, Civil Law, Damages, Collections, Contracts, Transportation Law, Corporations, Aeronautical/Maritime, Foreign Claims, Estates, Taxes, Government Relations, Labor Relations, Immigration, Auto/Accidents.

HUGHES & HUGHES
25 de Mayo 455, 2nd floor / Montevideo, Uruguay 11100
TEL: +598 2916 0988
FAX: +598 2916 1003
EMAIL: H&H@hughes.com.uy
WEBSITE: www.hughes.com.uy
FIELDS OF SPECIALIZATION: Insurance, Banking/Financial, Commercial/Business Law, Foreign Investments, Marketing Agreements, Civil Law, Damages, Contracts, Transportation Law, Corporations, Aeronautical/Maritime, Taxes, Government Relations, Labor Relations, Immigration.

JIMÉNEZ DE ARECHAGA, VIANA & BRAUSE
Zabala 1504 esq. Cerrito / Montevideo, Uruguay 11100

TEL: +598 2916 1460
FAX: +598 2916 3961
EMAIL: estudio@jimenez.com.uy
WEBSITE: www.jimenez.com.uy
FIELDS OF SPECIALIZATION: Banking & Finance, Corporate / Mergers & Acquisitions, Litigation / Arbitration, Labor & Employment, Real Estate, Tax, Energy and Natural Resources.

LOCKLING & LABRUNA – ABOGADOS
Río Negro 1354, 5th floor, Office 31 / Montevideo, Uruguay 11100
TEL: +598 2901 2867
FAX: +598 2901 2867 Ext. 2
EMAIL: contacto@locklinglabruna.com
FIELDS OF SPECIALIZATION: Transportation Law, Aeronautical/Maritime/Tourism, Family Law, Adoptions, Child Custody, Marriage/Divorce, Inheritance Law, Commercial/Business Law, Civil Law, Immigration, Litigation, Collections, Labor Relations and Foreign Claims.

ESTUDIO DR. MEZZERA
Plaza Independencia 811 / 1st Floor/ Montevideo, Uruguay 11100
TEL: +598 2902 9020 or +598 2915 0500
FAX: 598 2902-2415
EMAIL: postmaster@estudiomezzera.com.uy
WEB PAGE: www.estudiomezzera.com.uy
FIELDS OF SPECIALIZATION: Arbitration and Mediation, Banking and Financial Services, Civil/Commercial Law, Intellectual Property, Corporate Law, Environmental Law, Family Law, International Law and International Contracts, Internet and Communications, Insurance, Integration and Mercosur, Investment, Labor Law, Litigation, Real Estate and Vessels, Taxes, Transportation, Customs Law.

MEZZERA ABOGADOS
Plaza Independencia 831 office 405 / Montevideo, Uruguay 11100
TEL: (598) 2908 3333
FAX: (598) 2908 3333
EMAIL: rmezzera@mezzera.com.uy
WEB PAGE: www.mezzera.com.uy
FIELDS OF SPECIALIZATION: Commercial/Business Law, Contracts, Transportation Law, Corporations, Estates, Taxes, Labor Relations, Immigration, Insurance.

PÉREZ DEL CASTILLO & ASOCIADOS
Juncal 1327 D 1803 / Montevideo, Uruguay
TEL: +598 2915 0743
FAX: +598 2915 0762
EMAIL: estudio@pdelc.com.uy
WEBSITE: www.pdelc.com.uy
FIELDS OF SPECIALIZATION: Banking/Financial, Commercial/Business Law, Foreign Investments, Civil Law, Damages, Commercial Law, Contracts, Corporations, Labor Relations, Immigration, Translator and notary.
POSADAS, POSADAS & VECINO
Mones Roses 6937 / Montevideo, Uruguay 11500

TEL: +598 2604 1604
FAX: +598 2604 6604
EMAIL: mail@ppv.com.uy
WEBSITE: www.ppv.com.uy
FIELDS OF SPECIALIZATION: Insurance, Banking/Finance, Commercial/Business Law, Foreign investments, Civil Law, Patents/Trademarks/Copyrights, Contracts, Corporations, Litigation, Aeronautical/Maritime, Foreign Claims, Estates, Taxes, Labor Relations.

PREVE ABOGADOS
Circunvalación Durango 383 office 303 / Plaza Zabala, Montevideo 11000
TEL/FAX: (+598) 2916 5450
EMAIL: mpreve@preveabogados.com
WEBSITE: www.preveabogados.com

FIELDS OF SPECIALIZATION: Commercial/Business Law, Foreign Investments, Marketing Agreements, Civil Law, Damages, Commercial Law, Contracts, Transportation Law, Corporations, Aeronautical/Maritime, Foreign Claims, Estates, Government Relations.

RUEDA, ABADI & PEREIRA
Avda. Libertador 1680, 2nd floor / Montevideo, Uruguay 11100
TEL: +598 2901 3020
FAX: +598 2901 3020
EMAIL: rap@rap.com.uy
WEBSITE: www.rap.com.uy
FIELDS OF SPECIALIZATION: Insurance, Banking/Finance, Commercial/Business Law, Foreign Investments, Marketing Agreements, Patents/Trademarks/Copyrights, Civil Law, Damages, Collections, Contracts, Transportation Law, Corporations, Foreign Claims, Estates, Taxes, Labor Relations, Immigration, Accidents.

SANGUINETTI / FODERÉ ABOGADOS
Ituzaingó 1377, 2nd, 3rd, 4th, 5th floor / Montevideo, Uruguay 11000
TEL: +598 2915 0101
FAX: +598 2915 0101
EMAIL: sfb@sfb.com.uy
WEBSITE: www.sfb.com.uy
FIELDS OF SPECIALIZATION: Insurance, Banking/Financial, Commercial/Business Law, Foreign Investments, Marketing Agreements, Civil Law, Damages, Collections, Contracts, Transportation Law, Corporations, Aeronautical/Maritime, Foreign Claims, Estates, Taxes, Government Relations, Labor Relations, Immigration, Auto/Accidents.

SUR CONSULTORES
Av. Libertador 1513 office 14 / Montevideo, Uruguay
TEL: +598 2908 9569
EMAIL: info@surconsultores.com
WEBSITE: www.surconsultores.com
FIELDS OF SPECIALIZATION: Legal and Accountant Assistance, Insurance, Insurance, Business Matchmaking, Investment Advice, Trusteeships, Regional and Mercosur Regulations, Tax advice and Presentation, Book Keeping, Immigration & Residence for Foreign Citizens, Grupo Network and legal Offices all over Latin America.

URUGUAY RESIDENCY GROUP
Galeria Santos Dumont L. 12 No 230/ Punta Del Este, Uruguay 20100
TEL: +001 310 740 9966
FAX: +001 310 861 0474
EMAIL: info@uruguayresidencylawyers.com
WEBSITE: www.uruguayresidencylawyers.com
FIELDS OF SPECIALIZATION: Our firm, comprised of US licensed attorneys, specializes in providing high quality residency and immigration services to US citizens and businesses that wish to relocate to Uruguay.

VENEZUELA - INVESTMENT AND BUSINESS CLIMATE - STRATEGIC INFORMATION AND CONTACTS FOR STARTING BUSINESS

Venezuela is located on the northern coast of South America. Political tensions, state interventions in the economy, macroeconomic distortions, physical insecurity, corruption, and a volatile regulatory framework make Venezuela a difficult climate for foreign investors. Conditions for foreign investment are unlikely to improve in the near term. During 2014 the Venezuelan government (GBRV) passed new foreign investment laws that have made the country less hospitable to foreign investors. The falling oil prices, which started in the second quarter of last year, have aggravated Venezuela's economic crisis. Venezuela finished 2014 with an estimated 4 percent economic contraction, 68.4 percent inflation, and widespread shortages of consumer goods. For 2015, the International Monetary Fund (IMF) projects that the economy will shrink another 7 percent, with inflation reaching 80 percent. Financial analysts have raised concerns that strains on Venezuela's USD resources could exacerbate shortages of consumer goods and potentially force a default on its external debt.

The energy sector dominates Venezuela's import-dependent economy; the petroleum industry provides roughly 96 percent of export earnings, 40 percent of government revenues, and 11 percent of GDP. Falling petroleum export revenues and a corruption-plagued, mismanaged foreign exchange regime have deprived multinational firms of hard currency to repatriate earnings and import inputs and finished goods. Insufficient access to USD, price controls, and rigid labor regulations have compelled U.S. and multinational firms to reduce or shut down their Venezuelan operations, while high costs for oil production and state oil company Petroleos de Venezuela's (PDVSA) poor cash flow have slowed investment in the petroleum sector. Venezuela has traditionally been a destination for U.S. direct investment, especially in energy and manufacturing, and for exports of U.S. machinery, medical supplies, chemicals, agricultural products, and vehicles. Such investment and trade links have been weakened in recent years by GBRV efforts to build commercial relationships with ideological allies, strained U.S.-Venezuelan relations, and the deteriorating investment climate.

Under President Nicolas Maduro, the GBRV's policy response to Venezuela's economic crisis has centered on increasing state control over the economy. President Maduro has used decree powers to pass laws that implement former President Hugo Chavez's Second Socialist Plan for 2013-2019; erode foreign investors' rights; deepen the state's role as the primary buyer and marketer of imports; tighten the currency control regime; and empower the GBRV to cap business profits and regulate prices throughout the economy. The GBRV has promulgated regulations to open a new alternative foreign exchange mechanism for the private sector to buy and sell dollars, including for qualified oil sector inflows, but the new system has attracted limited hard currency in its first months of operation. The GBRV has implemented new laws and regulations to varying degrees, and their staying power remains unproven, increasing uncertainty in the investment climate.

U.S. and multinational firms contemplating business in Venezuela should weigh carefully the risks posed by an ongoing economic crisis, a non-transparent and heavily if unevenly regulated operating environment, and a foreign exchange regime that strictly limits access to hard currency.

1. OPENNESS TO, AND RESTRICTIONS UPON, FOREIGN INVESTMENT

ATTITUDE TOWARD FOREIGN DIRECT INVESTMENT

Recent changes to Venezuela's legal and regulatory regime reflect the GBRV's hardening posture toward foreign investment. The 1999 constitution generally provides for equal treatment of foreign and domestic investment. Article 301 provides for equal treatment of national and foreign investment. Article 302 reserves the petroleum industry and other strategic sectors of public interest for the state. In November 2014 a new foreign investment law was issued. While the new law has reduced foreign investors' statutory rights, it remains unclear how it will be enforced.

OTHER INVESTMENT POLICY REVIEWS

The World Trade Organization (WTO) last conducted a Trade Policy Review of Venezuela in 2002.

LAWS/REGULATIONS OF FOREIGN DIRECT INVESTMENT

In November 2014, a new foreign investment law went into effect. The new law, issued by presidential decree, has reduced foreign investors' statutory rights compared to the prior regime. The law abolishes the former Superintendent of Foreign Investment (SIEX) and declared the Venezuelan currency commission, the National Center for Foreign Commerce (CENCOEX), to be the new regulatory authority for foreign investment, under oversight of the Commerce Ministry. The Petroleum and Mining Ministry and the Economy, Finance, and Public Banking Ministry have concurrent authority with CENCOEX for regulating their respective sectors. CENCOEX and other competent authorities will have six months from the time this new law goes into effect to implement regulations.

This law stipulates the following legal entities and physical persons are subject to its measures; foreign businesses (51 percent or more owned by non-Venezuelans) and their affiliates and subsidiaries (50 percent or more owned by a foreign business), national companies subject to a strategic plan by two or more states; national companies that capture foreign investment as defined by the law; Venezuelans and non-Venezuelans resident abroad who invest in Venezuela; non-Venezuelans resident in Venezuela who undertake investments in Venezuela. This law defines an investment as any legally obtained resources used for the production of goods and services, particularly those of national origin or manufacturing, that contribute to creating jobs, promoting small and medium enterprises (SMEs), local production chains, and innovation. It also includes financial, tangible, and non-tangible assets, as well as reinvested earnings.

Tangible goods are required to make up at least 75 percent of the value of the foreign investment. Foreign investment must be for a minimum value of USD 1 million and for at least five years, although CENCOEX may exceptionally approve an investment of no less than USD 100,000 for the promotion of SMEs. After the initial five years and payment of any financial obligations, a foreign investor may repatriate up to 85 percent of the registered foreign investment. This condition is waived if the foreign investor instead sells the business to local investors who will continue to operate the business. In those cases, the foreign investor may repatriate 100 percent of their investment.

Likewise the pay out of earnings and dividends will now be done in the local currency in Venezuela. No more than 80 percent of earnings may be repatriated in hard currency in any fiscal year. The GBRV may undertake special measures regarding foreign investments and technology transfer, including limiting earnings and capital repatriation, if extraordinary circumstances affect Venezuela's balance of payments or international reserves. Neither CENCOEX, nor its predecessor, CADIVI, has authorized USD sales for purposes of earnings or capital repatriation since 2008 (see Conversion and Transfer Policies).

All foreign investors must, contribute to the production of goods and services to satisfy domestic demand and promote non-traditional exports; aid in economic development, research, and innovation; participate in Venezuelan government economic policies; implement responsible business conduct programs consistent with international standards; and align to the objectives of Venezuela's national economic policy. Failure to comply subjects a foreign investor to revocation of the foreign investment registration and monetary fines.

Foreign investors will enjoy rights as foreign investors once CENCOEX or another competent authority provides them with a foreign investment registration. CENCOEX had not published regulations pursuant to the new law as of the drafting of this report.

Comparative information on the former requirements for foreign investments under decree 2095 is still available at the SIEX website, although it is unclear whether such regulations are still valid: http://www.siex.gob.ve/. New regulations should eventually be available on CENCOEX's website: http://www.cencoex.gob.ve/.

INDUSTRIAL PROMOTION

Energy and Mining

The GBRV has made changes to contracts, royalty and tax policies that have expanded state control of the hydrocarbons sector. The 2001 Hydrocarbons Law did not grandfather contracts executed under earlier legislation. The 2001 hydrocarbons law reserved for the state the rights of exploration, production, transportation and storage of petroleum and associated natural gas. Under these regulations, hydrocarbon activities must be carried out by state-owned enterprises such as PDVSA, or by a public-private partnership with at least 50 percent state ownership.

In 2005, the GBRV informed companies operating under service contracts that they needed to convert their existing contracts into joint ventures to conform to the 2001 Hydrocarbons Law. That same year, the Venezuelan government threatened to seize 33 services contracts if these foreign investors did not migrate their existing contracts to the new format. Sixteen of those oil companies signed memoranda of understanding, converting their contracts to joint ventures. Exiting joint venture investments in the petroleum sector have proved problematic for minority partners seeking to sell their stakes, as GBRV approval is required.

In contrast to the framework for petroleum, the 1999 Gaseous Hydrocarbons Law offers more favorable terms to investors within the unassociated natural gas sector, which is mostly offshore This law opened the sector to private investment, both domestic and foreign, and created a licensing system for exploration and production regulated by the former Ministry of Energy and Mines (now the Ministry of Petroleum and Mining). Venezuela retained ownership of all natural gas in situ, but PDVSA involvement was not required for gas development projects (although the law allows PDVSA to back into 35 percent ownership of any natural gas project once the private partners have declared commerciality). The law prohibited vertical integration of the gas business from the wellhead to the consumer.

In 2008, the Organic Law on the Restructuring of the Internal Liquid Fuels Market came into effect. The law mandates government control of domestic transportation and wholesale of liquid fuels and set a 60-day period for negotiations with the affected companies. The law does not define liquid fuels, this created uncertainty as to whether it applies to products other than gasoline and diesel fuel. This law affected companies that had investments in the downstream sector.

In 2009, Venezuela enacted the Organic Law that Reserve to the State the Assets and Services related to Hydrocarbon Primary Activities. The law affected petroleum service companies involved in the injection of water, steam, or gas as secondary recovery methods, as well as services rendered for the performance of primary activities on Lake Maracaibo. It provided for the rendering of contracts previously executed between PDVSA and private companies. All contracts and activities governed by this law are subject to domestic law and are the exclusive jurisdiction of Venezuelan courts. The GBRV nationalized more than 75 companies, including three U.S. firms. In 2014, the GBRV announced it had reached an agreement to compensate the Venezuelan owners of a small number of the expropriated firms.

Despite Venezuela's expropriations in the petroleum sector and the costly and difficult operating environment, since 2009, several international companies have agreed to create joint venture companies with PDVSA to extract crude oil. A number of these joint ventures are in the Faja, where most of Venezuela's reserves are located. Venezuela's oil production and reserves also account for the continued presence of major foreign oilfield service companies. Nevertheless, some service companies operating in Venezuela have left and others have shrunk due to the problem of late payments from PDVSA that began in late 2008, nationalizations, and the threat of nationalizations.

In 2009, Venezuela's Organic Law for the Development of Petrochemical Activities entered into force. The law reserves basic and intermediate petrochemical activities to the state. It allows the state, through the Ministry of Petroleum and Mining, to create mixed companies in which the GBRV will control at least 50 percent of the shareholder equity and exercise effective control over company decisions. Such mixed companies can only exist for a maximum of 25 years, extendable for periods of 15 years by mutual agreement of the parties and with national assembly approval.

The GBRV has modified laws and regulations, and adjusted loan terms with foreign oil companies, to encourage investment in the energy sector. The GBRV revised in February 2013 the Law of Special Contributions for Extraordinary and Exorbitant Prices, commonly called the windfall profit tax. The revision reduced the measure's tax burden by raising the price per barrel at which a graduated scale of tax rates would apply. The rates are: 20 percent for USD 60-80/barrel; 80 percent for USD 81-100/barrel; 90 percent for USD 101-110/barrel; and 95 percent for more than USD 110/barrel. Foreign companies involved in joint ventures to develop the Orinoco Heavy Oil Belt have sought GBRV clarification regarding whether the new windfall profit tax rates would apply to the joint ventures' production of extra-heavy crude.

Limits on Foreign Control

Express limits on foreign ownership of investments are generally found in the energy and mining sector, as described in the Industrial Promotion section.

Privatization Program

Information not available.

Screening of FDI

Venezuela's current investment law contains language regarding, e.g., the development of local suppliers and non-traditional exports, but remains unclear on whether the authorities will use the law to screen applications for foreign investment registration and, if so, under what rules and procedures.

Competition Law

In 2014 a new competition law, the anti-monopoly law went into effect. The law provides for an independent anti-monopoly authority, headed by a superintendent, to implement and regulate compliance. The law prohibits anti-competitive conduct, restraints on trade, manipulative conduct, price fixing and other anti-competitive agreements. Violations may subject businesses to fines up to 40 percent of their gross revenues and 20 percent of their equity. The previous competition authority, Procompetencia (http://www.procompetencia.gob.ve/), will continue overseeing competition policy for 90 days after this law goes into effect; this period is renewable for 90 additional days by the Commerce Ministry.

INVESTMENT TRENDS

Political tensions, state interventions in the economy, corruption, and a volatile regulatory framework make Venezuela a difficult climate for foreign investors. Conditions for foreign investment are unlikely to improve in the near future. Venezuela has traditionally been a destination for U.S. direct investment in the energy and manufacturing sectors, as well as an importer of U.S. machinery, medical supplies, chemicals, agricultural products, and vehicles. Such investment and trade links have been weakened in recent years by GBRV efforts to build commercial relationships with ideological allies, strained U.S.-Venezuelan relations, and the deteriorating investment climate.

Table 1

Measure	Year	Index or Rank	Website Address
TI Corruption Perceptions index	2014	161 of 175	transparency.org/cpi2014/results
World Bank's Doing Business Report "Ease of Doing Business"	2014	182 of 189	doingbusiness.org/rankings
Global Innovation Index	2014	122 of 143	globalinnovationindex.org/content.aspx?page=data-analysis
World Bank GNI per capita	2013	USD 17,900	data.worldbank.org/indicator/NY.GNP.PCAP.CD

2. CONVERSION AND TRANSFER POLICIES

FOREIGN EXCHANGE

Venezuela's foreign exchange (FX) regime has been in flux for several years, with multiple FX mechanisms and exchange rates introduced, modified, and eliminated. The GBRV has described the current FX regime as transitory, increasing uncertainty for the near term. Since 2003, the GBRV has maintained strict currency controls. Venezuela authorizes three official FX mechanisms to sell USD to private sector firms and individuals.

The currency commission, CENCOEX, oversees two FX mechanisms. The first, CENCOEX, sells USD at the official exchange rate of 6.3 VEF/USD for imports of goods and services deemed national priorities, primarily food, medicine, and medical supplies. Firms and individuals soliciting dollars from CENCOEX must register with the body and obtain supporting documentation from various GBRV ministries, e.g., certificates of non-national production of the proposed imports and statements of good standing with the tax authorities. CENCOEX also operates a complementary FX mechanism, SICAD, which periodically sells USD to specific priority sectors at roughly 12 VEF/USD. Firms and individuals who wish to place bids for SICAD USD must separately register for the system. FX regulations state that CENCOEX will sell dollars for certain priority sectors, e.g., aviation, overseas travel, IT, IPR, capital goods, international investments, and insurance, through normal CENCOEX procedures, rather than ad hoc special sales, but use the prevailing exchange rate from the most recent SICAD sale, instead of the official exchange rate. Information about SICAD is available at http://www.bcv.org.ve/c5/sicad/c9/tme01.asp.

The Venezuelan central bank (BCV) oversees a third FX mechanism, SIMADI (http://www.bcv.org.ve/c5/simadi/simadi-02.asp), which was created in 2015. SIMADI allows for three distinct foreign exchange activities undertaken by different authorized agents: wholesale FX trading for firms by commercial banks; retail FX trading for individuals by commercial banks and exchange houses; and trading in dollar-denominated securities by commercial banks and stock brokers through the public-sector stock exchange. Participants in SICAD and SIMADI must hold dollar-denominated checking accounts in a Venezuelan bank. The BCV publishes daily SIMADI's exchange rate. The BCV has controlled SIMADI's exchange rate, which depreciated from 170 to 190 VEF/USD in its first two months of operations. Firms often wait 180-270 days to receive dollars, or never receive them, despite having had their applications approved.

Remittance Policies

Foreign investors in Venezuela have struggled to convert their VEF earnings into USD. Since 2008, CENCOEX and its predecessor, CADIVI, virtually ceased approving the sale of USD for earnings or capital repatriation. Multinational firms have announced numerous accounting losses due to the exchange rates. Venezuela's investment law limits earnings repatriation to a maximum of 80 percent of local currency earnings in any fiscal year. Legally, foreign investors could purchase dollars through SIMADI to repatriate earnings, at a 96 percent devaluation compared to the official exchange rate, but SIMADI has not been able to satisfy the demand for hard currency. There is also a parallel market for dollars. Private websites hosted outside of Venezuela publish the parallel exchange rate. They report that the rate has been depreciating steadily, reaching 260 VEF/USD in March 2015.

The OECD's Financial Action Task Force (FATF) announced in February 2013 that Venezuela was no longer subject to FATF's global anti-money-laundering/combatting terrorist finance (AML/CFT) monitoring process. FATF noted Venezuela would continue to work with the Caribbean FATF regional body to address AML/CFT deficiencies identified in Venezuela's mutual evaluation report.

3. EXPROPRIATION AND COMPENSATION

Since 1998, Venezuelan trade association Conindustria estimates the GBRV has expropriated more than 1,400 private businesses. The affected sectors included agribusiness, chemicals, construction, energy and mining, finance, food processing and packaging, information and communication technology, metals manufacturing, ports, real estate, and transportation. The GBRV has cited as valid reasons for these expropriations; abusive prices, economic sovereignty, excessive profits, food security, monopolistic behavior and public utility

The legal framework for expropriations is included in the Law of Expropriations, the Land and Agricultural Development Reform Law, the Urban Land Law and the Emergency Law of Urban Lands and Housing. These laws authorize expropriation by means of a presidential decree. The law provides for adequate and timely compensation, but the process has been slow and opaque, forcing companies to seek relief through international arbitration.

The 2005 land and agricultural development law calls for the redistribution of unproductive land, which in this context means land held by private owners that is considered idle by the government because it is currently not being used for agriculture or livestock production The GBRV continues to nationalize large tracts of land and farms. In 2013, the National Land Institute (NLI), which oversees expropriations of agricultural property, claimed to have seized over 8.9 million acres of land since 2002. The 2014 budget contained funding to seize up to an additional 865,000 acres.

4. DISPUTE SETTLEMENT

LEGAL SYSTEM, SPECIALIZED COURTS, JUDICIAL INDEPENDENCE, JUDGMENTS OF FOREIGN COURTS

Venezuela's legal system is based on the civil law tradition, reflecting Napoleonic and continental European influences. The commercial and civil codes address most business matters. The investment law stipulates that foreign investments shall be subject to the jurisdiction of Venezuelan courts and any bodies in which Venezuela might participate within the framework of Latin American and Caribbean integration. Venezuelan legal analysts have conflicting views regarding whether the new law eliminates the possibility of arbitration. The legal system is generally slow and inefficient, and lacks independence from the executive branch.

BANKRUPTCY

Venezuela's bankruptcy laws are outdated and inadequate to permit the reorganization of a debtor as a going concern. Currently insolvent companies that file for bankruptcy or reorganization generally lose control of their businesses and assets to a receiver and a bankruptcy judge, giving creditors fewer options to assert their interests in the process, compared to bankruptcy proceedings in other jurisdictions. All financial and commercial unsecured creditors are treated equally, but they are subordinated to the debtor's employees, who are due unpaid wages and other labor benefits, as well as to certain taxes. The bankruptcy trustee and advisors also have a statutory preference over all other creditors. Under the commercial code, all creditors that are not secured by a legal and valid security interest, or have a preference as mandated by law (e.g., the debtor's employees) must be treated equally by the bankruptcy court. Lawyers say Venezuela's bankruptcy laws incentivize debtors and creditors to negotiate settlements outside the context of formal bankruptcy proceedings.

INVESTMENT DISPUTES

The GBRV has not specifically targeted U.S. firms in its expropriations, but many expropriations and investment disputes have involved U.S. businesses. Roughly 15 investment disputes involving U.S. firms are ongoing at the International Centre for Settlement of Investment Disputes.

INTERNATIONAL ARBITRATION

Venezuelan law provides for commercial arbitration, based on UNCITRAL's model arbitration law. The private sector Venezuelan Business Center of Arbitration and Conciliation (CEDCA) offers arbitration services. Additional information is available at http://www.cedca.org.ve/.

ICSID Convention and New York Convention

On January 24, 2012, the GBRV withdrew as a member state from the convention on International Centre for Settlement of Investment Disputes (ICSID Convention). Withdrawal from ICSID does not offer any immediate benefits to Venezuela. Twenty cases pending before ICSID remain active. These pending cases are not affected by Venezuela's denunciation of the ICSID convention. Between the date of the notice of denunciation and the date when it became effective, foreign investors had an additional six months file new claims against Venezuela. Since 2013, ICSID has returned judgments in favor of several claimants. The GBRV has sought to annul ICSID's judgments within the ICSID forum and to challenge claimants' efforts to enforce the judgments in U.S. and European courts.

Venezuela is a signatory to the convention on the Recognition and Enforcement of Foreign Arbitral Awards (1958 New York Convention) and a member of the International Chamber of Commerce's International Court of Arbitration, which covers commercial disputes.

DURATION OF DISPUTE RESOLUTION

The legal system is generally slow and inefficient, and independent observers have said it suffers from corruption and a lack of independence from the executive branch. Venezuelan lawyers say routine commercial disputes can take up to five years to litigate in Venezuelan courts.

5. PERFORMANCE REQUIREMENTS AND INVESTMENT INCENTIVES

WTO/TRIMS

Venezuela is a member of the World Trade Organization (WTO_. Venezuela's only Trade Related Investment Measures (TRIMs) notification regards a 1995 agreement among Colombia, Ecuador, and Venezuela on local content requirements for automobile assemblers. Venezuela's new investment law contains mandatory language regarding the development of local suppliers and non-traditional exports, but it remains to be determined whether the GBRV will enforce these rules in a manner consistent with the agreement on TRIMs.

INVESTMENT INCENTIVES

Investment incentives are generally found in the energy and mining sector as described in the Industrial Promotion section.

PERFORMANCE REQUIREMENTS

Venezuela's new investment law contains mandatory language regarding the development of local suppliers, domestic research and development, and non-traditional exports, but it remains to be determined whether the GBRV will enforce these rules as performance requirements. PDVSA seeks to maximize local content and hiring in its deals with foreign companies. New agreements require technology transfers and also social contributions from companies. Foreign companies receive the same tax treatment as domestic companies, with the exception of the non-associated natural gas sector where foreign investors receive preferential tax treatment.

The Law for Communal Management of Responsibilities and Services outlined preferential treatment for companies that cooperate with the "communal state," including: access to the government's distribution and commercialization network; guarantees of technical assistance; access to GBRV's direct purchasing plans (i.e., closed bidding); access to credits and funds for production encouragement; preferential rates and conditions on manufacturing credits; access to technology; tax exemptions; and exemption from the Law of Public Contracts, which, among other things, gives the GBRV the right to expropriate a government contractor's equipment if the firm breaches its agreement.

Currently, government procurement is governed by the Partial Tender Reform Act and the Law of Public Contracts. The law has sought to increase participation by small and medium enterprises (SME). The law on public contracts has sought to enhance the role of communal councils in public procurement. Venezuela is not a signatory to the WTO Agreement on Government Procurement.

Data Storage

Venezuela's new investment law contains mandatory language regarding the development of local suppliers, domestic research and development, and non-traditional exports, but it remains to be determined whether the GBRV will enforce these rules in a manner that constitutes a local content requirement. Venezuela's telecommunications law gives regulatory authorities powers to access and intervene in telecommunications infrastructure and services in the interest of national security, defense, and public order. Venezuela's law against computer crimes criminalizes a range of conducts, including unauthorized access to systems, espionage, and sabotage. No information is available regarding requirements that foreign investors store data in Venezuela, although anecdotally many foreign firms store data outside the country.

6. RIGHT TO PRIVATE OWNERSHIP AND ESTABLISHMENT

There are legal limits on foreign ownership in certain sectors as noted in the 1999 constitution and special laws (reference Openness To, and Restrictions Upon, Foreign Investment).

7. PROTECTION OF PROPERTY RIGHTS

Real Property

Expropriations, weak public sector institutions, and lack of judicial independence undermine real property rights in Venezuela. Mortgages and property liens exist. Real estate lawyers say land registries are generally reliable, although in some cases are subject to abuse and corruption. In 2014, the World Bank ranked Venezuela 102 out of 189 countries for ease of registering property. The Bank said registering a property interest takes nine administrative procedures, 52 days, and costs 2.5 percent of the property value. Venezuela has a law on indigenous land rights which provides general definitions of indigenous peoples' lands and use rights and assigns the laws implementation to the environment ministry. Data are unavailable on the percentage of Venezuelan land lacking clear title.

A November 2013 presidential decree law capped commercial rental rates at 250 VEF/square-meter, which represented 50-75 percent reductions from prior market prices. The law prohibits commercial rent contracts in any currency other than VEF; private arbitration for the resolution of conflicts between landlords and tenants; and foreign companies administering commercial rental contracts.

Intellectual Property Rights

Venezuela's intellectual property regime provides ambiguous protections for rights holders under Article 98 of the 1999 constitution and the industrial property law of 1955. Under the constitution, intellectual property rights (IPR) are classified as cultural and educational rights rather than economic rights. In April 2006, Venezuela formally withdrew from the Andean Community (AC). Although there was legal uncertainty as to whether AC agreements still applied, the Venezuelan Supreme Court (TSJ) ruled in 2011 that Venezuela had reverted to the 1955 industrial property law (IPL) upon withdrawal from the AC. In its current form, the IPL is outdated and incapable of addressing modern IPR issues. It also conflicts with the WTO Trade-Related Aspects of Intellectual Property Rights (TRIPS) Agreement. The 2012 Organic Law of Labor and Workers further complicated Venezuela's IPR regime because article 325 provides that any intellectual property generated by public sector entities, or using public sector funds, automatically becomes part of the public domain. In July 2012, recognizing the 1955 industrial property law was outdated and at odds with multiple national and international legal structures, the Venezuelan Supreme Court (TSJ) urged the National Assembly to revise the industrial property law and reconcile it with Article 98 of the 1999 constitution. However, the initiative faltered and there have been no new developments since 2014.

As a WTO member, the GBRV is obligated to adhere to the requirement of the TRIPS Agreement. However, its failure to grant any patents since in 2007 violates TRIPS Articles 2.1 and 62.2. Venezuela is a member of the World Intellectual Property Organization (WIPO). It is also a party to the Berne Convention for the Protection of Literary and Artistic Works, the Convention for the Protection of Producers of Phonograms against Unauthorized Duplication of Their Phonograms, the Universal Copyright Convention, Paris Convention for the Protection of Industrial Property, and the Rome Convention for the Protection of Performers, Producers of Phonograms, and Broadcasting Organizations. Venezuela has not ratified the WIPO Copyright Treaty or the WIPO Performances and Phonograms Treaty, nor is it a party to the Madrid Protocol on Trademarks or the Patent Law Treaty.

Venezuela ranked as one of the top 20 economies worldwide for unlicensed software in 2014. An estimated 88 percent of the software used in Venezuela in 2014 was unlicensed. The commercial value, if all unlicensed products were purchased legally, would be roughly USD 1 billion. This figure more than doubled from 2007 to 2013. No Venezuelan markets were identified in this year's U.S. Department of Commerce "Notorious Markets" Report. The World Economic Forum's 2014-2015 World Competitive Report ranked Venezuela last out of 144 countries in intellectual property protection. The Property Rights Alliance's 2014 International Property Rights Index (IPRI) ranked it 131 out of the 131 countries, a decline of 3 positions from 2013.

Venezuela remained on the Priority Watch List in the 2014 Special 301 Report. Key concerns cited in the report are the deteriorating environment for the protection and enforcement of IPR in Venezuela.

Patents and Trademarks

The Autonomous Service of Intellectual Property (SAPI), the Venezuelan equivalent of the U.S. Patent and Trademark Office, has not issued a new patent since 2007. Venezuela's 1955 IPL provides that patents of invention, improvement, model, or industrial drawing can last five or ten years depending on the preference of the filer. Patents for technologies developed abroad may last five years or until the original foreign patent term expires, whichever is shorter. These patent durations violate the 20-year patent-term required under the TRIPS Agreement. Article 15 of the industrial property law excludes from patent protection medicine and pharmaceuticals, financial systems and plans, industrial processes, and speculative or theoretical inventions, in violation of Article 27 of the TRIPS Agreement. Several suits pertaining to data protection have been dismissed by the Supreme Court, which has ruled that allowing a third party to obtain a sanitary registration based on the information previously submitted by patent holder does not breach data protection and that obtaining a sanitary registration alone is not patent infringement.

SAPI's handling of trademarks is less hostile to rights-holders, but trademarks continue to be a problem. Trademarks must be filed with SAPI and published in the official gazette. SAPI grants trademarks for 15 years, and they may be renewed for successive 15-year periods. Trademarks are valid from the date SAPI publishes them in its bulletin. The registration process averages 12-14 months but can take significantly longer if a third party opposes the registration. SAPI continues to reject, under Article 33 of the IPL, most applications for trademarks bearing geographical indications.

Copyrights

Creative works are protected under the 1993 Copyright Law, the Berne Convention, and the Universal Copyright Convention. The law is modern and comprehensive and extends copyright protection to all creative works including computer software.

Enforcement

Low GBRV motivation, lengthy legal processes, inexperienced judges, and insufficient investigative and prosecutorial resources hamper IPR enforcement in Venezuela. In 2010, the GBRV abolished the Venezuelan copyright and trademark enforcement branch of the federal police. The GBRV dedicates only one prosecutor to IPR enforcement cases. IPR enforcement actions can only take place after a rights holder files a complaint. The complainant is then responsible for any storage costs of illicit goods—costs that may continue for years given the slowness of court proceedings. Prosecutors may only pursue violators operating at a fixed location, effectively shielding street vendors from sanctions. Venezuela's tax and customs service, SENIAT, occasionally conducts low-level raids against known illegal markets or small vendors of counterfeit goods, but these raids are random and officials are reportedly careful to avoid large markets that could create political repercussions for SENIAT. IPR laws are rarely enforced and cases take years to resolve. The process is slow and penalties do not deter counterfeiters. Post does not have any additional information on border enforcement or the legal authority of its customs officials to seize and destroy confiscated counterfeit goods.

The December 2010 anti-smuggling law criminalized contraband trade and strengthened customs controls. The law imposed penalties, such as imprisonment for customs officials convicted of smuggling, broadened the definition of contraband, and authorized the attorney general to carry out investigations of smuggling crimes along with SENIAT, the armed forces, and the national police. Venezuelan IP attorneys say constant rotation of personnel at SENIAT hinders the tax authorities' capability to enforce IPR-related disputes and investigations. Piracy and trademark infringement remain widespread, including on the Internet. Pirated software, music, and movies are readily available throughout the country.

For additional information about treaty obligations and points of contact at local IP offices, please see WIPO's country profiles at http://www.wipo.int/directory/en/.

Resources for Rights Holders
Embassy Caracas Economic Section: CaracasEcon@state.gov, 58-0212-975-6411
The Venezuela-American Chamber of Commerce: www.VenAmCham.org
U.S. Patent and Trademark Office (USPTO): www.uspto.gov, 1-800-786-9199
National Intellectual Property Rights Coordination Center: www.iprcenter.gov
International Trade Administration, U.S. Department of Commerce: www.stopfakes.gov

8. TRANSPARENCY OF THE REGULATORY SYSTEM

Venezuela's regulatory system lacks transparency, is unpredictable, and suffers from corruption. The GBRV's ruling United Socialist Party of Venezuela (PSUV) and its allies control the executive branch, including all regulatory agencies, the National Assembly, the judiciary, and the electoral authority. International observers believe the executive branch exercises undue influence over the legislative, judicial, regulatory, and electoral authorities. Proposed laws are generally presented for two rounds of discussion in the National Assembly, but opposition parties and private parties are limited in their ability to influence legislative outcomes. The National Assembly has granted the president the ability to issue new laws by decree, most recently for November 2013-November 2014 and again for March 2015-December 2015, circumventing the normal legislative process. Executive agencies generally develop and promulgate implementing regulations without consulting private sector representatives of the affected sectors.

9. EFFICIENT CAPITAL MARKETS AND PORTFOLIO INVESTMENT

Venezuela's financial services are heavily regulated. In 2010 the GBRV passed laws to reform the financial sector, including the Organic Law of the National Financial System , the regulatory framework for banks, insurance companies, and the capital markets; the Law for Insurance Activity ; the Capital Markets Law , which created a state-run securities exchange; the Bicentennial Public Securities Exchange (BPVB) ; and the Law of Banking Sector Institutions . Financial services account for a relatively small but growing share of GDP. According to BCV data, financial services represented 8 percent of GDP in the first three quarters of 2014. Financial services growth has been driven by increasing monetary liquidity (M2) resulting from loose fiscal and monetary policy and strict currency controls, which traps VEF earnings in Venezuela.

Venezuelan capital markets are underdeveloped and thinly traded. The leading Caracas stock market index, the Caracas Stock Exchange Index, was up roughly 80 percent in bolivar terms, year on year, in March 2015. Private analysts attribute the rise to government spending-driven increases in M2 and currency controls that trap the liquidity in Venezuela. Activity in Venezuela's securities market has decreased in recent years due to nationalizations of previously listed firms and the GBRV's seizure of 51 brokerages, since 2010, mostly on charges of illegal trading in a now defunct foreign exchange market.

Venezuela's primary stock market is the Caracas Stock Exchange (BVC). On January 31, 2011, the GBRV launched the BPVB, under the November 2010 securities market law, to sell government and corporate bonds and to compete with the BVC. The BPVB was empowered to trade both VEF- and USD-denominated securities, but as of April 2014 it had only traded VEF-denominated debt. Private brokerages have not been allowed to participate in the BPVB. Trading volumes in both the BVC and the BPVB are low and dominated by fixed-income public- and private-sector securities offering negative real interest rates due to an excess of VEF liquidity trapped in Venezuela by currency controls.

Foreign investors can buy or sell stocks and bonds in Venezuelan capital markets as long as they have registered with the securities regulator, the Superintendent of Securities (SNV). Venezuela's new foreign investment law requires foreign investors to obtain a foreign investment registration before they invest directly in Venezuelan firms.

MONEY AND BANKING SYSTEM, HOSTILE TAKEOVERS

Venezuelan credit markets are heavily regulated. The BCV and the Superintendent of Banks (SUDEBAN) regulate Venezuela's banking sector. The 2010 law of banking sector institutions describes banking as a public service and banks as public utilities, permitting the GBRV to nationalize financial institutions without National Assembly approval. The public sector's share of total bank assets has grown in recent years, primarily through GBRV nationalizations. According SUDEBAN data, in April 2014 there were 35 banking institutions—25 private and 10 public—down from 59 in November 2009. Public-sector banks held an estimated 32 percent of total banking sector assets in February 2015.

Venezuela's banking sector is heavily distorted by the GBRV's and BCV's expansive fiscal and monetary policies, which combined with currency controls trap local currency liquidity in the economy, fuel inflation, reduce loan default rates, and inflate banking sector profitability indicators. Universal and commercial banks enjoyed return on equity of roughly 51 percent in the twelve months to February 2015, with a sector-wide default rate of less than 1 percent, driven by M2 growth and currency controls that constrain capital transfers out of Venezuela. Financial analysts believe reform to the currency control regime would have to be paired with banking sector reforms to avoid widespread stress to the financial system.

The BCV sets maximum and minimum interest rates banks can charge. Recent limits included 24 percent on commercial and personal loans, 29 percent on credit cards, and 16 percent on car loans. With inflation ranging between 20 and 70 percent since 2009, real interest rates have generally been negative. Banks are required to allocate roughly 59 percent of their portfolio for loans to the housing, agriculture, small business, manufacturing, and tourism sectors, at preferential interest rates that have been negative, in real terms, since 2012. Universal and commercial banks are prohibited from making commercial loans for terms longer than three years. The BCV also regulates interest rates on savings accounts and time deposits. Recent limits have included 16 percent on savings account balances from 0 to VEF 20,000, 12.5 percent on savings account balances above VEF 20,000, and 14.5 percent on certificates of deposit. Such rates have been negative, in real terms, since 2009, discouraging household saving and incentivizing domestic consumption and the purchase of USD in the parallel market as a more stable store of value. Faced with negative real interest rates on bank deposits and VEF-denominated securities, multinationals with VEF earnings trapped in Venezuela have increasingly invested in commercial real estate in an attempt to mitigate inflation risks.

The majority of banking sector assets is concentrated in the country's five largest banks. Total banking assets, at roughly USD 420 billion (at the official exchange rate), grew 62 percent from February 2014 to February 2015. Public and private universal and commercial banks control 99 percent of total banking sector assets. The three largest private universal banks are: Banesco, with 16 percent of total sector assets in February 2015; Banco Provincial, with 13 percent; and, Banco Mercantil, with 12 percent. Banesco and Banco Mercantil are Venezuelan-owned, while Banco Provincial is majority-owned by BBVA of Spain. Citibank is the only U.S.-owned universal bank with a presence in Venezuela. The two largest state universal banks are Banco de Venezuela and Banco Bicentenario. The GBRV nationalized Banco de Venezuela from Spain-based Banco Santander in May 2009. Banco de Venezuela is now the country's largest bank, with 18 percent of total sector assets in February 2015. Banco Bicentenario was formed in 2010 through the nationalization of four private banks; it held 7 percent of assets as of February 2015.

The BCV promulgated regulations in September 2012 outlining conditions under which businesses and individuals may open USD-denominated bank accounts at Venezuelan universal and commercial banks. Venezuelan residents may use such accounts for international transfers, overseas debit card transactions, and transactions through Venezuela's alternative FX mechanisms, SICAD and SIMADI (see Conversion and Transfer Policies). Venezuelans may not withdraw dollars from such accounts in Venezuela, however.

10. COMPETITION FROM STATE-OWNED ENTERPRISES

State Owned Enterprises (SOEs) are dominant in diverse sectors of the Venezuelan economy, including agribusiness, food, hydrocarbons, media, mining, telecommunications, and tourism. Private firms are at a disadvantage when competing with public enterprises, specifically in terms of accessing foreign currency at the official exchange rate. SOEs generally do not need to go through CENCOEX to request hard currency at the official exchange rate, while private companies struggle with the official mechanisms' limitations and process delays (see Conversion and Transfer Policies).

In March 2012 the GBRV amended its customs and tax regimes to favor imports by the public sector over those of the private sector. The new rules exempt SOE importers from providing certain customs documentation and grant waivers on value-added taxes, customs duties, and fees on a broad range of imported products. The exemptions do not generally apply to the private sector. The GBRV has extended such benefits to certain private-sector firms. The BCV provides massive monetary financing to SOEs, especially PDVSA, to cover local currency operating deficits. Financial analysts generally believe Venezuela's SOEs contribute to macroeconomic imbalances and undermine domestic output.

OECD Guidelines on Corporate Governance of SOEs

The GBRV does not encourage its SOEs to adhere to the OECD Guidelines on Corporate Governance for SOEs. The CEO of PDVSA and the rest of PDVSA's board members are appointed by the President. GBRV direct appointment of SOE executives is commonplace, such as in the Venezuelan Corporation of Guayana (CVG), a state holding company that includes firms in basic industries such as aluminum, iron ore mining, electricity generation, and steel. Venezuela is not a party to the WTO's Agreement on

Government Procurement. Private sector firms are at a disadvantage vis-à-vis SOEs in Venezuelan courts.

11. RESPONSIBLE BUSINESS CONDUCT

Article 135 of the Venezuelan constitution declares a general duty for all non-state actors to respect laws regarding social responsibility. Venezuela's 2014 foreign investment law requires foreign investors to promote responsible business conduct (RBC) consistent with international standards. Various Venezuelan laws set forth requirements intended to advance principles generally included under the concept of RBC. GBRV regulation and enforcement of these laws is weak and uneven.

The Venezuelan private sector is generally aware of and promotes RBC. The Venezuelan-American Chamber of Commerce (VenAmCham), for its part, promotes RBC though its Social Alliance program, which organizes RBC-themed events. The Venezuelan Federation of Chambers of Commerce (Fedecamaras) promotes RBC through a standing working group devoted to the dissemination of best practices and an annual award to recognize RBC excellence.

OECD GUIDELINES FOR MULTINATIONAL ENTERPRISES

Venezuela does not encourage foreign or local firms to follow the OECD Guidelines for Multinational Enterprises or the UN Guiding Principles on Business and Human Rights.

12. POLITICAL VIOLENCE

Venezuela's political climate is polarized between supporters and opponents of the GBRV and policies of the PSUV. There were, however, no major incidents of political violence that specifically targeted foreign owned companies or installations through March 2015. The GBRV publicly accuses the United States and the private sector of waging an economic war against the Venezuelan people, fostering an atmosphere of hostility toward private business.

13. CORRUPTION

Venezuela has comprehensive anti-corruption laws but enforcement is weak, as indicated by Venezuela's ranking by Transparency International of 160 out of 177 countries in its corruption perceptions index. Corruption is endemic in Venezuela, including in government procurement; the awarding of authorizations, particularly in the foreign exchange regime; dispute settlement; the regulatory system; and customs and taxation. The GBRV does not provide protection to NGOs that investigate corruption and often subjects them to harassment.

UN Anticorruption Convention, OECD Convention on Combatting Bribery

Venezuela signed the UN Convention against Corruption on December 10, 2003, and ratified it on February 2, 2009. Venezuela has not adopted the OECD Convention on Combating Bribery of Foreign Public Officials in International Business Transactions.

Resources to Report Corruption

The GBRV's Public Ministry, roughly equivalent to the U.S. Attorney General's Office, has telephonic and e-mail resources for victims to report crimes, including corruption. The Public Ministry's contact information is:

Sede Principal del Ministerio Público

Esquinas de Misericordia a Pele El Ojo y Avenida México
Caracas
58-0212-509-7211 (main)
58-0212-509-7464 (main)
58-0-800-FISCA-00 (speak to a Public Ministry attorney)
58-0-800-VICTIMA (victim hotline)
mp@mp.gob.ve

Transparency International's Venezuela chapter, Transparencia Venezuela, offers consultation and services to victims of corruption. Transparencia Venezuela 's contact information is:

Avenida Andrés Eloy Blanco
Edificio Cámara de Comercio de Caracas
Piso 2
Oficina 2-15
Los Caobos
Caracas 1050
58-0212-576-0863
58-0212-573-3134
comunicaciones@transparencia.org.ve

14. BILATERAL INVESTMENT AGREEMENTS

Venezuela has bilateral investment treaties with Argentina, Barbados, Belarus, Belgium and Luxembourg, Brazil, Canada, Chile, Costa Rica, Cuba, Czech Republic, Denmark, Ecuador, France, Germany, Iran, Islamic Republic, Italy, Lithuania, Netherlands*, Paraguay, Peru, Portugal, Russian Federation, Spain, Sweden, Switzerland, United Kingdom, Uruguay, and Vietnam.

Effective November 1, 2008, Venezuela revoked its Bilateral Investment Treaty with the Netherlands. Revocation did not have immediate consequences for investments made prior to the date of revocation. The BIT remains in force for these investments for a period of 15 years.

BILATERAL TAXATION TREATIES

The United States and Venezuela have a bilateral tax treaty for the Avoidance of Double Taxation and the Prevention of Fiscal Evasion with Respect to Taxes on Income and Capital, signed in 1999. The provisions of the treaty apply to the following taxes in existence at the time of the entry into force: a) in Venezuela: the tax on income and the business assets tax; b) in the United States: the Federal income taxes imposed by the Internal Revenue Code (but excluding social security contributions), and to any identical or substantially similar taxes that imposed after the date of signature.

15. OPIC AND OTHER INVESTMENT INSURANCE PROGRAMS

Overseas Private Investment Corporation (OPIC) programs in Venezuela were suspended in 2005, due to Venezuela's failure to cooperate in suppressing international narcotics trafficking. In 2014, the United States determined that Venezuela failed to make sufficient or meaningful efforts to adhere to its obligations under international counter-narcotics agreements and conventions. However, President Obama issued a national interest waiver, determining that support for programs to aid Venezuela is vital to the national interest of the United States. Under this waiver, Venezuela is eligible for OPIC programs starting in 2015.

The U.S. Export-Import Bank (ExIm Bank) has not provided new financing for projects in Venezuela since April 2003. Both OPIC and the Ex-Im Bank still retain significant exposure in Venezuela prior to suspending operations.

16. LABOR

Several factors make human resources a challenge for domestic and foreign investors alike: heavily regulated labor markets; talent flight, as skilled Venezuelans have sought employment abroad due to physical insecurity and political and economic uncertainty; government programs that support poorer Venezuelans making it more difficult for companies to attract unskilled labor; and declining traditional trade unions, as the GBRV has supported the establishment of "parallel" unions aligned to government interests and new "workers militias" to monitor the activities of union members. Roughly 10 percent of the total workforce is unionized. The GBRV extended in December 2014 a firing freeze in place since 2002 that shields most private-sector workers from termination through December 31, 2015.

In April 2012, former President Chavez used a presidential decree law to pass a long-pending Organic Law of Labor and Workers. The law replaced a 1997 labor law, expanding workers' rights and benefits. The law prohibits employer discrimination on the basis of race, sex, age, civil status, religion, political beliefs, social class, nationality, sexual orientation, union membership, criminal record, or disability. The law prohibits termination without legal justification and requires employers to consult labor courts regarding the lawfulness of a termination. The law also prohibits employers from hiring third-party contractors to perform ongoing, regular duties as a means of avoiding legal obligations owed to those on one's payroll. The law guarantees a retirement pension for workers in both the formal and informal sectors.

The law reduced the legal workweek from 44 to 40 hours and guaranteed workers 15 days of vacation, plus one day for each additional year of employment, up to a total of 45 days per year. The law also introduced new rights for female workers with children, including: 26 weeks of paid maternity leave for mothers (six pre- and 20 post-natal); two breaks per day for mothers who are breastfeeding; and access to a lactation room, if they work for an employer with more than 20 employees. The law created guidelines for temporary workers, who can work 10-hours daily with a labor inspector's permission; shift workers may not work more than 42 hours per week, on average, over any eight-week period. The GBRV promulgated regulations implementing the new labor law in May 2013.

In 2014, Venezuela saw continued protests and work stoppages by unions across the public and private sectors. While no official statistics are available for 2014, the number of labor protests declined in 2014 compared to 2013. The Ministry of Labor reported 1,612 actions in 2013 and the non-governmental organization Venezuelan Observatory of Social Conflict registered 1,415 conflicts in 2014, a 21 percent decrease. Union protests in the state of Guayana have stopped operations at the Venezuelan Corporation of Guayana (CVG), the largest state-owned industrial conglomerate in the country. The GBRV has delayed negotiations over collective bargaining agreements for workers in the public sector, leaving more than two million public employees without collective contracts, including teachers and electrical workers. In February 2014, PDVSA and unions representing oil and gas industry employees agreed on a new collective bargaining agreement for the period of 2013-2015.

The GBRV's statistics agency estimated the unemployment rate at 7.9 percent in January 2015. The INE estimated 41 percent of the employed worked in the informal sector and 59 percent in the formal sector.

17. FOREIGN TRADE ZONES/FREE PORTS/TRADE FACILITATION

The Free-Trade Zone Law provides for free-trade zones and free ports. The three existing free-trade zones are located in the Paraguana Peninsula, in the state of Falcon, which also has a tourism investment promotion provision; Atuja in the state of Zulia; and the municipalities of Libertador, Campo Elias, Sucre; and Santos Marquina in the state of Merida, but only for cultural, scientific, and technological goods. These zones provide exemptions from most import and export duties and offer foreign-owned firms the same investment opportunities as Venezuelan firms. Venezuela has two free ports that also enjoy exemptions from most tariff duties: Margarita Island (part of Nueva Esparta state) and Santa Elena de Uairen in the state of Bolivar.

18. FOREIGN DIRECT INVESTMENT AND FOREIGN PORTFOLIO INVESTMENT STATISTICS

Table 2: Key Macroeconomic Data, U.S. FDI in Host Country/Economy

	HOST COUNTRY STATISTICAL SOURCE*		USG OR INTERNATIONAL STATISTICAL SOURCE		USG OR INTERNATIONAL SOURCE OF DATA: BEA; IMF; EUROSTAT; UNCTAD, OTHER
ECONOMIC DATA	YEAR	AMOUNT	YEAR	AMOUNT	
Host Country Gross Domestic Product (GDP) ($M USD)	2012	381,395	2013	438,238	www.worldbank.org/en/country
Foreign Direct Investment	Host Country Statistical source*		USG or international statistical source		USG or international Source of data: BEA; IMF; Eurostat; UNCTAD, Other
U.S. FDI in partner country ($M USD, stock positions)	NA	NA	2013	14,487	BEA data available 3/19/14 at http://bea.gov/international/direct_investment_multinational_companies_comprehensive_data.htm
Host country's FDI in the United States ($M USD, stock positions)	NA	NA	2012	4,683	BEA data available 3/19/14 at http://bea.gov/international/direct_investment_multinational_companies_comprehensive_data.htm
Total inbound stock of FDI as % host GDP	2012	12.8	2013	11.7	

Source: Venezuelan Central Bank

Table 3: Sources and Destination of FDI

DIRECT INVESTMENT FROM/IN COUNTERPART ECONOMY DATA

FROM TOP FIVE SOURCES/TO TOP FIVE DESTINATIONS (US DOLLARS, MILLIONS)					
INWARD DIRECT INVESTMENT			OUTWARD DIRECT INVESTMENT		
Total Inward	51,817	100%	Total Outward	NA	100%
Netherlands	10,693	21%			
United States	9,282	18%			
France	3,985	8%			
Spain	3,500	7%			
Switzerland	2,273	4%			
"0" reflects amounts rounded to +/- USD 500,000.					

Source: IMF Coordinated Direct Investment Survey

Table 4: Sources of Portfolio Investment

PORTFOLIO INVESTMENT ASSETS

TOP FIVE PARTNERS (MILLIONS, US DOLLARS)

TOTAL			EQUITY SECURITIES			TOTAL DEBT SECURITIES		
All Countries	8,228	100%	All Countries	79	100%	All Countries	8,149	100%
United States	4,726	57%	United States	69	87%	United States	4,657	57%
UK	894	11%	NA	NA	NA	UK	894	11%
Switzerland	754	9%	NA	NA	NA	Switzerland	754	9%
Germany	650	8%	NA	NA	NA	Germany	650	8%
Argentina	76	1%	NA	NA	NA	Argentina	76	1%

Source: IMF Coordinated Portfolio Investment Survey

IMPORTANT INVESTMENT AND BUSINESS CONTACTS

Contact for More Information

U.S. Embassy Caracas Economic Section
Calle F con Calle Suapure
Urbanización Colinas de Valle Arriba
Caracas, Venezuela
58-0212-907-8441
CaracasEcon@state.gov

LOCAL LAWYERS

FIRMAS	ESPECIALIZACION	IDIOMAS	INFORMACION DE CONTACTO
ANTEQUERA PARILLI & RODRIGUEZ	Intellectual Property - trademarks, patents, copyright- domain name, trade secrets, informatics law, e-commerce, franchises, advertising law, entertainment law, competition law, intangible assets valuation, litigation, anti piracy enforcement programs.	English, Spanish, French	Av. San Felipe, Edificio Centro COINASA, PH B, La Castellana, Caracas 1060, Venezuela Telf:0212-263-9944 - Fax: 212-2639908 Website: www.antequera.com.ve E-mail: info@antequera.com.ve
ARAQUE REYNA SOSA VISO & PITTIER ABOGADOS	General Corporate Law and Taxation; litigation; Labor Law (litigation, collective bargaining, general advisory); Trademarks; Antitrust; Oil and Mining; Mergers & Acquisitions; Securities Regulation; Foreign Investments; Corporate finance; Arbitration; Administrative Law; Listed: -Martindale Hubbell. Law Directory; -The International Bar; -Global Chambers; -Latin Lawyer; -Latin Counsel	English, Spanish, French, Portuguese and Italian.	Centro Lido, Torre C, piso 8. Av. Francisco de Miranda, El Rosal, Caracas. Venezuela. Tel: 0212-953-9244 Fax::953-7777 Website: www.araquereyna.com E-mail: info@araquereyna.com
BAKER & McKENZIE	All fields of law, including employment and labor law, taxation, energy and natural resources (major projects, oil and gas, energy, mining, water) environmental law, corporate law, commercial law, mergers and acquisitions, civil law, administrative law, economic law (customs, antidumping,	English, Spanish and German.	Centro Bancaribe, Intersección Av. Principal de Las Mercedes con inicio de Calle París Urb. Las Mercedes Caracas 1060, Venezuela

	antitrust, international trade regulations), intellectual property, telecommunications, electronic commerce, financial law (project finance, banking, capital markets), insurance, litigation and dispute resolution, criminal law, and foreign investments and transfer of technology. Members of the international law firm of Baker & McKenzie.		Tel: 0212-276-5111 Fax:993-0818 ; 993-9049 Website: http://www.bakermckenzie.com
BAUMEISTER & BREWER	Administrative, corporate, civil, foreign investment, constitutional, insurance, banking, urban development & construction law	English, Spanish, French & Italian	Avda. Venezuela, Torre América, PH-B, Bello Monte, Caracas 1050. Mailing address: Apartado 51322, Caracas 1050 Telf: 0212-762-2651 - 55 Fax: 761-7472 Website: www.bblegal.com
BENSON, PEREZ MATOS, ANTAKLY & WATTS	Corporate, private international, tax, labor, petroleum, mining, insurance, banking, contracts, e-commerce, Andean Pact, foreign investments, transfer of technology, privatization, debt/equity swap, mergers and acquisitions, capital markets law, stock exchange, securities, antitrust, antidumping, environmental, due diligence, litigation and maritime.	English and Spanish	Edificio Centro Altamira, Piso 7 y 8, Av. San Juan Bosco, Altamira, Caracas 1062. Tel: 0212-265-3801, 265-4279. FAX: 265-9252; 261-2493. Website: www.bpmaw.com E-mail: bpmawccs@bpmaw.com
BENTATA Abogados	Foreign investments, joint ventures, (banking, insurance) and taxation in general, planning and negotiations in labor law	English, Spanish, French and German	Torre Las Mercedes, Piso 2, Avda. La Estancia, Chuao, Caracas. Tel: 0212-600-7400, FAX: 600-7401. Website: www.bentata.com
ESCOVAR LEON Abogados	Civil Law, Labor Law, National & International Litigation	English & Spanish.	Av. Ppal El Bosque, Torre Credicard, Piso 6, Oficina 61, Urbanización El Bosque, Chacaíto, Caracas. Apartado: 1050 Tel: 0212-952-6332/ 3076. FAX: 954-0362. www.escovarleon.com
PARRA SALUZZO &	Child Protection, Marriage/Divorce, Banking/Financial,	English & Spanish.	Avenida Principal de la Castellana, Centro Letonia,

ASOCIADOS, S.C.	Commercial/Business Law, Foreign Investments, Marketing Agreements, Civil Law, Criminal Law, Damages, Commercial Law, Contracts, Transportation Law, Corporations, Foreign Claims, Government relations, Immigration, Auto/Accidents		Piso 12, Oficina 121, Chacao, Caracas Office Telephone: (+58) 0212-266-5355 Fax Number: (+58) 0212-264-4965 Webpage: www.psa-abogados.com

RETAINING A FOREIGN ATTORNEY

In retaining the services of a foreign attorney the following guidelines may assist you in protecting your interests.

I. Selecting an attorney

1. When you receive a list of attorneys, it would be wise for you to contact several, briefly describing the nature of the services you desire. Before you decide which attorney to employ, ask for a written schedule of fees generally charged for the services you need, ask whether the attorney is fluent in English, and become acquainted with him or her. Do not turn over your documents or funds until you are certain that the attorney understands your problem and is willing to handle your case.

II. Assistance of the U.S. Embassy

2. Should your association with a foreign attorney prove unsatisfactory, a U.S. consular officer can contact the attorney on your behalf in an effort to facilitate your communication. In addition, complaints against foreign lawyers whose names appear on the attorneys list can result in the removal of their names from that list.

III. Coordination with Counsel in the U.S.

3. American attorneys may not be in a position to represent your interests abroad, particularly because they will not be permitted to participate in foreign court proceedings under the laws of the foreign country. However, American attorneys experienced in international law may be helpful in explaining complex international issues involved in your case and some may have associates or partners abroad to whom they can refer you.

IV. How to deal with your foreign attorney?

a) Find out the attorney's qualifications and experience.

b) Find out how the attorney plans to represent you. Ask specific questions and expect the attorney to explain legal procedures in language that you can understand.

c) Find out what fees the attorney charges and how he expects to be paid. Some attorneys may expect to be paid in advance; some may demand payment after each action they take on your behalf, refusing to take further action until they are paid; and some may take the case on a percentage basis, collecting a pre-arranged percentage of the monies awarded to you by the foreign court. You may also want to consider setting up an escrow account from which the attorney can collect his fees only if and when he or she has had some success with your case.

d) Ask that your attorney keep you informed on the progress of your case according to a pre-arranged schedule. Remember that most foreign courts work rather slowly. You may, therefore, wish the attorney to send you monthly reports, even though no real developments have ensued, simply to satisfy your doubts about the progress of the case.

e) Have your attorney analyze your case, giving you the positive and negative aspects and probable outcome (if possible).

f) Do not expect your attorney to give a simple answer to a complex legal problem. Be sure that you understand the technical language of any contract or other legal document prepared by your attorney you sign it.

g) Keep your attorney fully informed of any new developments in the case.

h) If you need to provide complex or technical documents to your attorney, you may wish to consider having the documents translated into Spanish. Remember, an elementary knowledge of English may not be enough to enable the attorney to understand the documents you provide.

i) Be honest with your attorney. Tell him every relevant fact in order to get the best representation of your interests.

j) Find out how much time the attorney anticipates the case may take to complete.

k) Request copies of all letters and documents prepared on your behalf.

V. Assistance of the Department of State.

5. If you have additional questions, contact the Office of Citizen Consular Services, Room 4811, Department of State, Washington D.C. 20520.

6. BAR ASSOCIATION OF VENEZUELA

7. NATIONAL INTERNAL REGULATIONS CONCERNING LAWYER'S FEES

VI. In order to estimate fees lawyers must take into consideration the following:

a) The importance of the services;

b) The magnitude of the case;

c) The success obtained and the importance of the case;

d) The novelty or difficulty of the judicial problems discussed;

e) Their own experience or reputation;

f) The financial situation of the client;

g) The possibility that the lawyer may be prevented from pursuing other cases;

h) Whether the lawyer's services will be temporary or permanent;

i) The lawyer's personal responsibility and liability in the case;

j) The time required;

k) The degree of the lawyer's participation in the study, development and execution of the case;

l) If the lawyer is acting as counselor or attorney for the client;

m) The place where the services are rendered (whether inside or outside of the lawyer's domicile).

INTERNATIONAL ORGANIZATIONS CONDUCTING DIRECT INVESTMENTS AND PRIVATIZATION

FIAS - Foreign Investment Advisory Service

Mr. Nigel Twose
Manager
Tel: 1-202 473 0411
Fax: 1-202 974 4303
E-mail:Ntwose@worldbank.org

MIGA - Multilateral Investment Guarantee Agency

Ms. Tessie San Martin
Director
Investment Marketing Services
Tel: 1-202 458 48 76
Fax: 1-202 522 26 50
E-mail:tsanmartin@worldbank.org

OECD - Organisation for Economic Co-operation and Development

Mr. Pierre Poret
Head, Investment Division
Directorate for Financial
and Enterprise Affairs
Tel: 33-1 45 24 88 56
Fax: 33-1 44 30 61 35
E-mail:pierre.poret@oecd.org

UNCTAD - United Nations Conference on Trade and Development

Mr. Karl P. Sauvant
Director
Division on Investment, Technology
and Enterprise Development
Tel: 41-22 907 57 07
Fax: 41-22 907 01 97
E-mail:karl.sauvant@unctad.org

UNIDO - United Nations Industrial Development Organization

Ms. Dan Liang
Director
Investment and Technology
Promotion Branch
Tel: 43-1 26026 32 39
Fax: 43-1 26026 68 05
E-mail: dliang@unido.org

IMPORTANT INVESTMENT AND PRIVATIZATION ORGANIZATIONS BY COUNTRY

Country	Agency	Website
Afghanistan	Afghan Investment Support Agency AISA	www.aisa.org.af
Albania	Albanian Foreign Investment Promotion Agency ANIH	www.anih.com.al www.investalbania.com
Algeria	Agence Nationale de Developpément des Investissements ANDI	www.andi.dz www.andi.gov.dz
Angola	National Agency of Private Investment ANIP	www.investinangola.com
Anguilla	Ministry of Finance	www.gov.ai
Antigua and Barbuda	Industrial Development Board IDB	www.antigua-barbuda.com
Armenia	Armenian Development Agency ADA	www.businessarmenia.com
Aruba	Aruba Foreign Investment Agency AFIA	www.aruba.com
Australia	Invest Australia	www.investaustralia.gov.au
Australia	Invest Victoria	www.investvictoria.com
Austria	Austrian Business Agency ABA	www.aba.gv.at
Azerbaijan	Azerbaijan Investments Promotion and Advisory Foundation AIPAF	www.azerinvest.com
Bahrain	Bahrain Promotions and Marketing Board	www.bahrainedb.com

Bangladesh	Board of Investment BOI	www.boibd.org
Barbados	Barbados Investment and Development Corporation BIDC	www.bidc.com
Belarus	Belarusian Foreign Investment Promotion Agency BFIPA	www.export.by
Belgium	Flanders Foreign Investment Office FFIO	www.ffio.com
Belgium	Office for Foreign Investors Limited OFI Ltd in Wallonia S.A.	www.investinwallonia.be
Belize	Belize Trade and Investment Development Services BELTRAIDE	www.belizeinvest.org.bz
Benin	Centre de Promotion des Investissements	www.cpi-benin.org
Benin	S.K. Sarl, Agence des Promoteurs d'Investissements	
Bolivia	The Bolivian Agency for the Promotion of Exports and Investment CEPROBOL	www.ceprobol.gov.bo
Bosnia-Herzegovina	Foreign Investment Promotion Agency of Bosnia-Herzegovina FIPA	www.fipa.gov.ba
Botswana	Botswana Export Development and Investment Authority BEDIA	www.bedia.co.bw
Brazil	Agencia de Promoção de Exportações e Investimentos APEX Brazil	www.apexbrasil.com.br
Brazil	Banco do Nordeste	www.bnb.gov.br
Brazil	Instituto de Desenvolvimento Industrial de Minas Gerais INDI	www.indi.mg.gov.br
British West Indies	Turks and Caicos Islands Investment Agency TCInvest	www.tcinvest.tc
Bulgaria	Invest Bulgaria Agency BFIA	www.bfia.org
Cameroon	Cellule de Gestion du Code des Investissements CGCI	
Canada	Investment, Science and Technology Brance IIT	www.investincanada.ca

Cape Verde	Center for Tourism, Investment and Export Promotion PROMEX	www.promex.cv www.promex.org
Chile	Foreign Investment Committee FIC	www.foreigninvestment.cl www.inversionextranjera.cl
China	Ministry of Commerce MOFCOM	www.fdi.gov.cn
Hong Kong, China	InvestHK	www.investHK.gov.hk
Macao, China	Macao Trade and Investment Promotion Institute	www.ipim.gov.mo
Colombia	Invest in Colombia Corporation COINVERTIR	www.coinvertir.org
Congo Democratic Republic of the	Agence Nationale pour la Promotion des Investissements ANAPI	www.anapi.org
Costa Rica	Costa Rican Investment & Development Board CINDE	www.cinde.or.cr
Côte d'Ivoire	Centre de Promotion des Investissements en Côte d'Ivoire CEPICI	www.cepici.go.ci
Croatia	Trade and Investment Promotion Agency	www.mingo.hr
Cuba	Centro de Promoci6n de Inversiones CPI	www.cpi-minvec.cu
Curacao Netherlands Antilles	Curacao Industrial and International Trade Development Company CURINDE	www.curinde.com
Cyprus	Foreign Investors Service Centre	
Czech Republic	Czechlnvest	www.czechinvest.org
Denmark	Invest in Denmark	www.investindk.com
Djibouti	Agence nationale pour la promotion des investissements ANPI	www.djiboutinvest.dj
Dominica	National Development Corporation	www.dominica.dm
Dominican Republic	Center for Export and Investment of the Dominican Republic CEI-RD	www.cei-rd.gov.do
Ecuador	Corporaci6n de Promoci6n de Exportaciones e Inversiones CORPEI	www.corpei.org.ec
Egypt	General Authority for Investment & Free Zones GAFI	www.gafinet.org

El Salvador	Comision Nacional de Promocion de Inversiones PROESA	www.proesa.com.sv
Estonia	Estonian Investment Agency EIA	www.eia.ee
Ethiopia	Ethiopian Investment Commission EIC	www.ethioinvestment.org
Fiji	Fiji Islands Trade & Investment Board FITIB	www.ftib.org.fj www.investinfiji.com
Finland	Invest in Finland	www.investinfinland.fi
France	Invest in France	www.investinfrance.org
French Polynesia	Tahiti Invest	www.tahiti-invest.com
Gabon	Agence de Promotion des Investissements Privés APIP	www.invest-gabon.com
Gabon	Commmission Nationale de Mise en Place de la Zone Franche de l'Île Mandji	www.cnzf.dgi.gouv.ga
Gambia	The Gambia Investment Promotion and Free Zones Agency	www.gipfza.gm
Georgia	Georgian National Investment and Export Promotion Agency GNIEPA	www.investingeorgia.org
Germany	Invest in Germany	www.invest-in-germany.com
Ghana	Ghana Investment Promotion Centre GIPC	www.gipc.org.gh
Greece	Hellenic Centre for Investment S.A. ELKE S.A.	www.elke.gr
Guatemala	Guatemalan Development Foundation FUNDESA	www.guate.net/fundesa www.fundesa.guatemala.org
Guinea	Office de Promotion des Investissements Privés OPIP	www.mirinet.com/opip
Guyana	Guyana Office for Investment GO-INVEST	www.goinvest.gov.gy
Haiti	Ministère du Commerce & Industrie	
Honduras	Foundation for Investment and Development of Exports FIDE	www.hondurasinfo.hn

Hungary	Hungarian Investment and Trade and Development Agency ITDH	www.itdh.hu
Iceland	Invest in Iceland Agency	www.invest.is
India	Indian Investment Centre IIC	www.iic.nic.in
India	Investment Promotion and Infrastructure Development Division	www.dipp.nic.in
India	Bureau of Investment Promotion Rajasthan BIP	www.investrajasthan.com
India	India Brand Equity Foundation	www.ibef.org
Indonesia	Ministry of Investment & State Owned Enterprises	www.bkpm.go.id
Irak	Kurdistan Board of Promoting Investment KBPI	www.kinvest.org
Iran Islamic Republic of	Organization for Investment, Economic and Technical Assistance of Iran OIETAI	www.iraninvestment.org
Ireland	Industrial Development Agency of Ireland IDA Ireland	www.idaireland.com
Israel	Investment Promotion Centre IPC	www.investinisrael.gov.il
Italy	Italian Institute for Foreign Trade ICE	www.ice.it
Jamaica	Jamaica Promotions Corporation JAMPRO	www.investjamaica.com
Japan	Japan External Trade Organization JETRO	www.investjapan.org
Jordan	Jordan Investment Board JIB	www.jordaninvestment.com
Jordan	Aqaba Special Economic Zone Authority	www.aqabazone.com
Kazakhstan	Kazinvest	www.kazinvest.kz
Kenya	Investment Promotion Centre IPC	www.investmentkenya.com www.ipckenya.org
Kenya	Export Processing Zones Authority EPZA	www.epzakenya.com
Kiribati	Foreign Investment Commission	www.investinkiribati.com www.sptc.org.nz

Korea Republic of	Gyeonggi Provincial Government - Investment Promotion Division	www.invest.go.kr
Korea Republic of	Korea Trade-Investment Promotion Agency KOTRA	www.investkorea.org
Korea Republic of	Busan-Jinhae Free Economic Zone Authority	www.bjfez.net
Kosovo Serbia and Montenegro	Agency for Investment Promotion, Ministry of Trade and Industry	
Kuwait	The Inter Arab Investment Guarantee Corporation IAIGC	www.iaigc.org
Kuwait	Kuwait Foreign Investment Bureau KFIB	www.kfib.com
Kyrgyzstan	Investment Promotion Center	www.kyrgyzinvest.org
Latvia	Latvian Development Agency LDA	www.lda.gov.lv
Lebanon	Investment Development Authority of Lebanon IDAL	www.idal.com.lb
Lesotho	Lesotho Tourism Development Corporation	
Lesotho	Investment Promotion Center IPC	www.lndc.org.ls
Libya	Libyan Foreign Investment Board LFIB	www.investinlibya.com
Lithuania	Lithuanian Development Agency LDA	www.lda.lt
Macedonia	Privatisation Agency of the Republic of Macedonia	www.mpa.org.mk
Malawi	Malawi Investment Promotion Agency	www.mipa.malawi.net
Malaysia	Malaysian Industrial Development Authority MIDA	www.mida.gov.my
Malaysia	Selangor State Investment Centre SSIC	www.ssic.com.my
Malaysia	Kulim Technology Park Corp. Berhad	www.khtp.com.my
Malaysia	Melaka State Investment Centre Berhad MSIC	www.msic.com.my
Maldives	Foreign Investment Services Bureau FISB	www.investmaldives.org
Mali	Centre National de Promotion des	www.cnpi-mali.org

	Investissements CNPI	
Malta	Malta Enterprise Corporation	www.maltaenterprise.com
Mauritania	Direction de la Promotion de l'Investissement Privé	
Mauritius	Board of Investment of Mauritius	www.boimauritius.com
Mexico	Mexican Bank for Foreign Trade BANCOMEXT	www.bancomext.com
Mexico	Secretaria de Promocion Economica SEPROE	seproe.jalisco.gob.mx
Mexico	Industrial Development Commission of Mexicali	www.mexicaliindustrial.com
Moldova Republic of	Moldovan Export Promotion Organization MEPO	www.mida.md
Mongolia	Foreign Investment and Foreign Trade Agency FIFTA	www.investnet.mn
Morocco	Ministère de l'Economie et des Finances	www.invest-in-morocco.gov.ma
Namibia	Namibia Investment Centre NIC	www.grnnet.gov.na
Nepal	Industrial Promotion Division	www.yomari.com
Netherlands	Netherlands Foreign Investment Agency	www.minez.nl
Netherlands	West-Holland Foreign Investment Agency WFIA	www.wfia.nl
New Zealand	Investment New Zealand	www.investnewzealand.govt.nz
Nicaragua	ProNicaragua	www.pronicaragua.org.ni
Niger	Centre de Promotion des Investissements CPI	www.investir-au-niger.org
Nigeria	Nigerian Investment Promotion Commission NIPC	www.nipc-nigeria.org
Oman	Omani Centre for Investment Promotion & Export Development OCIPED	www.ociped.com
Pakistan	Board of Investment BOI	www.pakboi.gov.pk

Palestine National Authority	Palestinian Investment Promotion Agency PIPA	www.pipa.gov.ps
Papua New Guinea	Investment Promotion Authority IPA	www.ipa.gov.pg www.investinpng.com
Paraguay	Proparaguay	www.stp.gov.py
Peru	Prolnversión	www.proinversion.gob.pe
Philippines	Board of Investments BOI	www.boi.gov.ph
Poland	Polish Information and Foreign Investment Agency PAIiIZ	www.paiz.gov.pl
Portugal	Invest in Portugal	www.investinportugal.pt
Qatar State of	Investment Promotion Department	www.mec.gov.qa
Romania	Romanian Agency for Foreign Investments ARIS	www.arisinvest.ro
Russian Federation	Trade and Investment Promotion Agency TIPA	www.inves.ru
Rwanda	Rwanda Investment and Export Promoting Agency	www.rwandainvest.com
Saint Lucia	National Development Corporation	www.stluciandc.com
Saint Vincent and the Grenadines	National Investment Promotions Incorporated	www.svg-nipi.com
Samoa	Department of Trade, Commerce and Industry	www.tradeinvestsamoa.ws
Saudi Arabia	Saudi Arabia General Investment Authority SAGIA	www.sagia.org
Saudi Arabia	Royal Commission for Jubail and Yanbu	www.rcjy.gov.sa
Senegal	Investment Promotion and Major Works Agency APIX	www.apix.sn
Serbia and Montenegro	Montegegrin Investment Promotion Agency MIPA	www.mipa.cg.yu
Seychelles	Seychelles International Business Authority SIBA	www.siba.net

Seychelles	Seychelles Investment Bureau SIB	www.sib.sc
Sierra Leone	Ministry of Trade, Industry and State Enterprises	www.sierra-leone.gov.sl
Slovakia	Slovak Investment and Trade Development Agency SARIO	www.sario.sk
Slovenia	Slovenian Trade and Investment Promotion Agency TIPO	www.investslovenia.org
Solomon Islands	Ministry of Commerce and Tourism	www.commerce.gov.sb
South Africa	Durban Investment Promotion Agency	www.dipa.co.za
South Africa	Gauteng Economic Development Agency GEDA	www.geda.co.za
South Africa	Invest North West	www.inw.org.za
South Africa	Trade and Investment KwaZulu-Natal TIK	www.tikzn.co.za
South Africa	Trade and Investment Limpopo TIL	www.til.co.za
Spain	Subdirección General de Inversiones Exteriores	www.investinspain.org
Spain	Investment Promotion Agency of Catalonia CIDEM	www.catalonia.com
Spain	Service Center for the internationalisation of the Catalan Companies	www.copca.com
Sri Lanka	Board of Investment of Sri Lanka BOI	www.boi.lk
Sudan	Sudanese Investment Authority	www.sudaninvest.org
Swaziland	Swaziland Investment Promotion Authority SIPA	www.sipa.org.sz
Sweden	Invest in Sweden Agency ISA	www.isa.se
Tadjikistan	Agency for Promotion of Foreign Investments APFI	www.rambler.ru
Tanzania United Republic of	Tanzania Investment Centre TIC	www.tic.co.tz
Tanzania United	Zanzibar Investment Promotion Agency ZIPA	www.investzanzibar.org

Republic of		
Thailand	Office of the Board of Investment BOI	www.boi.go.th
Trinidad and Tobago	Tourism and Industrial Development Company TIDCO	www.tidco.co.tt
Tunisia	Foreign Investment Promotion Agency FIPA	www.investintunisia.com
Turkey	Under Secretariat for Treasury, General Directorate for Foreign Investment	www.treasury.gov.tr
Uganda	Uganda Investment Authority UIA	www.ugandainvest.com
Ukraine	Ukrainian Center for Foreign Investments Promotion	www.investukraine.org
United Arab Emirates	Dubai Development and Investment Authority DDIA	www.ddia.ae
United Arab Emirates	Dubai Airport Free Zone Authority DAFZA	www.dafza.gov.ae
United Arab Emirates	Ras Al Khaimah Free Trade Zone Authority	www.rakiftz.com
United Kingdom	UK Trade & Investment	www.uktradeinvest.gov.uk
United Kingdom	Manchester Investment Development Agency Service MIDAS	www.investinmanchester.com
Uzbekistan	Foreign Investment Agency	
Vanuatu	Vanuatu Investment Promotion Authority VIPA	www.investinvanuatu.com www.vanuatuinvest.vu
Venezuela	Consejo Nacional de Promoción de Inversiones CONAPRI	www.conapri.org
Yemen Republic of	General Investment Authority GIA	www.giay.gov.ye
Zambia	Zambia Investment Centre ZIC	www.zic.org.zm
Zambia	COMESA Regional Investment Agency	www.comesa.int
Zimbabwe	Zimbabwe Investment Centre	www.zimtrade.co.zw

KEY ORGANIZATION CONDUCTING DEVELOPMENT FINANCING AND PRIVATIZATION WORLDWIDE

1. Donor Organizations
Economic development organizations providing privatization technical assistance.
2. Sources of Investment Finance
National and multinational organizations that provide equity or loan financing, guarantees and other support for private investment into emerging markets.
3. Privatization Agencies
Government agencies in charge of divesting state-owned assets.

SOURCES OF INVESTMENT FINANCE

1. Korea Trade-Investment Promotion Agency KOTRA
   While principally facilitating FDI into Korea, KOTRA also provides overseas market information to Korean businesses.

2. Singapore -- Economic Development Board EDB
   Through several finance initiatives, EDBI encourages Singapore companies to seek out new technologies and new markets overseas. Also finances investments in Singapore.

3. African Development Bank, Private Sector Department
   Provides assistance directly to private enterprises local or foreign-owned incorporated in member countries in Africa through term loans, equity participations, quasi-equity investments, guarantees, underwriting and advisory services. The Bank also extends lines of credit to financial institutions for on-lending to small and medium enterprises.

4. Commonwealth Development Corporation
   Makes direct investments and provides finance to companies in emerging markets.

5. AIG Silk Road Fund
   A direct equity fund managed and sponsored by AIG Capital Partners for investments in Central Asia.

6. DFID Financial Deepening Challenge Funds
   The fund encourages initiatives from financial institutions in developing countries and the United Kingdom to develop profitable financial services accessible and beneficial to the poor. Funding awards may cover credit, savings, leasing, insurance or investment capital services.

7. DFID Ghana Business Linkages Challenge Funds
   A cost-sharing grant scheme that provides grants towards the costs incurred in the development of commercially sustainable business linkages that will benefit the poor.

8. European Bank for Reconstruction and Development EBRD

Provides project financing for banks, industries and businesses, both new ventures and investments in existing companies. It also works with publicly owned companies to support privatization, restructuring state-owned firms and improvement of municipal services. EBRD invests mainly in private enterprises, usually together with commercial partners. EBRD also mobilises significant FDI beyond its own financing.

9. United States -- OPIC Investment Funds
List of all OPIC-supported funds.

10. Japan External Trade Organization JETRO
In addition to promoting FDI into Japan, JETRO helps Japanese enterprises, particularly small and medium-sized ones, to build stronger business ties in Asia and to support their efforts to develop their international business.

11. The Norwegian Guarantee Institute for Export Credits GIEK
Official agency responsible for providing guarantees and insurance to promote Norwegian investment abroad.

12. China -- Ministry of Commerce
In charge of approving Chinese companies to set up overseas establishments excluding financial companies.

13. Italy -- Servizi Assicurativi del Commercio Estero SACE
Grants political and commerical risk insurance and reinsurance to support the internationalization of Italy's economy.

14. Italy -- SIMEST
Italy's development finance institution charged with supporting and promoting Italian companies' activities abroad. Also finances prefeasibility and feasibility studies and technical assistance programs.

15. China Export and Credit Insurance Corporation Sinosure
China's official export credit insurance agency, offering export credit, as well as political risk insurance to inbound foreign investors.

16. Finland -- FINPRO
Finpro provides services, support and information to Finnish companies to assist in their internationalization. It also provides Project Advisory Services, assisting Finnish companies and other organizations in their international operations through EU, IFI and UN financed projects in developing and transition economy countries.

17. UBIFRANCE
Assists French enterprises to take advantage and capitalize on investment opportunities abroad.

18. India -- Export Credit Guarantee Corporation
Essentially an export promotion and export credit guarantee organization, also offering overseas investment insurance to Indian companies investing in joint ventures abroad in the

form of equity or loans.

19. Export Development Canada
Offers Canadian companies access to its extensive international banking network to find a workable solution for financing their foreign investments, as well as political risk insurance

20. International Trade Canada
Offers strategic advice on doing business, including intelligence on opportunities, insight into emerging trends, as well as access to reports on foreign markets organized by industry sector.

21. Slovene Export Corporation
Slovenia's export credit agency finances international trade and investment transactions and insures outward investments against non-commercial risks.

22. Austrian Federal Economic Chamber WKÖ - Wirtschaftskammer Österreich
Provides information, advisory and business support services to Austrian businesses through field offices around the world and a network of experts.

23. Belgium -- Ducroire-Delcredere
An autonomous public body whose mission is to protect its clients against risks in connection with international transactions, such as exporting and investing abroad.

24. Southeast Europe Enterprise Development SEED
A five-year, US$25 million initiative managed by the International Finance Corporation to strengthen small and medium enterprises SMEs in the Balkan region.

25. International Finance Corporation
The largest multilateral source of loan and equity financing for private sector projects in developing countries.

26. OPEC Fund for International Development:
The OPEC Fund for International Development is a multilateral development finance institution established in January 1976 by the member countries of the Organization of the Petroleum Exporting Countries OPEC. The aim of this fund is, among other things, participating in the financing of private sector activities in developing countries outside OPEC members.

27. Baltic-American Enteprise Fund
Through Hanseatic Capital, a wholly-owned subsidiary, the fund provides mezzanine investments in growth-oriented businesses in the Baltic States.

28. Denmark -- Investment Fund for Central and Eastern Europe
Provides finance to Danish investors in Central and Eastern Europe non-EU accession countries.

29. European Union -- The Tacis Programme
Provides grant-financed technical assistance to transition economies, including for the promotion of investment. In its present form, the Tacis Programme will expire at the end of

2006.

30. Sources of Finance for Trade and Investments in the NIS
Overview of finance sources by BISNIS in PDF format.

31. The U.S. Russia Investment Fund
The US Russia Investment Fund was established in 1994 and has invested about US$300 million in 44 Russian companies. In 2004 its successor, the Delta Russia Fund, was set up.

32. Canada -- CIDA: Private Sector Development Program
A variety of private sector programs run by CIDA, which include microfinance and support to SMEs in developing countries.

33. Canada -- CIDA's Industrial Cooperation Program
This program provides financial support and advice to Canadian businesses planning sustainable business activities in developing countries in a variety of sectors.

34. International Enterprise Singapore
IE Singapore's mission is to help Singapore-based companies grow and internationalize successfully.

35. European Investment Bank EIB
An EU institution furnishing loan and equity capital for investment projects in developing and transition countries, as well as EU members, including the 'accession' countries.

36. Greece -- Export Credit Insurance Organization ECIO
Offers insurance programs against political risks concerning overseas investments.

37. Malaysian South South Corporation Berhad
Seeks to promote bilateral trade and investment between Malaysia and developing countries

38. Export-Import Bank of India
Provides equity loans to Indian companies for setting up overseas joint ventures or wholly owned subsidiaries.

39. Norwegian Investment Fund for Developing Countries Norfund
Supports commercially sustainable business ventures in developing countries through direct investments, as well as investments in local investment funds.

40. Belgian Corporation for International Investment BMI - SBI
An investment company whose main objective is to provide medium to long-term co-financing of foreign investments by Belgian companies.

41. France -- Investment and Promotion Company for Economic Cooperation PROPARCO
Supports private sector development in emerging markets by providing loans to companies in these markets, making minority equity investments and issuing guarantees.

42. Netherlands Development Finance Company
Offers loans to companies in emerging markets, or participates as a minority holder in their share capital. Also runs an Investment Promotion and Technical Assistance program running on a limited basis in 2004 to promote investment, international business partnerships and improve business operations for companies in developing countries.

43. Japan Bank for International Cooperation JBIC
Provides overseas investment loans, or participates in equity form in overseas business ventures of Japanese corporations.

44. Islamic Corporation for the Insurance of Investment and Export Credit
Provides investment guarantees to companies in member states investing in other member states.

45. United Kingdom -- Export Credits Guarantee Department ECGD
The country's official export credit agency also insures U.K. companies investing overseas against political risk.

46. Export-Import Bank of Thailand
The national export credit agency, providing financial facilities and information to Thai investors.

47. Nordic Development Fund
Co-finances private sector projects, or engages in joint ventures, in cooperation with Nordic companies, or Nordic regional and international development institutions.

48. Finland -- FINNVERA PLC
A state-owned specialised financing company offering financing services to promote the domestic operations of Finnish businesses, as well as to futher exports and the internationalization of Finnish enterprises.

49. Czech Republic -- Export Guarantee and Insurance Corporation EGAP
An export guarantee agency, also providing political risk insurance to Czech Republic legal entities investing abroad .

50. Canada -- Export Development Corporation
Supports Canadian exports and FDI abroad through trade finance and political risk insurance.

51. Inter-Arab Investment Guarantee Corporation
Provides insurance coverage for inter-Arab investments and export credits against non-commercial risks and seeks to promote inter-Arab investment flows.

52. KfW - The German Development Bank
KfW Entwicklungsbank finances investments and provides consulting services in developing countries.

53. South Africa -- Industrial Development Corporation, Department of Trade and Industry,

The Industrial Development Corporation is a self-financing state-owned development finance institution providing financing to entrepreneurs engaged in competitive industries.

54. Export-Import Bank of Malaysia
Provides financial support to Malaysian exporters and investors, as well as to foreign buyers of Malaysian products and services. The Bank's Overseas Investment Credit Facility supports Malaysian investors undertaking manufacturing, infastructure or other projects overseas.

55. Malaysia Export Credit Insurance Berhad
Malaysia's export credit insurance agency also supports outward FDI by Malaysian multinationals by providing overseas investment insurance.

56. United States -- Overseas Private Investment Corporation OPIC
OPIC helps U.S. businesses invest overseas by providing investment insurance, medium- to long-term financing for projects with significant U.S. participation and by sponsoring several investment funds for specific countries, regions or sectors.

57. Switzerland -- Swiss Organisation For Facilitating Investments SOFI
An outward investment promotion organization assisting Swiss companies in identifying business opportunities abroad, as well as helping enterprises in developing countries seek partners or financing. Priority countries/regions are: Burkina Faso, Ghana, Mozambique, Tanzania, South Africa, Egypt, Jordan, Morocco, Tunisia, Bolivia, Brazil, Central America, Peru, China, India, Indonesia, Vietnam, Albania, Bosnia-Herzegovina, Bulgaria, Macedonia, Romania, Serbia & Montenegro, Azerbaijan, Kyrgyzstan, Tajikistan, Uzbekistan, Russia and the Ukraine.

58. Finland -- The Finnish Fund for Industrial Corporation Ltd. FINNFUND
A development finance company that provides long-term risk capital for private projects in developing countries. Apart from co-investing with Finnish companies, Finnfund finances ventures that use Finnish technology, cooperate with Finnish partners on a long-term basis, or generate major environmental or social benefits.

59. Sweden -- Swedfund International AB
A state-owned risk capital company offering risk capital and know-how for investments in Central and Eastern Europe, Africa, Asia and Latin America.

60. Spain -- The Spanish Development Finance Company COFIDES
A partially state-owned corporation created to support Spanish companies investing in developing countries through loans, technical assistance and, to a limited extent, equity participation in Spanish.

61. Germany -- The German Investment and Development Company DEG
Provides a range of financing and consultancy services to investors, including long-term loans, risk management services and investment project support services.

62. Denmark -- The Industrialisation Fund for Developing Countries IFU
Promotes Danish investments and economic activity in developing countries with GNP per capita of less than US$5,115 through loans, guarantees and equity investments. Greenfield

projects, expansion of existing projects and privatisation of state-owned enterprises are eligible.

63. Korea Eximbank
Korea's official export credit agency providing comprehensive export credit and project finance to support Korean enterprises in conducting business internationally and engaging in overseas investment.

64. Austria -- Austria Wirtschaftsservice AWS
A state-owned financing company that primarily provides guarantees for international and domestic investment projects and manages funds.

65. Austria -- Oesterreichische Kontrollbank AG
Austria's Export Credit Agency offering the business community customized instruments in the area of risk management for a variety of exports.

66. BID Facility
The mission of this joint IFC-USAID facility is to identify, analyze, structure, and develop viable infrastructure private sector participation projects in energy, transport and water and sanitation that have a tangible impact and contribute to the economic development of the Balkan region.

67. South Africa -- Development Bank of South Africa DBSA
DBSA promotes public and private partnerships in infrastructure by co-financing public- and private-sector investments, and by providing technical assistance for strengthening policy, institutional capacity and environmental management, as well as loans, equity and guarantees to private investors in infrastructure.

68. Canada -- Strategis: Finance Finder
An online directory and search engine to connect users and sources of finance for business and investment in Canada.

69. Barbados -- Central Bank - Barbados Investment Fund
A close-ended equity fund established by the Central Bank of Barbados and the Caribbean Financial Services Corporation to provide equity financing for SMEs.

70. European Union -- Asia - Invest Programme
An initiative that provides financial support to facilitate business co-operation between companies from the European Union and Asia.

71. Andean Finance Corporation Corporaci□n Andina de Fomento
Provides loans, technical cooperation, equity investments and guarantees to private companies.

72. Black Sea Trade and Development Bank
Provides loans, equity and guarantees to private and state-owned enterprises.

73. Western NIS Enterprise Fund

A private equity fund established by the U.S. Congress in 1996 with US$150 million under management. The fund supports small businesses and entrepreneurs via microlending institutions.

74. Innova Capital
A US$300+ million private-equity fund for Central Europe.

75. Kula Fund Limited
Provides risk capital for business proposals in the Pacific Islands with strong commercial potential, backed by proven management capability.

76. Emerging Africa Infrastructure Fund

77. BISNIS FinanceLink
A resource for helping U.S. companies seeking financing by distributing to U.S.-incorporated financial service providers summaries about transactions or projects where the U.S. company has already identified a buyer or partner in the newly independent states.

78. China -- Sino-Swiss Partnership Fund
Provides equity investments in joint ventures between Chinese enterprises and small and medium-sized Swiss and German companies.

79. World Bank Group
Offers loans, technical assistance and guarantees to encourage private investment in developing countries.

80. SFI Corporation
Homepage of the SFI Corporation, which offers commercial factoring and short term lending

81. Centre for the Development of Enterprise
Although not a financial institution, CDE assists ACP industries in the creation, expansion, diversification, rehabilitation or privatization of industrial entreprises, and can help to together a financing package.

82. Commonwealth Disaster Management Agency

83. Japan -- Development Bank of Japan
Provides loans, funds and guarantees for direct investments to foreign companies, including joint ventures with Japanese companies, investing in Japan.

84. World Bank Capital Markets Development Department -- Fundline
A listing of investment funds and equity resources for Eastern Europe and the former Soviet Union countries.

85. South Africa -- Business Partners
Provides a variety of financing options to small and medium-sized enterprises located in South

Africa.

86. Singapore -- National Science and Technology Board, Technology Development Fund
Provides venture capital for technology-based companies in their early stages of development. The Fund supports the growth of local technology start-ups in Singapore, as well as foreign-owned technology start-ups seeking to establish a base in Singapore.

87. Portugal -- Banco BPI S.A.

88. North American Development Bank NADB
Information on advisory and financial services, loan and guarantee programs and other activities of the NADB.

89. Mexico -- Mexican Bank for Foreign Trade Bancomext
Supports FDI into Mexico by providing information, advice and appraisal services.

90. Inter-American Investment Corporation
Makes direct and indirect investments through the granting of loans to Latin American companies.

91. European Commission -- Al-Invest
Meetings between companies in Europe and Latin America organized and financed under this program often lead to the formation of joint ventures and other cross-border investments and business agreements. Over 6,000 companies in Europe and Latin America have benefited from this program so far.

92. Central Asian - American Enterprise Fund
Promotes the development of private enterprise in Central Asia by operating as a venture capital institution to companies operating in the region, and to companies seeking to invest in the region.

93. Central American Bank for Economic Integration CABEI
Finances medium and long-term fixed investments in Central America's industry, as well as micro and SME investments in the form of credit, cofinancing, loans and guarantees.

94. Bulgarian - American Enterprise Fund
Private U.S. corporation established to promote entrepreneurship and investment opportunities in Bulgaria and to establish joint ventures and new business.

95. Brazil -- Banco Nacional de Desenvolvimento Economic e Social BNDES

Lends to legally incorporated private-sector companies with operations established in Brazil.

96. Asian Finance and Investment Corporation Ltd.

The Asian Finance and Investment Corporation Ltd., established under the auspices of the Asian Development Bank, concentrates largely on mid-sized projects in manufacturing and other sectors.

97. Asian Development Bank ADB

The Asian Development Bank provides finance directly to private enterprises and financial institutions through loans, underwriting, investment in equity securities, co-financing and guarantees.

98. Argentina -- Fundacion Invertir Argentina

Assists small and medium-sized companies seeking finance for investment projects.

99. Palestine Development and Investment Ltd. PADICO

Establishes and manages projects and investment funds and undertakes direct investments in real estate, housing and industrial projects.

DONOR ORGANIZATIONS

1. German Technical Cooperation GTZ

German development organization providing also assistance in privatization

2. International Finance Corporation IFC

Provides information on the activities of the world's largest multilateral source of financing for projects in emerging economies

3. European Bank for Reconstruction and Development EBRD

Established to foster the transition towards open market-oriented economies and to promote private and entrepreneurial initiatives in the countries of Central and Eastern Europe and the Commonwealth of Independent States.

4. The World Bank Group

A development institution whose goal is to reduce poverty by promoting sustainable economic growth in its client countries.

5. OECD: Directorate for Financial, Fiscal and Enterprise Affairs

Presents information on international investment and capital movements, privatization and enterprise reform, as well as information on the review process of the OECD Guidelines on Multinational Enterprises.

6. Association of Southeast Asian Nations

Contains information on ASEAN's activities, as well as on economic cooperation in private sector development, small and medium-sized enterprises, infrastructural development, investment promotion and the ASEAN Investment Area.

7. United States Agency for International Development USAID

US government agency for development aid; also providing technical assistance in privatization

8. Asian Development Bank

Information about the activities of the ADB, a development finance institution promoting the economic and social progress of its developing member countries in the Asian and Pacific region.

9. Department for International Development - United Kingdom

   UK development aid agency; provides also technical assistance in privatization

10. African Development Bank

    Multilateral development bank promoting economic development and social progress in Africa.

11. Canadian International Development Agency CIDA

    Canadian development agency, also providing technical assistance in the area of privatization

12. European Union: EuropeAid Cooperation Office

    The EU is involved in a number of privatization-related technical assistance projects in the Former Soviet Union and other regions.

PRIVATIZATION AGENCIES

1. Pakistan -- Corporate and Industrial Restructuring Organization
2. Executive Privatization Commission - Jordan
3. Agency of Montenegro for Economic Restructuring and Foreign Investments
4. Romania -- The Authority for State Assets Recovery
5. China -- Shanghai United Assets and Equity Exchange
6. Ministry of Economic Development: Privatization - Georgia
7. Egypt -- Ministry of Investment
8. Kyrgyzstan -- State Committee on State Property and Direct Investments
9. Bulgaria -- Privatization Agency
10. Bosnia-Herzegovina -- Privatization Agency
11. Bulgaria -- Sofia Municipal Privatisation Agency
12. Nigeria -- Bureau of Public Enterprises
13. Gambia Divestiture Agency
14. China -- Zhuhai Municipal State-owned Assets Management Bureau
15. China -- Wuhan Administrative Bureau of the State Property
16. China Beijing Equity Exchange
17. National Investment Bank of Jamaica
18. Directorate of Disinvestment, Punjab - India
19. Albania -- National Agency for Privatization
20. Costa Rica -- Ministerio de Planificacion Nacional y Politica Economica
21. Rwanda -- Privatization Secretariat
22. Bangladesh -- Privatization Commission
23. Privatisation Commission of Malawi
24. Bosnia - Herzegovina -- Republika Srpska Directorate for Privatization
25. Ministry of Economic Development, Dept. of Privatization - Azerbaijan
26. India -- Department of Public Enterprises
27. Pakistan -- Privatisation Commission
28. Armenia -- Ministry of State Property Management
29. Lithuania -- State Property Fund
30. Poland -- Ministry of the Treasury
31. Uganda -- Ministry of Finance, Planning and Economic Development, Privatization Unit
32. Turkey -- Privatization Administration

33. Equador -- Council for the Modernization of the State CONAM under construction
34. Thailand -- State Enterprise Policy Office
35. Uzbekistan -- State Property Committee
36. China -- State-owned Assets Supervision & Administration Commission of the State Council
37. Tanzania -- Parastatal Sector Reform Commission
38. Peru -- Comission for the Promotion of Private Investment COPRI
39. Kosovo Trust Agency
40. Republic of Serbia Privatization Agency
41. India -- Ministry of Disinvestment
42. Russian Federal Property Fund
43. South Africa -- Department of Public Enterprises
44. Indonesian Ministry of State Owned Enterprises, Restructuring and Privatization Division
45. Ministry of Economy and Privatisation - Republic of Serbia
46. Israel -- Government Companies Authority
47. Madagascar -- Comite de Privatisation
48. Singapore -- Temasek Holdings
49. Zimbabwe -- Privatisation Agency
50. Mexico -- Ministry of Finance and Public Credit
51. Sri Lanka -- Public Enterprise Reform Commission
52. Zambia Privatization Agency ZPA
53. Latvian Privatization Agency
54. Croatian Privatization Fund
55. Macedonia Privatization Agency
56. Ethiopian Privatization Aency EPA
57. Moldova -- Department of Privatization and State Property Administration
58. Slovak Republic -- National Property Fund
59. Nepal -- Ministry of Finance, Privatisation Cell
60. Hungarian Privatization and State Holding Company
61. Mongolia State Property Committee
62. Ukraine -- State Property Fund
63. Brazil -- Brazilian Development Bank BNDES
64. Republic of Korea -- Ministry of Planning and Budget
65. Czech Republic -- National Property Fund

INVESTMENT PROMOTION ORGANIZATIONS

AUSTRALIA

Australian Agency for International Development AusAID

Focuses on developing countries in the Asia-Pacific region, harnessing the expertise and capacity of Australian enterprises to work with counterpart organizations in the area.

Australian Trade Commission AUSTRADE

Promotes Australian industry abroad and identifies business opportunities.

Environment Australia

Promotes Australian environment industry capabilities domestically and internationally and identifies and contributes to environment capacity building opportunities in developing countries.

Export Finance and Insurance Corporation EFIC

Insures investment exposed to heightened political risks in emerging markets.

AUSTRIA

Bürgesförderungsbank Gesellschaft

FDI scheme for small-and medium-sized enterprises and financial aid for a long-term partnership between an Austrian SME and a private company.

Erp-Fonds European Recovery Programme Fund

Supports Austrian companies investing home or abroad.

Financing Guarantee Company East-West Fund

Eases the long-term project financing by Austrian companies abroad. It is now merged with the Finance Guarantee Company in Austria is now AWS

BELGIUM

Belgian Corporation for International Investment BMI-SBI

An investment company whose main objective is to provide medium to long-term co-financing for Belgian companies investing abroad.

BRUNEI

Ministry of Industry and Primary Resources

Spearheads industrial and commercial development through investment in key industrial sectors in the interest of Brunei's business.

CANADA

Africa Direct - Canadian International Development Agency CIDA

Initiative led by the Government of Canada to build stronger Canadian–African business linkages.

Industrial Cooperation Programme - Canadian International Development Agency CIDA

Provides finance to Canadian business planning sustainable activities in developing countries in various sectors.

Export Development Corporation

Promotes Canadian outward investment through direct loans, lines of credit and equity. participation.

CZECH REPUBLIC

Export Guarantee and Insurance Corporation EGAP

Insurance against non-marketable commercial and political risks with state support.

DENMARK

Danish International Development Agency DANIDA

Provides capital and know-how for investments in developing countries.

Danish Co-operation for Environment and Development DANCED

Promotes the transfer of environmental know-how and technology from Danish companies to developing countries.

The Industrialization Fund for Developing Countries IFU and the Investment Fund for Emerging marketS IFV

Promotes Danish investment and economic activity in developing countries and emerging markets and contributes to a positive and environmentally responsible industrial development of these markets.

FINLAND

FINNFUND

Investment finance company for emerging markets through equity participation, loans and fund management.

FINN VERA PLC

Specialized financing company offering financing services to promote the internationalization of Finnish business.

FRANCE

French Global Environment Facility GEF

Provides funding to encourage developing countries and economies in transition to incorporate protection of the global environment into their development Programmes and projects.

Investment and Promotion Company for Economic Cooperation PROPARCO

A subsidiary of the Agence Française de Développement, PROPARCO provides support to SMEs in developing countries.

GERMANY

Bundestelle für Aussenhandelsinformation

Fosters outward investment through research and dissemination of information about potential investment destinations.

The German Investment and Development Company DEG

Provides a range of financing and consultancy services to investors and promotes private enterprise as a contribution to sustainable growth in developing and transition economies.

KFW-The German Development Bank

Provides finances for investments and project-related consultancy services to expand social, economic and industrial infrastructure in developing countries.

ICELAND

Overseas Business Services OBS

Disseminates information on potential destinations for outward investment such as country profiles and investment opportunities database.

INDIA

Indian Investment Centre ICC

Deals with policy matters relating to Indian investment abroad, both direct and portfolio.

ITALY

Instituto per la Promozione Industriale IPI

Provides a range of financing and consultancy services to Italian companies seeking to invest abroad.

Mondimpresa

Fosters Italian entrepreneurs, specially small and medium-sized companies by informing about investment opportunities and giving technical assistance.

Prometeo SRL

Gives technical assistance for manufacturing and technological projects abroad with Italian participation.

Instituto per i Servizi Assicurativi del Commercio Estero SACE

Insures Italian companies investing abroad.

Società Italiana per le Imprese Miste all'Estero Spa SIMEST

Finances up to 25% of Italian equity investment abroad.

JAPAN

Japan International Development Organization Ltd. JAIDO

Promotes joint ventures which contribute to the growth of private sectors in developing countries.

Japan Bank for International Cooperation JBIC

Provides private sector investment finance through loan financing for and equity investment in private companies in developing countries.

Japan External Trade Organization JETRO

Promotes Japanese direct investment abroad through a variety of services.

Export-Import Bank of Japan JEXIM

Finances Japanese firms' equity acquisition abroad.

Japan International Cooperation Agency JICA

JICA provides long-term, low-interest loans to Japanese enterprises for projects which do not qualify for loans from the Overseas Economic Cooperation Fund or the Export-Import Bank of Japan.

Japan Institute for Overseas Investment JOI

Promotes Japanese direct investment abroad through research and training.

KINGDOM OF SAUDI ARABIA

Saudi Fund for Development SFD

articipates in the financing of development projects in developing countries through the granting of loans.

KOREA

The Export-Import Bank of Korea

Provides overseas investment credits to Korean nationals who invest abroad in the form of capital subscription, acquisition stock, and extension of long-term credit.

KUWAIT

Kuwait Fund for Arab Economic Development

Assists Arab and other developing countries in developing their economies particularly by providing loans and grants to facilitate the implementation of development programmes.

MALAYSIA

Malaysia External Trade Development Corporation MATRADE

Provides information on investment opportunities abroad for Malaysian business.

MEXICO

Banco Nacional de Comercio Exterior BANCOMEXT

Informs Mexican companies of business opportunities abroad.

NETHERLANDS

The Netherlands Foreign Trade Agency EVD

Databank of trade and investment opportunities worldwide.

Dutch Credit Insurance Company NCM NV

Offers a range of credit management solutions to support companies with their national and international trading activities.

Netherlands Development Finance Company FMO

Promotes investment and international business partnerships in Africa, Asia and Latin America.

Senter

Is responsible for the execution of grant schemes in the fields of technology, energy, environment, exports or international partnerships and offers financial assistance for the realization of projects.

NEW ZEALAND

Ministry of Foreign Affairs and Trade Development Cooperation Division

Promotes the development of the private sector in the Pacific Islands and builds links between New Zealand and Pacific Islands private sectors.

South Pacific Trade Commission SPTC

Identifies of joint venture investment partners and promotion of the Pacific Islands Investment and Development Scheme PIIDS.

NORWAY

Norwegian Agency for Development Cooperation NORAD

Finances projects in development cooperation in partnership with the central government and local authorities, civil society and the business sector.

Norwegian Investment Fund for Developing Countries NORFUND

Contributes to the success of the projects by providing not only risk capital but also expertise, increasing the value of the investments through active participation on the board and by providing commercial and financial expertise and access to an extensive international network.

PORTUGAL

Investimentos, Comercio e Turismo de Portugal ICEP

Assists home entrepreneurs in identifying opportunities for investment abroad as well as giving credit solutions.

SINGAPORE

Economic Development Board of Singapore EDB

Networks to provide investment information and technical advice to firms seeking expanding abroad.

SOUTH AFRICA

Development Bank of Southern Africa DBSA

Invest in infrastructure and facilitates the provision of infrastructural development finance, finances sustainable development business in partnership with the private sector, also acts as a catalyst for investment.

SPAIN

Compañia Española de Financiación del Desarrollo COFIDES

Fosters Spanish investment in developing countries and economies in transition by providing project feasibility studies, mediating in the application for subsidies, and also providing financial support.

Instituto Español de Comercio Exterior ICEX

Informs, advises and finances Spanish companies with outward investment projects.

SWEDEN

Swedfund International AB

Provides capital and know-how for investments in developing countries primarily in partnership with Swedish companies.

SWITZERLAND

Swiss Agency for Development and Cooperation SDC

Provides funding as well as financial services for investment projects in developing countries.

State Secretariat for Economic Affairs SECO

Promotes investment in developing countries and emerging countries mainly through risk-sharing schemes.

Swiss Organization for Facilitating Investments SOFI

Encourages, facilitates and contributes to the effective implementation of investment projects between Swiss companies and counterparts from developing and transition countries.

THAILAND

Export-Import Bank of Thailand EXIM BANK

Provides financial services and medium and long-term credit facilities to Thai companies investing abroad. Additionally it is able to joint-invest in their ventures through equity participation. It also has a special support programme for neighboring countries.

UNITED KINGDOM

Commonwealth Development Corporation CDC

The CDC is the UK Government's main instrument for directly mobilizing private investment in developing countries.

Department for International Development DFID

Promotes UK private sector trade and investment in developing countries through the collaboration with business on individual projects.

Department of Trade and Industry

Promotes a wide range of policies that support technology development, foreign investment, trade, technical, managerial and other capacity building.

Export Credits Guarantee Department ECGD

Promotes UK firms investment overseas by providing guarantees, insurance and reinsurance against loss.

Trade Partners UK

Provides advice on market condition and matchmaking with local firms to UK firms looking to invest in developing countries.

UNITED STATES

Overseas Private Investment Corporation OPIC

Provides political risk insurance and project financing for investment projects abroad.

Environmental Exports Programme - Export-Import Bank of the United States EX-IM

Provides enhanced short-term, multi-buyer and single-buyer insurance coverage for small business.

Trade and Development Agency TDA

Enable American businesses to compete for infrastructure and industrial projects in middle-income and developing countries through the funding of feasibility studies, site visits, specialized training grants, business workshops and various forms of technical assistance.

United States Agency for International Development USAID

Provides business-matching programmes.

REGIONAL DEVELOPMENT BANKS INVOLVED IN PRIVATIZATION PROGRAMS

- African Development Bank AfDB
- African Export-Import Bank Afreximbank

- Andean Development Corporation CAF
- Arab Bank for Economic Development in Africa BADEA
- Arab Fund for Economic and Social Development AFESD
- Asia-Africa Investment and Technology Promotion Centre AAITPC
- Asia-Europe Investment Promotion Action Plan IPAP
- Asian Development Bank AsDB
- Asia-Pacific Economic Co-operation APEC
- Black Sea Trade and Development Bank BSTDB
- Caribbean Development Bank CDB
- Central American Bank for Economic Integration CABEI
- Eastern and Southern Africa Trade and Development Bank PTA
- European Bank for Reconstruction and Development EBRD
- European Development Finance Institutions EDFI
- European Investment Bank EIB
- European Investment Fund EIF
- Inter-American Development Bank IADB
- Inter-Arab Investment Guarantee Corporation IAIGC
- Islamic Corporation for the Insurance of Investment and Export Credit ICIEC
- Islamic Development Bank IDB
- Nordic Development Fund NDF
- Nordic Investment Bank NIB
- OPEC Fund for International Development

SUPPLEMENTS

STRATEGIC STATISTICS

ECONOMIC STATISTICS

Name	Currency	GDP (PPP) per capita (est. in U.S. dollars)
Argentina	Argentine peso	14,200
Bolivia	Boliviano	4,500
Brazil	Brazilian real	10,100
Chile	Chilean peso	14,900
Colombia	Colombian peso	8,900
Ecuador	United States dollar	7,500
Falkland Islands (UK)	Falkland Islands pound	35,400 (2002 est.)
French Guiana (France)	Euro	6,000 (2001 est.)
Guyana	Guyanese dollar	3,900
Paraguay	Paraguayan guaraní	4,200
Peru	Peruvian nuevo sol	8,400
Suriname	Surinamese dollar	8,900
Uruguay	Uruguayan peso	12,200
Venezuela	Venezuelan bolívar	13,500

SOUTH AMERICAN COUNTRIES BY POPULATION

Rank	Country(or dependent territory)	July 1, 2015 projection	% of pop.	Average relative annual growth (%)	Average absolute annual growth	Estimated doubling time (years)	Official figure (where available)
1	Brazil	204,519,000	49.36	0.86	1,750,000	81	206,075,000
2	Colombia	48,549,000	11.64	1.16	555,000	60	48,728,000
3	Argentina	43,132,000	10.41	1.09	463,000	64	43,590,368
4	Peru	31,153,000	7.52	1.10	338,000	64	31,488,625
5	Venezuela	30,620,000	7.39	1.37	414,000	51	31,028,637
6	Chile	18,006,000	4.35	1.05	187,000	66	18,191,884
7	Ecuador	16,279,000	3.93	1.57	252,000	44	16,529,300
8	Bolivia	10,520,000	2.54	1.73	179,000	40	10,985,059
9	Paraguay	7,003,000	1.69	1.58	109,000	44	6,854,536

Rank	Country(or dependent territory)	July 1, 2015 projection	% of pop.	Average relative annual growth (%)	Average absolute annual growth	Estimated doubling time (years)	Official figure (where available)
10	Uruguay	3,310,000	0.80	0.18	6,000	382	3,480,222
11	Guyana	747,000	0.18	0.00	0	-	747,884
12	Suriname	560,000	0.14	1.08	6,000	64	541,638
13	French Guiana	262,000	0.06	2.75	7,000	26	239,648
14	Falkland Islands(UK)	3,000	0.00	0.00	0	-	2,563
	Total	414,663,000	100.00	1.04	4,266,000	67	

SOVEREIGN STATES AND DEPENDENT TERRITORIES IN SOUTH AMERICA BY POPULATION DENSITY

Rank	Country / Territory	Population	Area (km²)	Density (persons/km²).
1	Ecuador	15,007,343	283,561	52.9
2	Colombia	44,725,543	1,138,914	39.3
3	Venezuela	27,635,743	912,050	30.3
4	Brazil	203,429,773	8,547,403	23.8
5	Peru	29,248,943	1,285,216	22.8
6	Chile	16,888,760	756,626	22.3
7	Uruguay	3,308,535	175,016	18.9
8	Paraguay	6,459,058	406,752	15.9
9	Argentina	41,769,726	2,780,400	15.0
10	Bolivia	10,118,683	1,098,581	9.2
11	Guyana	744,768	214,969	3.5
12	French Guiana	274,652	90,000	3.1
13	Suriname	491,989	163,265	3.0
14	Falkland Islands	3,140	12,173	0.26
	Total	400,106,656	17,864,926	22.4

SOUTH AMERICAN COUNTRIES BY GDP (PPP) PER CAPITA

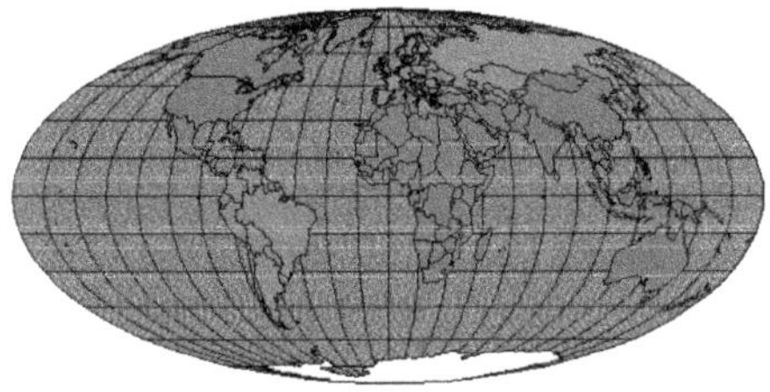

GLOBAL DIRECT FOREIGN INVESTMENT LAWS, REGULATIONS AND OPPORTUNITIES LIBRARY

Price: $149.95 Each

1. Albania Direct Foreign Investments Laws, Regulations and Opportunities Handbook
2. Algeria Direct Foreign Investments Laws, Regulations and Opportunities Handbook
3. Angola Direct Foreign Investments Laws, Regulations and Opportunities Handbook
4. Antigua & Barbuda Direct Foreign Investments Laws, Regulations and Opportunities Handbook
5. Antilles (Netherlands) Direct Foreign Investments Laws, Regulations and Opportunities Handbook
6. Argentina Direct Foreign Investments Laws, Regulations and Opportunities Handbook
7. Armenia Direct Foreign Investments Laws, Regulations and Opportunities Handbook
8. Australia Direct Foreign Investments Laws, Regulations and Opportunities Handbook
9. Austria Direct Foreign Investments Laws, Regulations and Opportunities Handbook
10. Azerbaijan Direct Foreign Investments Laws, Regulations and Opportunities Handbook
11. Bahamas Direct Foreign Investments Laws, Regulations and Opportunities Handbook
12. Bangladesh Direct Foreign Investments Laws, Regulations and Opportunities Handbook
13. Barbados Direct Foreign Investments Laws, Regulations and Opportunities Handbook
14. Belarus Direct Foreign Investments Laws, Regulations and Opportunities Handbook
15. Belgium Direct Foreign Investments Laws, Regulations and Opportunities Handbook
16. Belize Direct Foreign Investments Laws, Regulations and Opportunities Handbook
17. Bermuda Direct Foreign Investments Laws, Regulations and Opportunities Handbook
18. Bolivia Direct Foreign Investments Laws, Regulations and Opportunities Handbook
19. Bosnia and Herzegovina Direct Foreign Investments Laws, Regulations and Opportunities Handbook
20. Botswana Direct Foreign Investments Laws, Regulations and Opportunities Handbook
21. Brazil Direct Foreign Investments Laws, Regulations and Opportunities Handbook
22. Brunei Direct Foreign Investments Laws, Regulations and Opportunities Handbook
23. Bulgaria Direct Foreign Investments Laws, Regulations and Opportunities Handbook
24. Cambodia Direct Foreign Investments Laws, Regulations and Opportunities Handbook
25. Cameroon Direct Foreign Investments Laws, Regulations and Opportunities Handbook
26. Canada Direct Foreign Investments Laws, Regulations and Opportunities Handbook
27. Cayman Islands Direct Foreign Investments Laws, Regulations and Opportunities Handbook
28. Chile Direct Foreign Investments Laws, Regulations and Opportunities Handbook
29. China Direct Foreign Investments Laws, Regulations and Opportunities Handbook
30. Colombia Direct Foreign Investments Laws, Regulations and Opportunities Handbook
31. Comoros Direct Foreign Investments Laws, Regulations and Opportunities Handbook
32. Cook Islands Direct Foreign Investments Laws, Regulations and Opportunities Handbook
33. Costa Rica Direct Foreign Investments Laws, Regulations and Opportunities Handbook
34. Croatia Direct Foreign Investments Laws, Regulations and Opportunities Handbook
35. Cuba Direct Foreign Investments Laws, Regulations and Opportunities Handbook

36.	Cyprus Direct Foreign Investments Laws, Regulations and Opportunities Handbook
37.	Czech Republic Direct Foreign Investments Laws, Regulations and Opportunities Handbook
38.	Denmark Direct Foreign Investments Laws, Regulations and Opportunities Handbook
39.	Dominica Direct Foreign Investments Laws, Regulations and Opportunities Handbook
40.	Dominican Republic Direct Foreign Investments Laws, Regulations and Opportunities Handbook
41.	Dubai Direct Foreign Investments Laws, Regulations and Opportunities Handbook
42.	Ecuador Direct Foreign Investments Laws, Regulations and Opportunities Handbook
43.	Egypt Direct Foreign Investments Laws, Regulations and Opportunities Handbook
44.	El Salvador Direct Foreign Investments Laws, Regulations and Opportunities Handbook
45.	Equatorial Guinea Direct Foreign Investments Laws, Regulations and Opportunities Handbook
46.	Estonia Direct Foreign Investments Laws, Regulations and Opportunities Handbook
47.	Falkland Islands Direct Foreign Investments Laws, Regulations and Opportunities Handbook
48.	Fiji Direct Foreign Investments Laws, Regulations and Opportunities Handbook
49.	Finland Direct Foreign Investments Laws, Regulations and Opportunities Handbook
50.	France Direct Foreign Investments Laws, Regulations and Opportunities Handbook
51.	Georgia Direct Foreign Investments Laws, Regulations and Opportunities Handbook
52.	Germany Direct Foreign Investments Laws, Regulations and Opportunities Handbook
53.	Gibraltar Direct Foreign Investments Laws, Regulations and Opportunities Handbook
54.	Greece Direct Foreign Investments Laws, Regulations and Opportunities Handbook
55.	Grenada Direct Foreign Investments Laws, Regulations and Opportunities Handbook
56.	Guam Investment & Business Guide
57.	Guatemala Direct Foreign Investments Laws, Regulations and Opportunities Handbook
58.	Guernsey Direct Foreign Investments Laws, Regulations and Opportunities Handbook
59.	Guyana Direct Foreign Investments Laws, Regulations and Opportunities Handbook
60.	Haiti Direct Foreign Investments Laws, Regulations and Opportunities Handbook
61.	Honduras Direct Foreign Investments Laws, Regulations and Opportunities Handbook
62.	Hungary Direct Foreign Investments Laws, Regulations and Opportunities Handbook
63.	Iceland Direct Foreign Investments Laws, Regulations and Opportunities Handbook
64.	India Direct Foreign Investments Laws, Regulations and Opportunities Handbook
65.	Indonesia Direct Foreign Investments Laws, Regulations and Opportunities Handbook
66.	Iran Direct Foreign Investments Laws, Regulations and Opportunities Handbook
67.	Iraq Direct Foreign Investments Laws, Regulations and Opportunities Handbook
68.	Ireland Direct Foreign Investments Laws, Regulations and Opportunities Handbook
69.	Israel Direct Foreign Investments Laws, Regulations and Opportunities Handbook
70.	Italy Direct Foreign Investments Laws, Regulations and Opportunities Handbook
71.	Jamaica Direct Foreign Investments Laws, Regulations and Opportunities Handbook
72.	Japan Direct Foreign Investments Laws, Regulations and Opportunities Handbook
73.	Jersey Direct Foreign Investments Laws, Regulations and Opportunities Handbook
74.	Jordan Direct Foreign Investments Laws, Regulations and Opportunities Handbook
75.	Kazakhstan Direct Foreign Investments Laws, Regulations and Opportunities Handbook
76.	Kenya Direct Foreign Investments Laws, Regulations and Opportunities Handbook
77.	Kiribati Direct Foreign Investments Laws, Regulations and Opportunities Handbook
78.	Korea, North Direct Foreign Investments Laws, Regulations and Opportunities Handbook

79. Korea, South Direct Foreign Investments Laws, Regulations and Opportunities Handbook
80. Kuwait Direct Foreign Investments Laws, Regulations and Opportunities Handbook
81. Kyrgyzstan Direct Foreign Investments Laws, Regulations and Opportunities Handbook
82. Laos Direct Foreign Investments Laws, Regulations and Opportunities Handbook
83. Latvia Direct Foreign Investments Laws, Regulations and Opportunities Handbook
84. Lebanon Direct Foreign Investments Laws, Regulations and Opportunities Handbook
85. Libya Direct Foreign Investments Laws, Regulations and Opportunities Handbook
86. Liechtenstein Direct Foreign Investments Laws, Regulations and Opportunities Handbook
87. Lithuania Direct Foreign Investments Laws, Regulations and Opportunities Handbook
88. Luxemburg Direct Foreign Investments Laws, Regulations and Opportunities Handbook
89. Macao Direct Foreign Investments Laws, Regulations and Opportunities Handbook
90. Macedonia, Republic Direct Foreign Investments Laws, Regulations and Opportunities Handbook
91. Madagascar Direct Foreign Investments Laws, Regulations and Opportunities Handbook
92. Malaysia Direct Foreign Investments Laws, Regulations and Opportunities Handbook
93. Malta Direct Foreign Investments Laws, Regulations and Opportunities Handbook
94. Man Direct Foreign Investments Laws, Regulations and Opportunities Handbook
95. Mauritius Direct Foreign Investments Laws, Regulations and Opportunities Handbook
96. Mauritius Direct Foreign Investments Laws, Regulations and Opportunities Handbook
97. Mexico Direct Foreign Investments Laws, Regulations and Opportunities Handbook
98. Micronesia Direct Foreign Investments Laws, Regulations and Opportunities Handbook
99. Moldova Direct Foreign Investments Laws, Regulations and Opportunities Handbook
100. Monaco Direct Foreign Investments Laws, Regulations and Opportunities Handbook
101. Mongolia Direct Foreign Investments Laws, Regulations and Opportunities Handbook
102. Morocco Direct Foreign Investments Laws, Regulations and Opportunities Handbook
103. Myanmar Direct Foreign Investments Laws, Regulations and Opportunities Handbook
104. Namibia Direct Foreign Investments Laws, Regulations and Opportunities Handbook
105. Netherlands Direct Foreign Investments Laws, Regulations and Opportunities Handbook
106. New Caledonia Direct Foreign Investments Laws, Regulations and Opportunities Handbook
107. New Zealand Direct Foreign Investments Laws, Regulations and Opportunities Handbook
108. Nicaragua Direct Foreign Investments Laws, Regulations and Opportunities Handbook
109. Nigeria Direct Foreign Investments Laws, Regulations and Opportunities Handbook
110. Northern Mariana Islands Direct Foreign Investments Laws, Regulations and Opportunities Handbook
111. Norway Direct Foreign Investments Laws, Regulations and Opportunities Handbook
112. Pakistan Direct Foreign Investments Laws, Regulations and Opportunities Handbook
113. Panama Direct Foreign Investments Laws, Regulations and Opportunities Handbook
114. Peru Direct Foreign Investments Laws, Regulations and Opportunities Handbook
115. Philippines Direct Foreign Investments Laws, Regulations and Opportunities Handbook
116. Poland Direct Foreign Investments Laws, Regulations and Opportunities Handbook
117. Portugal Direct Foreign Investments Laws, Regulations and Opportunities Handbook
118. Romania Direct Foreign Investments Laws, Regulations and Opportunities Handbook
119. Russia Direct Foreign Investments Laws, Regulations and Opportunities Handbook
120. Samoa (American) Investment & Business Guide
121. Samoa (Western) Direct Foreign Investments Laws, Regulations and Opportunities Handbook

122. Saudi Arabia Direct Foreign Investments Laws, Regulations and Opportunities Handbook
123. Scotland Direct Foreign Investments Laws, Regulations and Opportunities Handbook
124. Serbia Direct Foreign Investments Laws, Regulations and Opportunities Handbook
125. Singapore Direct Foreign Investments Laws, Regulations and Opportunities Handbook
126. Slovakia Direct Foreign Investments Laws, Regulations and Opportunities Handbook
127. Slovenia Direct Foreign Investments Laws, Regulations and Opportunities Handbook
128. South Africa Direct Foreign Investments Laws, Regulations and Opportunities Handbook
129. Spain Direct Foreign Investments Laws, Regulations and Opportunities Handbook
130. Sri Lanka Direct Foreign Investments Laws, Regulations and Opportunities Handbook
131. St. Helena Direct Foreign Investments Laws, Regulations and Opportunities Handbook
132. Sudan Direct Foreign Investments Laws, Regulations and Opportunities Handbook
133. Suriname Direct Foreign Investments Laws, Regulations and Opportunities Handbook
134. Sweden Direct Foreign Investments Laws, Regulations and Opportunities Handbook
135. Switzerland Direct Foreign Investments Laws, Regulations and Opportunities Handbook
136. Syria Export Import & Business Directory
137. Taiwan Direct Foreign Investments Laws, Regulations and Opportunities Handbook
138. Tajikistan Direct Foreign Investments Laws, Regulations and Opportunities Handbook
139. Thailand Direct Foreign Investments Laws, Regulations and Opportunities Handbook
140. Tunisia Direct Foreign Investments Laws, Regulations and Opportunities Handbook
141. Turkey Direct Foreign Investments Laws, Regulations and Opportunities Handbook
142. Turkmenistan Direct Foreign Investments Laws, Regulations and Opportunities Handbook
143. Uganda Direct Foreign Investments Laws, Regulations and Opportunities Handbook
144. Ukraine Direct Foreign Investments Laws, Regulations and Opportunities Handbook
145. United Arab Emirates Direct Foreign Investments Laws, Regulations and Opportunities Handbook
146. United Kingdom Direct Foreign Investments Laws, Regulations and Opportunities Handbook
147. United States Direct Foreign Investments Laws, Regulations and Opportunities Handbook
148. Uruguay Direct Foreign Investments Laws, Regulations and Opportunities Handbook
149. US Direct Foreign Investments Laws, Regulations and Opportunities Handbook
150. Uzbekistan Direct Foreign Investments Laws, Regulations and Opportunities Handbook
151. Venezuela Direct Foreign Investments Laws, Regulations and Opportunities Handbook
152. Vietnam Direct Foreign Investments Laws, Regulations and Opportunities Handbook

www.ingramcontent.com/pod-product-compliance
Ingram Content Group UK Ltd.
Pitfield, Milton Keynes, MK11 3LW, UK
UKHW051510290926
15471UKWH00008B/1532

9 780739 727638